NATIONALISM INDUSTRIALIZ... AND DEMOCRACY 1815-1914

A Documentary History Of Modern Europe Volume III

Edited by

Thomas G. Barnes
Gerald D. Feldman
University of California, Berkeley

Originally Published by
Little, Brown and Company

UNIVERSITY
PRESS OF
AMERICA

LANHAM • NEW YORK • LONDON

University Press of America,™ Inc.

4720 Boston Way
Lanham, MD 20706

3 Henrietta Street
London WC2E 8LU England

ISBN (Perfect): 0-8191-1079-5

Library of Congress Catalog Card Number : **80-5383**

PREFACE

"For I do not see the whole of anything; neither do those who promise to show it to us." Michel de Montaigne's frank disclaimer of his own capacity and scathing rejection of the vaunted capacities of others to see all was written almost exactly four centuries ago, in an age of fanaticisms and all-embracing visions. It is relevant for our own age of fanaticisms and all-embracing visions. Fanaticism aside, it is a particularly apt motto for authors and editors of books for introductory courses in history. Where not downright messianic, or even prophetical, such books tend to be pontifical — if not by the authors' intentions, then at least in the student's reading of them. Some notions guided us in this compilation, and it is good to make those notions and their manifestations clear at the outset, not only that we might not be thought messianic, prophetical, or pontifical, but also that those who choose and those who use this book will know what we think it does and does not do. At the outset, we make no claim that it will enable the student to "see the whole" of modern European history, or even as much of it as is treated here.

We believe that even the most general study of history requires awareness of historians' dependence upon the sources for history. It is as well that the novice understands from the start that all historiography is based on a broad but still selected body of sources. The very selectiveness of this collection reflects the nature of the historian's job in writing history. We believe that the student cannot begin to understand either history or the historian's task without himself exercising his intellect on the sources of history. This compilation, highly selective though it is, demands that the student use his critical faculties in weighing what he reads as historical evidence; indeed, it demands that he determine from the variety of sources presented what constitutes historical evidence and how evidence can be analyzed and understood in different ways. For example, a student with the psychological interests of Erik H. Erikson, another with the politico-social bent of Roland H. Bainton, and another given to the avowedly theological focus of James Atkinson would all approach Martin Luther differently, but they would all have to meet and begin with Luther's own writings.

For that reason, if for no other, this series includes a major segment of Luther, which, though it comprises only a fraction of his considerable output, provides a common ground for all who would understand Luther and Lutheranism and a common origin for each interpretation of the man and his movement. So have we in every volume of this series aimed at providing a large enough selection from major historical figures (both thinkers and doers), commentaries by lesser men, descriptions of events, laws and government directives, manifestoes and platforms, some correspondence and belles lettres, to suggest the variety of sources for Europe's past, to allow each student to bring into play his own critical acumen, and to provide illustration of men, events, and ideas which might otherwise prove elusive.

This series is intended to be a *documentary history* of Europe. By this we mean that a student using — not merely reading — these volumes can come to some understanding of modern Europe's past by the documents alone aided by the explanation of the headnotes to the selections and the longer introductory essay to each chapter, which provides context and continuity both to the documents in that chapter and with the chapters preceding and succeeding. The series is not meant to serve as a substitute for a text, but it is intended to be as self-sufficient as is necessary to fit with any textbook or narrative history, sometimes in agreement with and sometimes in contrast to the interpretations that will be found elsewhere in what a student can be expected to read in an introductory course in modern European history at any college level. We have sought to make the selections long enough to give real substance for reflection and analysis. Perforce, this has limited the number of selections and therefore has caused us to exclude some men, events, and ideas that others would think of prime importance. We have felt no call to mirror the broad consensus as to which documents are and are not important. Although our colleagues will find a number of selections that all agree are "major," they will also find many that are rarely if ever found in books of readings and a few that have not previously appeared in English. We have sought significance, freshness, insightfulness, and incisiveness in our selections, and these concerns rather than idiosyncrasy, a penchant for novelty, or a commitment to a specific historical interpretation have determined that much of the material in this series will be new and different.

ACKNOWLEDGMENTS

The permission of authors and publishers in whom copyright is vested has been acknowledged where the selection appears. We would, however, tender special thanks to those holders of copyright who allowed us to use material either gratis or for a nominal fee, a practice that is no longer universal. A number of our colleagues assisted us with sage advice and tips for finding materials, and we are in yet greater debt to Lawrence Levine, Martin Malia, Robert Middlekauff, William Slottman, and Engel Sluiter than that already incurred by many years' close service together at Berkeley. Two students, Murray Bilby and Jeffrey Diefendorf, served us as bibliographical assistants and rendered aid beyond what we paid them. Malgorzata I. Winkler of the University of California, Berkeley, Library translated the Union of Lublin from Polish, a difficult task well done. The College Department of Little, Brown and Co. was always helpful, and we perhaps tumble into invidiousness in singling out the history editor, Charles Christensen, and the three copyeditors who wrestled with the series and its authors, Jane Aaron, Lynne Marcus Gould, and Patricia Herbst. To all, our most sincere thanks.

T. G. B.
G. D. F.

CONTENTS

NATIONALISM, INDUSTRIALIZATION, AND DEMOCRACY
1815–1914

ROMANTICISM
AND REACTION

Chapter 1

The allied victory over Napoleon at Waterloo on June 18, 1815, marked
the end of almost a quarter-century of European upheaval. The French
Revolution and the Napoleonic imperium had transformed the political and social character of much of the European continent. France's
armies brought oppression and exploitation, but they also promoted
territorial rationalization, administrative reorganization, the reformation of legal codes, and many of the ideals of the French Revolution. It
was impossible to truly restore the world that had existed in 1789, and
the rulers and statesmen who reordered Europe at the Congress of
Vienna during 1814 and 1815 were interested more in peace and stability than in completely setting back the clock. They disregarded the
principle of nationality in eastern, central, and southern Europe, and
they asserted the doctrine of legitimacy by restoring the old ruling
houses. They made no effort to restore the Holy Roman Empire and
its more than three hundred states, however, and the statesmen at
Vienna went even further than Napoleon in disregarding territorial
boundaries and claims of sovereignty when they established the new
German Confederation.

Even more revealing of their attitude was their regulation of French
affairs. The Bourbons were restored to France and France was restored
to Europe, but in both instances some account was taken of the lessons
of the recent past. Louis XVIII did not try to rule in the manner of his
unfortunate brother Louis XVI, and he gave France the Charter of
1814, which established a parliament based on limited suffrage, left the
initiation of legislation in the hands of the royal ministers, and retained many of the rights and legal reforms won during the Revolution.
In contrast to the treatment of Germany at Versailles a century later,
the victors of 1814–1815 invited France back into the European community as a great power and were remarkably lenient in their terms.
The First Treaty of Paris (signed in May, 1814) actually permitted
France to keep some of the territory it had conquered in the early years

of the Revolution. France's skillful minister Talleyrand was able to gain a powerful position at the Vienna Congress by joining with Count Metternich of Austria and Lord Castlereagh of England to oppose Russia's attempt to gain control over the whole of Poland and Prussia's effort to annex Saxony.

Napoleon's return from Elba and his warm reception by large segments of the French population caused the allies to take a more punitive attitude toward France, but the loss of a few fortresses, a small indemnity, and a brief occupation imposed by the Second Treaty of Paris (signed in November, 1815) were relatively mild measures compared with the renewed offense France had given to Europe.

At the same time that the allies sought to restore France, they attempted to protect Europe from renewed French aggression by means of the Quadruple Alliance, which included England, Austria, Prussia, and Russia. This alliance called for mutual assistance in the event France violated the treaties, and it provided for periodic conferences to retain the peace of Europe. Much vaguer in its intention and applicability was the Holy Alliance signed in September, 1815, by Russia, Prussia, and Austria at Czar Alexander I's instigation. The ambiguity of the so-called Restoration was quite evident in the contrast between the fairly precise and pragmatic Quadruple Alliance and the quasi-religious Holy Alliance. England's refusal to join the Holy Alliance portended the rift that was to grow between the eastern and western powers after 1815.

A similar ambiguity appears in the romantic movement that dominated the artistic and intellectual life of the first half of the nineteenth century. Romanticism was a reaction against the Enlightenment's stress upon reason and intellect, and it was characterized by an emphasis upon emotion, feeling, nature, the organic, and the historical. Although this switch in emphasis could and did serve the cause of conservatism, romanticism received much inspiration from the Enlightenment philosophe Jean Jacques Rousseau and included such champions of liberalism and nationalism as the painter Eugène Delacroix and the poets Heinrich Heine and Lord Byron. Often, and especially in Germany, the homeland of romanticism, it could be remarkably unpolitical. Nevertheless, romanticism was quite compatible with the burgeoning conservative movement that had first defined itself in reaction to the French Revolution and had received much inspiration from the writings of Edmund Burke, the great English opponent of the Revolution. Where Burke was at least prepared to accept organic change and gradual reform, however, romantic conservatives such as Sir Walter Scott, Joseph de Maistre, Novalis (Friedrich von Hardenberg), and René de Chateaubriand idealized the medieval world, in which every man had had the security of knowing his place and in which the domination of the Church preserved men from sinful efforts to create heaven on earth.

The major concern of Europe's rulers in the years following the peace settlement was the prosaic one of maintaining the status quo, and this was not easy. In England, economic difficulties led to demands for the repeal of the Corn Law and to public disturbances that culminated in the Peterloo Massacre of 1819 and in Parliament's Six Acts, which were designed to curb radical protest. In France, the government sought to chart a course between the ultraroyalist extremists and the liberals, but the assassination of the duc de Berry in 1820 unleashed a period of repression and reaction. In central Europe, Metternich, with the assistance of the conservative rulers of Prussia, sought to put down nationalist and liberal sentiment in the press and universities by means of the Carlsbad Decrees of 1819. Similarly, in 1820 he tried to mobilize the conservative forces of Europe against the revolutionary outbursts in Spain, Portugal, and Italy. His efforts, however, revealed that the alliance forged to defeat France was too divided to confront the forces that the French Revolution had unleashed.

The Conflict Between Metternich and Castlereagh

Although the Holy Alliance and the Quadruple Alliance became identified together by European liberals and other enemies of the 1815 settlement, the origins and character of the two compacts differ greatly. The former was the brainchild of Alexander I, who was given to fantasy and mysticism and who was probably acting under the influence of his friend, the religious mystic Baroness von Krüdener. The British foreign minister, Lord Castlereagh, thought the whole idea "a piece of sublime mysticism and nonsense," and Metternich seems to have treated the affair with great cynicism himself. Austria and Prussia joined largely in order to please the tsar, and England was able to avoid signing on constitutional grounds. The Quadruple Alliance, in contrast, had the enthusiastic support of both Metternich and Castlereagh and was a direct continuation of the anti-Napoleonic coalition formed at Chaumont in March, 1814. It was specifically designed to enforce the peace treaty with France and to maintain the peace of Europe. The regulation of European affairs by conferences, as provided in Article VI, led to a series of conferences between 1818 and 1822.

During these conferences, a major rift between England and her east-ern allies became clear. Clemens von Metternich increasingly inter-preted the Quadruple Alliance in the spirit of the Holy Alliance and urged intervention in the internal affairs of other states to prevent change and revolution. This change in attitude, reflecting his own growing rigidity, was expressed in his political confession of faith. Met-ternich was so opposed to change that, even though he hated constitu-tions, he demanded that rulers who had been foolish enough to grant them refrain from violating them or altering them even in a conserva-tive manner. Metternich's attitude was something of a personal tragedy for Lord Castlereagh, who was deeply committed to maintaining the balance of power in Europe by means of the Quadruple Alliance and the conference system, but who could not condone, and knew the British people would never condone, the use of these instruments to interfere in the internal affairs of other states. In the face of Metter-nich's and Alexander's persistent call for intervention against revolu-tion in Spain, Castlereagh gave classic expression to the British position in his state paper of May 5, 1820.

The Holy Alliance of September 26, 1815

In the name of the Most Holy and Indivisible Trinity,

Their Majesties, the Emperor of Austria, the King of Prussia and the Emperor of Russia, having — in consequence of the great events which have marked the course of the three last years in Europe, and especially of the blessings which it has pleased Divine Providence to shower down upon those States which place their confidence and their hope on it alone — acquired the intimate conviction of the necessity of founding the con-duct to be observed by the Powers, in their reciprocal relations, upon the sublime truths which the holy religion of our Saviour teaches;

They solemnly declare that the present Act has no other object than to publish in the face of the whole world their fixed resolution, both in the ad-ministration of their respective States, and in their political relations with every other Government, to take for their sole guide the precepts of that holy religion, namely, the precepts of justice, Christian charity, and peace, which, far from being applicable only to private concerns, must have an immediate influence on the councils of princes, and guide all their steps, as being the only means of consolidating human institutions, and remedying their imperfections.

In consequence their Majesties have agreed on the following Articles:

Article 1. Conformably to the words of the holy Scriptures, which com-mand all men to consider each other as brethren, the three contracting

From *Cobbett's Parliamentary Debates*, vol. 32, pp. 355–57.

monarchs will remain united by the bonds of a true and indissoluble fraternity, and considering each other as fellow-countrymen, they will, on all occasions, and in all places, lend each other aid and assistance, and regarding themselves towards their subjects and armies as fathers of families, they will lead them in the same spirit of fraternity with which they are animated, to protect religion, peace and justice.

Article 2. In consequence, the sole principle in force, whether between the said Governments, or between their subjects, shall be, that of doing each other reciprocal service, and of testifying by unalterable goodwill, the mutual affection with which they ought to be animated, to consider themselves all as members of one and the same Christian nation; the three Allied Princes looking on themselves as merely delegated by Providence to govern three branches of the one family, namely, Austria, Prussia and Russia: thus confessing that the Christian nation, of which they and their people form a part, has in reality no other Sovereign than Him to whom alone power really belongs, because in Him alone are found all the treasures of love, science, and infinite wisdom; that is to say, God, our Divine Saviour, the word of the Most High, the Word of Life. Their Majesties consequently recommend to their people, with the most tender solicitude, as the sole means of enjoying that peace which arises from a good conscience, and which alone is durable, to strengthen themselves every day more and more in the principles and exercise of the duties which the Divine Saviour has taught to mankind.

Article 3. All the Powers who shall choose solemnly to avow the sacred principles which have dictated the present Act, and shall acknowledge how important it is for the happiness of nations, too long agitated, that those truths should henceforth exercise over the destinies of mankind all the influence which belongs to them, will be received with equal ardour and affection into this Holy Alliance.

Done in triplicate, and signed at Paris the year of Grace, 1815, 14–26 September.

Francis
Frederick William
Alexander

The Quadruple Alliance of November 20, 1815

The purpose of the Alliance concluded at Vienna the 25th day of March 1815, having been happily attained by the re-establishment in France of the order of things which the last criminal attempt of Napoleon Bonaparte had momentarily subverted; their Majesties the King of

From *British and Foreign State Papers, 1815–1816*, pp. 273–80. Reprinted by permission of Her Majesty's Stationery Office.

the United Kingdom and Ireland, the Emperor of Austria, King of Hungary and Bohemia, the Emperor of all the Russias, and the King of Prussia, considering that the repose of Europe is essentially interwoven with the confirmation of the order of things founded on the maintenance of the royal authority and of the Constitutional Charter, and wishing to employ all their means to prevent the general tranquillity (the object of the wishes of mankind and the constant end of their efforts) from being again disturbed; desirous moreover to draw closer the ties which unite them for the common interests of their people, have resolved to give to the principles solemnly laid down in the Treaties of Chaumont of the 1st of March 1814, and of Vienna of the 25th of March 1815, the application the most analogous to the present state of affairs, and to fix beforehand by a solemn Treaty the principles which they propose to follow, in order to guarantee Europe from the dangers by which she may still be menaced. . . .

enforce the Treaty

Article I. The High Contracting Parties reciprocally promise to maintain, in its force and vigour, the Treaty signed this day with His Most Christian Majesty, and to see that the stipulations of the said Treaty, as well as those of the Particular Conventions which have reference thereto, shall be strictly and faithfully executed in their fullest extent.

II. The High Contracting Parties, having engaged in the War which is just terminated, for the purpose of maintaining inviolably the arrangements settled at Paris last year, for the safety and interest of Europe, have judged it advisable to renew the said engagements by the present Act, and to confirm them as mutually obligatory — subject to the modifications contained in the Treaty signed this day with the Plenipotentiaries of His Most Christian Majesty — and particularly those by which Napoleon Bonaparte and his family, in pursuance of the Treaty of the 11th of April 1814, have been for ever excluded from the Supreme Power in France, which exclusion the Contracting Powers bind themselves, by the present Act, to maintain in full vigour, and, should it be necessary, with the whole of their forces. And as the same revolutionary principles which upheld the last criminal usurpation might again, under other forms, convulse France, and thereby endanger the repose of other States; under these circumstances the High Contracting Parties, solemnly admitting it to be their duty to redouble their watchfulness for the tranquillity and interests of their people, engage, in case so unfortunate an event should again occur, to concert amongst themselves, and with His Most Christian Majesty, the measures which they may judge necessary to be pursued for the safety of their respective States, and for the general tranquillity of Europe.

will intervene in France again if necessary

III. The High Contracting Parties, in agreeing with His Most Christian Majesty that a line of military positions in France should be occupied by a Corps of Allied troops, during a certain number of years, had in view to secure, as far as lay in their power, the effect of the Stipulations contained in Articles I and II of the present Treaty; and, uniformly disposed to adopt every salutary measure calculated to secure the tranquillity of Europe by maintaining the order of things re-established in France, they engage that, in case the said body of troops should be attacked or menaced with an attack on the part of France, the said Powers should be again obliged to place themselves on a war establishment against that Power, in order to maintain either of the said stipulations, or to secure and support the great interests to which they relate, each of the High Contracting Parties shall furnish, without delay, according to the stipulations of the Treaty of Chaumont, and especially in pursuance of the VIIth and VIIIth Articles of this Treaty, its full contingent of 60,000 men, in addition to the forces left in France, or such part of the said contingent as the exigency of the case may require, should be put in motion.

IV. If, unfortunately, the forces stipulated in the preceding Article should be found insufficient, the High Contracting Parties will concert together, without loss of time, as to the additional number of troops to be furnished by each for the support of the common cause; and they engage to employ, in case of need, the whole of their forces, in order to bring the war to a speedy and successful termination; reserving to themselves the right to prescribe, by common consent, such conditions of peace as shall hold out to Europe a sufficient guarantee against the recurrence of a similar calamity.

V. The High Contracting Parties, having agreed to the dispositions laid down in the preceding Articles, for the purpose of securing the effect of their engagements during the period of the temporary occupation, declare, moreover, that even after the expiration of this measure, the said engagements shall still remain in full force and vigour, for the purpose of carrying into effect such measures as may be deemed necessary for the maintenance of the stipulations contained in the Articles I and II of the present Act.

VI. To facilitate and to secure the execution of the present Treaty, and to consolidate the connections which at the present moment so closely unite the four Sovereigns for the happiness of the world, the High Contracting Parties have agreed to renew their meetings at fixed periods, *Congresses* either under the immediate auspices of the Sovereigns themselves, or by their respective Ministers, for the purpose of consulting upon their common interests, and for the consideration of the measures which at each of those periods shall be considered the most salutary for the repose and prosperity of nations, and for the maintenance of the peace of Europe.

VII. The present Treaty shall be ratified, and the ratifications shall be exchanged within two months, or sooner, if possible. . . .

Metternich's Secret Memorandum to Tsar Alexander, Containing His Political Confession of Faith, December 15, 1820

Union between the monarchs is the basis of the policy which must now be followed to save society from total ruin.

What is the particular object towards which this policy should be directed? The more important this question is, the more necessary it is to solve it. A principle is something, but it acquires real value only in its application.

The first sources of the evil which is crushing the world have been indicated by us in a paper which has no pretension to be anything more than a mere sketch. Its further causes have also there been pointed out if, with respect to individuals, it may be defined by the word *presumption,* in applying it to society, taken as a whole, we believe we can best describe the existing evil as the *confusion of ideas,* to which too much generalisation constantly leads. This is what now troubles society. Everything which up to this time has been considered as fixed in principle is attacked and overthrown.

In religious matters criticism and inquiry are to take the place of faith, Christian morality is to replace the Law of Christ as it is interpreted by Christian authorities. . . .

If the same elements of destruction which are now throwing society into convulsion have existed in all ages — for every age has seen immoral and ambitious men, hypocrites, men of heated imaginations, wrong motives, and wild projects — yet ours, by the single fact of the liberty of the press, possesses more than any preceding age the means of contact, seduction, and attraction whereby to act on these different classes of men.

We are certainly not alone in questioning if society can exist with the liberty of the press, a scourge unknown to the world before the latter half of the seventeenth century, and restrained until the end of the eighteenth, with scarcely any exceptions but England — a part of Europe separated from the continent by the sea, as well as by her language and by her peculiar manners.

The first principle to be followed by the monarchs, united as they are by the coincidence of their desires and opinions, should be that of maintaining the stability of political institutions against the disorganised excitement which has taken possession of men's minds; the immutability of principles against the madness of their interpretation; and respect for laws actually in force against a desire for their destruction.

The hostile faction is divided into two very distinct parties. One is

From *Memoirs of Prince Metternich, 1815–1829,* vol. 3, ed. Prince Richard Metternich, trans. Alexander Napier (New York: Scribner's, 1881), pp. 471–76.

that of the Levellers; the other, that of the Doctrinaires. United in times of confusion, these men are divided in times of inaction. It is for the Governments to understand and estimate them at their just value.

In the class of Levellers there are found men of strong will and determination. The Doctrinaires can count none such among their ranks. If the first are more to be feared in action, the second are more dangerous in that time of deceitful calm which precedes it; as with physical storms, so with those of social order. Given up to abstract ideas inapplicable to real wants, and generally in contradiction to those very wants, men of this class unceasingly agitate the people by their imaginary or simulated fears, and disturb Governments in order to make them deviate from the right path. The world desires to be governed by facts and according to justice, not by phrases and theories; the first need of society is to be maintained by strong authority (no authority without real strength deserves the name) and not to govern itself. In comparing the number of contests between parties in mixed Governments, and that of just complaints caused by aberrations of power in a Christian State, the comparison would not be in favour of the new doctrines. The first and greatest concern for the immense majority of every nation is the stability of the laws, and their uninterrupted action — never their change. Therefore let the Governments govern, let them maintain the groundwork of their institutions, both ancient and modern; for if it is at all times dangerous to touch them, it certainly would not now, in the general confusion, be wise to do so.

Let them announce this determination to their people, and demonstrate it by facts. Let them reduce the Doctrinaires to silence within their States, and show their contempt for them abroad. Let them not encourage by their attitude or actions the suspicion of being favourable or indifferent to error: let them not allow it to be believed that experience has lost all its rights to make way for experiments which at the least are dangerous. Let them be precise and clear in all their words, and not seek by concessions to gain over those parties who aim at the destruction of all power but their own, whom concessions will never gain over, but only further embolden in their pretensions to power.

Let them in these troublous times be more than usually cautious in attempting real ameliorations, not imperatively claimed by the needs of the moment, to the end that good itself may not turn against them — which is the case whenever a Government measure seems to be inspired by fear.

Let them not confound concessions made to parties with the good they ought to do for their people, in modifying, according to their recognised needs, such branches of the administration as require it.

Let them give minute attention to the financial state of their kingdoms, so that their people may enjoy, by the reduction of public burdens, the real, not imaginary, benefits of a state of peace.

Let them be just, but strong; beneficent, but strict.

Let them maintain religious principles in all their purity, and not allow the faith to be attacked and morality interpreted according to the *social contract* or the visions of foolish sectarians.

Let them suppress Secret Societies, that gangrene of society.

In short, let the great monarchs strengthen their union, and prove to the world that if it exists, it is beneficent, and ensures the political peace of Europe: that it is powerful only for the maintenance of tranquillity at a time when so many attacks are directed against it; that the principles which they profess are paternal and protective, menacing only the disturbers of public tranquillity.

The Governments of the second order will see in such a union the anchor of their salvation, and they will be anxious to connect themselves with it. The people will take confidence and courage, and the most profound and salutary peace which the history of any time can show will have been effected. This peace will first act on countries still in a good state, but will not be without a very decided influence on the fate of those threatened with destruction, and even assist the restoration of those which have already passed under the scourge of revolution.

To every great State determined to survive the storm there still remain many chances of salvation, and a strong union between the States on the principles we have announced will overcome the storm itself.

Lord Castlereagh's State Paper of May 5, 1820

. . . The People of this Country would probably not recognise (unless Portugal was attacked) that our Safety could be so far menaced by any State of things in Spain, as to Warrant their Government in sending an Army to that Country to meddle in it's internal affairs; We cannot conceal from ourselves how generally the Acts of the King of Spain since His Restoration have rendered His Government unpopular, and how impossible it would be to reconcile the People of England to the use of force, if such a Proceeding could for a moment be thought of by the British Cabinet for the purpose of replacing Power in His hands, however he might engage to qualify it. The principle upon which the British Government acted in the discussions with respect to the Colonies, (viz: never to employ forcible means for their reduction) would equally preclude them from any intervention of such a character with regard to Old Spain. The interposition of our good offices, whether singly, or in concert with the Allied Govts., if uncalled for by any authority within Spain, even by

From A. W. Ward and G. P. Gooch, *The Cambridge History of British Foreign Policy, 1783–1919*, vol. 2 (Cambridge: Cambridge University Press, 1923), pp. 628–30. Reprinted by permission of Cambridge University Press.

the King Himself, is by no means free from a like inconvenience as far as regards the Position of the British Government at home. This species of Intervention especially when coming from five great Powers, has more or less the air of dictation and of menace, and the possibility of it's being intended to be pushed to a forcible intervention is always assumed or imputed by an adverse party. The grounds of the intervention thus become unpopular, the intention of the parties is misunderstood, the public Mind is agitated and perverted, and the General Political situation of the Government is thereby essentially embarrassed.

This Statement is only meant to prove that We ought to see somewhat clearly to what purpose of real Utility our Effort tends, before We embark in proceedings which can never be indifferent in their bearings upon the Government taking part in them. In this country at all times, but especially at the present conjuncture, when the whole Energy of the State is required to unite reasonable men in defence of our existing Institutions, and to put down the spirit of Treason and Disaffection which in certain of the Manufacturing Districts in particular, pervades the lower orders, it is of the greatest moment, that the public sentiment should not be distracted or divided, by any unnecessary interference of the Government in events, passing abroad, over which they can have none, or at best but very imperfect means of controul. Nothing could be more injurious to the Continental Powers than to have their affairs made matter of daily Discussion in our Parliament, which nevertheless must be the consequence of Their precipitately mixing themselves in the affairs of other States, if We should consent to proceed pari passu with them in such interferences. It is not merely the temporary inconvenience produced to the British Government by being so committed, that is to be apprehended, but it is the exposing ourselves to have the public Mind soured by the effects of a meddling policy, when it can tend to nothing really effectual, and pledged perhaps, beforehand against any exertion whatever in Continental Affairs; the fatal effects of such a false Step might be irreparable when the moment at which we might be indispensably called upon by Duty and Interest to take a part should arise.

These considerations will suggest a doubt whether that extreme degree of unanimity and supposed concurrence upon all political subjects would be either a practicable or a desirable principle of action among the Allied States, upon Matters not essentially connected with the main purposes of the Alliance. If this Identity is to be sought for, it can only be obtained by a proportionate degree of inaction in all the States. The position of the Ministers at Paris for instance can never be altogether uniform, unless their language upon Public affairs is either of the most general description, or they agree to hold no public language whatever. The latter Expedient is perhaps the most prudent, but then the Unanimity of the Sentiment, thus assumed to be established, will not be free from inconvenience to some of the parties, if the Cabinets of other States by their public documents assign objects to that Concert, to which, at least as described by them, the others cannot conveniently subscribe.

The fact is that we do not, and cannot feel alike upon all subjects. Our Position, our Institutions, the Habits of thinking, and the prejudices of our People, render us essentially different. We cannot in all matters reason or feel alike; we should lose the Confidence of our respective Nations if we did, and the very affectation of such an Impossibility would soon render the Alliance an Object of Odium, and Distrust, whereas, if we keep it within its *common Sense* limits, the Representative Governments, and those which are more purely Monarchical, may well find each a common Interest, and a common facility in discharging their Duties under the Alliance, without creating an Impression that they have made a surrender of the first principles upon which their respective Governments are founded. Each Government will then retain it's due faculty of independent Action, always recollecting, that they have all a common Refuge in the Alliance, as well as a common Duty to perform, whenever such a Danger shall really exist, as that against which the Alliance was specially intended to provide. There is at present very naturally a widespread apprehension of the fatal Consequences to the publick tranquillity of Europe, that may be expected to flow from the dangerous principles of the present Day, at work more or less in every European State. Consequences which no human foresight can presume to estimate. In all dangers the first Calculation of Prudence is to consider what we should avoid and on what we should endeavour to rely. . . . The principle of one State interfering by force in the internal affairs of another, in order to enforce obedience to the governing authority, is always a question of the greatest possible moral as well as political delicacy, and it is not meant here to examine it. It is only important on the present occasion, to observe that to generalize such a principle and to think of reducing it to a System, or to impose it as an obligation, is a Scheme utterly impracticable and objectionable. There is not only the physical impossibility of giving execution to such a System, but there is the moral impracticability arising from the inaptitude of particular States to recognize or to act upon it. No Country having a Representative System of Govt. could act upon it — and the sooner such a Doctrine shall be distinctly abjured as forming in any Degree the Basis of our Alliance, the better; in order that States, in calculating the means of their own Security may not suffer Disappointment by expecting from the Allied Powers, a support which, under the special Circumstances of the National Institutions they cannot give — Great Britain has perhaps equal Power with any other State to oppose herself to a practical and intelligible Danger, capable of being brought home to the National Feeling — When the Territorial Balance of Europe is disturbed, she can interfere with effect, but She is the last Govt. in Europe, which can be expected, or can venture to commit Herself on any Question of an abstract character.

These Observations are made to point attention to what is practicable and what is not. If the dreaded moral Contagion should unfortunately extend itself into Germany and if the flame of Military Revolt should for example, burst forth in any of the German States, it is in vain for that State, however anxiously and sincerely we deprecate such a Calamity, to turn it's Eyes to this Country for the means of effectually suppressing such a Danger — If external means are indispensable for it's Suppression, such State must not reckon for assistance upon Govts. constituted as that of Great Britain but it is not therefore without it's Resource.

The Internal peace of each German State is by Law placed under the protection of the Army of the Empire: The Duty which is imposed by the Laws of the Confederacy upon all German States, to suppress, by the Military Power of the whole mass, Insurrection within the Territories of Each and Every, of the Co-Estates, is an immense Resource in itself, and ought to give to the Centre of Europe a sense of Security which previous to the Reunion of Vienna was wholly wanting. The Importance of preventing the Low Countries, the Military Barrier of Europe, from being lost, by being melted down into the general Mass of French Power, whether by Insurrection, or by Conquest, might enable the British Govt. to act more promptly upon this, than perhaps upon any other Case of an internal Character that can be stated. But upon all such Cases we must admit ourselves to be, and our Allies should in fairness understand that we are, a Power that must take our Principle of action, and our Scale of acting, not merely from the Expediency of the Case, but from those Maxims, which a System of Government strongly popular, and national in it's character, has irresistibly imposed upon us.

We shall be found in our Place when actual danger menaces the System of Europe; but this Country cannot, and will not, act upon abstract and speculative Principles of Precaution. The Alliance which exists had no such purpose in view in its original formation. It was never so explained to Parliament; if it had, most assuredly the sanction of Parliament would never have been given to it; and it would now be a breach of faith, were the Ministers of the Crown to acquiesce in a construction being put upon it, or were they to suffer themselves to be betrayed into a course of Measures, inconsistent with those Principles which they avowed at the time, and which they have since uniformly maintained both at Home and Abroad.

Romanticism

Madame de Staël (1766–1817), without a doubt one of the most inter-
esting women of her age, gave the romantic movement its name. The
daughter of Louis XVI's famous minister, Jacques Necker, and the
lover of such remarkable men as the French statesman Talleyrand and
the liberal philosopher Benjamin Constant, Madame de Staël came
into contact with many of the great political and artistic personalities
of her time. Although a refugee from the French Revolution and
Napoleon, she was nevertheless moderate in her politics and cosmopoli-
tan in her attitude. Yet she was forceful and passionate in her approach
to life and art. Her wide travels and empathetic attitude toward the
variety of European cultural expressions made her an ideal interpreter
of the peculiar genius in the various cultures she surveyed. This ability
is particularly evident in her book On Germany *(1813), which discussed*
the roots of German romanticism in the folklore, customs, and religion
of the German people. Madame de Staël defended romanticism against
its critics by pointing out that the romantic style was as appropriate for
the Germans as the classical style was for the Latin peoples. The Ger-
man poet and writer Heinrich Heine (1797–1856) almost perfectly illus-
trates the romanticism discussed by Madame de Staël in his charming
description of his journey through the Harz mountains, Harzreise, *pub-*
lished in 1824.

Madame de Staël: On Classic Poetry
and Romantic Poetry

The name *romantic* has been recently introduced in Germany to desig-
nate the poetry whose source is the songs of the troubadours and which
arose from chivalry and Christianity. If we do not acknowledge that paganism and Christianity, the North and the South, antiquity and the
Middle Ages, chivalry and Greek and Roman institutions, have divided
the realm of literature, then we shall never succeed in judging ancient
and modern taste philosophically.

The word *classic* is sometimes taken as a synonym for perfection. I use it
here in another sense, regarding classic poetry as that of the ancients, and
romantic poetry as related in some way to the traditions of chivalry. This
division is equally appropriate to the two historical eras of the world:
that which preceded the establishment of Christianity and that which
followed it.

From *On Germany*, ch. 11, in *Madame de Staël on Politics, Literature and National Character*, ed. Morroe Berger (Garden City, N.Y.: Doubleday, 1964), pp. 311–14. Re-printed by permission of Doubleday & Company, Inc., and Sidgwick & Jackson Ltd.

In various German works ancient poetry has been likened to sculpture and romantic poetry to painting. In short, the progress of the human mind has been described in every way in its passage from materialist to spiritual religions, from nature to divinity.

The French nation, the most cultivated of the Latin nations, inclines toward classic poetry modeled upon the Greeks and Romans. The English nation, the most renowned of the Germanic nations, prefers romantic and chivalrous poetry and is proud of its masterpieces in this *genre*. I shall not examine here which of these two kinds of poetry merits preference; it is enough to show that diversity of taste in this connection arises not merely from accidental causes but also from primitive sources of the imagination and thought.

There is a kind of simplicity in the epic poems and tragedies of the ancients that arises from man's identification with nature in that era and his belief that he was controlled by fate just as nature was controlled by necessity. Not very reflective, man still manifested externally all the workings of his mind. Even conscience was represented by external things, and the torches of the Furies shook remorse over the heads of the guilty. The event was everything in antiquity, but character has more importance in modern times.

The ancients had, so to speak, a corporeal soul all of whose emotions were strong, direct, and pronounced. It is not the same with the human heart unfolded by Christianity; modern men have derived from Christian repentance the habit of constantly turning inward upon themselves.

But to reveal this inward existence, a great variety of external events must display the infinite subtleties of the soul in all their forms. If in our day the fine arts were confined to the simplicity of the ancients, we would not attain their characteristic pristine power, but we would lose the intimate and manifold feelings of which we are capable. Simplicity in art, among the moderns, could easily turn into coldness and abstraction, whereas among the ancients it was full of life. Honor and love, valor and pity are the sentiments that marked Christianity in the age of chivalry; and these tendencies of the soul could manifest themselves only through perils, exploits, loves, misfortunes — in short, romantic concerns that ceaselessly vary the scene of action. Thus the sources of the effects of art differ, in many respects, in classic poetry and romantic poetry. In the one it is fate that rules, in the other it is Providence. Fate ignores the feelings of men, while Providence judges deeds only in accordance with these feelings. Poetry must indeed create a world of an entirely different nature when it seeks to describe the workings of a destiny that is blind and deaf, always in a struggle with mortals, or that intelligent order guided by a Supreme Being to whom our heart may address itself and be answered.

Pagan poetry is necessarily as simple and pronounced as external objects, but Christian poetry needs the myriad colors of the rainbow to prevent it from being lost in the clouds. The poetry of the ancients is purer as art, whereas that of the moderns makes us shed more tears. But the issue for us is not between classic poetry and romantic poetry but between imitation in the former and inspiration in the latter. To the modern era the literature of the ancients is a transplanted literature; romantic literature is indigenous to us, and it is our religion and customs that have made it blossom. Writers who imitate the ancients have submitted to the strictest rules of taste; not being able to consult their own nature or their own recollections, they must conform to those formulas by which the masterpieces of the ancients may be adapted to our taste, even though all the political and religious conditions that gave birth to those masterpieces are changed. But poems modeled on the ancient, however perfect they may be, are seldom popular, for they do not relate in our own time to anything native to us.

French being the most classic of all modern poetry, it is the only one not familiar to the populace. The stanzas of Tasso are sung by the gondoliers of Venice, Spaniards and Portuguese of all social classes know by heart the verses of Calderón and Camões. Shakespeare is as much admired by the populace in England as by the upper classes. The poems of Goethe and Bürger are set to music and you can hear them repeated from the banks of the Rhine to the Baltic. Our French poets are admired by all cultivated minds among ourselves and in the rest of Europe, but they are completely unknown to the common people and even to the middle class in the cities, because the arts in France are not, as elsewhere, native to the country where their beauty is revealed.

Some French critics maintain that the literature of the German people is still in its infancy as art. This view is entirely wrong. The most learned men in languages and the works of the ancients are certainly not ignorant of the disadvantages and advantages of the *genre* they adopt or reject, but their character, habits, and reflections have led them to prefer the literature based upon memories of chivalry, on the wonders of the Middle Ages, to that based upon Greek mythology. Romantic literature alone is still capable of improvement because, having its roots in our own soil, it alone can grow and revitalize itself. It expresses our religion and recalls our history. Its source is old but not antique.

Classic poetry must pass through the recollection of paganism in order to reach us, but the poetry of the Germans belongs to the Christian era of the fine arts: it uses our personal impressions to move us. The spirit that inspires it appeals directly to our heart and seems to recall our very existence like the most powerful and awful of phantoms.

Heine's *Harzreise*

Most of the miners live in Klausthal, or in the little mountain village of Zellerfeld. I sought these simple folk in their homes; saw their modes of life, heard many an old folk-song accompanied on the zither — their best loved music. And they told me strange legends of the mountains, mines, and woods, and repeated their prayers on going to work in the dark and dismal mines. I also joined in their prayers. One old guide asked me to share his cottage, and work as a miner. And when I said farewell he gave me a message for his brother near Goslar, and lots of kisses for his dearly-loved little niece.

Still and peaceful is the life of these honest people, but it is true genuine life. The old, old grandmother, sitting opposite the stove near the great clothes press, may have been sitting there for five and twenty years, and her thoughts and feelings have grown into every crack and cranny of the stove, every moulding of the press. And press and stove are living things, for a human soul has breathed into them a portion of itself.

Only by this direct nature-life has the German fairy tale evolved, the peculiarity of which is that not only beasts and plants, but objects that seem to us quite inanimate, both speak and act. To watchful, simple folk, in their quiet and peaceful lowly homes on the mountain or in the forest, the inner life of such objects revealed itself; each acquired in their eyes an essential consequence and consistent character of its own; a sweet blending of fantasy and purely human sentiment. This is why these fairy stories are wonderful; but always methodical and consistent. Needle and pin come from the tailor's shop and lose their way in the dark; straw and coal try to cross the stream and fall in; dustpan and broom stand on the stairs, and quarrel and fight; the glass, when questioned, shows the image of the loveliest woman; the blood-drops begin to speak dark words of heart-felt compassion. This, too, is why our life in childhood is so full of infinite significance. Then, all is of equal importance to us; we hear all, we see all, all impressions affect us equally; whereas, later on, we act with well considered motives, and occupy ourselves more exclusively with detail, and laboriously exchange the pure gold of instinct for the paper-money of book definitions, and our lives gain in breadth what they lose in depth and intensity. Now we are grown up and are people of importance, we are always getting into new houses. The maid goes sweeping every day, and moves at her pleasure the furniture which has so little interest for us, for it is either new, or perhaps it may be ours to-day and be gathered into Abraham's bosom to-morrow. Our clothes even are strange. We do not know how many buttons there are on the back of our coat.

From Heinrich Heine, *Pictures of Travel* (*Reisebilder*), trans. Russell Davis Gillman (New York: Scribner's, 1907), pp. 24–27. Reprinted by permission of Low (Sampson), Marston & Company Ltd.

We change our things so frequently that there is no longer any connection between the real man and his outward clothing. Already we have almost forgotten that old brown waistcoat we once wore, which evoked so much laughter, and on whose broad stripes the loving hand of our sweetheart once rested!

The old woman sitting opposite the stove, near the great press, wore a flowered dress of faded silk — the wedding dress of her dead mother. Her great grandson, a golden-haired, blue-eyed boy, dressed like a little miner, sat at her feet and counted the flowers on her gown. And what pretty tales she has told him about this old gown; many a little romance that the youngster will not soon forget. When he is a man, working in the dark and dreary Carolina mine, he will remember the old-time tales; and, when he is a feeble old man, sitting with silvery beard amongst his grandchildren, opposite the stove near the great press, he, too, will tell the tales told him by his great-grandmother, so long in her grave.

Romantic Conservatism

The reaction against the French Revolution and its excesses expressed itself by rejecting the mechanistic thought of the Enlightenment with its belief in the perfectibility of man, by attacking the idea of the social contract, and by condemning the godlessness of the revolutionary age. Joseph de Maistre (1753–1821), a Savoyard who served as Sardinian ambassador to Russia for fourteen years, was one of the most extreme proponents of this reaction, and his work On the Generative Principle of Political Constitutions *(1810) is one of the classics of European conservatism. For De Maistre, the political and social order was literally God-given and had to remain unquestioned if state and society were to hold together. Only the rule of the Catholic Church could save them from the chaos of the secular modern world and its works. De Maistre, in short, was more than a conservative; he was a true reactionary who wished to restore the organic society of the Middle Ages and establish a theocracy. Nevertheless, he exerted a powerful influence on French conservative and even protofascist thought because of his insistence on the organic nature of the state and the need for unquestioning agreement on basic sociopolitical values.*

De Maistre: On the Generative Principle
of Political Institutions

I. One of the greatest errors of a century which professed them all was to believe that a political constitution could be created and written *a priori*, whereas reason and experience unite in proving that a constitution is a divine work and that precisely the most fundamental and essentially constitutional of a nation's laws could not possibly be written.

II. Certain people have thought to perpetrate an excellent witticism at the expense of Frenchmen by asking, *"In what book was Salic law written?"* But Jérôme Bignon [1] answered quite appropriately, very likely without knowing how right he was, *"that it is written in the hearts of Frenchmen."* Indeed, let us suppose that such an important law existed only because it was written. Surely whatsoever authority had written it would have the right to annul it, and the law would not have that quality of divine immutability which characterizes truly constitutional laws. The essence of a fundamental law is that no one has the right to abolish it. For how could it stand above *all men,* if *some men* had made it? Popular agreement is not possible. And even if it were, an agreement is still not a *law* at all and obligates no one unless a higher power guarantees its enforcement. . . . "Promises, contracts, and oaths are mere words. It is as easy to break this trifling bond as to make it. Without the doctrine of a Divine Legislator, all moral obligation becomes illusory. Power on one side, weakness on the other: this constitutes all the bonds of human societies."

That is what a wise, profound theologian has said of moral obligation. It is equally true of political and civil obligations. Law is only truly sanctioned, and properly *law,* when assumed to emanate from a higher will, so that its essential quality is to be *not the will of all* [*la volonté de tous*]. Otherwise, laws would be *mere ordinances.* As the author just quoted states, "those who were free to make these conventions have not deprived themselves of the power of revocation, and their descendants, with no share in making these regulations, are bound even less to observe them." This is the reason that primitive common sense, which, fortunately, is anterior to sophism, has always sought the sanction of laws in a superhuman power, whether recognizing that sovereignty comes from God or in worshiping certain unwritten laws as given by Him. . . .

From Joseph de Maistre, *On God and Society: Essay on the Generative Principle of Political Constitutions and Other Human Institutions,* ed. Elisha Greifer, trans. Laurence M. Porter (Chicago: Regnery, Gateway Edition, 1959), pp. 3–6, 14–20, 54–58, 83–88, 90–92. Reprinted by permission of Henry Regnery Company.

1 Jérôme Bignon, 1589–1656, lawyer, writer, and tutor of Louis XIII. The Salic law prohibited the accession of women to the throne.

IX. The more one examines the role of human agency in forming political constitutions, the more one becomes convinced that it enters only in an infinitely subordinate manner, or as a simple instrument and I do not believe that the slightest doubt remains as to the unquestionable truth of the following propositions:

1. The fundamental principles of political constitutions exist prior to all written law.

2. Constitutional law [*loi*] is and can only be the development or sanction of a pre-existing and unwritten law [*droit*].

3. What is most essential, most inherently constitutional and truly fundamental law is never written, and could not be, without endangering the State.

4. The weakness and fragility of a constitution are actually in direct proportion to the number of written constitutional articles.

X. On this point, we are often deceived by a sophism so natural that it escapes our notice entirely. Because man acts, he thinks he acts alone. Because he is aware of his freedom, he forgets his dependence. He is more reasonable about the physical world, for although he can, for example, plant an acorn, water it, etc., he is convinced that he does not make oaks, since he has witnessed them growing and perfecting themselves without the aid of human power. Besides, he has not made the acorn. But in the social order, where he is always present and active, he comes to believe that he is the sole author of all that is done through his agency. In a sense, it is as if the trowel thought itself an architect. Doubtless, man is a free, intelligent, and noble creature; *nevertheless, he is an instrument of God.* . . .

XI. If anything be familiar, it is Cicero's analogy on the subject of the Epicurean system, which claimed that the world had been made from atoms falling randomly in space. I would rather believe, said the great orator, that letters thrown into the air would fall so as to form a poem. Thousands have repeated this thought and praised it. Yet as far as I know, no one has thought to give it the completeness which it lacks. Imagine that handfuls of printed characters thrown from the top of a tower should on landing make Racine's *Athalia*. What could one infer? *That a mind had directed their fall and arrangement.* Common sense will never find another answer.

XII. Let us now examine any particular political constitution, England's for example. It certainly was not made *a priori*. Her statesmen never assembled to say, *Let us create three powers, balancing them in such a manner, etc.* No one of them ever thought of such a thing. The constitution is the work of circumstances whose number is infinite. Roman laws, ecclesiastical laws, feudal laws, Saxon, Norman, and Danish customs; the privileges, prejudices, and pretentions of every segment of society; wars, rebellions, revolutions, the Conquest, the Crusades, every virtue, every vice, all sorts of knowledge, and all errors and passions; in sum, all these factors acting together and forming by their admixture and interdependent effects countless millions of combinations have at last produced, after several centuries, the most complex unity and the most propitious equilibrium of political powers that the world has ever seen.

XIII. Now since these agencies, thus tossed into the air, so to speak, have arranged themselves so neatly, although no man among the vast multitude which acted in this vast world ever knew what he was doing in relation to the whole or foresaw the outcome, it follows that these agencies were guided in their course by an infallible power. Perhaps the greatest misconception in a century of follies was that fundamental laws could be written *a priori,* while they are obviously the work of a higher power, and committing them to writing long after is the surest way of proving that they are no longer valid.

XIV. It is quite remarkable that God, having condescended to speak to man, has Himself shown these truths in the two revelations His goodness has given us. There was a clever man who marked a sort of era in our century through the desperate conflict his works exhibit between the worst prejudices of the period, of sect, of habit, etc., and the purest intentions, the most sincere sentiment and the most valuable knowledge. He decided that *instruction coming directly from God, or given only according to His commands, should primarily certify to man His existence.*[2] Precisely the opposite is true. For the prime characteristic of this teaching is not to reveal God's existence or attributes but to suppose the whole already known without our understanding why or how. Therefore it does not state *there is* or *you shall believe in only one God, omnipotent and everlasting,* etc. It begins in purely narrative form: *In the beginning, God created,* etc., which assumes that the dogma was known before the writing. . . .

XL. Creation is not man's province. Nor does his *unassisted* power even appear capable of improving on institutions already established. If anything is apparent to man, it is the existence of two opposing forces in the universe in continual conflict. Nothing good is unsullied or unaltered by evil. Every evil is repressed and assailed by good, which continually impels all existence towards a more perfect state. These two forces are present everywhere. We observe them equally in the growth of plants, the development of animals, the formation of languages and empires (two inseparable things), etc. Probably, human powers extend only to removing or resisting evil in order to separate from it the good, which may then develop freely according to its nature. The illustrious Zanotti has said: *It is difficult to change things for the better.* This thought conceals a great meaning under the guise of extreme simplicity. It agrees perfectly with

2 Maistre perhaps refers to the credo of the Savoyard priest in Rousseau's *Émile,* which must have seemed to him, if sincere, nevertheless lacking in orthodoxy.

another thought of Origen which alone is worth a volume. *Nothing,* says he, *can be altered for the better among men* WITHOUT GOD. All men sense this truth, even without consciously realizing it. From it derives the innate aversion of all intelligent persons to innovations. The word *reform,* by itself and prior to any scrutiny, will always be suspect to wisdom, and the experience of every generation justifies this instinct. We know all too well the fruit of the most attractive speculations of this kind.

XLI. Apply these general maxims to an individual example, the great question of parliamentary reform which has so powerfully stirred English minds for so long. Without being in a position to have a settled opinion, I am constrained to believe, from the mere consideration of the extreme danger of innovations founded upon purely human theories, that the idea of such reform is pernicious and that if the English yield too hastily to it, they will have occasion to repent. *But,* say the partisans of reform (for this is the classic argument), *the abuses are striking, undeniable; and can a formal abuse, a defect, be constitutional?* Yes indeed, for every political constitution has faults in its nature which cannot possibly be extracted from it. Moreover — and all would-be reformers should quail at the thought — these faults may change with circumstances, so that in showing that they are new, we have not yet proved them unnecessary. What prudent man, then, would not shudder in setting to work? Social harmony, like musical harmony, obeys the law of *just proportions* in the *keyboard of the universe.* Tune the *fifths* rigorously and the *octaves* will be dissonant, and conversely. Since discord is inevitable, instead of eliminating it, which is impossible, we must moderate it by a general distribution. Thus, in all parts, *imperfection is an element of the perfection possible.* This proposition is a paradox in form only. *But,* one may still object, *where is the rule for distinguishing the accidental flaw from that which belongs to the nature of things and is impossible to exclude?* Men upon whom nature has merely bestowed ears ask such questions, while those who have a good ear shrug their shoulders in reply. . . .

LXI. There have always been some forms of religion in the world and wicked men who opposed them. Impiety was always a crime, too. Since there can be no false religion without some ingredients of truth, all impiety does attack some divine verity, however disfigured. *But only in the bosom of the true religion can there be real impiety.* From which it inevitably results that impiety has never produced in times past the evils which it has brought forth in our day, for its guilt is always directly proportional to the enlightenment which surrounds it. By this rule must we judge the eighteenth century, for in this respect it is unlike any other. It is often said that *all ages are alike and men have always been the same.* But we must beware of these general maxims, which are invented by the lazy and frivolous to spare themselves the trouble of thinking. On the contrary, every age and every nation has a special distinctive nature which must be carefully considered. Undoubtedly, vice has always existed in the world, but it can differ in quantity, essence, dominant characteristics, and intensity. Although impious men have always existed, there never was before the eighteenth century, and in the heart of Christendom, *an insurrection against God.* Never before, above all, has there been a sacrilegious conspiracy of every human talent against its Creator. For this is what we have witnessed in our time. Vaudeville has blasphemed, as well as tragedy, and the novel, along with history and the physical sciences. Men of this age have prostituted genius to irreligion and, according to the admirable phrase of Saint Louis on his deathbed, THEY HAVE WAGED WAR AGAINST GOD WITH HIS OWN GIFTS. . . .

LXIII. Not until the first half of the eighteenth century did impiety really become a force. We see it at first spreading in every direction with amazing energy. From palaces to hovels, it insinuates itself everywhere, infesting everything. It follows invisible paths, acting secretly but infallibly, so that the most acute observer, seeing the effect, cannot always discover the means. By an unimaginable delusion, it even wins the affections of those to whom it is most deadly, and the authority it is preparing to sacrifice embraces it stupidly before receiving the blow. Soon a simple scheme becomes a formal association, which by degrees rapidly transforms itself into a confederacy and at length into a grand conspiracy which covers all Europe.

LXIV. Then that species of impiety which belongs only to the eighteenth century discloses itself for the first time. It is no longer the cold tone of indifference, of, at worst, the malignant irony of skepticism. It is a mortal hatred, the tone of anger and often of fury. The writers of that period, at least the most distinguished among them, no longer treat Christianity as an unimportant human error. They pursue it like a formidable enemy. They oppose it to the last extreme. It is a war to the death. What would seem incredible, if our own eyes had not seen the sad proofs of it, is that several of these men, who call themselves *philosophers,* advanced from hatred of Christianity to personal hatred of its Divine Author. They truly hated Him, as one would hate a living enemy. Two men especially,[3] who will forever be covered with the anathemas of posterity, have distinguished themselves in this form of villainy, which seemed beyond the powers of human nature, however depraved. . . .

LXVII. Europe is guilty for having shut her eyes to these great truths, and she suffers on account of her guilt. Yet still she rejects the light and does not acknowledge the Arm which strikes her. Few men, indeed, of this materialistic generation are in a condition to recognize the *date,* the

---

[3] Many would qualify for this distinction, but Maistre certainly means Voltaire, and the second is probably Condorcet, whom Maistre elsewhere has called "the most ardent enemy of Christianity." Cf. *Reflections on Protestantism,* written 1798 and later published posthumously.

nature, and the *enormity* of certain crimes perpetrated by individuals, by nations, and by sovereignties. Still less are they able to understand the sort of expiation which these sins demand and the worshipful marvel which compels evil to purify with its own hands the place which the eternal Architect has already measured for His marvelous constructions. The men of this age have chosen their lot. *They have sworn to fix their eyes upon the earth.* But it would be useless, even dangerous perhaps, to go into further detail. We are exhorted to *profess the truth in love.* Moreover, on certain occasions we must speak it only with respect, and despite every conceivable precaution, this step would be slippery for even the calmest and best-intentioned author. Besides, the world still contains a countless horde of men so perverse, so profoundly corrupt, that if they should bring themselves to suspect the truth of certain things, their wickedness might redouble in consequence, making them, so to speak, as guilty as the rebel angels. Oh! May their brutishness become instead even greater, if possible, in order that they cannot become even as guilty as men can be. Surely blindness is a dreadful punishment. Sometimes, however, it can still recognize love. That is all that can be usefully said at this time.

The German Universities and the Carlsbad Decrees

The German universities were important centers of political dissent during the first half of the nineteenth century. This was particularly true immediately following the Congress of Vienna, when many students who had participated in the War of Liberation (1813–1815) against Napoleon felt outraged by their rulers' disregard of the national and liberal ideals for which young men had fought and died. These views were shared by many professors, some of whom had been instrumental in calling their students to the colors in 1813. Student societies (Burschenschaften) became centers of liberalism and radicalism, but some of their most extreme behavior proved both tasteless and shortsighted. The three-hundredth anniversary of the Reformation was celebrated by Jena students at the so-called Wartburg Festival with the burning of books of reactionary authors. More serious were the activities of an extremist student group, the Unconditionals, who sought to achieve their ends by violence. The assassination of the reactionary poet and Russian spy, August von Kotzebue, in March, 1819, by a crazed student acting under extremist influence played right into the hands of

Metternich and his aide, Friedrich von Gentz, the ideologue of the Restoration and the translator of Burke's work on the French Revolution. In alliance with Prussia and other German states, they forced the Carlsbad Decrees through the Diet in September, 1819. These decrees imposed severe restrictions upon the universities and the press, and they established a central investigating committee to discover subversive activities. Gentz's justification for the decrees demonstrates that he was particularly anxious to terminate subversive teaching and activities in the universities and restore to them their function of providing loyal state servants. The decree pertaining to the universities proved remarkably effective in its intent and probably had a permanently devastating effect upon the political character of the German universities. In any case, university life under the decrees proved frustrating for liberal students such as Heinrich Heine, who "celebrated" the city of Göttingen and his alma mater in the opening pages of his Harzreise. *Heine's ironical portrait reveals another side of his talent and is suggestive of what university life must have been like in the heyday of the Carlsbad Decrees.*

Von Gentz's Introduction to the Carlsbad Decrees: Defects in the Schools and Universities

The attention of the Diet and of individual German governments was long ago directed to this subject, the exceptional importance of which has vividly impressed all Germany. A proper and wholesome leadership of the public educational system in general, but especially that of the higher institutions which prepare for direct entrance into practical life, is regarded in every state as one of the most urgent. A special duty and more than customary responsibility, however, rests on the German governments. This is so in the first place because in Germany education for public effectiveness and state service is left entirely to the upper schools; thus, because these upper schools are a main link in the chain of German unity, and as the benefit accruing from them is spread over the entire body of the nation, their defects are sure to be more or less felt; finally, because Germany owes a part of its reputation and therefore its place in the European community to its famous educational institutions, which up to now Germany has successfully maintained and in whose continued maintenance His Majesty will take the warmest and most active interest at all times.

From *Europe in the Nineteenth Century: A Documentary Analysis of Change and Conflict. Volume I: 1815–1870,* ed. Eugene N. Anderson, Stanley J. Pincetl, Jr., Donald J. Ziegler, pp. 80–83. Copyright © 1961, by the Bobbs-Merrill Company, Inc. Reprinted by permission of the publisher.

It can hardly be doubted that the actual situation of the German universities, with some recognized worthy exceptions, in many respects no longer corresponds to the reputation gained in better times. For some time thoughtful and well-meaning leaders have noticed and complained that these institutions have departed in more than one respect from their original character and from the purposes intended by their illustrious founders and patrons. Swept along by the stream of an age which is undermining everything, a large part of the academic profession has misunderstood the true function of the universities and has substituted an arbitrary and often pernicious one. Instead of training the youth entrusted to it for civil service, which was its first duty, and awakening in them the feeling from which the fatherland could expect mature fruits, they have pursued the phantom of a so-called cosmopolitan education, which fills minds ready to receive truth and error alike with empty dreams and infuses in them, if not bitterness, at least disrespect for and opposition to the established order. From a perverted course of this kind there have gradually developed illusions of higher wisdom, a disdain for all positive values, and the claim of a right to re-create the social order according to their own untried systems, to the great disadvantage of both the common good and the next generation; and a considerable number of the youth has transformed itself into teachers and reformers.

The dangerous deterioration of the upper schools has not escaped the attention of the German governments; but in part the praiseworthy desire not to hinder freedom of instruction so long as it did not directly and disturbingly affect civil relationships, and in part the confusion and distress brought about by twenty years of war, have prevented them from fighting the progress of the evil with thoroughgoing countermeasures.

Today, however, although we enjoy the beneficent influence of restored external peace and the honest and active effort of many German rulers to prepare for their peoples a happy future, and although we might expect the upper schools too to regain those limits within which they previously functioned so well for the country and for humanity, the strongest antagonism to the principles and measures upon which the present constitutions and the internal peace of Germany rest has come from this quarter. Because of the culpable cooperation or the unpardonable carelessness of the teachers, the best talents and instincts of our youth have been abused and made instruments of adventurous political plans and frivolous, even if unsuccessful, schemes. Since these dangerous byways have led to deeds which stain the German name, further indulgence would deteriorate into censurable weakness, and indifference to further misuse of such mistaken academic freedom would make all German governments responsible before the world and eternity.

Clearly, in this serious situation, the maintenance of public order must precede every other consideration; but the governments of the Confederation will not lose sight of the great question of how to help in overcoming the internal and perhaps very deep-seated defection of the schools from their original wholesome purpose. His Majesty therefore maintains that the Diet is obligated to take up this question, one so important to knowledge and public life, to family welfare, and to the solidity of the states; and it should not desist from the matter until its efforts shall have led to thorough and satisfactory results.

First, however, we must meet the trouble directly threatening us and take measures so that thoughtless enthusiasts or declared enemies of the existing order, in the present ruptured condition of several German universities, will be prevented from finding either material for arousing feeling further and deluded instruments for promoting plans, subjects, or weapons against the personal security of the citizens of the state. His Imperial Majesty therefore has no hesitation, in consequence of the preliminary memorandum on this matter, in recommending the accompanying plan of provisional measures proposed to this Assembly for immediate consideration and further discussion.

Provisional Decree Relating to the Universities, Unanimously Adopted, September 20, 1819

Decreed that, with a view to the fundamental improvement of the whole system of schools and universities a series of provisional measures shall, pending further deliberations of the Diet, be adopted without delay, for remedying the defects of the same. For this purpose the draft in question shall be adopted. This law of the Confederation shall, in accordance with its provisions, go into force immediately in all the states of the Union.

1. A special representative of the ruler of each state shall be appointed for each university with appropriate instructions and extended powers, and who shall reside in the place where the university is situated. This office may divolve upon the existing Curator or upon any other individual whom the government may deem qualified.

The function of this agent shall be to see to the strictest enforcement of existing laws and disciplinary regulations; to observe carefully the spirit which is shown by the instructors in the university in their public lectures

From *Translations and Reprints from the Original Sources in European History,* vol. 1: *The Reaction After 1815 and European Policy of Metternich,* ed. James Harvey Robinson (Philadelphia: University of Pennsylvania, Department of History, 1902), pp. 16–17. Reprinted by permission of Alfred J. Rieber, Chairman of the Department of History, University of Pennsylvania.

and regular courses, and, without directly interfering in scientific matters or in the methods of teaching, to give a salutary direction to the instruction, having in view the future attitude of the students. Lastly, they shall devote unceasing attention to everything that may promote morality, good order and outward propriety among the students.

The relation of these special agents to the Senate of the university, as well as all details relating to the extent of their duties and to their manner of action, shall be included in the instructions furnished by the superior government officials. These instructions shall be as precise as the circumstances which have dictated the appointment of the agents in question shall permit.

2. The confederated governments mutually pledge themselves to remove from the universities or other public educational institutions all teachers who, by obvious deviation from their duty or by exceeding the limits of their functions, or by the abuse of their legitimate influence over the youthful minds, or by propagating harmful doctrines hostile to public order or subversive of existing governmental institutions, shall have unmistakably proved their unfitness for the important office intrusted to them. No obstacle whatever shall prevent the execution of this provision so long as it shall remain in force and until such time as this matter shall be definitely regulated. Removals of this character shall however, never be made except upon the recommendation, accompanied with full reasons, of the aforesaid special agent of the government at the university or in view of a report previously required from him.

No teacher who shall have been removed in this manner shall be again appointed to a position in any public institution of learning in another state of the Union.

3. Those laws which have for a long period been directed against secret and unauthorized societies in the universities, shall be strictly enforced. These laws apply especially to that association established some years since under the name Universal Students' Union (*Allegmeine Burschenschaft*), since the very conception of the society implies the utterly unallowable plan of permanent fellowship and constant communication between the various universities. The duty of especial watchfulness in this matter should be impressed upon the special agents of the government.

The governments mutually agree that such persons as shall, after the publication of the present decree, be shown to have remained in secret or unauthorized associations or shall have entered such associations, shall not be admitted to any public office.

4. No student, who shall be expelled from a university by a decision of the University Senate, which was ratified or prompted by the agent of the government, or who shall have left the institution in order to escape

expulsion, shall be received in any other university. Nor, in general, shall any student be admitted to another university without a satisfactory certificate of his good conduct at the university he has left.

Heine's *Harzreise*

The City of Göttingen, famed for its sausages and its University, is in the Kingdom of Hanover. It has nine-hundred-and-ninety-nine houses, sundry Churches, a Library, a Lying-in-hospital, a University prison, an Observatory, and a Rathskeller where they sell excellent beer. The river Leine flows past the town, and in the summer it is used for bathing. It is cold, and in some places so broad that my dog Luder has to take quite a good run before jumping across it. It is a pretty little town, and the best view of it is obtained by turning your back to it. Nobody can deny its antiquity, for when I matriculated there five years ago (just before rustication) it presented the same grey, winking appearance that it does to-day, and was as plentifully provided with watchmen, beadles, theses, tea-parties, drinking clubs, smoking clubs, laundresses, cramming books, decoration ribbons, pigeon pies, councillors, dons, professors, and other kittle-kattle. It is maintained by some antiquarians that the city dates from the days of the Wandering of the Races, and that as each tribe passed on its way it dropped a microcosmic copy of itself, thus accounting for the multifarious Vandals, Frisians, Suabians, Saxons, Teutons, and Thuringians, who inhabit the town to the present day. Still the young barbarians who wander in hordes, may be distinguished by the colours of their caps and by the tassels of their pipes. Still they stroll along the Weenderstrasse to the bloody battlefields of Rasenmuhle, Richtenburg and Bovden, where they settle their disputes in the same old way. Their manners and customs date from the invasion of the barbarians, and they are governed by the leaders of their cock-pits, and by the code of honour which has their allegiance — A code which deserves its place among the *Leges Barbarorum*.[1]

The Göttingers may be classified under the headings of students, professors, philistines, and beasts — but there is no well-defined distinction between the four classes, perhaps the beasts are the most important. Far would it transcend my limits to denominate all the students, and professors — ordinary and extraordinary. The names of the students I don't

From Heinrich Heine, *Pictures of Travel (Reisebilder)*, trans. Russell Davis Gillman (New York: Scribner's, 1907), pp. 2–6. Reprinted by permission of Low (Sampson), Marston & Company Ltd.
[1] The law of the Barbarians. The reference is to the student custom of duelling. — G. D. F.

remember. As for the professors, they have yet their names to make. Numberless as the sands by the sea-side (or shall I say the scum on the shore) are the philistines. When one sees them day by day, writing in front of the University doors, with clean bills and dirty faces, one asks why the Good Lord could ever have created so many scoundrels?

For further particulars of the City the reader may refer to "Topography of Göttingen" by R. F. H. Mark. Although my attachment to the author is great, (he was my doctor, and dosed me with nothing but kindness) it is impossible to bestow unqualified praise upon his work. It is, indeed, my painful duty to correct him for not having given an emphatic contradiction to the scandalous tradition that the women of Göttingen have big feet. I have been employed for some time in controverting this rumour, and in order to enable me to do so with the more complete success, I became a member of a class for the study of comparative anatomy. My studies have enabled me to make extracts from the rarest works in the library. I have stood for many hours together in the Weenderstrasse in order to examine the feet of the ladies who walked by, and in the exhaustive essay which comprises the results of my studies, I deal with (a) Feet in general: (b) Feet in the Olden Times: (c) Elephants' Feet: (d) The Feet of the Women of Göttingen: (e) A precis of the conversation respecting their feet, overheard in Ulrich's tea-gardens: (f) Reflections on the collateral relations of these feet, with observations on calves, knees, etc., etc.: and (g) some copperplate facsimiles of the Göttingen famale foot, if I am able to obtain paper of a sufficiently large size.

Early in the morning I left Göttingen. Doubtless the learned ———— was still in his bed, dreaming that he was walking in a pleasant garden, full of flower-beds planted with strips of paper on each of which was inscribed a quotation. All radiant with sunlight were these paper flowers, and the dreaming Professor wandered from one to the other, carefully plucking and transplanting them to new beds, while the nightingales enraptured his old heart with the sweetness of their melodies.

At the Weendenthor I met two little boys — genuine aborigines. Said one to the other, "I will have nothing to do with Theodore; he is a boor. Yesterday he did not know the genitive of *mensa*." I must record these words, trivial as they may seem, for I should like them to be engraven on the portals of the town gate as the motto of the city, and a visible token of the musty pedantry of the learned University of Göttingen.

A sweet little breeze greeted me as I left the streets for the country road. The birds sang gleefully, and I also felt fresh and gay. The tonic was needed, for too long had I allowed myself to be bound in the stables of the Pandects; too long had my brain been clouded with the cobwebs of Roman casuists. My heart had been iron-bound by the bars of illiberal philosophies, and my ears were bedinned with Justinian, Tribonian, Hermogenian and Dummerjahn. I actually mistook a pair of lovers sitting hand-in-hand under a May tree for a clasped volume of the Corpus Juris. Even at this early hour, the road was lively with market-women and donkey drivers. Passing the village of Weende, I saw Shepherd and Doris [2] — not Gessner's idyllic pair — but a couple of orthodox University bull-bogs, intent upon stopping students' duels at Bovden, and resolutely determined to prevent the smuggling of any new ideas into the University, by any speculative tutor or student whatsoever, without the customary tedious quarantine at Göttingen! The Shepherd gave me a cordial greeting, for he, too, is an author, and has repeatedly named me in his bi-annual publications — to say nothing of his citations of me and his pressing invitations, written with chalk on my door, when he did not find me at home. Merrily the post chaises rolled by, filled with students, some of them going home for the holidays, some going never to return. Innumerable are the changes in a University town like Göttingen. Ever coming, ever going; a new generation every three years. Life there is like the sea; term after term, like wave upon wave, presses on that which has gone before; and amidst all this mutability nothing is stagnant but the Professors, and they are changeless as the Pyramids of Egypt. Yet there is a difference. In these Pyramids of Göttingen no wisdom is concealed!

[2] Heine is using the literary reference to satirize the university officials charged with discipline and censorship. As the lines which follow show, they had demonstrated considerable "interest" in Heine. — G. D. F.

THE RISING TIDE
OF REVOLUTION
Chapter 2

The early 1820's were good years for the forces of reaction, and from the British Isles to Russia repressive measures seemed to be achieving their goals. Austria crushed the Neapolitan Revolution of 1820 and the Piedmontese Revolution of 1821; France acted as the agent of the "concert of Europe" and in 1823 put down the forces of revolution in Spain. Reactionary Tsar Nicholas I began his reign as the "policeman of Europe" by liquidating the Decembrist Revolt of 1825 in Russia. Unfortunately for Metternich, however, even these joyous events were marred by untoward developments that proved destructive to his basic goals. Castlereagh committed suicide in 1822, and English support for the congress system died with him. Castlereagh had been committed to the system despite his refusal to sanction interference in the affairs of other states, but his successor, George Canning, was hostile to the system itself. The Congress of Verona (1822), the last of the congresses, sent France into Spain without British sanction. Even in his central European bailiwick, Metternich was unable to succeed fully in his policy of repression because of the strength of liberalism and constitutionalism in southern Germany. Finally, Nicholas I, normally to be relied upon in crushing revolutions and preventing change, found it in Russia's interest to support the Greeks in their successful war of independence against the Ottoman Empire from 1821 to 1829.

In the long run, liberalism and nationalism could receive only fresh impetus from the political stagnation of Metternichean Europe and Tory England. The gap between state and society widened, and the middle class of property and education was alienated. Liberalism was revolutionary only when it was forced to be. The liberals demanded constitutional government, suffrage for the propertied, freedom of conscience, freedom of speech, assembly, and press, and the right to pursue economic interests without irritating restrictions. In Germany, Italy, Greece, and Poland, liberalism and nationalism were virtually synonymous because the opponents of the existing order correctly recognized

that national disunity and foreign domination went hand in hand with
political repression.

Liberalism, however, was not an entirely homogeneous movement.
The differing forms it took reflected the variety of Europe's historical
experience. In England, with its political revolution already accomplished and its industrial revolution in process, liberalism was more self-
confident and pragmatic than it was on the Continent. Appropriately,
it found its major expression in Jeremy Bentham's philosophy of Utilitarianism. In France, the liberalism of Benjamin Constant was more
rationalistic and bore the obvious influence of the French Enlightenment. Liberal doctrine became more confusing and less certain of itself
as it moved eastward across the Continent. In southern Germany,
where French ideas and liberal politics were strong, Karl Welcker and
Carl von Rotteck, both professors at the University of Freiburg, assumed a doctrinaire posture resembling that of their French colleagues,
but they were unable to find a successful formula for asserting the sovereignty of the people and emphasized the sovereignty of constitutionally
formulated law instead. In northern Germany, where English influences were strong, a more moderate, classical liberalism, typified by
Göttingen history professor Friedrich Christoph Dahlmann, argued the
case for constitutionalism and organic reform within a monarchical
order. The liberal movement in Prussia was strongest in the Rhineland,
a center of French influence and industrial development. In Berlin,
however, was an important group of bureaucratic liberals who, as in
the days of Napoleon and the Prussian Reform Movement, hoped to
accomplish by good administration what France and England had
achieved by revolution.

Between 1830 and 1832 Europe experienced another round of up-
heavals that with some accuracy reflected the strength and character of
the liberal-nationalist forces. England chose reform rather than revolution. The victor at Waterloo, the duke of Wellington, demonstrated
the bankruptcy of Tory rule by opposing Catholic emancipation (that
is, the right of Catholics to hold office) and then turning to support it
from fear of civil war in Ireland. The resultant confusion in Tory
ranks enabled the Whigs to assume office in 1830 and to force through a
Reform Bill in a bitter parliamentary and electoral battle in 1831 and
1832. The bill was moderate, but it began suffrage and parliamentary
reform that eventually culminated in democratic suffrage. France suffered under the reactionary and short-sighted rule of Charles X, who
sincerely believed in the divine right of kings and who was foolish
enough to attempt a reversal of liberal election victories by unilateral
change of the electoral law. In the July Revolution of 1830, he was
overthrown by force and replaced by Louis-Philippe, duke of Orleans,
who could be counted on to behave in a constitutional manner and to

serve the interests of the upper bourgeoisie who had put him in office. As in England, reform and revolution in France at this time served the interests of the propertied middle class. The impulse from Paris spread rapidly to Belgium, which won its independence from Holland, and to Poland and parts of Italy and Germany. The uprisings in Poland and Italy were crushed by Prussia and Austria, and in Germany, Metternich and his Prussian allies responded to the liberal measures in some of the smaller states by introducing a new series of repressive acts in the Diet of the Confederation. Ironically, Metternich, the archenemy of German unity, was constantly trying to strengthen the powers of the diet over the states in order to fight the forces of nationalism and liberalism!

Utilitarianism

The conservatives who opposed change on the grounds of the sanctity of history and tradition found a forceful and effective opponent in Jeremy Bentham (1748–1832). Bentham and the philosophical radicals he influenced, such as James Mill, attempted to base ethics and politics on the fundamental and observable tendency of men to seek pleasure and avoid pain. However unsatisfactory such an approach might be to students of depth psychology, it was liberating in the context of early nineteenth-century thought because it provided a rational foundation for reform, a kind of calculus by which men could judge the value and propriety of their laws and institutions. On the one hand, Bentham's doctrines supported the laissez faire dogma of Adam Smith and other liberal economists because of the assumption that men will do the proper thing if they pursue their own nature and interest. In short, Bentham's philosophy was individualistic and opposed organic theories of state and society. On the other hand, Bentham's work did much to promote reform of all kinds — political, social, legal, and penal — and Bentham himself contributed directly to such efforts. Bentham's insistence that all institutions had to be tested according to their usefulness meant that it was appropriate and necessary to question the existing order. Utilitarianism opened the way for reforms that were often at variance with strict laissez faire doctrine. Also, once common law and the penal code were subjected to rational inspection according to the principle of utility, reforms of the rather antiquated English legal and penal codes became an obvious necessity. Bentham's most famous work,

An Introduction to the Principles of Morals and Legislation (*1780*), *was designed to bring about some of those reforms.*

Bentham's *Introduction to the Principles of Morals and Legislation*

OF THE PRINCIPLE OF UTILITY

I. Nature has placed mankind under the governance of two sovereign masters, *pain* and *pleasure*. It is for them alone to point out what we ought to do, as well as to determine what we shall do. On the one hand the standard of right and wrong, on the other the chain of causes and effects, are fastened to their throne. They govern us in all we do, in all we say, in all we think: every effort we can make to throw off our subjection, will serve but to demonstrate and confirm it. In words a man may pretend to abjure their empire: but in reality he will remain subject to it all the while. The *principle of utility* recognises this subjection, and assumes it for the foundation of that system, the object of which is to rear the fabric of felicity by the hands of reason and of law. Systems which attempt to question it, deal in sounds instead of sense, in caprice instead of reason, in darkness instead of light.

But enough of metaphor and declamation: it is not by such means that moral science is to be improved.

II. The principle of utility is the foundation of the present work: it will be proper therefore at the outset to give an explicit and determinate account of what is meant by it. By the principle of utility is meant that principle which approves or disapproves of every action whatsoever, according to the tendency which it appears to have to augment or diminish the happiness of the party whose interest is in question: or, what is the same thing in other words, to promote or to oppose that happiness. I say of every action whatsoever; and therefore not only of every action of a private individual, but of every measure of government.

III. By utility is meant that property in any object, whereby it tends to produce benefit, advantage, pleasure, good, or happiness, (all this in the present case comes to the same thing) or (what comes again to the same thing) to prevent the happening of mischief, pain, evil, or unhappiness to the party whose interest is considered: if that party be the community in general, then the happiness of the community: if a particular individual, then the happiness of that individual.

IV. The interest of the community is one of the most general expressions that can occur in the phraseology of morals: no wonder that the

From Jeremy Bentham, *An Introduction to the Principles of Morals and Legislation*, chs. 1 and 4 (London, 1923), pp. 1–7, 29–32.

meaning of it is often lost. When it has a meaning, it is this. The community is a fictitious *body,* composed of the individual persons who are considered as constituting as it were its *members.* The interest of the community then is, what? — the sum of the interests of the several members who compose it.

V. It is in vain to talk of the interest of the community, without understanding what is the interest of the individual. A thing is said to promote the interest, or to be *for* the interest, of an individual, when it tends to add to the sum total of his pleasures: or, what comes to the same thing, to diminish the sum total of his pains.

VI. An action then may be said to be conformable to the principle of utility, or, for shortness sake, to utility, (meaning with respect to the community at large) when the tendency it has to augment the happiness of the community is greater than any it has to diminish it.

VII. A measure of government (which is but a particular kind of action, performed by a particular person or persons) may be said to be conformable to or dictated by the principle of utility, when in like manner the tendency which it has to augment the happiness of the community is greater than any which it has to diminish it.

VIII. When an action, or in particular a measure of government, is supposed by a man to be conformable to the principle of utility, it may be convenient, for the purposes of discourse, to imagine a kind of law or dictate, called a law or dictate of utility: and to speak of the action in question, as being conformable to such law or dictate.

IX. A man may be said to be a partisan of the principle of utility, when the approbation or disapprobation he annexes to any action, or to any measure, is determined by and proportioned to the tendency which he conceives it to have to augment or to diminish the happiness of the community: or in other words, to its conformity or unconformity to the laws or dictates of utility.

X. Of an action that is conformable to the principle of utility one may always say either that it is one that ought to be done, or at least that it is not one that ought not to be done. One may say also, that it is right it should be done; at least that it is not wrong it should be done: that it is a right action; at least that it is not a wrong action. When thus interpreted, the words *ought* and *right* and *wrong,* and others of that stamp, have a meaning: when otherwise, they have none.

XI. Has the rectitude of this principle been ever formally contested? It should seem that it had, by those who have not known what they have been meaning. Is it susceptible of any direct proof? it should seem not: for that which is used to prove every thing else, cannot itself be proved: a chain of proofs must have their commencement somewhere. To give such proof is as impossible as it is needless.

XII. Not that there is or ever has been that human creature breathing, however stupid or perverse, who has not on many, perhaps on most occasions of his life, deferred to it. By the natural constitution of the human frame, on most occasions of their lives men in general embrace this principle, without thinking of it: if not for the ordering of their own actions, yet for the trying of their own actions, as well as of those of other men. There have been, at the same time, not many, perhaps, even of the most intelligent, who have been disposed to embrace it purely and without reserve. There are even few who have not taken some occasion or other to quarrel with it, either on account of their not understanding always how to apply it, or on account of some prejudice or other which they were afraid to examine into, or could not bear to part with. For such is the stuff that man is made of: in principle and in practice, in a right track and in a wrong one, the rarest of all human qualities is consistency.

XIII. When a man attempts to combat the principle of utility, it is with reasons drawn, without his being aware of it, from that very principle itself. His arguments, if they prove any thing, prove not that the principle is *wrong*, but that, according to the applications he supposes to be made of it, it is *misapplied*. Is it possible for a man to move the earth? Yes; but he must first find out another earth to stand upon.

XIV. To disprove the propriety of it by arguments is impossible; but, from the causes that have been mentioned, or from some confused or partial view of it, a man may happen to be disposed not to relish it. Where this is the case, if he thinks the settling of his opinions on such a subject worth the trouble, let him take the following steps, and at length, perhaps, he may come to reconcile himself to it.

1. Let him settle with himself, whether he would wish to discard this principle altogether; if so, let him consider what it is that all his reasonings (in matters of politics especially) can amount to?

2. If he would, let him settle with himself, whether he would judge and act without any principle, or whether there is any other he would judge and act by?

3. If there be, let him examine and satisfy himself whether the principle he thinks he has found is really any separate intelligible principle; or whether it be not a mere principle in words, a kind of phrase, which at bottom expresses neither more nor less than the mere averment of his own unfounded sentiments; that is, what in another person he might be apt to call caprice?

4. If he is inclined to think that his own approbation or disapprobation, annexed to the idea of an act, without any regard to its consequences, is a sufficient foundation for him to judge and act upon, let him ask himself whether his sentiment is to be a standard of right and wrong, with respect to every other man, or whether every man's sentiment has the same privilege of being a standard to itself?

5. In the first case, let him ask himself whether his principle is not despotical, and hostile to all the rest of human race?

6. In the second case, whether it is not anarchial, and whether at this

rate there are not as many different standards of right and wrong as there are men? and whether even to the same man, the same thing, which is right to-day, may not (without the least change in its nature) be wrong to-morrow? and whether the same thing is not right and wrong in the same place at the same time? and in either case, whether all argument is not at an end? and whether, when two men have said, 'I like this,' and 'I don't like it,' they can (upon such a principle) have any thing more to say?

7. If he should have said to himself, No: for that the sentiment which he proposes as a standard must be grounded on reflection, let him say on what particular the reflection is to turn? if on particulars having relation to the utility of the act, then let him say whether this is not deserting his own principle, and borrowing assistance from that very one in opposition to which he sets it up: or if not on those particulars, on what other particulars?

8. If he should be for compounding the matter, and adopting his own principle in part, and the principle of utility in part, let him say how far he will adopt it?

9. When he has settled with himself where he will stop, then let him ask himself how he justifies to himself the adopting it so far? and why he will not adopt it any farther?

10. Admitting any other principle than the principle of utility to be a right principle, a principle that it is right for a man to pursue; admitting (what is not true) that the word *right* can have a meaning without reference to utility, let him say whether there is any such thing as a *motive* that a man can have to pursue the dictates of it: if there is, let him say what that motive is, and how it is to be distinguished from those which enforce the dictates of utility: if not, then lastly let him say what it is this other principle can be good for?

VALUE OF A LOT OF PLEASURE OR PAIN; HOW TO BE MEASURED

I. Pleasures then, and the avoidance of pains, are the *ends* which the legislator has in view: it behoves him therefore to understand their *value*. Pleasures and pains are the *instruments* he has to work with: it behoves him therefore to understand their force, which is again, in other words, their value.

II. To a person considered *by himself,* the value of a pleasure or pain considered *by itself,* will be greater or less, according to the four following circumstances:

1. Its *intensity.*
2. Its *duration.*
3. Its *certainty* or *uncertainty.*
4. Its *propinquity* or *remoteness.*

III. These are the circumstances which are to be considered in estimating a pleasure or a pain considered each of them by itself. But when the value of any pleasure or pain is considered for the purpose of estimating the tendency of any *act* by which it is produced, there are two other circumstances to be taken into the account; these are,

5. Its *fecundity,* or the chance it has of being followed by sensations of the *same* kind: that is, pleasures, if it be a pleasure: pains, if it be a pain.

6. Its *purity,* or the chance it has of *not* being followed by sensations of the *opposite* kind: that is, pains, if it be a pleasure: pleasures, if it be a pain.

These two last, however, are in strictness scarcely to be deemed properties of the pleasure or the pain itself; they are not, therefore, in strictness to be taken into the account of the value of that pleasure or that pain. They are in strictness to be deemed properties only of the act, or other event, by which such pleasure or pain has been produced; and accordingly are only to be taken into the account of the tendency of such act or such event.

IV. To a *number* of persons, with reference to each of whom the value of a pleasure or a pain is considered, it will be greater or less, according to seven circumstances: to wit, the six preceding ones; *viz.*

1. Its *intensity.*
2. Its *duration.*
3. Its *certainty* or *uncertainty.*
4. Its *propinquity* or *remoteness.*
5. Its *fecundity.*
6. Its *purity.*

And one other; to wit:

7. Its *extent;* that is, the number of persons to whom it *extends;* or (in other words) who are affected by it.

V. To take an exact account then of the general tendency of any act, by which the interests of a community are affected, proceed as follows. Begin with any one person of those whose interests seem most immediately to be affected by it: and take an account,

1. Of the value of each distinguishable *pleasure* which appears to be produced by it in the *first* instance.

2. Of the value of each *pain* which appears to be produced by it in the *first* instance.

3. Of the value of each pleasure which appears to be produced by it *after* the first. This constitutes the *fecundity* of the first pleasure and the *impurity* of the first *pain.*

4. Of the value of each *pain* which appears to be produced by it after the first. This constitutes the *fecundity* of the first *pain,* and the *impurity* of the first pleasure.

5. Sum up all the values of all the *pleasures* on the one side, and those

of all the pains on the other. The balance, if it be on the side of pleasure, will give the *good* tendency of the act upon the whole, with respect to the interests of that *individual* person; if on the side of pain, the *bad* tendency of it upon the whole.

6. Take an account of the *number* of persons whose interests appear to be concerned; and repeat the above process with respect to each. *Sum up* the numbers expressive of the degrees of *good* tendency, which the act has, with respect to each individual, in regard to whom the tendency of it is *good* upon the whole: do this again with respect to each individual, in regard to whom the tendency of it is *good* upon the whole: do this again with respect to each individual, in regard to whom the tendency of it is *bad* upon the whole. Take the *balance;* which, if on the side of *pleasure,* will give the general *good tendency* of the act, with respect to the total number or community of individuals concerned; if on the side of pain, the general *evil tendency,* with respect to the same community.

VI. It is not to be expected that this process should be strictly pursued previously to every moral judgment, or to every legislative or judicial operation. It may, however, be always kept in view: and as near as the process actually pursued on these occasions approaches to it, so near will such process approach to the character of an exact one.

VII. The same process is alike applicable to pleasure and pain, in whatever shape they appear: and by whatever denomination they are distinguished: to pleasure, whether it be called *good* (which is properly the cause or instrument of pleasure) or *profit* (which is distant pleasure, or the cause or instrument of distant pleasure,) or *convenience,* or *advantage, benefit, emolument, happiness,* and so forth: to pain, whether it be called *evil,* (which corresponds to *good*) or *mischief,* or *inconvenience,* or *disadvantage,* or *loss,* or *unhappiness,* and so forth.

VIII. Nor is this a novel and unwarranted, any more than it is a useless theory. In all this there is nothing but what the practice of mankind, wheresoever they have a clear view of their own interest, is perfectly conformable to. An article of property, an estate in land, for instance, is valuable, on what account? On account of the pleasures of all kinds which it enables a man to produce, and what comes to the same thing the pains of all kinds which it enables him to avert. But the value of such an article of property is universally understood to rise or fall according to the length or shortness of the time which a man has in it: the certainty or uncertainty of its coming into possession: and the nearness or remoteness of the time at which, if at all, it is to come into possession. As to the *intensity* of the pleasures which a man may derive from it, this is never thought of, because it depends upon the use which each particular person may come to make of it; which cannot be estimated till the particular pleasures he may come to derive from it, or the particular pains he may come to exclude by means of it, are brought to view. For the same reason, neither does he think of the *fecundity* or *purity* of those pleasures.

Thus much for pleasure and pain, happiness and unhappiness, in *general*. We come now to consider the several particular kinds of pain and pleasure.

Three Revolutionary Movements

The spectrum of revolutionary activity in Europe between 1820 and 1830 was remarkably variegated and revealed the extent to which even the most autocratic of empires experienced serious unrest. In Russia, Tsar Alexander I himself incited a measure of unrest by toying with liberal ideas before 1818 and actually introducing a constitution in Russia's portion of Poland before dismissing his liberal advisers and embarking upon the reactionary and obscurantist path already indicated by his advocacy of the Holy Alliance. Alexander, however, was not the only Russian influenced by the new revolutionary ideas. Many of his officers and officials who had served in western Europe against Napoleon had returned impressed by what they had seen and profoundly disturbed by the backwardness of their homeland. Betrayed by Alexander in their hopes for reform, they sought to achieve their aims by secret organizations and conspiracy. Some of them tried to take advantage of the confusion over the succession following Alexander's death in December, 1825, by supporting Prince Constantine for the throne instead of the future Tsar Nicholas I. Unhappily, the movement was badly divided and disorganized, Nicholas was informed in advance, and the Decembrist Revolt was crushed. Some of the conspirators were executed; others were sent to Siberia. One of those executed was Peter Kakhovsky, an intellectual of means who had traveled extensively in Europe and was a member of the terroristic Northern Society. Impatient and romantic, he had played a major role in the uprising and had longed to emulate the German terrorist, Karl Sand, who had assassinated the poet Kotzebue. His motives are revealed in a letter to General Levashev, the head of the committee assigned by Tsar Nicholas to investigate the conspiracy. The explanation for the uprising given by Alexander Bestuzhev, another member of the Northern Society, is less romantic and shows an obvious concern with the economic development of Russia and the influence of industrializing England. He was more fortunate than Kakhovsky and was imprisoned in Siberia.

Although Greek independence was won finally because of a successful Russian war against the Ottoman Empire in 1828 and 1829, the heroic Greek struggle, which lasted from 1821 to 1829, inspired an outburst of Philhellenism throughout Europe. In Metternich's Europe, the Greeks gave nationalists and liberals a cause to idealize. *Romantic revolutionaries such as Kakhovsky fought in the Greek revolution, as did the radical and romantic poet Lord Byron (1788–1824). The poem that follows, written shortly before Byron's death in Greece, expresses the Philhellenism that swept Europe and an idealistic yearning for a heroic death in the cause of Greek liberty.*

Although by the beginning of the nineteenth century France had become the traditional land of revolution, the French revolution of 1830, though certainly not lacking in heroism and bloodshed, did lack the pathos of the Decembrist uprising and the glory of the Greek revolt. Charles X was ludicrously out of step with the French nation, and both the parliament and the press protested his high-handed tactics in trying to change the electoral law and muzzle the newspapers. They made the revolution, which the people of Paris carried out and the middle-class politicians then took over. Indeed, liberals such as Adolphe Thiers, historian and editor of the influential newspaper Le National, *had a candidate to replace the Bourbons, Louis-Philippe, who, as his proclamation shows, knew his part. France remained a monarchy and the charter was retained, but without the long preamble declaring it a grant of the king who ruled by the "grace of God." Louis-Philippe was simply the "King of France."*

The Decembrists in Russia, 1825

Peter Kakhovsky to General Levashev
Your Excellency,
Dear Sir!

The uprising of December 14 is a result of causes related above. I see, Your Excellency, that the Committee established by His Majesty is making a great effort to discover all the members of the secret Society. But the government will not derive any notable benefit from that. We were not trained within the Society but were already ready to work when we joined it. The origin and the root of the Society one must seek in the spirit of the time and in our state of mind. I know a few belonging to the secret Society but am inclined to think the membership is not very large. Among my many acquaintances who do not adhere to secret societies very few are opposed to my opinions. Frankly I state that among thousands of young men there are hardly a hundred who do not passionately

From Anatole G. Mazour, *The First Russian Revolution, 1825. The Decembrist Movement: Its Origins, Development, and Significance* (Berkeley: University of California Press, 1937), pp. 274–79. Originally published by the University of California Press; reprinted by permission of the Regents of the University of California.

long for freedom. These youths, striving with pure and strong love for the welfare of their Fatherland, toward true enlightenment, are growing mature.

The people have conceived a sacred truth — that they do not exist for governments, but that governments must be organized for them. This is the cause of struggle in all countries; peoples, after tasting the sweetness of enlightenment and freedom, strive toward them; and governments, surrounded by millions of bayonets, make efforts to repel these peoples back into the darkness of ignorance. But all these efforts will prove in vain; impressions once received can never be erased. Liberty, that torch of intellect and warmth of life, was always and everywhere the attribute of peoples emerged from primitive ignorance. We are unable to live like our ancestors, like barbarians or slaves. . . .

Emperor Alexander promised us much; he, it could be said, enormously stirred the minds of the people toward the sacred rights of humanity. Later he changed his principles and intentions. The people became frightened, but the seed had sprouted and the roots grew deep. So rich with various revolutions are the latter half of the past century and the events of our own time that we have no need to refer to distant ones. We are witnesses of great events. The discovery of the New World and the United States, by virtue of its form of government, have forced Europe into rivalry with her. The United States will shine as an example even to distant generations. The name of Washington, the friend and benefactor of the people, will pass from generation to generation; the memory of his devotion to the welfare of the Fatherland will stir the hearts of citizens. In France the revolution which began so auspiciously turned, alas, at the end from a lawful into a criminal one. However, not the people but court intrigues and politics were responsible for that. The revolution in France shook all the thrones of Europe and had a greater influence upon the governments and peoples than the establishment of the United States.

The dominance of Napoleon and the war of 1813 and 1814 united all the European nations, summoned by their monarchs and fired by the call to freedom and citizenship. By what means were countless sums collected among citizens? What guided the armies? They preached freedom to us in Manifestoes, Appeals, and in Orders! We were lured and, kindly by nature, we believed, sparing neither blood nor property. Napoleon was overthrown! The Bourbons were called back to the throne of France and, submitting to circumstances, gave that brave, magnanimous nation a constitution, pledging themselves to forget the past. The Monarchs united into a Holy Alliance; congresses sprang into existence, informing the nations that they were assembled to reconcile all classes and introduce political freedom. But the aim of these congresses was soon revealed; the nations learned how greatly they had been deceived. The Monarchs thought only of how to retain their unlimited power, to support their shattered thrones, and to extinguish the last spark of freedom and enlightenment.

Offended nations began to demand what belonged to them and had been promised to them — chains and prisons became their lot! Crowns transgressed their pledges, the constitution of France was violated at its very base. Manuel, the representative of the people, was dragged from the Chamber of Deputies by gendarmes! Freedom of the press was restricted, the army of France, against its own will, was sent to destroy the lawful liberty of Spain. Forgetting the oath given by Louis XVIII, Charles X compensates *émigrés* and for that purpose burdens the people with new taxes. The government interferes with the election of deputies, and in the last elections, among the deputies only thirty-three persons were not in the service and payment of the King, the rest being sold to the Ministers.

Spain

The firm, courageous Spanish people at the cost of blood rose for the liberty of their country, saved the King, the Monarchy, and the honor of the Fatherland; of their own volition the people themselves received Ferdinand as King. The King took the oath to safeguard the rights of the people. As early as the year 1812, Alexander I recognized the constitution of Spain.

Then the Alliance itself assisted France by sending her troops, and thus aided in dishonoring her army in the invasion of Spain. . . . Instead of the promised liberty the nations of Europe found themselves oppressed and their educational facilities curtailed. The prisons of Piedmont, Sardinia, Naples, and, in general, of the whole of Italy and Germany were filled with chained citizens. The lot of the people became so oppressive that they began to regret the past and to bless the memory of Napoleon the conqueror! These are the incidents which enlightened their minds and made them realize that it was impossible to make agreements with Sovereigns. . . .

The story told to Your Excellency that, in the uprising of December 14 the rebels were shouting "Long live the Constitution!" and that the people were asking "What is Constitution, the wife of His Highness the Grand Duke?" is not true. It is an amusing invention. We knew too well the meaning of a constitution and we had a word that would equally stir the hearts of all classes — LIBERTY! . . .

> Most obedient and devoted servant of Your Excellency,
> Peter Kakhovsky

February, 24th day, 1826

Alexander Bestuzhev to Nicholas I
Your Imperial Highness!

Convinced that You, Sovereign, love the truth, I dare to lay before You the historical development of free thinking in Russia and in general of many ideas which constitute the moral and political basis of the events of December 14. I shall speak in full frankness, without concealing evil, without even softening expressions, for the duty of a loyal subject is to tell his Monarch the truth without any embellishment. I commence.

The beginning of the reign of Emperor Alexander was marked with bright hopes for Russia's prosperity. The gentry had recuperated, the merchant class did not object to giving credit, the army served without making trouble, scholars studied what they wished, all spoke what they thought, and everyone expected better days. Unfortunately, circumstances prevented the realization of these hopes, which aged without their fulfillment. The unsuccessful, expensive war of 1807 and others disorganized our finances, though we had not yet realized it when preparing for the national war of 1812. Finally, Napoleon invaded Russia and then only, for the first time, did the Russian people become aware of their power; only then awakened in all our hearts a feeling of independence, at first political and finally national. That is the beginning of free thinking in Russia. The government itself spoke such words as "Liberty, Emancipation!" It had itself sown the idea of abuses resulting from the unlimited power of Napoleon, and the appeal of the Russian Monarch resounded on the banks of the Rhine and the Seine. The war was still on when the soldiers, upon their return home, for the first time disseminated grumbling among the masses. "We shed blood," they would say, "and then we are again forced to sweat under feudal obligations. We freed the Fatherland from the tyrant, and now we ourselves are tyrannized over by the ruling class." The army, from generals to privates, upon its return, did nothing but discuss how good it is in foreign lands. A comparison with their own country naturally brought up the question, Why should it not be so in our own land?

At first, as long as they talked without being hindered, it was lost in the air, for thinking is like gunpowder, only dangerous when pressed. Many cherished the hope that the Emperor would grant a constitution, as he himself had stated at the opening of the Legislative Assembly in Warsaw, and the attempt of some generals to free their serfs encouraged that sentiment. But after 1817 everything changed. Those who saw evil or who wished improvement, thanks to the mass of spies were forced to whisper about it, and this was the beginning of the secret societies. Oppression by the government of deserving officers irritated men's minds. Then the military men began to talk: "Did we free Europe in order to be ourselves placed in chains? Did we grant a constitution to France in order that we dare not talk about it, and did we buy at the price of blood priority among nations in order that we might be humiliated at home?" The destructive policy toward schools and the persecution of education forced us in utter despair to begin considering some important measures. And since the grumbling of the people, caused by exhaustion and the abuses of national and civil administrations, threatened bloody revolution, the Societies intended to prevent a greater evil by a lesser one and began their activities at the first opportunity. . . .

You, Sovereign, probably already know how we, inspired by such a situation in Russia and seeing the elements ready for change, decided to bring about a *coup d'état.* . . . Here are the plans we had for the future. We thought of creating a Senate of the oldest and wisest Russian men of the present administration, for we thought that power and ambition would always have their attraction. Then we thought of having a Chamber of Deputies composed of national representatives. . . . For enlightenment of the lower classes we wished everywhere to establish Lancasterian schools. And in order to bring about moral improvement we thought of raising the standard of the clergy by granting to them a means of livelihood. Elimination of nearly all duties, freedom from distillation and road improvement for the state, encouragement of agriculture and general protection of industry would result in satisfying the peasants. Assurance and stability would attract to Russia many resourceful foreigners. Factories would increase with the demand for commodities, while competition would stimulate improvement, which rises along with the prosperity of the people, for the need of commodities for life and luxury is constant. . . .

Most devoted servant of *Your Imperial Highness,*
Alexander Bestuzhev

[No date]

Economic vision for Russia [handwritten margin note]

Byron: "On This Day I Complete
My Thirty-sixth Year"

'Tis time this heart should be unmoved,
　Since others it hath ceased to move;
Yet, though I cannot be beloved,
　　Still let me love!

My days are in the yellow leaf;
　The flowers and fruits of love are gone;
The worm, the canker, and the grief
　　Are mine alone!

The fire that on my bosom preys
　Is lone as some volcanic isle;
No torch is kindled at its blaze —
　　A funeral pile!

The hope, the fear, the jealous care,
   The exalted portion of the pain
And power of love, I cannot share,
      But wear the chain.

But 'tis not *thus* — and 'tis not *here* —
   Such thoughts should shake my soul, nor *now*,
Where glory decks the hero's bier,
      Or binds his brow.

The sword, the banner, and the field,
   Glory and Greece, around me see!
The Spartan, borne upon his shield,
      Was not more free.

Awake! (not Greece — she *is* awake!)
   Awake, my spirit! Think through *whom*
Thy life-blood tracks its parent lake,
      And then strike home!

Tread those reviving passions down,
   Unworthy manhood! — unto thee
Indifferent should the smile or frown
      Of beauty be.

If thou regret'st thy youth, *why live?*
   The land of honourable death
Is here: — up to the field, and give
      Away thy breath!

Seek out — less often sought than found —
   A soldier's grave, for thee the best;
Then look around, and choose thy ground,
      And take thy rest.

The July Revolution in France

PROTEST OF THE PARIS JOURNALISTS, JULY 26, 1830

The legal régime is interrupted, that of force is begun. The government has violated legality, we are absolved from obedience. We shall attempt to publish our papers without asking for the authorisation which

From *The Constitutions and Other Select Documents Illustrative of the History of France, 1789–1907,* ed. Frank Maloy Anderson, 2d ed. 1908 (New York: Russell & Russell, 1967), pp. 501–05. Reprinted by permission of Russell & Russell.

is imposed upon us. The government has to-day lost the character which commands obedience. We are resisting it in that which concerns us; it is for France to decide how far its own resistance must extend.

PROTEST OF THE PARIS DEPUTIES, JULY 26, 1830

The undersigned, regularly elected [to the Chamber of Deputies] and at present in Paris, consider themselves absolutely obliged by their duty and their honor to protest against the measures which the councillors of the crown have recently made to prevail for the overthrow of the legal system of elections and the ruin of the liberty of the press.

The said measures, contained in the ordinances of July 25, are, in the eyes of the undersigned, directly contrary to the constitutional rights of the Chamber of Peers, to the public law of the French, to the prerogatives and decrees of the tribunals, and calculated to throw the whole state into a confusion which would compromise both present peace and future security.

In consequence, the undersigned, inviolably faithful to their oath, protest with one accord, not only against the said measures, but also against all the acts which may be the consequence of them.

And seeing, on the one hand, that the Chamber of Deputies, not having been constituted, cannot be legally dissolved; and on the other hand that the attempt to form another Chamber of Deputies by a new and arbitrary method is in formal contradiction to the Constitutional Charter and the acquired rights of the electors, the undersigned declare that they still consider themselves as legally elected to the deputation by the district and department colleges whose suffrages they have obtained, and that they cannot be replaced except in virtue of elections conducted according to the principles and forms determined by the laws.

And if the undersigned do not effectively exercise the rights and do not discharge all the duties which spring from their legal election, it is because they have been prevented from so doing by physical violence.

[Signatures.]

THIERS' ORLEANIST MANIFESTO, JULY 30, 1830

Charles X can no longer return to Paris: he has caused the blood of the people to flow. The Republic would expose us to frightful divisions; it would embroil us with Europe. The Duke of Orleans is a prince devoted to the cause of the revolution. The Duke of Orleans did not fight against us. The Duke of Orleans was at Jemmapes.[1] The Duke of Orleans is a citizen king. The Duke of Orleans has borne the tricolors with ardor. The

---

[1] The French won a victory over Austria and Prussia in 1792 at Jemmapes. The point is that Louis-Philippe fought on the side of the Revolution. — G. D. F.

Duke of Orleans alone can again bear them; we do not wish for any others. The Duke of Orleans does not declare himself. He awaits our will. Let us proclaim that will, and he will accept the Charter as we have always understood and wanted it. It is from the French people that he will hold the crown.

PROCLAMATION OF THE DEPUTIES, JULY 31, 1830

Frenchmen,

France is free. The absolute power was raising its flag; the heroic population of Paris overthrew it. Paris attacked has made to triumph in arms the sacred cause which in the elections had just triumphed in vain. A power, the usurper of our rights and the disturber of our repose, was threatening at the same time order and liberty; we re-enter into possession of order and liberty. No more fear for acquired rights; no further barrier between us and the rights which we still lack.

A government which, without delay, will guarantee us these blessings is to-day the first need of the fatherland. Frenchmen, those of your deputies who happen to be already at Paris have assembled; and, while awaiting the regular action of the chambers, they have invited a Frenchman who has never fought except for France, Monsieur, the Duke of Orleans, to exercise the functions of lieutenant-general of the kingdom. This is in their eyes the surest method to complete by peace the success of the most lawful defence.

The Duke of Orleans is devoted to the national and constitutional cause; he has always defended its interests and professed its principles. He will respect our rights, for he will hold his from us. We shall assure ourselves by laws all the necessary guarantees in order to render liberty strong and durable:

The re-establishment of the national guard, with the participation of the national guards in the choice of the officers;

The participation of the citizens in the formation of the department and municipal administrations;

The jury for press offences;

Legally organized responsibility of ministers and the subordinate agents of the administration;

The status of military men legally assured;

The re-election of the deputies promoted to public offices.

Finally, we shall in concert with the head of the state give to our institutions the development which they need.

Frenchmen, the Duke of Orleans himself has already spoken, and his language is that which befits a free country, "The chambers are about to meet," he tells you, "they will deliberate upon the means to assure the reign of the laws and the maintenance of the rights of the nation."

"The Charter shall henceforth be a reality."

Were present Messrs.:

[Here follow the names of eighty-nine deputies.]

PROCLAMATION BY LOUIS-PHILIPPE, AUGUST 1, 1830

Inhabitants of Paris,

The deputies of France, at this moment assembled in Paris, have expressed to me a desire that I should proceed into this capital in order to exercise here the functions of lieutenant-general of the kingdom.

I have not hesitated to come to share your dangers, to place myself in the midst of your heroic population, and to use all my endeavors to preserve you from the calamities of civil war and of anarchy.

In re-entering the city of Paris, I bear with pride the glorious colors which you have resumed and which I have myself for a long time borne.

The chambers are about to convene and will deliberate upon the means to assure the reign of the laws and the maintenance of the rights of the nation.

The Charter shall henceforth be a reality.

Louis-Philippe d'Orleans

DECLARATION OF THE CHAMBER OF DEPUTIES, AUGUST 7, 1830

The Chamber of Deputies, taking into consideration the imperative necessity which results from the events of July 26, 27, 28, 29 and the days following and the general situation in which France is placed in consequence of the violation of the Constitutional Charter;

Considering besides that, in consequence of that violation and of the heroic resistance of the citizens of Paris, His Majesty Charles X, His Royal Highness Louis-Antoine, dauphin, and all the members of the elder branch of the royal house have at this moment left French territory;

Declares that the throne is vacant in fact and in right, and that it is indispensable to provide therefor.

The Chamber of Deputies declares secondly that,

In accordance with the wish and in the interest of the French people, the preamble of the Constitutional Charter is suppressed, as wounding the national dignity, in appearing to *grant* to Frenchmen the rights which essentially belong to them, and that the following articles of the same Charter must be suppressed or modified in the manner which is about to be indicated.

Europe and the Independence of Latin America

Questions of imperial ambition and political principle were inextricably bound up in the European attitude toward the revolt of Spain's Latin American colonies. The British had been alarmed by France's decision to invade Spain and put down the Spanish revolution in 1823, because they feared not only for the continental balance of power, but also that France would take advantage of the situation to gain a foothold in South America and try to establish there the kind of exclusive commercial rights previously claimed by Spain. These fears were exaggerated, but Castlereagh's successor, George Canning, who had gained great popularity by attacking the Holy Alliance, discussed the British position in no uncertain terms with the French ambassador, the Prince de Polignac. Their discussion was recorded in the memorandum that follows. He warned against intervention, threatened recognition of the revolting colonies, and insisted that the United States be invited to attend any conference summoned by the European powers on the situation. The last was a very radical position since the European powers were not in the habit of attending congresses on an equal footing with republics. As it turned out, there was neither intervention nor a congress, but Britain did begin recognizing the new South American republics in 1824. Britain's position and the power of the British fleet gave substance to America's famous Monroe Doctrine during this period.

The Polignac Memorandum, October, 1823

The Prince de Polignac having announced to Mr. Canning, that His Excellency was now prepared to enter with Mr. Canning into a frank explanation of the views of his Government respecting the question of Spanish America, in return for a similar communication which Mr. Canning had previously offered to make to The Prince de Polignac, on the part of the British Cabinet; Mr. Canning stated that the British Cabinet has no disguise or reservation on that subject:

That the near approach of a crisis, in which the Affairs of Spanish America must naturally occupy a great share of the attention of both

From *Foundations of British Foreign Policy from Pitt (1792) to Salisbury (1902) or Documents Old and New,* ed. Harold Temperley and Lillian Penson (Cambridge: Cambridge University Press, 1938), pp. 70–75. Reprinted by permission of Cambridge University Press.

Powers, made it desirable that there should be no misunderstanding between them on any part of a subject so important.

That the British Government were of opinion, that any attempt to bring Spanish America again under its ancient submission to Spain, must be utterly hopeless; that all Negotiation for that purpose would be unsuccessful; and that the prolongation or renewal of War for the same object, would be only a waste of human life, and an infliction of calamity upon both parties to no end.

That the British Government would, however, not only abstain from interposing any obstacle, on their part, to any attempt at Negotiation which Spain might think proper to make, but would aid and countenance such Negotiation, provided it were founded upon a basis which appeared to them to be practicable, and that they would, in any case, remain strictly neutral in a War between Spain and the Colonies, if War should unhappily be prolonged; but that the junction of any foreign Power in an enterprise of Spain against the Colonies, would be viewed by them as constituting an entirely new question; and one upon which they must take such decision as the interest of Great Britain might require.

That the British Government absolutely disclaimed, not only any desire of appropriating to itself any portion of the Spanish Colonies; but any intention of forming a political connection with them, beyond that of Amity and Commercial Intercourse.

That, in these respects, so far from seeking an exclusive preference for its Subjects over those of other foreign States, it was prepared, and would be contented, to see the Mother Country (by virtue of an amicable arrangement) in possession of that preference; and to be ranked, after her, equally with others, only on the footing of the most favoured Nation.

That, completely convinced that the ancient system of the Colonies could not be restored, the British Government could not enter into any stipulation binding Itself either to refuse or to delay its recognition of their Independence.

That the British Government has had no desire to precipitate that recognition, so long as there was any reasonable chance of an accommodation with the Mother Country, by which such a recognition might come first from Spain; but that It could not wait indefinitely for that result; that It could not consent to make Its recognition of the New States *dependent* upon that of Spain; and that It would consider any foreign interference by force or by menace in the dispute between Spain and the Colonies, as a Motive for recognizing the latter without delay.

That the mission of Consuls to the several Provinces of Spanish America, was no new Measure on the part of this Country; that it was one which had, on the contrary, been delayed, perhaps too long, in consideration of the state of Spain, after having been announced to the Spanish Government, in the Month of December last, as settled; and even after a

List had been furnished to that Government of the Places to which such Appointments were intended to be made.

That such Appointments were absolutely necessary for the protection of British Trade in those Countries. That the old pretension of Spain to interdict all Trade with those Countries was, in the opinion of the British Government, altogether obsolete. . . .   ⌐ Trade

That Great Britain, however, had no desire to set up any separate right to the free enjoyment of this Trade. That She considered the force of circumstances, and the irreversible progress of events, to have already determined the question of the existence of that freedom for all the World; but that, for Herself, She claimed and would continue to use it; and should any attempt be made to dispute that claim, and to renew the obsolete interdiction, such attempt might be best cut short by a speedy and unqualified recognition of the Independence of the Spanish American States.

That, with these general opinions, and with these peculiar claims, England could not go into a joint deliberation upon the subject of Spanish America, upon an equal footing with other Powers, whose opinions were less formed upon that question, and whose interests were no way implicated in the decision of it. . . .

In observing upon what Mr. Canning had said with respect to the peculiar situation of Great Britain in reference to such a concert the Prince de Polignac declared he saw no difficulty to prevent England from taking part in the Congress however She might now announce the difference in the view which She took of the Question from that taken by the allies. The refusal of England to cooperate in the work of reconciliation might afford reason to think either that She did not really wish for that reconciliation, or that She had some ulterior object in contemplation, two suppositions equally injurious to the Honour and Good Faith of the British Cabinet. The Prince de Polignac further declared that he could not conceive what could be meant, under present circumstances, by a pure and simple acknowledgement of the Independence of the Spanish Colonies; since those Countries being actually distracted by civil Wars, there existed no Government in them which could offer any appearance of solidity and that the acknowledgement of American Independence, so long as such a state continued, appeared to him to be nothing less than a real sanction of Anarchy.

Polignac's reply

The Prince de Polignac observed that in the interest of humanity, and especially in that of the Spanish Colonies, it would be worthy of the European Governments to concert together the means of calming in those distant and scarcely civilized regions passions blinded by party Spirit; and to endeavour to bring back to a principle of Union in Government, whether Monarchical or Aristocratical People among whom absurd and dangerous theories were now keeping up Agitation and Disunion.

Mr. Canning without entering into any discussion upon abstract principles contented himself with saying that however desirable the Establishment of a Monarchical Form of Govern[men]t in any of those Provinces might be, he saw great difficulties in the way of it, nor could his Government take upon itself to recommend it.

Mr. Canning further remarked that he could not understand how an *European* Congress could discuss Spanish American Affairs without calling to their Counsels a Power so eminently interested in the result, as the United States of *America,* while Austria, Russia and Prussia, Powers so much less concerned in the subject were in consultation upon it.

The Prince de Polignac professed himself unprovided with any opinion of His Government upon what respected the United States of America; but did not *for himself* see any insuperable difficulty to such an Association. . . .

The British Reform Bill of 1832

A threat to pack the House of Lords was required before the Lords finally agreed to pass the Reform Bill in 1832. Yet the bill was hardly radical. It gave the vote to one out of every thirty inhabitants of Britain, and it gave some representation to the large urban centers. It increased the number of voters by one-half, an indication of how inequitable the old system had been as well as of how far England had to go before it became a true democracy. The July Revolution in France strongly affected the campaign for the bill. The revolution was a warning of what would happen if reform was not undertaken, and this warning was reinforced by numerous riots and threats of nonpayment of taxes by supporters of the bill. At the same time, the July Revolution demonstrated that a bourgeois revolution did not need to overturn the social and political order — the French Electoral Law of 1832 gave the vote to only one out of every two hundred citizens — and that it was better to enfranchise men of property than to drive them further on the path to radicalism. Perhaps the classic argument for the Reform Bill was presented by the historian and politician Thomas Babington Macaulay (1800–1859). Macaulay, whose "whig interpretation" of British history glorified the growing power of England over the centuries and the development of English constitutional liberties, praised the Reform Bill for its moderation and as an antidote to revolution. A brilliant writer and speaker, Macaulay presented a compelling case in the House of Commons on March 2, 1831, for giving suffrage to the

*propertied members of the urban communities that had developed as a
consequence of the industrial revolution.*

Macaulay's Speech in Parliament

I will not, Sir, at present express any opinion as to the details of the
Bill; but having during the last twenty-four hours, given the most diligent consideration to its general principles, I have no hesitation in pro-
nouncing it a wise, noble, and comprehensive measure, skilfully framed
for the healing of great distempers, for the securing at once of the public
liberties and of the public repose, and for the reconciling and knitting together of all the orders of the State. The hon. Baronet (Sir John Walsh)
who has just sat down has told us, that the Ministers have attempted to
unite two inconsistent principles in one abortive measure. He thinks, if I
understand him rightly, that they ought either to leave the representative
system such as it is, or to make it symmetrical. I think, Sir, that they
would have acted unwisely if they had taken either of these courses. Their
principle is plain, rational, and consistent. It is this — to admit the middle
class to a large and direct share in the Representation, without any violent shock to the institutions of our country. [*Hear!*] I understand those
cheers — but surely the Gentlemen who utter them will allow, that the
change made in our institutions by this measure is far less violent than
that which, according to the hon. Baronet, ought to be made if we make
any Reform at all. I praise the Ministers for not attempting, under existing circumstances, to make the Representation uniform — I praise them
for not effacing the old distinction between the towns and the counties,
for not assigning Members to districts, according to the American practice, by the Rule of Three. They have done all that was necessary for the
removing of a great practical evil, and no more than was necessary. I consider this, Sir, as a practical question. I rest my opinion on no general
theory of government — I distrust all general theories of government. I
will not positively say, that there is any form of polity which may not,
under some conceivable circumstances, be the best possible. I believe that
there are societies in which every man may safely be admitted to vote.
[*Hear!*] Gentlemen may cheer, but such is my opinion. I say, Sir, that
there are countries in which the condition of the labouring classes is such
that they may safely be intrusted with the right of electing Members of
the Legislature. If the labourers of England were in that state in which
I, from my soul, wish to see them — if employment were always plentiful,

From *Hansard's Parliamentary Debates*, vol. 2, 3d series, pp. 1191–1200, 1202, 1204–05.
Reprinted by permission of Her Majesty's Stationery Office.

wages always high, food always cheap, if a large family were considered not as an encumbrance, but as a blessing, the principal objections to Universal Suffrage would, I think, be removed. Universal Suffrage exists in the United States without producing any very frightful consequences; and I do not believe, that the people of those States, or of any part of the world, are in any good quality naturally superior to our own countrymen. But, unhappily, the lower orders in England, and in all old countries, are occasionally in a state of great distress. Some of the causes of this distress are, I fear, beyond the control of the Government. We know what effect distress produces, even on people more intelligent than the great body of the labouring classes can possibly be. We know that it makes even wise men irritable, unreasonable, and credulous — eager for immediate relief — heedless of remote consequences. There is no quackery in medicine, religion, or politics, which may not impose even on a powerful mind, when that mind has been disordered by pain or fear. It is therefore no reflection on the lower orders of Englishmen, who are not, and who cannot in the nature of things be highly educated, to say that distress produces on them its natural effects, those effects which it would produce on the Americans, or on any other people — that it blunts their judgment, that it inflames their passions, that it makes them prone to believe those who flatter them, and to distrust those who would serve them. For the sake, therefore, of the whole society, for the sake of the labouring classes themselves, I hold it to be clearly expedient, that in a country like this, the right of suffrage should depend on a pecuniary qualification. Every argument, Sir, which would induce me to oppose Universal Suffrage, induces me to support the measure which is now before us. I oppose Universal Suffrage, because I think that it would produce a destructive revolution. I support this measure, because I am sure that it is our best security against a revolution. The noble Paymaster of the Forces hinted, delicately indeed and remotely, at this subject. He spoke of the danger of disappointing the expectations of the nation; and for this he was charged with threatening the House. Sir, in the year 1817, the late Lord Londonderry proposed a suspension of the Habeas Corpus Act. On that occasion he told the House, that, unless the measures which he recommended were adopted, the public peace could not be preserved. Was he accused of threatening the House? Again, in the year 1819, he brought in the bills known by the name of the Six Acts. He then told the House, that, unless the executive power were reinforced, all the institutions of the country would be overturned by popular violence. Was he then accused of threatening the House? Will any Gentleman say, that it is parliamentary and decorous to urge the danger arising from popular discontent as an argument for severity; but that it is unparliamentary and indecorous to urge that same danger as an argument for conciliatory measures? I, Sir, do entertain great apprehension for the fate of my country. I do in my conscience believe, that unless this measure, or some similar measure, be speedily adopted, great and terrible calamities will befall us. Entertaining this opinion, I think myself bound to state it, not as a threat, but as a reason. I support this measure as a measure of Reform: but I support it still more as a measure of conservation. That we may exclude those whom it is necessary to exclude, we must admit those whom it may be safe to admit. At present we oppose the schemes of revolutionists with only one half, with only one quarter of our proper force. We say, and we say justly, that it is not by mere numbers, but by property and intelligence, that the nation ought to be governed. Yet, saying this, we exclude from all share in the government vast masses of property and intelligence — vast numbers of those who are most interested in preserving tranquillity, and who know best how to preserve it. We do more. We drive over to the side of revolution those whom we shut out from power. Is this a time when the cause of law and order can spare one of its natural allies? My noble friend, the Paymaster of the Forces, happily described the effect which some parts of our representative system would produce on the mind of a foreigner, who had heard much of our freedom and greatness. If, Sir, I wished to make such a foreigner clearly understand what I consider as the great defects of our system, I would conduct him through that great city which lies to the north of Great Russell-street and Oxford-street — a city superior in size and in population to the capitals of many mighty kingdoms; and probably superior in opulence, intelligence, and general respectability, to any city in the world. I would conduct him through that interminable succession of streets and squares, all consisting of well-built and well-furnished houses. I would make him observe the brilliancy of the shops, and the crowd of well-appointed equipages. I would lead him round that magnificent circle of palaces which surrounds the Regent's-park. I would tell him, that the rental of this district was far greater than that of the whole kingdom of Scotland, at the time of the Union. And then I would tell him, that this was an unrepresented district! It is needless to give any more instances. It is needless to speak of Manchester, Birmingham, Leeds, Sheffield, with no representation; or of Edinburgh and Glasgow with a mock representation. If a property-tax were now imposed on the old principle, that no person who had less than 150*l.* a year should contribute, I should not be surprised to find, that one-half in number and value of the contributors had no votes at all; and it would, beyond all doubt, be found, that one-fiftieth part in number and value of the contributors had a larger share of the representation than the other forty-nine-fiftieths. This is not government by property. It is government by certain detached portions and fragments of property, selected from the rest, and preferred to the rest, on no rational principle whatever. To say that such a system is ancient is no defence. My hon. friend, the member for the University of

Oxford (Sir R. Inglis) challenges us to show, that the Constitution was ever better than it is. Sir, we are legislators, not antiquaries. The question for us is, not whether the Constitution was better formerly, but whether we can make it better now. In fact, however, the system was not in ancient times by any means so absurd as it is in our age. One noble Lord (Lord Stormont) has to-night told us, that the town of Aldborough, which he represents, was not larger in the time of Edward 1st than it is at present. The line of its walls, he assures us, may still be traced. It is now built up to that line. He argues, therefore, that, as the founders of our representative institutions gave Members to Aldborough when it was as small as it now is, those who would disfranchise it on account of its smallness have no right to say, that they are recurring to the original principle of our representative institutions. But does the noble Lord remember the change which has taken place in the country during the last five centuries? Does he remember how much England has grown in population, while Aldborough has been standing still? Does he consider, that in the time of Edward 1st this part of the island did not contain two millions of inhabitants? It now contains nearly fourteen millions. A hamlet of the present day would have been a place of some importance in the time of our early Parliaments. Aldborough may be absolutely as considerable a place as ever. But compared with the kingdom, it is much less considerable, by the noble Lord's own showing, than when it first elected burgesses. . . . It is now time for us to pay a decent, a rational, a manly reverence to our ancestors — not by superstitiously adhering to what they, under other circumstances, did, but by doing what they, in our circumstances, would have done. All history is full of revolutions, produced by causes similar to those which are now operating in England. A portion of the community which had been of no account, expands and becomes strong. It demands a place in the system, suited, not to its former weakness, but to its present power. If this is granted, all is well. If this is refused, then comes the struggle between the young energy of one class, and the ancient privileges of another. Such was the struggle between the Plebeians and the Patricians of Rome. Such was the struggle of the Italian allies for admission to the full rights of Roman citizens. Such was the struggle of our North American colonies against the mother country. Such was the struggle which the *Tiers Etat* of France maintained against the aristocracy of birth. Such was the struggle which the Catholics of Ireland maintained against the aristocracy of creed. Such is the struggle which the free people of colour in Jamaica are now maintaining against the aristocracy of skin. Such, finally, is the struggle which the middle classes in England are maintaining against an aristocracy of mere locality — against an aristocracy, the principle of which is to invest 100 drunken pot-wallopers in one place, or the owner of a ruined hovel in another, with powers which are withheld from cities renowned to the furthest ends of the earth, for the marvels of their wealth and of their industry. . . . If it be said, that there is an evil in change as change, I answer, that there is also an evil in discontent as discontent. This, indeed, is the strongest part of our case. It is said that the system works well. I deny it. I deny that a system works well, which the people regard with aversion. We may say here, that it is a good system and a perfect system. But if any man were to say so to any 658 respectable farmers or shop-keepers, chosen by lot in any part of England, he would be hooted down, and laughed to scorn. Are these the feelings with which any part of the Government ought to be regarded? Above all, are these the feelings with which the popular branch of the Legislature ought to be regarded? It is almost as essential to the utility of a <u>House of Commons</u>, that it <u>should possess the confidence of the people</u>, as that it should deserve that confidence. Unfortunately, that which is in theory the popular part of our Government, is in practice the unpopular part. Who wishes to dethrone the King? Who wishes to turn the Lords out of their House? Here and there a crazy radical, whom the boys in the street point at as he walks along. Who wishes to alter the constitution of this House? The whole people. It is natural that it should be so. The House of Commons is, in the language of Mr. Burke, a check for the people — not on the people, but for the people. While that check is efficient, there is no reason to fear that the King or the nobles will oppress the people. But if that check requires checking, how is it to be checked? If the salt shall lose its savour, wherewith shall we season it? The distrust with which the nation regards this House may be unjust. But what then? Can you remove that distrust? That it exists cannot be denied. That it is an evil cannot be denied. That it is an increasing evil cannot be denied. One Gentleman tells us that it has been produced by the late events in France and Belgium; another, that it is the effect of seditious works which have lately been published. If this feeling be of origin so recent, I have read history to little purpose. Sir, this alarming discontent is not the growth of a day or of a year. If there be any symptoms by which it is possible to distinguish the chronic diseases of the body politic from its passing inflammations, all these symptoms exist in the present case. The taint has been gradually becoming more extensive and more malignant, through the whole life-time of two generations. We have tried anodynes. We have tried cruel operations. What are we to try now? Who flatters himself that he can turn this feeling back? Does there remain any argument which escaped the comprehensive intellect of Mr. Burke, or the subtlety of Mr. Wyndham? Does there remain any species of coercion which was not tried by Mr. Pitt and by Lord Londonderry? We have had laws. We have had blood. New treasons have been created. The Press has been shackled. The Habeas Corpus Act has been suspended. Public meetings have been prohibited. The event has proved that these expedients were mere palliatives. You are at the end of your palliatives. The evil remains. It is more

formidable than ever. What is to be done? Under such circumstances, a
great measure of reconciliation, prepared by the Ministers of the Crown,
has been brought before us in a manner which gives additional lustre to
a noble name, inseparably associated during two centuries with the dearest liberties of the English people. I will not say, that the measure is in
all its details precisely such as I might wish it to be; but it is founded on
a great and a sound principle. It takes away a vast power from a few. It
distributes that power through the great mass of the middle order. Every
man, therefore, who thinks as I think, is bound to stand firmly by Ministers, who are resolved to stand or fall with this measure. Were I one of
them, I would sooner — infinitely sooner — fall with such a measure than
stand by any other means that ever supported a Cabinet. My hon. friend,
the member for the University of Oxford tells us, that if we pass this law,
England will soon be a republic. The reformed House of Commons will,
according to him, before it has sat ten years, depose the King, and expel
the Lords from their House. Sir, if my hon. friend could prove this, he
would have succeeded in bringing an argument for democracy, infinitely
stronger than any that is to be found in the works of Paine. His proposition is in fact this — that our monarchical and aristocratical institutions
have no hold on the public mind of England; that those institutions are
regarded with aversion by a decided majority of the middle class. This,
Sir, I say, is plainly deducible from his proposition; for he tells us, that
the Representatives of the middle class will inevitably abolish royalty
and nobility within ten years: and there is surely no reason to think that
the Representatives of the middle class will be more inclined to a democratic revolution than their constituents. Now, Sir, if I were convinced
that the great body of the middle class in England look with aversion on
monarchy and aristocracy, I should be forced, much against my will, to
come to this conclusion, that monarchical and aristocratical institutions
are unsuited to this country. Monarchy and aristocracy, valuable and useful as I think them, are still valuable and useful as means, and not as
ends. The end of government is the happiness of the people: and I do
not conceive that, in a country like this, the happiness of the people can
be promoted by a form of government, in which the middle classes place
no confidence, and which exists only because the middle classes have no
organ by which to make their sentiments known. But, Sir, I am fully
convinced that the middle classes sincerely wish to uphold the Royal prerogatives, and the constitutional rights of the Peers. . . . Every Gentleman, I think, who has spoken from the other side of the House has
alluded to the opinions which some of his Majesty's Ministers formerly
entertained on the subject of Reform. It would be officious in me, Sir, to
undertake the defence of Gentlemen who are so well able to defend themselves. I will only say, that, in my opinion, the country will not think
worse either of their talents or of their patriotism, because they have

shown that they can profit by experience, because they have learned to see the folly of delaying inevitable changes. There are others who ought to have learned the same lesson. I say, Sir, that there are those who, I should have thought, must have had enough to last them all their lives of that humiliation which follows obstinate and boastful resistance to measures rendered necessary by the progress of society, and by the development of the human mind. Is it possible that those persons can wish again to occupy a position, which can neither be defended, nor surrendered with honour. . . . Do they wait for that last and most dreadful paroxysm of popular rage — for that last and most cruel test of military fidelity? Let them wait, if their past experience shall induce them to think that any high honour or any exquisite pleasure is to be obtained by a policy like this. Let them wait, if this strange and fearful infatuation be indeed upon them — that they should not see with their eyes, or hear with their ears, or understand with their heart. But let us know our interest and our duty better. Turn where we may — within, around — the voice of great events is proclaiming to us, Reform, that you may preserve. Now, therefore, while every thing at home and abroad forebodes ruin to those who persist in a hopeless struggle against the spirit of the age — now, while the crash of the proudest throne of the continent is still resounding in our ears — now, while the roof of a British palace affords an ignominious shelter to the exiled heir of forty kings — now, while we see on every side ancient institutions subverted, and great societies dissolved — now, while the heart of England is still sound — now, while the old feelings and the old associations retain a power and a charm which may too soon pass away — now, in this your accepted time — now in this your day of salvation — take counsel, not of prejudice, not of party spirit, not of the ignominious pride of a fatal consistency, but of history, of reason, of the ages which are past, of the signs of this most portentous time. Pronounce in a manner worthy of the expectation with which this great Debate has been anticipated, and of the long remembrance which it will leave behind. Renew the youth of the State. Save property divided against itself. Save the multitude, endangered by their own ungovernable passions. Save the aristocracy, endangered by its own unpopular power. Save the greatest, and fairest, and most highly civilized community that ever existed, from calamities which may in a few days sweep away all the rich heritage of so many ages of wisdom and glory. The danger is terrible. The time is short. If this Bill should be rejected, I pray to God that none of those who concur in rejecting it may ever remember their votes with unavailing regret, amidst the wreck of laws, the confusion of ranks, the spoliation of property, and the dissolution of social order.

THE REVOLUTION
IN ECONOMIC LIFE

Chapter 3

The industrial revolution was the most profound and permanent revolution of modern times. As in most major revolutions, the way in which it took place and its contribution to mankind have been hotly debated from its beginning. The industrial revolution would not have been possible without the rationalization of agriculture. In England, this took the form of the enclosure movement, whereas in Prussia, and later in Russia, it was preceded by the emancipation of the serfs and the creation of a landless agrarian proletariat, which either stayed on the land as agricultural laborers or drifted into the cities to provide the manpower for the new industrial order. Whatever form it took, agrarian rationalization meant a diminution of the number of independent farmers, and it was a critical first step toward the creation of an urban industrial society. The industrial revolution also settled the fate of the old system of domestic industry based on the so-called putting out system. Mechanical spinning and weaving were more productive and efficient than the laborious methods employed by domestic workers and their families in their homes, and the locus of textile production shifted from the home to the large factory with its power-driven machinery. On the Continent, the guild system, with its strict hierarchy of masters, journeymen, and apprentices, and its stress on craftsmanship and quality production, was another major victim of industrialization, although the destruction of the old crafts was much slower than the elimination of cottage industry. Indeed, it continues to this day and is always bitterly resented by those who are forced to give up their way of life. Industrialization is criticized for separating man from the products of his labor. Finally, the industrial revolution, at least in its initial phases, always was associated with exploitation involving child labor, long hours of employment for women and children, miserable working conditions, and the squalor of the early industrial city. Thus critics have complained not only that industrialization destroyed "merry old England" and "old Germany" but also that it turned England and, much later, Germany, into a kind of hell.

Nevertheless, from a more objective and long-range perspective, the industrial revolution appears as a beneficient necessity. The last half of the eighteenth century was marked by an enormous increase in the population of Europe, a phenomenon that demographers have yet to satisfactorily explain. Feeding and employing this population required agricultural rationalization and industrialization. To be sure, industrialization itself in its early phases promotes population growth, but the vast amount of pauperism in the nonindustrial areas of Europe between 1750 and 1848, when contrasted with the relatively small number of floating unemployed in the industrialized portions of Europe during the second half of the nineteenth century, demonstrates the capacity of industrialization to solve problems it helps to create. Similarly, hindsight demonstrates that the further industrialization and technological development advances, the better is the position of the working class and the sooner the odious conditions of the early factory system are mitigated or swept away. Once they can rise above the level of subsistence, workers begin to be conscious of their collective strength, and society and employers begin to do something about the grossest forms of exploitation once industrialization has taken root and industrial enterprise has become more secure.

One of the major questions of the industrial revolution was the role to be played by the state both in encouraging industrialization and in mitigating its hardships. In England, where the industrial revolution began earliest and was most profound, the laissez faire doctrines of Adam Smith (1723–1790), Thomas Malthus (1766–1835), and David Ricardo (1772–1823) were rigorously propagated and popularized by economic writers such as John Ramsay M'Culloch (1789–1864) and were warmly supported by businessmen and the Whig party. According to these classical economists and their supporters, the basic functions of the state were the negative ones of removing restraints on trade and free enterprise and making sure that the law was obeyed. The state was to serve as a "night watchman" and was to avoid interfering with the "laws of economics" by social and economic legislation. Supporters of this position achieved their greatest successes in the Poor Law of 1834, which made it extremely difficult and onerous for the indigent to receive relief, and in the repeal of the Corn Law in 1846, which ended the protection of English agriculture and made it possible for the urban population to buy food cheaply. However, at no time did laissez faire exist in pure form. The British shipping industry, for example, was given various forms of government help, and businessmen did not object to such assistance. Similarly, in the face of the desperate need for the regulation of child labor, Parliament passed the Factory Act of 1833, which marked the beginning of a continuous stream of social legislation.

On the Continent, the traditions of bureaucratic and centralized government made the continuation of mercantilist practices and the employment of state intervention more natural and acceptable. Economic historians differ on the role played by the state in European industrialization. Some argue that the state, especially in Prussia, played a positive role by running enterprises, training technical personnel, building railroads, and granting privileges. The dominant feeling today is that the most important work in the industrialization process on the Continent was done by private initiative and that the state's direct intervention in economic affairs was clumsy and often ill conceived. The state played its most valuable role indirectly by bringing about the legal and social reforms necessary for industrialization to progress: the elimination of serfdom, the destruction of guild privileges, and the creation of modern corporation laws.

Pauperism and Unemployment in France

Two of the most alarming phenomena of the industrial revolution were pauperism and unemployment, particularly in the depressed years immediately following the Napoleonic Wars. Industry was insufficient to absorb the population of the countryside, and bad economic conditions exacerbated the situation. The state frequently took remedial action by means of the dole and public works projects, but the potential unrest of what, by 1848, was increasingly identified as a "proletariat" caused the authorities no little anxiety.

Police Bulletin, Paris, March 8–9, 1817

This is the time of year when the provinces unload onto Paris part of their population, from that class which is simultaneously the most hard-working and also the laziest. Those who come to look for work enter into competition with local artisans and workers who are themselves far from fully employed. The newcomers can only increase the number of beggars and criminals. The Prefects have been asked to exercise more restraint and care in the granting of passports. In Paris bread is cheaper; it

From *Documents of European Economic History. Volume 1: The Process of Industrialization, 1750–1870,* ed. S. Pollard and C. Holmes (London: Edward Arnold, 1968), pp. 525. Reprinted by permission of Edward Arnold Ltd.

is a great attraction; but it entails sacrifices which are becoming increasingly burdensome. Paris has its resources; the country areas have theirs; the equilibrium in the division of taxation is very difficult to maintain. Abundance could solve everything, and policy could not have a more useful ally; but after eighteen months of rain the March storms are causing general gloom; there does not seem to be any end to the floods. . . . The worker who has passed his time on the wharves without seeing any work come his way begins to murmur; he makes his complaints heard, even if they are still discreet and subdued. Those who are employed speak of wage increases; observers have noticed for some time more agitation amongst this class, which never escapes from the surveillance of the police, and which is often saved from despair by the Government's help. However, the men can be seen in the bars spending what bit of money they have; they no longer have sufficient money to buy bread for their families, they have enough, however, to get drunk.

Prefect of Police to Minister, April 24, 1817

Every year about this time workers of all kinds, and especially those concerned with construction work, pour into Paris, where they hope to find work. The appalling food situation in several parts of France, and the advantages enjoyed in this respect by the capital, as a result of Government assistance, have again this year increased immigration from the Departments to Paris. A large number of workers can be found in Paris — and their number is increasing every day — who flock into the areas which attract them and wait until they are hired; but although the season is rather advanced there is not enough work available for those who seek employment. The embarrassment experienced at present by most businessmen does not permit the belief that they could undertake important construction or repair work before next year. It would appear very necessary for the Government to inaugurate a public works scheme to provide large scale employment. Public order has been maintained up to now among the workers; but it must be feared that a longer period of idleness and the resultant misery for these individuals may induce them into excesses which would be very difficult to repress. This object is too closely related to the maintenance of good order for me not to inform you about it; doubtless it will be presumed useful to call the attention of the Conseil des Ministres to such a state of affairs.

Among the works which the government could introduce to give employment and subsistence to large numbers, I feel that those concerned

From *Documents of European Economic History. Volume 1: The Process of Industrialization, 1750–1870,* ed. S. Pollard and C. Holmes (London: Edward Arnold, 1968), pp. 525–26. Reprinted by permission of Edward Arnold Ltd.

with the continuation of the Ourcq canal would offer a double advantage, since they would involve the movement out of Paris of a large number of workers who are at present in the capital. Inside the town, construction work would not be less useful for the maintenance of public order and the improvement of opinion. You know how Parisians value the attention paid by the authorities to work devoted to the improvement and salubrity of the capital. This method was constantly used by the last Government, even in the most critical circumstances, and the present dearness of foodstuffs appears to me to demand the employment of such measures at least until 1 August. By that time work in the countryside could occupy some of those who are at present unemployed; but the months of May and June will be especially difficult months to overcome.

Luddism in England,
France, and Germany

Both the large number of unskilled workers and the factories that could employ them were a threat to the artisans, who fell victim to technological unemployment. These artisans often responded to their economic deprivations by machine breaking, or Luddism, which received its name from the English Luddite riots that took place in 1811 and 1812. Although the English machine breakers were dealt with harshly, Luddism remained a problem both in England and on the Continent, as amply illustrated in the French city of Vienne and in the German state of Saxony, where artisan unrest was one of the most important social undercurrents of the Revolution of 1848.

The Sentencing of the Luddites

John Swallow, John Batley, Joseph Fisher, John Lumb, Job Hey, John Hill, William Hartley, James Hey, Joseph Crowther, Nathan Hoyle, James Haigh, Jonathan Dean, John Ogden, Thomas Brook, John Walker, you, unhappy prisoners at the bar, stand convicted of various offences, for which your lives are justly forfeited to the injured laws of your Country. You have formed a part of that desperate association of men, who, for a great length of time, have disturbed the peace and tranquillity of the West Riding of this county. You have formed yourselves into bodies; you

From Proceedings at York Special Commission (January, 1813).

have proceeded to the most serious extremities against the property of many individuals. The cause of your so associating appears to have been a strange delusion, which you entertained, that the use of machinery in the woollen manufacture was a detriment to the hands that were employed in another way in it; a grosser delusion never could be entertained, proceeding probably from the misrepresentations of artful and designing men, who have turned it to the very worst purpose which riot and sedition could produce. You have proceeded to great extremities. The first object, perhaps, seems to have been that of your procuring arms, in order to carry on your nefarious designs. With that view, it seems that some of you went about inquiring for such arms at different houses, and getting them wherever you could find them.

But not stopping there, and not contenting yourselves with getting what arms you could lay your hands upon, you proceeded to plunder the habitations with a great degree of force, and took from them property of every description, which you could find in those houses. An offence of that nature is brought home, and sufficiently established against you the prisoners *John Swallow, John Batley, Joseph Fisher, John Lumb, Job Hey, John Hill, William Hartley, James Hey, Joseph Crowther,* and *Nathan Hoyle.*

You the prisoners, *Job Hey, John Hill,* and *William Hartley,* did upon the occasion, when you went to the house of your prosecutor, carrying away certainly nothing but arms, but you carried them away with great terror, and under circumstances which were sufficient unquestionably to make him deliver what he had. The other prisoners, whose names I have last recited, have been concerned in breaking a dwelling-house in the night time, some of them getting notes, money, and other things; and the last prisoners, *James Hey, Joseph Crowther,* and *Nathan Hoyle,* for robbing a person in his dwelling-house.

The evidence, that has been given against you all, was too clear to admit of any doubt; and you have all been convicted of these offences upon the most satisfactory evidence.

You, the other prisoners, *James Haigh, Jonathan Dean, John Ogden, Thomas Brook,* and *John Walker,* have been guilty of one of the greatest outrages that ever was committed in a civilized country. You had been long armed and organized, you had assembled upon this night, when the mill of Mr. Cartwright was attacked; you had assembled at the dead hour of night in great numbers; you had formed yourselves into companies under the command of different leaders; you were armed with different instruments of offence, with guns, with pistols, with axes, and with other weapons; you marched in military order and array to the mill, which was afterwards in part pulled down; you began there your attack with firearms, discharged into that mill, and kept up a most dreadful fire, and at the same time applied the instruments, which you had brought there, of a description calculated to do the worst of mischief, in beginning to demolish the mill, intending, as it is obvious, to do also mischief to and to demolish the machinery which that mill contained. The cries and exclamations that proceeded from this riotous tumultuous mob thus assembled, of which you formed a very powerful part, were such as were enough to alarm a man of less firmness than that man possessed, who was the owner of the mill so attacked. Your cry was, "Get in, get in, kill them all"; and there is but little doubt, it is to be feared, that if you had made good your entry into that mill, these threats would have been put into execution, and that the mischief done would hardly have been confined to the machinery which was there. The courage and resolution, however, which that individual displayed, had the effect of making you desist at that time from the attack. . . .

In the awful situation in which you, prisoners, stand, let me seriously exhort you to set about the great work of repentance, and to spend the very short time that you must be allowed to remain in this world, in endeavouring to make your peace with your God, and to reconcile him by deep repentance. A full confession of your crime is the only atonement you can make for that which you have committed. Give yourselves up to the pious admonitions of the reverend Clergyman, whose office it will be to prepare you for your awful change; and God grant, that, worthily lamenting your sins, and acknowledging your wretchedness, you may obtain of the God of all mercy perfect remission and forgiveness.

Hear the sentence which the Laws of man pronounce upon your crimes. The sentence of the Law is, and this Court doth adjudge, That you, the several Prisoners at the bar, be taken from hence to the place from whence you came, and from thence to the place of execution, where you shall be severally hanged by the neck until you are dead. The Lord have mercy upon your souls.

Prefect of the Isère Department to the Sub-Prefect of Vienne, January 29, 1819

In the past the introduction of new machines has alarmed the working class, and experience has proved that economical processes have on the contrary improved its position, inasmuch as the manufacturers, with higher output at reduced prices, paid their workers at increased rates, and were never compelled to slow down or even to interrupt their work. Employees therefore benefit in such cases. The workers in your district ap-

From *Documents of European Economic History. Volume 1: The Process of Industrialization, 1750–1870*, ed. S. Pollard and C. Holmes (London: Edward Arnold, 1968), pp. 525–26. Reprinted by permission of Edward Arnold Ltd.

pear to fear that the machine for clipping cloth will throw idle those who do this work by the methods now in use. But these new processes are only brought in gradually, the manufacture expands with its increased man-power, a new classification of work is made, and in no case does a ✓ willing worker lack employment.

There is no question here of a new method peculiar to the town of Vienne. This machine is already used in a great number of factories and soon will be in all; thus the factories of Sedan and of Louviers, being no longer able to sustain the competition, were obliged to adopt the machines used at Verviers, for otherwise they would have had to close. These factories have prospered and the workers of all kinds, instead of lacking work, are now better off.

The same thing will undoubtedly happen at Vienne. Place the real position of affairs before the workers of that factory, reassure them, tell them that the paternal government of the King keeps a watch on their needs, and tell them also that if, contrary to what is expected of them by authority, they are guilty of disorders, they will incur a degree of severity which, far from improving their condition, will make it much worse. Their leaders are known, and they will be held responsible for all reprehensible acts.

I enjoin you to act with prudence and firmness, to gather around you all the force at your disposal, to keep an active watch, and, if you become aware of instigators of troubles, do not hesitate to have them charged and handed over to the tribunals.

I beg that you will communicate this letter to the Mayor of Vienne.

Official Report of Procurator-General Badin, February 26, 1819

We, procurator-royal of the tribunal of first instance at Vienne, Department of the Isère, report that, immediately on receiving information that today, 26 February, at half-past one in the afternoon, the new cloth-clipping machine belonging to Messrs Gentin and Odoard had just arrived at the bank of the River Gere, near its destination; that a great crowd of workers had rushed towards that place crying "Down with the clipper"; that carbine shots were heard, and finally that everything pointed to the mob's determination to resort to open pillage of a piece of movable property. We were taken to the spot, where the Sub-Prefect, the Mayor and the Commissioner of Police joined with us to authorise the

From *Documents of European Economic History. Volume 1: The Process of Industrialization, 1750–1870*, ed. S. Pollard and C. Holmes (London: Edward Arnold, 1968), pp. 527–29. Reprinted by permission of Edward Arnold Ltd.

use of armed force, and afterwards to note the nature and extent of the offence committed, the condition of the place of its occurrence, and to hear with us the declarations of those able to furnish particulars.

Having reached the entrance to Messrs Odoard and Gentin's workshop on the right bank of the river, we saw in the stream, at a distance of about fifteen feet, a wagon without horses, its shafts in the air, loaded with four or five boxes, of which one was visibly broken, and at three or four paces' distance in the water an instrument of iron or other metal of the same size as the box, as regards length; several posts of cavalry and of gendarmerie on foot and on horseback, placed at different distances along both banks of the Gere and on the heights, guarding all the avenues of approach; some of the windows overlooking the river were closed.

M. Despremenil, lieutenant-colonel of dragoons, commandant of the place, stated that some minutes before our arrival, when the armed force had not yet been able to disperse the mob on the right bank, several lightly-clad individuals whom he did not know, but whom he presumed to be workers, dashed into the water and threw themselves on the wagon, armed with wooden bars and with a cutting instrument or iron used by cloth-clippers; that they broke the first box they came upon and threw into the water one of the instruments it contained; that they were about to continue when Messieurs d'Augereauville, adjutant-major of the dragoons of the Gironde, de Verville, commandant of the gendarmerie, and afterwards brigadiers, dragoons, and gendarmes appeared on the scene and put the assailants to flight in spite of a hail of stones from the windows and from both sides of the Gere. Our special attention was called to the windows closest to the spot we were on, those of M. Tachet. M. d'Augereauville, who came up just then, lent confirmation to this by showing us his bleeding cheek, caused by a stone. There now appeared in succession, Messieurs Clement, Commissioner of Police; Chassin, police constable; Guillot, clerk of the firm Gentin and Odoard; Pierre Allard — Channerin, junior; Charreton, manufacturer, of the Becourdau firm; Charreton (the son) grocer; the two Rousset sons, the one a cloth manufacturer and the other a spinner, working with his brother, and Bizet (son) who gave us the following particulars.

Edlon Montal (Jean or Pierre) of Grenoble or of Baurepaire who has been an apprentice cloth-clipper with the firm of Bomières Junior, at Vienne, and who worked on the new road, was the one who used an iron instrument to break the boxes.

Pontet, known as Simon, a worker with the firm of Donnat and Boussut, was the head of the workers; he carried a wooden bar to break the machine. He was one of the first to get on to the wagon along with Hubert Richard, who works with Jean-Francois Ozier, clipper, at Vienne.

Jacques Ruffe, clipper with his cousin Dufieux, was on the wagon, breaking the boxes and throwing them into the water.

Imbert Claude, working with Darrieux on the new road, was likewise on the wagon, as were also Labre, who lives at the ambulance station, and Jean-Pierre Plasson, working with Dufieux.

The daughter of Claude Tonnerieux, butcher, threw stones at the dragoons and egged on the workers by her cries: 'Break them! smash them! go it!' and so on. The woman Lacroix, who has only one eye, also incited them.

Marguerite Dupon, spinner at Fremy's, used most abusive language to the lieutenant-colonel of dragoons.

Pierre Dejean de Saint-Priest, working with Velay Pourret, clipper, went round the shops yesterday, asking the clippers to assemble on the square.

Jacques Boulle, glass-maker, was observed to be shouting among the first workers who came down the Saint-Martin bridge.

Basset, weaver, said, 'We'll find the machine, sure enough,' and Rousset, living at the ambulance station, used these words: 'We'll get hold of Gentin' (one of the owners of the machine). 'It isn't the machine that we must knock to bits.'

One of the Linossier sons, called Flandre, was seen at the entrance to the steps leading down to the river, inciting his comrades by saying to them, 'Come along, let's go down.'

Jean-Baptiste Gros, working with Ozier the elder, threw a stone that hit his cousin, who is in the dragoons.

The woman Garauda shouted, 'The clipper must be broken.'

The woman Mange and one of her sisters also attracted attention by their shouts and their remarks.

Being unable to obtain further particulars, we asked M. Clement, commissioner of police, to transmit to us all those which he might eventually obtain; and exercising the right given to us by Article 40 of the Code of Criminal Instruction, we decide to issue a writ of arrest against the nineteen persons named and described above.

Luddism in Annaberg, Saxony, 1846–1848

According to the report of Police Sergeant Hirsch, there assembled on the afternoon of 9 November 1846, 'without prior permission of the Town Council, a large number of ribbon- and lace-makers and journeymen,' at the Annaberg 'hostel for ribbon- and lace-makers, coming from Annaberg, Bucholz and Schlettau. The purpose of the assembly was to destroy or put out of use the lace-twist machine erected at Eisenstuck &

From *Documents of European Economic History. Volume 1: The Process of Industrialization, 1750–1870*, ed. S. Pollard and C. Holmes (London: Edward Arnold, 1968), pp. 529–30. Reprinted by permission of Edward Arnold Ltd.

Co.' The impulse to the action by the ribbon- and lace-makers arose — as the court records show — from a mere rumour about such a machine at the above-named firm, which was going to 'make many workers redundant and create pauperism' in a population consisting mostly of ribbon- and lace-makers. Eisenstuck, who had got wind of the intentions of the ribbon- and lace-makers, sent a message to the hostel, and offered to allow a deputation of workers to search his rooms and convince themselves that there was no such machine. This was agreed to, and all ribbon- and lace-makers present attached themselves to the deputation. No damage to property ensued during the search, apart from a window pane broken by a flying stone, and no machine was brought to light. Nevertheless it seemed as though the affair would have serious consequences for many of the participants, since the Town Court of Annaberg ordered a police inquiry into the offences of obstructing public authority, breach of the peace, intended liberation of the leading ribbon- and lace-makers arrested on suspicion of rioting, and unauthorised gild assembly. If, after all this, the charges against the ribbon- and lace-makers were nevertheless withdrawn, 'following a royal command of 17 April 1848 based on the hearing before the Royal Court of Appeal at Zwickau, on 7 inst.,' the accused owed this above all to the fact that the State showed some understanding for their irritation, first caused by the rising prices of 1847 and then turned to recklessness by an irresponsible rumour, evidently wanting to avoid the antagonism between classes for tactical reasons, in the highly charged political situation just before the revolution.

The Population Problem

The most miserable aspects of the industrial revolution were intensified in theory and practice by the transformation of economics into the dismal science that Adam Smith and his French counterpart Jean-Baptiste Say had never meant it to be. A good measure of the credit for this transformation belongs to Thomas Malthus, an Anglican minister, whose Essay on the Principle of Population, *first published in 1798, presented the thesis that the basic and natural tendency of population to outstrip the means of subsistence meant that neither the condition of the lower classes in particular nor the condition of man in general was likely to improve unless population was checked. Although Malthus strongly attacked the facile optimism of Enlightenment thinkers, he was not without hope that the working man, once he came to realize the source of his misery, would exercise self-restraint and thereby reduce the supply of labor and increase its value. As a cleric, Malthus could justify no other mode of limiting population growth. Malthus' theory and David Ricardo's contention that the price of labor tends toward the level necessary to sustain the working class at the subsistence level — the iron law of wages — were used by opponents of social reform to oppose all measures designed to alleviate the condition of the working class on the grounds that they did not deal with the real problem and only further encouraged the improvidence and lack of restraint of the workers. The brutal English Poor Law of 1834 was one practical implementation of these theories.*

Malthus' *Essay on the Principle of Population* 1798

The great and unlooked for discoveries that have taken place of late years in natural philosophy; the increasing diffusion of general knowledge from the extension of the art of printing; the ardent and unshackled spirit of inquiry that prevails throughout the lettered, and even unlettered world; the new and extraordinary lights that have been thrown on political subjects, which dazzle, and astonish the understanding; and particularly that tremendous phenomenon in the political horizon, the French revolution, which, like a blazing comet, seems destined either to inspire with fresh life and vigour, or to scorch up and destroy the shrinking inhabitants of the earth, have all concurred to lead many able men into the opinion, that we were touching on a period big with the most important changes, changes that would in some measure be decisive of the future fate of mankind.

It has been said, that the great question is now at issue, whether man shall henceforth start forwards with accelerated velocity towards illimitable, and hitherto unconceived improvement; or be condemned to a perpetual oscillation between happiness and misery, and after every effort remain still at an immeasurable distance from the wished-for goal.

Yet, anxiously as every friend of mankind must look forwards to the termination of this painful suspense; and, eagerly as the inquiring mind would hail every ray of light that might assist its view into futurity, it is much to be lamented, that the writers on each side of this momentous question still keep far aloof from each other. Their mutual arguments do not meet with a candid examination. The question is not brought to rest on fewer points; and even in theory scarcely seems to be approaching to a decision.

From Thomas Malthus, *An Essay on the Principle of Population as It Affects the Future Improvement of Society, with Remarks on the Speculations of Mr. Goodwin, M. Condorcet, and Other Writers* (London, 1798), pp. 1–7, 11–17, and 6th ed., vol. 2 (London, 1826), pp. 283–84.

The advocate for the present order of things, is apt to treat the sect of speculative philosophers, either as a set of artful and designing knaves, who preach up ardent benevolence, and draw captivating pictures of a happier state of society, only the better to enable them to destroy the present establishment, and to forward their own deep-laid schemes of ambition: or, as wild and mad-headed enthusiasts, whose silly speculations, and absurd paradoxes, are not worthy the attention of any reasonable man.

The advocate for the perfectibility of man, and of society, retorts on the defender of establishments a more than equal contempt. He brands him as the slave of the most miserable, and narrow prejudices; or, as the defender of the abuses of civil society, only because he profits by them. He paints him either as a character who prostitutes his understanding to his interest; or as one whose powers of mind are not of a size to grasp any thing great and noble; who cannot see above five yards before him: and who must therefore be utterly unable to take in the views of the enlightened benefactor of mankind.

In this unamicable contest, the cause of truth cannot but suffer. The really good arguments on each side of the question are not allowed to have their proper weight. Each pursues his own theory, little solicitous to correct, or improve it, by an attention to what is advanced by his opponents.

The friend of the present order of things condemns all political speculations in the gross. He will not even condescend to examine the grounds from which the perfectibility of society is inferred. Much less will he give himself the trouble in a fair and candid manner to attempt an exposition of their fallacy.

The speculative philosopher equally offends against the cause of truth. With eyes fixed on a happier state of society, the blessings of which he paints in the most captivating colours, he allows himself to indulge in the most bitter invectives against every present establishment, without applying his talents to consider the best and safest means of removing abuses, and without seeming to be aware of the tremendous obstacles that threaten, even in theory, to oppose the progress of man towards perfection.

It is an acknowledged truth in philosophy, that a just theory will always be confirmed by experiment. Yet so much friction, and so many minute circumstances occur in practice, which it is next to impossible for the most enlarged and penetrating mind to foresee, that on few subjects can any theory be pronounced just, that has not stood the test of experience. But an untried theory cannot fairly be advanced as probable, much less as just, till all the arguments against it, have been maturely weighed, and clearly and consistently refuted.

I have read some of the speculations on the perfectibility of man and

of society, with great pleasure. I have been warmed and delighted with
the enchanting picture which they hold forth. I ardently wish for such
happy improvements. But I see great, and, to my understanding, uncon-
querable difficulties in the way to them. These difficulties it is my present
purpose to state; declaring, at the same time, that so far from exulting in
them, as a cause of triumph over the friends of innovation, nothing
would give me greater pleasure than to see them completely removed. . . .

I think I may fairly make two postulata.

First, That food is necessary to the existence of man.

Secondly, That the passion between the sexes is necessary, and will
remain nearly in its present state.

These two laws ever since we have had any knowledge of mankind, appear to have been fixed laws of nature; and, as we have not hitherto seen
any alteration in them, we have no right to conclude that they will ever
cease to be what they now are, without an immediate act of power in that
Being who first arranged the system of the universe; and for the advantage of his creatures, still executes, according to fixed laws, all its various
operations. . . .

Assuming then, my postulata as granted, I say, that the power of population is indefinitely greater than the power in the earth to produce
subsistence for man.

Population, when unchecked, increases in a geometrical ratio. Subsistence increases only in an arithmetical ratio. A slight acquaintance
with numbers will shew the immensity of the first power in comparison
of the second.

By that law of our nature which makes food necessary to the life of
man, the effects of these two unequal powers must be kept equal.

This implies a strong and constantly operating check on population
from the difficulty of subsistence. This difficulty must fall some where;
and must necessarily be severely felt by a large portion of mankind.

Through the animal and vegetable kingdoms, nature has scattered the
seeds of life abroad with the most profuse and liberal hand. She has been
comparatively sparing in the room, and the nourishment necessary to
rear them. The germs of existence contained in this spot of earth, with
ample food, and ample room to expand in, would fill millions of worlds
in the course of a few thousand years. Necessity, that imperious all per-
vading law of nature, restrains them within the prescribed bounds. The
race of plants, and the race of animals shrink under this great restrictive
law. And the race of man cannot, by any efforts of reason, escape from it.
Among plants and animals its effects are waste of seed, sickness, and premature death. Among mankind, misery and vice. The former, misery, is
an absolutely necessary consequence of it. Vice is a highly probable con-

sequence, and we therefore see it abundantly prevail; but it ought not, perhaps, to be called an absolutely necessary consequence. The ordeal of virtue is to resist all temptation to evil.

This natural inequality of the two powers of population, and of production in the earth, and that great law of our nature which must constantly keep their effects equal, form the great difficulty that to me appears insurmountable in the way to the perfectibility of society. All other arguments are of slight and subordinate consideration in comparison of this. I see no way by which man can escape from the weight of this law which pervades all animated nature. No fancied equality, no agrarian regulations in their utmost extent, could remove the pressure of it even for a single century. And it appears, therefore, to be decisive against the possible existence of a society, all the members of which, should live in ease, happiness, and comparative leisure; and feel no anxiety about providing the means of subsistence for themselves and families.

Consequently, if the premises are just, the argument is conclusive against the perfectibility of the mass of mankind.

I have thus sketched the general outline of the argument; but I will examine it more particularly; and I think it will be found that experience, the true source and foundation of all knowledge, invariably confirms its truth.

.   .   .   .   .   .

OF THE ONLY EFFECTUAL MODE OF IMPROVING THE CONDITION OF THE POOR

He who publishes a moral code, or system of duties, however firmly he may be convinced of the strong obligation on each individual strictly to conform to it, has never the folly to imagine that it will be universally or even generally practised. But this is no valid objection against the publication of the code. If it were, the same objection would always have applied; we should be totally without general rules; and to the vices of mankind arising from temptation would be added a much longer list, than we have at present, of vices from ignorance.

Judging merely from the light of nature, if we feel convinced of the misery arising from a redundant population on the one hand, and of the evils and unhappiness, particularly to the female sex, arising from promiscuous intercourse, on the other, I do not see how it is possible for any person who acknowledges the principle of utility, as the great criterion of moral rules, to escape the conclusion, that moral restraint, or the abstaining from marriage till we are in a condition to support a family, with a perfectly moral conduct during that period, is the strict line of duty; and when revelation is taken into the question, this duty undoubtedly receives very powerful confirmation. At the same time I believe that few of my readers can be less sanguine than I am in their expectations of any sudden and great change in the general conduct of men on this subject. . . .

However powerful may be the impulses of passion, they are generally in some degree modified by reason. And it does not seem entirely visionary to suppose that, if the true and permanent cause of poverty were clearly explained and forcibly brought home to each man's bosom, it would have some, and perhaps not an inconsiderable influence on his conduct: at least the experiment has never yet been fairly tried. Almost every thing, that has been hitherto done for the poor, has tended, as if with solicitous care, to throw a veil of obscurity over this subject, and to hide from them the true cause of their poverty. When the wages of labour are hardly sufficient to maintain two children, a man marries, and has five or six; he of course finds himself miserably distressed. He accuses the insufficiency of the price of labor to maintain a family. He accuses his parish for their tardy and sparing fulfilment of their obligation to assist him. He accuses the avarice of the rich, who suffer him to want what they can so well spare. He accuses the partial and unjust institutions of society, which have awarded him an inadequate share of the produce of the earth. He accuses perhaps the dispensations of Providence, which have assigned to him a place in society so beset with unavoidable distress and dependence. In searching for objects of accusation, he never adverts to the quarter from which his misfortunes originate. The last person that he would think of accusing is himself, on whom in fact the principal blame lies, except so far as he has been deceived by the higher classes of society. He may perhaps wish that he had not married, because he now feels the inconveniences of it; but it never enters into his head that he can have done any thing wrong. He has always been told, that to raise up subjects for his king and country is a very meritorious act. He has done this, and yet is suffering for it; and it cannot but strike him as most extremely unjust and cruel in his king and country, to allow him thus to suffer, in return for giving them what they are continually declaring that they particularly want.

Till these erroneous ideas have been corrected, and the language of nature and reason has been generally heard on the subject of population, instead of the language of error and prejudice, it cannot be said, that any fair experiment has been made with the understandings of the common people; and we cannot justly accuse them of improvidence and want of industry, till they act as they do now, after it has been brought home to their comprehensions, that they are themselves the cause of their own poverty; that the means of redress are in their own hands, and in the hands of no other persons whatever; that the society in which they live and the government which presides over it, are without any *direct* power in this respect; and that however ardently they may desire to relieve them, and whatever attempts they may make to do so, they are really and truly unable to execute what they benevolently wish, but unjustly promise; that, when the wages of labour will not maintain a family, it is an incontrovertible sign that their king and country do not want more subjects, or at least that they cannot support them; that, if they marry in this case, so far from fulfilling a duty to society, they are throwing an useless burden on it, at the same time that they are plunging themselves into distress; and that they are acting directly contrary to the will of God, and bringing down upon themselves various diseases, which might all, or the greater part, have been avoided, if they had attended to the repeated admonitions which he gives by the general laws of nature to every being capable of reason.

Paley, in his Moral Philosophy, observes, that "in countries in which subsistence is become scarce, it behoves the state to watch over the public morals with increased solicitude; for nothing but the instinct of nature, under the restraint of chastity, will induce men to undertake the labour, or consent to the sacrifice of personal liberty and indulgence, which the support of a family in such circumstances requires." That it is always the duty of a state to use every exertion likely to be effectual in discouraging vice and promoting virtue, and that no temporary circumstances ought to cause any relaxation in these exertions, is certainly true. The means therefore proposed are always good; but the particular end in view in this case appears to be absolutely criminal. We wish to force people into marriage, when from the acknowledged scarcity of subsistence they will have little chance of being able to support their children. We might as well force people into the water who are unable to swim. In both cases we rashly tempt Providence. Nor have we more reason to believe that a miracle will be worked to save us from the misery and mortality resulting from our conduct in the one case than in the other.

The object of those who really wish to better the condition of the lower classes of society, must be to raise the relative proportion between the price of labour and the price of provisions, so as to enable the labourer to command a larger share of the necessaries and comforts of life. We have hitherto principally attempted to attain this end by encouraging the married poor, and consequently increasing the number of labourers, and overstocking the market with a commodity which we still say that we wish to be dear. It would seem to have required no great spirit of divination to foretell the certain failure of such a plan of proceeding. There is nothing however like experience. It has been tried in many different countries, and for many hundred years, and the success has always been answerable to the nature of the scheme. It is really time now to try something else.

When it was found that oxygen, or pure vital air, would not cure consumptions as was expected, but rather aggravated their symptoms, trial was made of an air of the most opposite kind. I wish we had acted with the same philosophical spirit in our attempts to cure the disease of poverty; and having found that the pouring in of fresh supplies of labour only tended to aggravate the symptoms, had tried what would be the effect of withholding a little these supplies.

In all old and fully-peopled states it is from this method, and this alone, that we can rationally expect any essential and permanent melioration in the condition of the labouring classes of the people.

In an endeavor to raise the proportion of the quantity of provisions to the number of consumers in any country, our attention would naturally be first directed to the increasing of the absolute quantity of provisions; but finding that, as fast as we did this, the number of consumers more than kept pace with it, and that with all our exertions we were still as far as ever behind, we should be convinced, that our efforts directed only in this way would never succeed. It would appear to be setting the tortoise to catch the hare. Finding, therefore, that from the laws of nature we could not proportion the food to the population, our next attempt should naturally be, to proportion the population to the food. If we can persuade the hare to go to sleep, the tortoise may have some chance of overtaking her.

We are not however to relax our efforts in increasing the quantity of provisions, but to combine another effort with it; that of keeping the population, when once it has been overtaken, at such a distance behind, as to effect the relative proportion which we desire; and thus unite the two grand *desiderata*, a great actual population, and a state of society, in which abject poverty and dependence are comparatively but little known; two objects which are far from being incompatible.

If we be really serious in what appears to be the object of such general research, the mode of essentially and permanently bettering the condition of the poor, we must explain to them the true nature of their situation, and shew them, that the withholding of the supplies of labour is the only possible way of really raising its price, and that they themselves, being the possessors of this commodity, have alone the power to do this.

I cannot but consider this mode of diminishing poverty as so perfectly clear in theory, and so invariably confirmed by the analogy of every other commodity which is brought to market, that nothing but its being shewn to be calculated to produce greater evils than it proposes to remedy, can justify us in not making the attempt to put it into execution.

Defense of the Factory System

*The proponents of the dismal science notwithstanding, it became in-
creasingly difficult for parliamentarians to neglect the findings of their
own commissions about the conditions in the early factories. The result
was a series of Factory Acts, beginning in 1833. The attack upon exploitation in the factories induced Andrew Ure (1778–1857), a Scottish
chemist, to produce his famous apology,* The Philosophy of Manufactures *(1835). Ure's rosy picture of working conditions in the factories
is often irritating, but his work is of extraordinary value for the way it
reveals the essential character and problem of the factory system. On
the one hand, the factory system sought to replace men and their skills
by machines. On the other hand, it demanded a new labor discipline.
In the long run, the factory was beneficent. In the short run, however,
it demanded a change of work habits and the development of a discipline that seemed unnatural and produced great resentment. Implicit
in Ure's description is the assumption that labor management was one
of the main problems of the industrial revolution, and it is now easy to
see that there was a lag between technological innovation and the development of the managerial techniques needed to create a stable and
relatively well satisfied labor force. The risks of early industrial en-
trepreneurship were too great, however, for most businessmen to care
much about the happiness of their workers, just as the hardships of the
early factory were too great for workers to surrender their earliest
forms of protest: inattention, lack of punctuality, frequent job changing, and drinking.*

Ure's *Philosophy of Manufactures*

The term *Factory*, in technology, designates the combined operation of
many orders of work-people, adult and young, in tending with assiduous
skill a system of productive machines continuously impelled by a central
power. This definition includes such organizations as cotton-mills, flax-
mills, silk-mills, woollen-mills, and certain engineering works; but it excludes those in which the mechanisms do not form a connected series, nor
are dependent on one prime mover. Of the latter class, examples occur in
ironworks, dye-works, soap-works, brass-foundries, &c. Some authors, indeed, have comprehended under the title *factory*, all extensive establish-

From Andrew Ure, *The Philosophy of Manufactures or an Exposition of the Scientific
and Commercial Economy of the Factory System of Great Britain* (London, 1835), pp.
13–20.

ments wherein a number of people co-operate towards a common purpose of art; and would therefore rank breweries, distilleries, as well as the workshops of carpenters, turners, coopers, &c., under the factory system. But I conceive that this title, in its strictest sense, involves the idea of a vast automation, composed of various mechanical and intellectual organs, acting in uninterrupted concert for the production of a common object, all of them being subordinated to a self-regulated moving force. If the marshalling of human beings in systematic order for the execution of any technical enterprise were allowed to constitute a factory, this term might embrace every department of civil and military engineering; a latitude of application quite inadmissible.

In its precise acceptation, the Factory system is of recent origin, and may claim England for its birthplace. The mills for throwing silk, or making organzine, which were mounted centuries ago in several of the Italian states, and furtively transferred to this country by Sir Thomas Lombe in 1718, contained indeed certain elements of a factory, and probably suggested some hints of those grander and more complex combinations of self-acting machines, which were first embodied half a century later in our cotton manufacture by Richard Arkwright, assisted by gentlemen of Derby, well acquainted with its celebrated silk establishment. But the spinning of an entangled flock of fibres into a smooth thread, which constitutes the main operation with cotton, is in silk superfluous; being already performed by the unerring instinct of a worm, which leaves to human art the simple task of doubling and twisting its regular filaments. The apparatus requisite for this purpose is more elementary, and calls for few of those gradations of machinery which are needed in the carding, drawing, roving, and spinning processes of a cotton-mill.

When the first water-frames for spinning cotton were erected at Cromford, in the romantic valley of the Derwent, about sixty years ago, mankind were little aware of the mighty revolution which the new system of labour was destined by Providence to achieve, not only in the structure of British society, but in the fortunes of the world at large. Arkwright alone had the sagacity to discern, and the boldness to predict in glowing language, how vastly productive human industry would become, when no longer proportioned in its results to muscular effort, which is by its nature fitful and capricious, but when made to consist in the task of guiding the work of mechanical fingers and arms, regularly impelled with great velocity by some indefatigable physical power. What his judgment so clearly led him to perceive, his energy of will enabled him to realize with such rapidity and success, as would have done honour to the most influential individuals, but were truly wonderful in that obscure and indigent artisan. The main difficulty did not, to my apprehension, lie so much in the invention of a proper self-acting mechanism for drawing

out and twisting cotton into a continuous thread, as in the distribution
of the different members of the apparatus into one co-operative body, in
impelling each organ with its appropriate delicacy and speed, and above
all, in training human beings to renounce their desultory habits of work,
and to identify themselves with the unvarying regularity of the complex
automaton. To devise and administer a successful code of factory discipline, suited to the necessities of factory diligence, was the Herculean enterprise, the noble achievement of Arkwright. Even at the present day,
when the system is perfectly organized, and its labour lightened to the
utmost, it is found nearly impossible to convert persons past the age of
puberty, whether drawn from rural or from handicraft occupations, into
useful factory hands. After struggling for a while to conquer their listless
or restive habits, they either renounce the employment spontaneously, or
are dismissed by the overlookers on account of inattention.

If the factory Briareus could have been created by mechanical genius
alone, it should have come into being thirty years sooner; for upwards of
ninety years have now elapsed since John Wyatt, of Birmingham, not
only invented the series of fluted rollers, (the spinning fingers usually
ascribed to Arkwright,) but obtained a patent for the invention, and
erected "a spinning engine without hands" in his native town. The details of this remarkable circumstance, recently snatched from oblivion,
will be given in our Treatise on the Cotton Manufactures. Wyatt was a
man of good education, in a respectable walk of life, much esteemed by
his superiors, and therefore favourably placed, in a mechanical point of
view, for maturing his admirable scheme. But he was of a gentle and passive
spirit, little qualified to cope with the hardships of a new manufacturing
enterprise. It required, in fact, a man of a Napoleon nerve and ambition,
to subdue the refractory tempers of work-people accustomed to irregular
paroxysms of diligence, and to urge on his multifarious and intricate
constructions in the face of prejudice, passion, and envy. Such was Arkwright, who, suffering nothing to stay or turn aside his progress, arrived
gloriously at the goal, and has for ever affixed his name to a great era in
the annals of mankind, an era which had laid open unbounded prospects
of wealth and comfort to the industrious, however much they may have
been occasionally clouded by ignorance and folly.

Prior to this period, manufacturers were everywhere feeble and fluctuating in their development; shooting forth luxuriantly for a season, and
again withering almost to the roots, like annual plants. Their perennial
growth now began in England, and attracted capital in copious streams
to irrigate the rich domains of industry. When this new career commenced, about the year 1770, the annual consumption of cotton in British
manufactures was under four millions of pounds weight, and that of the
whole of Christendom was probably not more than ten millions. Last
year the consumption in Great Britain and Ireland was about two hun-

dred and seventy millions of pounds, and that of Europe and the United States together four hundred and eighty millions. This prodigious increase is, without doubt, almost entirely due to the factory system founded and upreared by the intrepid native of Preston. If then this system be not merely an inevitable step in the social progression of the world, but the one which gives a commanding station and influence to the people who most resolutely take it, it does not become any man, far less a denizen of this favoured land, to vilify the author of a benefaction, which, wisely administered, may become the best temporal gift of Providence to the poor, a blessing destined to mitigate, and in some measure to repeal, the primeval curse pronounced on the labour of man, "in the sweat of thy face shalt thou eat bread." Arkwright well deserves to live in honoured remembrance among those ancient master-spirits, who persuaded their roaming companions to exchange the precarious toils of the chase, for the settled comforts of agriculture.

In my recent tour, continued during several months, through the manufacturing districts, I have seen tens of thousands of old, young, and middle-aged of both sexes, many of them too feeble to get their daily bread by any of the former modes of industry, earning abundant food, raiment, and domestic accommodation, without perspiring at a single pore, screened meanwhile from the summer's sun and the winter's frost, in apartments more airy and salubrious than those of the metropolis, in which our legislative and fashionable aristocracies assemble. In those spacious halls the benignant power of steam summons around him his myriads of willing menials, and assigns to each the regulated task, substituting for painful muscular effort on their part, the energies of his own gigantic arm, and demanding in return only attention and dexterity to correct such little aberrations as casually occur in his workmanship. The gentle docility of this moving force qualifies it for impelling the tiny bobbins of the lace-machine with a precision and speed inimitable by the most dexterous hands, directed by the sharpest eyes. Hence, under its auspices, and in obedience to Arkwright's polity, magnificent edifices, surpassing far in number, value, usefulness, and ingenuity of construction, the boasted monuments of Asiatic, Egyptian, and Roman despotism, have, within the short period of fifty years, risen up in this kingdom, to show to what extent, capital, industry, and science may augment the resources of a state, while they meliorate the condition of its citizens. Such is the factory system, replete with prodigies in mechanics and political economy, which promises, in its future growth, to become the great minister of civilization to the terraqueous globe, enabling this country, as its heart, to diffuse along with its commerce, the life-blood of science and religion to myriads of people still lying "in the region and shadow of death."

When Adam Smith wrote his immortal elements of economics, automatic machinery being hardly known, he was properly led to regard the division of labour as the grand principle of manufacturing improvement; and he showed, in the example of pin-making, how each handicraftsman, being thereby enabled to perfect himself by practice in one point, became a quicker and cheaper workman. In each branch of manufacture he saw that some parts were, on that principle, of easy execution, like the cutting of pin wires into uniform lengths, and some were comparatively difficult, like the formation and fixation of their heads; and therefore he concluded that to each a workman of appropriate value and cost was naturally assigned. This appropriation forms the very essence of the division of labour, and has been constantly made since the origin of society. The ploughman, with powerful hand and skilful eye, has been always hired at high wages to form the furrow, and the ploughboy at low wages, to lead the team. But what was in Dr. Smith's time a topic of useful illustration, cannot now be used without risk of misleading the public mind as to the right principle of manufacturing industry. In fact, the division, or rather adaptation of labour to the different talents of men, is little thought of in factory employment. On the contrary, wherever a process requires peculiar dexterity and steadiness of hand, it is withdrawn as soon as possible from the *cunning* workman, who is prone to irregularities of many kinds, and it is placed in charge of a peculiar mechanism, so self-regulating, that a child may superintend it. Thus — to take an example from the spinning of cotton — the first operation in delicacy and importance, is that of laying the fibres truly parallel in the spongy slivers, and the next is that of drawing these out into slender spongy cords, called rovings, with the least possible twist; both being perfectly uniform throughout their total length. To execute either of these processes tolerably by a hand-wheel, would require a degree of skill not to be met with in one artisan out of a hundred. But fine yarn could not be made in factory-spinning except by taking these steps, nor was it ever made by machinery till Arkwright's sagacity contrived them. Moderately good yarn may be spun indeed on the *hand-wheel* without any drawings at all, and with even indifferent rovings, because the thread, under the two-fold action of twisting and extension, has a tendency to equalize itself.

The principle of the factory system then is, to substitute mechanical science for hand skill, and the partition of a process into its essential constituents, for the division or graduation of labour among artisans. On the handicraft plan, labour more or less skilled, was usually the most expensive element of production — *Materiam superabat opus;* but on the automatic plan, skilled labour gets progressively superseded, and will, eventually, be replaced by mere overlookers of machines.

The Protection
of Underdeveloped Countries

In England, support for free trade and for industrialization tended to be synonymous, and English manufacturers were far ahead of their counterparts abroad and could afford to face any and all competition. Where English agrarians sought protection and English manufacturers sought free trade, the reverse was often true in Germany. In Prussia, large estate owners, the Junkers, were most anxious to sell their grains to England and to permit the entry of English manufactured goods. Naturally, Prussian and German manufacturers took a different view of the matter and constantly called upon their state governments to tear down trade barriers within Germany while protecting native German production from non-German competition. They supported the Customs Union (Zollverein), established under Prussian leadership in 1834, and called for protection of infant industries. One of the chief spokesmen for this position was Friedrich List, a liberal who fled to the United States in 1825 and who served the cause of American and German economic nationalism until his death in 1846. List criticized the classical economists for paying insufficient heed to the special problems of developing nations and argued for protection not as an end in itself but rather as a means of bringing nations to the point where they could freely compete with one another. At the same time, List's emphasis upon the national aspect of economic development and his schemes for a kind of continental economic union based on German leadership influenced nationalist and imperialist Germans of a later age.

List's *National System of Political Economy*

The system of the [classical] school suffers, as we have already shown in the preceding chapters, from three main defects: firstly, from boundless *cosmopolitanism,* which neither recognises the principle of nationality, nor takes into consideration the satisfaction of its interests; secondly, from a dead *materialism,* which everywhere regards chiefly the mere exchangeable value of things without taking into consideration the mental and political, the present and the future interests, and the productive powers of the nation; thirdly, from *a disorganising particularism* and *individualism,* which, ignoring the nature and character of social labour and the operation of the union of powers in their higher consequences, considers private industry only as it would develop itself under a state of free interchange with society (i.e. with the whole human race) were that race not divided into separate national societies.

Between each individual and entire humanity, however, stands the nation, with its special language and literature, with its peculiar origin and history, with its special manners and customs, laws and institutions, with the claims of all these for existence, independence, perfection, and continuance for the future, and with its separate territory; a society which, united by a thousand ties of mind and of interests, combines itself into one independent whole, which recognises the law of right for and within itself, and in its united character is still opposed to other societies of a similar kind in their national liberty, and consequently can only under the existing conditions of the world maintain self-existence and independence by its own power and resources. As the individual chiefly obtains by means of the nation and in the nation mental culture, power of production, security, and prosperity, so is the civilisation of the human race only conceivable and possible by means of the civilisation and development of the individual nations.

Meanwhile, however, an infinite difference exists in the condition and circumstances of the various nations: we observe among them giants and dwarfs, well-formed bodies and cripples, civilised, half-civilised, and barbarous nations; but in all of them, as in the individual human being, exists the impulse of self-preservation, the striving for improvement which is implanted by nature. It is the task of politics to civilise the barbarous nationalities, to make the small and weak ones great and strong, but, above all, to secure to them existence and continuance. It is the task of national economy to accomplish *the economical development of the nation,* and to prepare it for admission into the universal society of the future.

A nation in its normal state possesses one common language and literature, a territory endowed with manifold natural resources, extensive, and with convenient frontiers and a numerous population. Agriculture, manufactures, commerce, and navigation must be all developed in it proportionately; arts and sciences, educational establishments, and universal cultivation must stand in it on an equal footing with material production. Its constitution, laws, and institutions must afford to those who belong to it a high degree of security and liberty, and must promote religion, morality, and prosperity; in a word, must have the well-being of its citizens as their object. It must possess sufficient power on land and at sea to defend its independence and to protect its foreign commerce. It will possess the power of beneficially affecting the civilisation of less advanced nations, and by means of its own surplus population and of their mental and material capital to found colonies and beget new nations.

A large population, and an extensive territory endowed with manifold national resources, are essential requirements of the normal nationality; they are the fundamental conditions of mental cultivation as well as of material development and political power. A nation restricted in the number of its population and in territory, especially if it has a separate language, can only possess a crippled literature, crippled institutions for promoting art and science. A small State can never bring to complete perfection within its territory the various branches of production. In it all protection becomes mere private monopoly. Only through alliances with more powerful nations, by partly sacrificing the advantages of nationality, and by excessive energy, can it maintain with difficulty its independence.

A nation which possesses no coasts, mercantile marine, or naval power, or has not under its dominion and control the mouths of its rivers, is in its foreign commerce dependent on other countries; it can neither establish colonies of its own nor form new nations; all surplus population, mental and material means, which flows from such a nation to uncultivated countries, is lost to its own literature, civilisation and industry, and goes to the benefit of other nationalities.

A nation not bounded by seas and chains of mountains lies open to the attacks of foreign nations, and can only by great sacrifices, and in any case only very imperfectly, establish and maintain a separate tariff system of its own.

Territorial deficiencies of the nation can be remedied either by means of hereditary succession, as in the case of England and Scotland; or by purchase, as in the case of Florida and Louisiana; or by conquests, as in the case of Great Britain and Ireland.

In modern times a fourth means has been adopted, which leads to this object in a manner much more in accordance with justice and with the prosperity of nations than conquest, and which is not so dependent on accidents as hereditary succession, namely, the union of the interests of various States by means of free conventions.

By its Zollverein, the German nation first obtained one of the most important attributes of its nationality. But this measure cannot be considered complete so long as it does not extend over the whole coast, from the mouth of the Rhine to the frontier of Poland, including *Holland* and *Denmark*. A natural consequence of this union must be the admission of both these countries into the German Bund, and consequently into the German nationality, whereby the latter will at once obtain what it is now in need of, namely, fisheries and naval power, maritime commerce and colonies. Besides, both these nations belong, as respects their descent and whole character, to the German nationality. The burden of debt with which they are oppressed is merely a consequence of their unnatural endeavours to maintain themselves as independent nationalities, and it is in the nature of things that this evil should rise to a point when it will become intolerable to those two nations themselves, and when incorporation with a larger nationality must seem desirable and necessary to them.

Belgium can only remedy by means of confederation with a neighbouring larger nation her needs which are inseparable from her restricted territory and population. *The United States* and *Canada,* the more their population increases, and the more the protective system of the United States is developed, so much the more will they feel themselves drawn towards one another, and the less will it be possible for England to prevent a union between them.

As respects their economy, nations have to pass through the following stages of development: original barbarism, pastoral condition, agricultural condition, agricultural-manufacturing condition, and agricultural-manufacturing-commercial condition.

The industrial history of nations, and of none more clearly than that of England, proves that the transition from the savage state to the pastoral one, from the pastoral to the agricultural, and from agriculture to the first beginnings in manufacture and navigation, is effected most speedily and advantageously by means of free commerce with further advanced towns and countries, but that a perfectly developed manufacturing industry, an important mercantile marine, and foreign trade on a really large scale, can only be attained by means of the interposition of the power of the State.

The less any nation's agriculture has been perfected, and the more its foreign trade is in want of opportunities of exchanging the excess of native agricultural products and raw materials for foreign manufactured goods, the deeper that the nation is still sunk in barbarism and fitted only for an absolute monarchical form of government and legislation, the more will free trade (i.e. the exportation of agricultural products and the importation of manufactured goods) promote its prosperity and civilisation.

On the other hand, the more that the agriculture of a nation, its industries, and its social, political, and municipal conditions, are thoroughly developed, the less advantage will it be able to derive for the improvement of its social conditions, from the exchange of native agricultural products and raw materials for foreign manufactured goods, and the greater disadvantages will it experience from the successful competition of a foreign manufacturing power superior to its own.

Solely in nations of the latter kind, namely, those which possess all the necessary mental and material conditions and means for establishing a manufacturing power of their own, and of thereby attaining the highest degree of civilisation, and development of material prosperity and political power, but which are retarded in their progress by the competition of a foreign manufacturing Power which is already farther advanced than their own — only in such nations are commercial restrictions justifiable for the purpose of establishing and protecting their own manufacturing power; and even in them it is justifiable only until that manfacturing power is strong enough no longer to have any reason to fear foreign competition, and thenceforth only so far as may be necessary for protecting the inland manufacturing power in its very roots.

The system of protection would not merely be contrary to the principles of cosmopolitical economy, but also to the rightly understood advantage of the nation itself, were it to exclude foreign competition at once and altogether, and thus isolate from other nations the nation which is thus protected. If the manufacturing Power to be protected be still in the first period of its development, the protective duties must be very moderate, they must only rise gradually with the increase of the mental and material capital, of the technical abilities and spirit of enterprise of the nation. Neither is it at all necessary that all branches of industry should be protected in the same degree. Only the most important branches require special protection, for the working of which much outlay of capital in building and management, much machinery, and therefore much technical knowledge, skill, and experience, and many workmen are required, and whose products belong to the category of the first necessaries of life, and consequently are of the greatest importance as regards their total value as well as regards national independence (as, for example, cotton, woollen and linen manufactories, &c.). If these main branches are suitably protected and developed, all other less important branches of manufacture will rise up around them under a less degree of protection. It will be to the advantage of nations in which wages are high, and whose population is not yet great in proportion to the extent of their territory, e.g. in the United States of North America, to give less protection to manufactures in which machinery does not play an important part, than to those in which machinery does the greater part of the work, providing that those nations which supply them with similar goods allow in return free importation to their agricultural products.

The popular school betrays an utter misconception of the nature of national economical conditions if it believes that such nations can promote and further their civilisation, their prosperity, and especially their social progress, equally well by the exchange of agricultural products for manufactured goods, as by establishing a manufacturing power of their own. A mere argicultural nation can never develop to any considerable extent its home and foreign commerce, its inland means of transport, and its foreign navigation, increase its population in due proportion to their well-being, or make notable progress in its moral, intellectual, social, and political development: it will never acquire important political power, or be placed in a position to influence the cultivation and progress of less advanced nations and to form colonies of its own. A mere agricultural

State is an infinitely less perfect institution than an agricultural-manufacturing State. The former is always more or less economically and politically dependent on those foreign nations which take from it agricultural
products in exchange for manufactured goods. It cannot determine for
itself how much it will produce; it must wait and see how much others
will buy from it. These latter, on the contrary (the agricultural-manufacturing States), produce for themselves large quantities of raw materials
and provisions, and supply merely the deficiency by importation from the
purely agricultural nations. The purely agricultural nations are thus in
the first place dependent for their power of effecting sales on the chances
of a more or less plentiful harvest in the agricultural-manufacturing nations; in the next place they have to compete in these sales with other
purely agricultural nations, whereby their power of sale, in itself very
uncertain, thus becomes still more uncertain. Lastly, they are exposed to
the danger of being totally ruined in their trading with foreign manufacturing nations by wars, or new foreign tariff regulations whereby they suffer
the double disadvantage of finding no buyers for their surplus agricultural products, and of failing to obtain supplies of the manufactured
goods which they require. An agricultural nation is, as we have already
stated, an individual with *one* arm, who makes use of a foreign arm, but
who cannot make sure of the use of it in all cases; an agricultural-manufacturing nation is an individual who has *two* arms *of his own* always at
his disposal.

It is a fundamental error of the school when it represents the system of
protection as a mere device of speculative politicians which is contrary to
nature. History is there to prove that protective regulations originated
either in the natural efforts of nations to attain to prosperity, independence, and power, or in consequence of wars and of the hostile commercial legislation of predominating manufacturing nations.

REVOLUTION
AT FLOODTIDE

Chapter 4

In 1848 most of continental Europe was in a state of revolution. As usual, the major revolutionary proceedings begin in France with an uprising in Paris in February, 1848, and then the revolutions spread to central Europe and Italy. The initial successes of the revolutions were considerable. Louis-Philippe abdicated his throne, and France became a republic. In Berlin, Frederick William IV yielded to the revolutionary and national sentiments of his "beloved Berliners," removing his troops from the city and declaring that Prussia would be "merged into Germany." At the same time, a National Assembly met at Frankfurt am Main to frame a constitution for all Germany. Revolution in Vienna compelled Metternich to resign and flee to England, where undoubtedly he had a very touching reunion with the duke of Wellington when he debarked from his ship. In Prague, the Czechs, and in Budapest, the Hungarians, began the assertion of their national identity with demands for autonomy, and in Italy there was a string of revolts encouraging Charles Albert of Sardinia to give way to liberal pressure and take up arms against Austria in the name of Italian liberalism and nationalism.

Yet by 1850 the revolutions had failed. Prince Louis Napoleon was president of France, and his dictatorial behavior was paving the way for his assumption of the imperial crown. In Prussia and Austria reaction was triumphant; in Italy revolution had been suppressed by the Austrians, and in Hungary it was suppressed by the Austrians and Russians. One historian has compared the revolutions of 1848 to a fever creating all kinds of delusions while it lasted but leaving the revolutionaries without strength once the initial crisis had abated. The speedy surrender or retreat of the conservative forces had been premature, and when they realized their error, they were ruthless in correcting it. The failure of the revolutions demonstrated that the bourgeois revolution that had haunted Europe since 1789 was reaching the limits of its creative capacity because it was unable to cope with the social question on the one hand and the conflict between state power and national aspirations on the other.

Economic and social problems were major causes of the revolutions of 1848. An agricultural depression due to bad harvests from 1845 to 1847 depressed business conditions, and high unemployment led to unrest among the low orders of the population. Intellectuals and socially concerned businessmen expressed a growing awareness of the "social question" and the "proletariat," and some bourgeois reformers, anxious to create an alternative to the miseries of urban industrial life and the revolutionary sentiments that it spread, devised schemes for social reform and change that violated the principles of economic liberalism. Continental social reformers were particularly alarmed by conditions in England and hoped that they could benefit from their late start in industrializing by avoiding England's mistakes.

Robert Owen (1771–1858) in England and Charles Fourier (1772–1837) in France produced schemes for communal associations of limited size in which there would be a balance between industrial and agricultural activity. Henri de Saint Simon (1760–1825) created a technocratic vision of a society that would provide a just reward for all producers and would be scientifically managed by philosophers and engineers. The faith in voluntary association and cooperation expressed by Owen and Fourier was also shared by the anarchist Pierre Joseph Proudhon (1809–1865), but Proudhon wished to eliminate the state and every form of coercion. This attitude was not shared by Louis Blanc (1811–1882), whose role in the French Revolution of 1848 was important. Blanc believed that government was necessary and that it had to serve the people by guaranteeing their right to work. At the same time, he believed the workers should destroy capitalism by creating worker-managed national workshops to compete against capitalistic enterprise. These various schemes and programs were rejected as utopian by the fathers of "scientific socialism," Karl Marx (1818–1883), a German intellectual and newspaper editor, and Friedrich Engels (1820–1895), a German businessman. In their view, the triumph of the bourgeois order and exploitative capitalism was necessary in order for the proletariat to become conscious of its collective condition and overthrow the bourgeois state and system of private property on which its power was based.

Marx and Engels' expectations of the bourgeoisie and the workers were to be largely disappointed in 1848. In France and Germany the bourgeoisie retreated from its revolution and allied with the forces of conservatism rather than employ the lower classes to complete the demolition of the monarchical and aristocratic order. The French lower classes revolted in Paris in June, 1848, when the liberal government abolished the National Workshops it had set up to fight unemployment. The government ordered that the uprising be ruthlessly suppressed. The "June Days" in Paris frightened the German middle classes, and the Frankfurt Parliament responded to lower-class protests in September, 1848, by calling upon Prussian troops. In reality, the German factory workers, who were few in number, were not influential in the revolution, and the peasantry, artisans, and journeymen provided the mass base for the uprisings. Once the revolution eliminated the remaining feudal burdens, the peasants resumed their traditional conservative posture, and the artisans actually often turned against the Frankfurt Assembly because of its support of economic liberalism.

The experience of 1848 made it clear that the national question was one of power. Piedmont could not liberate Italy without outside help against Austria, nor could revolutionaries such as Mazzini and Garabaldi do the job themselves. In Germany, the disproportionately large Prussian state would not surrender its sovereignty to the Frankfurt Parliament, and Austria would neither divest itself of its non-German territories nor permit Prussia to assume the leadership of Germany. Whatever the mistakes and failings of the liberal revolutionaries in 1848, it is important not to overlook the fact that the social question and, in central Europe and Italy, the national question as well, fearfully complicated their traditional quest for political freedom.

Robert Owen's Rational System of Society

Robert Owen, a factory manager in New Lanarck, Scotland, viewed the social question primarily as economic and cultural, rather than political, reform. To overcome the alienation of the worker from the tools and products of his labor and the destruction of the community entailed by urbanization, he turned the factory, which he partly owned, and adjacent land in New Lanarck into a model "village of cooperation." His object was to create a self-sufficient community of producers who owned and managed their own property. Since the government of the period was interested more in repression than reform, Owen went to Indiana in 1824 to implement his socialist (he was the first to use the word) experiment by creating the community of New Harmony. It failed because of disharmony among the members, and Owen returned to Scotland more convinced than ever that education for cooperation was essential if his scheme was to work. Subsequently, Owen encouraged worker association and cooperation and is regarded as one of the founders of English trade unionism. His model "constitution" for an Owenite community demonstrates his faith in self-help, communitarianism, and education for cooperative living.

Rules and Regulations of an Owenite Community

It is proposed,

I. That the community shall consist of persons who have agreed to mutually co-operate with their labour and skill, in measures for producing, distributing and enjoying, in the most advantageous manner, a full supply of the necessaries and comforts of life; and for securing, for their children, the best physical and intellectual education.

II. That, at the commencement, the number of persons shall not much exceed five hundred, including their families.

III. That, as it is of great importance that the community should produce within itself a full supply of the first necessaries of life, there shall be attached to the establishment a sufficient extent of land, to render it essentially agricultural.

IV. That a village, to be situate as near the centre of the land as local circumstances may permit, be built. . . . In this village, the dwelling-houses, dormitories, &c. form the sides of a large square, in the centre of which are placed the requisite public buildings, surrounded by public walks and exercise grounds. This form has been adopted as giving superior accommodation to the dwelling-houses, and admitting the application, at the least expense, of scientific improvements in all the departments of domestic economy.

V. That the manufactories, workshops, granaries, stores, washing and drying houses, be placed at the most convenient distance beyond the gardens which surround the village — and that the farm offices be situate according to the localities of the land.

VI. That, whenever the capital advanced by its own members shall have been repaid, and the education of all be sufficiently advanced, the management of the establishment shall be confided to a committee, composed of all the members between certain ages; as, for example, between forty and fifty. But that until such period, the committee shall consist of twelve persons to be elected at an annual general meeting; eight to be chosen from among those members who have advanced capital to the amount of £100 or upwards, and four from the other members. The committee to be empowered to elect the treasurers and secretaries. . . .

From *Report of the Proceedings at the Several Public Meetings Held in Dublin, by Robert Owen, Esq.* (Dublin, 1823), pp. 82–91.

IX. That the books of accounts and transactions of the society be opened to the inspection of all its members.

X. That the business of the community be divided into the following departments:

1. Agriculture and gardening.

2. Manufactures and trades.

3. Commercial transactions.

4. Domestic economy, comprehending the arrangements for heating, ventilating, lighting, cleansing, and keeping in repair the dwelling-houses and public buildings of the village — the arrangements connected with the public kitchens and dining halls — those for the furnishing of clothes, linen and furniture, and for washing and drying — and the management of the dormitories.

5. Health, or the medical superintendence of the sick, including arrangements to prevent contagion or sickness.

6. Police, including the lighting and cleansing the square, the repairing of the roads and walks, guarding against fire, and the protection of the property of the community from external depredation.

7. Education, or the formation of character from infancy. To this department will also belong the devising of the best means of recreation.

XI. That for the general superintendence of these departments, the committee appoint sub-committees from their own number, or from the other members of the society. Each of the sub-committees shall lay a weekly report before the committee, to be examined and passed, with such observations as may be deemed necessary.

XII. That should there not be, at first, a sufficient number of persons in the community, fully competent to the management of the different branches of industry, which it may be desirable to establish, the committee be empowered to engage the assistance of skillful practical men from general society.

XIII. That in regulating the employments of the members according to their age, abilities, previous acquirements and situation in life, the committee pay every regard to the inclinations of each, consistent with the general good; and that the employment be, if possible, so ordered as to permit every individual, who may be so disposed, to occupy part of his time in agriculture. Great facilities are afforded to agriculture by the power which the community will always possess of calling out an extra number of hands, at those times and seasons, when it is of the utmost importance to have additional aid.

XIV. That, as under the proposed arrangements, every invention for the abridgment of human labour will bring an increase of benefit to all, it be a primary object with the committee to introduce to the utmost practical extent, all those modern scientific improvements, which, if rightly applied, are calculated to render manual labour only a healthy and agreeable exercise.

XV. That the first object of the community be to produce a full supply of the necessaries and comforts of life for domestic consumption; and, as far as localities will permit, directly from their own land and labour.

XVI. That in regard to domestic consumption, each member of the community shall be fully supplied with the necessaries and comforts of life.

XVII. That, within the community, all the members be equal in rights and privileges, according to their respective ages.

XVIII. That, to avoid the evils arising from a system of credit, the commercial transactions of the community be conducted for ready money only — that these transactions on the part of the community be always performed in good faith, and without the slightest attempt to deceive buyer or seller — and that, when any individuals, with whom they deal, show a disposition to impose upon the community, all dealings with such individuals shall from that time cease.

XIX. That the surplus proceeds of the united exertions of the community, which remain after discharging rent, interest, taxes, and other expenses, be regularly applied to the liquidation of the capital borrowed upon the establishment; and when this debt is cancelled, it is proposed, that the future surplus be invested to form a fund for the establishment of a second community, should the encreased population of the first require it.

XX. That in the domestic department the following arrangements and regulations be adopted:

1. The heating, ventilating, and lighting of the dwelling-houses and public buildings, shall be effected according to the most approved methods.

2. An ample supply of water shall be provided, and distributed to each building, for domestic purposes, and as a security against fire.

3. Provisions of the best quality only shall be cooked in the public kitchen, and it shall be a special object to those persons, who have the direction of this department, to ascertain and put in practice the best and most economical means of preparing nutritious and agreeable food. Any parties being ill, or desirous of having their meals alone, may have them sent to their private apartments.

4. The furniture of the dwelling houses, dormitories, and public buildings, (as far as the same to be provided out of the public funds,) shall be devised in reference to intrinsic use and comfort. A similar regulation will apply to the clothing of the community. Among the children, very essential improvements may be introduced, which will not only save much useless expense, but be the means of increasing, in a very high degree, the strength of the constitution.

5. The dormitories designed for the children above two years of age, and those for the youth of the community until the period of marriage, shall be divided into compartments, and furnished with the accommodations suited to the different ages.

XXI. That the employments of the female part of the community consist, in preparing food and clothing — in the care of the dwelling houses, dormitories, and public buildings — in the management of the washing and drying-houses — in the education (in part) of the children, and other occupations suited to the female character. By the proposed domestic arrangements one female will, with great ease and comfort, perform as much as twenty menial servants can do at present; and instead of the wife of a working man with a family being a drudge and slave, she will be engaged only in healthy and cleanly employments, acquire better manners, and have sufficient leisure for mental improvement, and rational enjoyment.

XXII. That it be a general rule, that every part of the establishment be kept in the highest state of order and neatness, and that the utmost personal cleanliness be observed. . . .

XXIV. That as the right education of the rising generation is, under Divine Providence, the base upon which the future prosperity and happiness of the community must be founded, the committee shall regard this as the most important of all the departments committed to their direction, and employ in its superintendance, those individuals whose talents, attainments, and dispositions, render them best qualified for such a charge.

The children of the community will be educated together, and as one family, in the schools and exercise-grounds provided for them in the centre of the square, where they will, at all times, be under the eye and inspection of their parents.

By properly conducting their education, it will be easy to give to each child good temper and habits, with as sound a constitution as air, exercise, and temperance can bestow.

A facility in reading, writing and accounts.

The elements of the most useful sciences, including geography and natural history.

A practical knowledge of agriculture and domestic economy, with a knowledge of some one useful manufacture, trade, or occupation, so that his employment may be varied, for the improvement of his mental and physical powers.

And lastly, a knowledge of himself and of human nature, to form him into a rational being, and render him charitable, kind and benevolent to all his fellow creatures.

XXV. That when the youth of the community shall have attained their sixteenth year, they be permitted either to become members, or to go out into general society, with every advantage which the community can afford them.

XXVI. That intelligent and experienced matrons be appointed to instruct the young mothers in the best mode of treating and training children from birth until they are two years old — the age at which it is proposed to send them to the schools and dormitories — that their constitutions, habits, and dispositions may not be injured during that period.

XXVII. That in winter and unfavourable weather, a sufficient variety of amusements and recreations proper for the members of such a community, be prepared within doors, to afford beneficial relaxation from employment and study.

XXVIII. That as liberty of conscience, religious and mental liberty, will be possessed by every member of the community, arrangements be made to accommodate all denominations with convenient places of worship, and that each individual be strongly recommended to exhibit, in his whole conduct, the utmost forbearance, kindness and charity towards all who differ from him.

XXIX. That in advanced age, and in cases of disability from accident, natural infirmity, or any other cause, the individual shall be supported by the community, and receive every comfort which kindness can administer.

XXX. That on the death of parents, the children shall become the peculiar care of the community, and proper persons be appointed to take the more immediate charge of them, and, as far as possible, supply the place of their natural parents.

XXXI. That the committee of management, shall not be empowered to admit a new member without the consent of three-fourths of the members of the community, obtained at a general meeting.

XXXII. That, although at the period when all the members shall have been trained and educated under the proposed arrangements, any regulations against misconduct will probably be unnecessary — and although it is anticipated, that the influence of these new circumstances upon the character of the individuals, whose habits and dispositions have been formed under a different system, will be sufficiently powerful, to render any serious differences of rare occurrence amongst them — yet in order to provide against such, it shall be a law of the community, that when differences arise, they be referred to the decision of arbitrators, to be elected by the society, who, after hearing the parties, shall decide upon the case.

XXXIII. That if the conduct of any individual be injurious to the well-being of the community, and it be so decided by three-fourths of the members assembled at a general meeting, the committee shall explain to him in what respect his conduct has been injurious, and at the same time intimate to him, that, unless the cause of complaint be removed, they are instructed to expel him from the community. . . .

XXXVII. That, in order to extend the benefits of a system of union and co-operation, which is applicable to mankind in every part of the world, measures be adopted by the committee to disseminate knowledge of the new principles and arrangements.

XXXVIII. That as this system is directly opposed to secrecy and exclusion of any kind, every practicable facility shall be given to strangers, to enable them to become acquainted with the constitution, laws and regulations of the community — and to examine the results which these have produced in practice. . . .

Uniting and Inciting
the Workers

Marx and Engels were asked to write The Communist Manifesto *at the November, 1847, meeting of the Communist League. It appeared in January, 1848. The word "Communist" was chosen deliberately because Marx and his colleagues did not want to be identified with bourgeois "Socialism." The* Manifesto *was meant to present the doctrine and program of a proletarian movement. It is the classic statement of dialectical materialism. Marx was strongly influenced by the German idealist philosopher Georg Wilhelm Friedrich Hegel (1770–1831), who sought to understand historical development as a dialectical process in which each stage of history bears within it the seeds of its own destruction — its antithesis — thus providing the conflict from which a new historical stage develops. Hegel sought to demonstrate the realization of Freedom in history, and he identified Freedom with the development of the State.*

The dialectical method, with its emphasis upon process and change, had radical implications. Marx shared Hegel's concern with spiritual freedom, but he was convinced that it was unattainable so long as man was enslaved by material conditions. Consequently, he rooted the dialectical development of history in material conditions, the changing forms of production, and predicted that just as feudalism had brought forth the bourgeoisie and its capitalist revolution, so capitalism would create a new proletarian class that would rebel against the increasing misery caused by the contradictions of the capitalist system to create the Communist society of the future. In Marx's view, it was the task of the Communists, the vanguard of the proletariat, to bring the proletariat to a greater consciousness of its conditions and mission.

Marx and Engels' *Communist Manifesto*

A spectre is haunting Europe — the spectre of Communism. All the Powers of old Europe have entered into a Holy Alliance to exorcise this spectre; Pope and Czar, Metternich and Guizot, French Radicals and German police-spies.

Where is the party in opposition that has not been decried as communistic by its opponents in power? Where the opposition that has not hurled back the branding reproach of Communism against the more advanced opposition parties, as well as against its reactionary adversaries?

Two things result from this fact.

I. Communism is already acknowledged by all European Powers to be itself a Power.

II. It is high time that Communists should openly, in the face of the whole world, publish their views, their aims, their tendencies, and meet this nursery tale of the Spectre of Communism with a Manifesto of the party itself.

To this end, Communists of various nationalities have assembled in London and sketched the following Manifesto, to be published in the English, French, German, Italian, Flemish, and Danish languages.

BOURGEOIS AND PROLETARIANS

The history of all hitherto existing society is the history of class struggles.

Freeman and slave, patrician and plebeian, lord and serf, guild-master and journeyman, in a word, oppressor and oppressed, stood in constant opposition to one another, carried on uninterrupted, now hidden, now open fight, a fight that each time ended, either in a revolutionary reconstitution of society at large, or in the common ruin of the contending classes.

In the earlier epochs of history we find almost everywhere a complicated arrangement of society into various orders, a manifold gradation of social rank. In ancient Rome we have patricians, knights, plebeians, slaves; in the middle ages, feudal lords, vassals, guild-masters, journeymen, apprentices, serfs; in almost all of these classes, again, subordinate gradations.

The modern bourgeois society that has sprouted from the ruins of feudal society has not done away with class antagonisms. It has but established new classes, new conditions of oppression, new forms of struggle in place of the old ones.

From *The Essentials of Marx,* introduction and notes by Algernon Lee (New York: Vanguard Press, 1926), pp. 30–33, 35–44.

Our epoch, the epoch of the bourgeoisie, possesses, however, this distinctive feature; it has simplified the class antagonisms. Society as a whole is more and more splitting up into two great hostile camps, into two great classes directly facing each other: Bourgeoisie and Proletariat.

From the serfs of the Middle Ages sprang the chartered burghers of the earliest towns. From these burgesses the first elements of the bourgeoisie were developed.

The discovery of America, the rounding of the Cape, opened up fresh ground for the rising bourgeoisie. The East Indian and Chinese markets, the colonization of America, trade with the colonies, the increase in the means of exchange and in commodities generally, gave to commerce, to navigation, to industry, an impulse never before known, and thereby, to the revolutionary element in the tottering feudal society, a rapid development.

The feudal system of industry, under which industrial production was monopolized by those guilds, now no longer sufficed for the growing wants of the new market. The manufacturing system took its place. The guild-masters were pushed on one side by the manufacturing middle class; division of labor between the different corporate guilds vanished in the face of division of labor in each single workshop.

Meantime the markets kept ever growing, the demand ever rising. Even manufacture no longer sufficed. Thereupon, steam and machinery revolutionized industrial production. The place of manufacture was taken by the giant Modern Industry, the place of the industrial middle-class, by industrial millionaires, the leaders of whole industrial armies, and modern bourgeois.

Modern industry has established the world-market, for which the discovery of America paved the way. This market has given an immense development to commerce, to navigation, to communication by land. This development has, in its turn, reacted on the extension of industry; and in proportion as industry, commerce, navigation, railways extended, in the same proportion the bourgeoisie developed, increased its capital, and pushed into the background every class handed down from the Middle Ages.

We see, therefore, how the modern bourgeoisie is itself the product of a long course of development, of a series of revolutions in the modes of production and of exchange.

Each step in the development of the bourgeoisie was accompanied by a corresponding political advance of that class. An oppressed class under the sway of the feudal nobility; an armed and self-governing association in the medieval commune, (here independent urban republic, as in Italy and Germany, there taxable "third estate" of the monarchy, as in France); afterwards, in the period of manufacture proper, serving either the semifeudal or the absolute monarchy as a counterpoise against the nobility, and in fact corner stone of the great monarchies in general — the bourgeoisie has at last, since the establishment of modern industry and of the world-market, conquered for itself, in the modern representative state, exclusive political sway. The executive of the modern state is but a committee for managing the common affairs of the whole bourgeoisie.

The bourgeoisie, historically, has played a most revolutionary part.

The bourgeoisie, wherever it has got the upper hand, has put an end to all feudal, patriarchal, idyllic relations. It has pitilessly torn asunder the motley feudal ties that bound man to his "natural superiors," and has left no other nexus between man and man than naked self-interest, than callous "cash payment." It has drowned the most heavenly ecstasies of religious fervor, of chivalrous enthusiasm, of philistine sentimentalism, in the icy water of egotistical calculation. It has resolved personal worth into exchange value, and in place of the numberless indefeasible chartered freedoms, has set up that single, unconscionable freedom — Free Trade. In one word, for exploitation, veiled by religious and political illusions, it has substituted naked, shameless, direct, brutal exploitation.

The bourgeoisie has stripped of its halo every occupation hitherto honored and looked up to with reverent awe. It has converted the physician, the lawyer, the priest, the poet, the man of science, into its paid wage laborers.

The bourgeoisie has torn away from the family its sentimental veil, and has reduced the family relation to a mere money relation.

The bourgeoisie has disclosed how it came to pass that the brutal display of vigor in the Middle Ages, which reactionists so much admire, found its fitting complement in the most slothful indolence. It has been the first to show what man's activity can bring about. It has accomplished wonders far surpassing Egyptian pyramids, Roman aqueducts, and Gothic cathedrals; it has conducted expeditions that put in the shade all former exoduses of nations and crusades. . . .

The bourgeoisie keeps more and more doing away with the scattered state of the population, of the means of production, and of property. It has agglomerated population, centralized means of production, and has concentrated property in a few hands. The necessary consequence of this was political centralization. Independent, or but loosely connected provinces, with separate interests, laws, governments, and systems of taxation, became lumped together in one nation, with one government, one code of laws, one national class-interest, one frontier and one customs' tariff.

The bourgeoisie, during its rule of scarce one hundred years, has created more massive and more colossal productive forces than have all preceding generations together. Subjection of nature's forces to man, machinery, application of chemistry to industry and agriculture, steam-navigation, railways, electric telegraphs, clearing of whole continents for cultivation, canalization of rivers, whole populations conjured out of the ground — what earlier century had even a presentiment that such productive forces slumbered in the lap of social labor?

We see then, the means of production and of exchange on whose foundation the bourgeoisie built itself up, were generated in feudal society. At a certain stage in the development of these means of production and of exchange, the conditions under which feudal society produced and exchanged, the feudal organization of agriculture and manufacturing industry — in one word, the feudal relations of property — became no longer compatible with the already developed productive forces; they became so many fetters. They had to burst asunder; they were burst asunder.

Into their places stepped free competition, accompanied by a social and political constitution adapted to it, and by the economical and political sway of the bourgeois class.

A similar movement is going on before our own eyes. Modern bourgeois society with its relations of production, of exchange, and of property, a society that has conjured up such gigantic means of production and of exchange, is like the sorcerer, who is no longer able to control the powers of the nether world whom he has called up by his spells. For many a decade past, the history of industry and commerce is but the history of the revolt of modern productive forces against modern conditions of production, against the property relations that are the conditions for the existence of the bourgeoisie and of its rule. It is enough to mention the commercial crises that by their periodical return put on its trial, each time more threateningly, the existence of the entire bourgeois society. In these crises a great part not only of the existing products, but also of the previously created productive forces, are periodically destroyed. In these crises there breaks out an epidemic that, in all earlier epochs, would have seemed an absurdity — the epidemic of over-production. Society suddenly finds itself put back into a state of momentary barbarism; it appears as if a famine, a universal war of devastation, had cut off the supply of every means of subsistence; industry and commerce seem to be destroyed; and why? Because there is too much civilization, too much means of subsistence, too much industry, too much commerce. The productive forces at the disposal of society no longer tend to further the development of the conditions of bourgeois property; on the contrary, they have become too powerful for these conditions by which they are confined, and as soon as they overcome these limitations they bring disorder into the whole of bourgeois society, endanger the existence of bourgeois property. The conditions of bourgeois society are too narrow to comprise the wealth created by them. And how does the bourgeoisie get over these crises? On the one hand by enforced destruction of a mass of productive forces; on the other, by the conquest of new markets, and by the more thorough exploitation of the old ones. That is to say, by paving the way for more extensive and more destructive crises, and by diminishing the means whereby crises are prevented.

The weapons with which the bourgeoisie felled feudalism to the ground are now turned against the bourgeoisie itself.

But not only has the bourgeoisie forged the weapons that bring death to itself; it has also called into existence the men who are to wield those weapons — the modern working class — the proletarians.

In proportion as the bourgeoisie — that is, as capital, is developed, in the same proportion is the proletariat, the modern working class, developed, a class of laborers who live only so long as they find work, and who find work only so long as their labor increases capital. These laborers, who must sell themselves piecemeal, are a commodity, like every other article of commerce, and are consequently exposed to all the vicissitudes of competition, to all the fluctuations of the market.

Owing to the extensive use of machinery and to division of labor, the work of the proletarians has lost all individual character, and, consequently, all charm for the workman. He becomes an appendage of the machine, and it is only the most simple, most monotonous, and most easily acquired knack that is required of him. Hence, the cost of production of a workman is restricted almost entirely to the means of subsistence that he requires for his maintenance, and for the propagation of his race. But the price of a commodity, and also of labor, is equal to its cost of production. In proportion, therefore, as the repulsiveness of the work increases the wage decreases. Nay more, in proportion as the use of machinery and division of labor increase, in the same proportion the burden of toil increases, whether by prolongation of the working hours, by increase of the work enacted in a given time, or by increased speed of the machinery, and so forth.

Modern industry has converted the little workshop of the patriarchal master into the great factory of the industrial capitalist. Masses of laborers, crowded into factories, are organized like soldiers. As privates of the industrial army they are placed under the command of a perfect hierarchy of officers and sergeants. Not only are they the slaves of the bourgeois class and of the bourgeois state, they are daily and hourly enslaved by the machine, by the foreman, and, above all, by the individual bourgeois manufacturer himself. The more openly this despotism proclaims gain to be its end and aim, the more petty, the more hateful and the more embittering it is.

The less the skill and exertion or strength implied in manual labor, in other words, the more modern industry becomes developed, the more is the labor of men superseded by that of women. Differences of age and sex have no longer any distinctive social validity for the working class. All are instruments of labor, more or less expensive to use, according to their age and sex.

No sooner is the exploitation of the laborer by the manufacturer so far at an end that he receives his wages in cash, than he is set upon by the other portions of the bourgeoisie, the landlord, the shopkeeper, the pawn-broker, and so forth.

The lower strata of the middle class — the small trades-people, shop-keepers and retired tradesmen generally, the handicraftsmen and peasants — all these sink gradually into the proletariat, partly because their dimin-utive capital does not suffice for the scale on which modern industry is carried on, and is swamped in the competition with the large capitalists, partly because their specialized skill is rendered worthless by new methods of production. Thus the proletariat is recruited from all classes of the population.

The proletariat goes through various stages of development. With its birth begins its struggle with the bourgeoisie. At first the contest is carried on by individual laborers, then by the workpeople of a factory, then by the operatives of one trade, in one locality, against the individual bour-geois who directly exploits them. They direct their attacks not against the bourgeois conditions of production, but against the instruments of pro-duction themselves; they destroy imported wares that compete with their labor, they smash machinery, they set factories ablaze, they seek to restore by force the vanished status of the workman of the Middle Ages.

At this stage the laborers still form an incoherent mass scattered over the whole country, and broken up by their mutual competition. If any-where they unite to form more compact bodies, this is not yet the conse-quence of their own active union, but of the union of the bourgeoisie, which class, in order to attain its own political ends, is compelled to set the whole proletariat in motion, and is moreover, for a time, still able to do so. At this stage, therefore, the proletarians do not fight their enemies, but the enemies of their enemies, the remnants of absolute mon-archy, the landowners, the non-industrial bourgeois, the petty bour-geoisie. Thus the whole historical movement is concentrated in the hands of the bourgeoisie, every victory so obtained is a victory for the bour-geoisie.

But with the development of industry the proletariat not only increases in number; it becomes concentrated in greater masses, its strength grows and it feels that strength more. The various interests and conditions of life within the ranks of the proletariat are more and more equalized, in proportion as machinery obliterates all distinctions of labor, and nearly everywhere reduces wages to the same low level. The growing competition among the bourgeois, and the resulting commercial crises, make the wages of the workers ever more fluctuating; the unceasing improvement of machinery, ever more rapidly developing, makes their livelihood more and more precarious; the collisions between individual workmen and individual bourgeois take more and more the character of collisions between two classes. Thereupon the workers begin to form combinations (trade unions) against the bourgeois; they club together in order to keep up the rate of wages; they found permanent associations in order to make provision beforehand for these occasional revolts. Here and there the contest breaks out into riots.

Now and then the workers are victorious, but only for a time. The real fruit of their battle lies not in the immediate result, but in the ever expanding union of workers. This union is helped on by the improved means of communication that are created by modern industry, and that places the workers of different localities in contact with one another. It was just this contact that was needed to centralize the numerous local struggles, all of the same character, into one national struggle between classes. But every class struggle is a political struggle. And that union, to attain which the burghers of the Middle Ages with their miserable highways, required centuries, the modern proletarians, thanks to railways, achieve in a few years.

This organization of the proletarians into a class, and consequently into a political party, is continually being upset again by the competition between the workers themselves. But it ever rises up again, stronger, firmer, mightier. It compels legislative recognition of particular interests of the workers by taking advantage of the divisions among the bourgeoisie itself. Thus the Ten-Hours-Bill in England was carried.

Altogether collisions between the classes of the old society further, in many ways, the development of the proletariat. The bourgeoisie finds itself involved in a constant battle — at first with the aristocracy; later on, with those portions of the bourgeoisie itself whose interests have become antagonistic to the progress of industry; at all times, with the bourgeoisie of foreign countries. In all these battles it sees itself compelled to appeal to the proletariat, to ask for its help, and thus to drag it into the political arena. The bourgeoisie itself, therefore, supplies the proletariat with its own elements of political and general education; in other words, it furnishes the proletariat with weapons for fighting the bourgeoisie.

Further, as we have already seen, entire sections of the ruling classes are, by the advance of industry, precipitated into the proletariat, or are at least threatened in their conditions of existence. These also supply the proletariat with fresh elements of enlightenment and progress.

Finally, in times when the class-struggle nears the decisive hour, the process of dissolution going on within the ruling class, in fact within the whole range of an old society, assumes such a violent, glaring character that a small section of the ruling class cuts itself adrift and joins the revolutionary class, the class that holds the future in its hands. Just as, therefore, at an earlier period, a section of the nobility went over to the bourgeoisie, so now a portion of the bourgeoisie goes over to the proletariat, and in particular, a portion of the bourgeois ideologists, who have raised themselves to the level of comprehending theoretically the historical movements as a whole.

Of all the classes that stand face to face with the bourgeoisie today the proletariat alone is a really revolutionary class. The other classes decay and finally disappear in the face of modern industry; the proletariat is its special and essential product.

The lower middle-class, the small manufacturer, the shopkeeper, the artisan, the peasant, all these fight against the bourgeoisie, to save from extinction their existence as fractions of the middle class. They are therefore not revolutionary, but conservative. Nay, more; they are reactionary, for they try to roll back the wheel of history. If by chance they are revolutionary, they are so only in view of their impending transfer into the proletariat; they thus defend not their present, but their future interests; they desert their own standpoint to place themselves at that of the proletariat.

The "dangerous class," the social scum, that passively rotting mass thrown off by the lowest layers of the old society, may here and there be swept into the movement by a proletarian revolution; its conditions of life, however, prepare it far more for the part of a bribed tool of reactionary intrigue.

In the conditions of the proletariat, those of old society at large are already virtually swamped. The proletarian is without property; his relation to his wife and children has no longer anything in common with the bourgeois family relations; modern industrial labor, modern subjection to capital, the same in England as in France, in America as in Germany, has stripped him of every trace of national character. Law, morality, religion, are to him so many bourgeois prejudices, behind which lurk in ambush just as many bourgeois interests.

All the preceding classes that got the upper hand sought to fortify their already acquired status by subjecting society at large to their conditions of appropriation. The proletarians cannot become masters of the productive forces of society, except by abolishing their own previous mode of appropriation, and thereby also every other previous mode of appropriation. They have nothing of their own to secure and to fortify; their mission is to destroy all previous securities for and insurance of individual property.

All previous historical movements were movements of minorities, or in the interest of minorities. The proletarian movement is the self-conscious, independent movement of the immense majority. The proletariat, the lowest stratum of our present society, cannot stir, cannot raise itself up without the whole superincumbent strata of official society being sprung into the air.

Though not in substance, yet in form, the struggle of the proletariat with the bourgeoisie is at first a national struggle. The proletariat of each country must, of course, first of all settle matters with its own bourgeoisie.

In depicting the most general phases of the development of the proletariat, we have traced the more or less veiled civil war, raging within existing society, up to the point where that war breaks out into open revolution, and where the violent overthrow of the bourgeoisie, lays the foundation for the sway of the proletariat.

Hitherto every form of society has been based, as we have already seen, on the antagonism of oppressing and oppressed classes. But in order to oppress a class, certain conditions must be assured to it under which it can at least continue its slavish existence. The serf, in the period of serfdom, raised himself to membership in the commune, just as the petty bourgeois, under the yoke of feudal absolutism, managed to develop into a bourgeois. The modern laborer, on the contrary, instead of rising with the progress of industry, sinks deeper and deeper below the conditions of existence of his own class. He becomes a pauper, and pauperism develops more rapidly than population and wealth. And here it becomes evident that the bourgeoisie is unfit any longer to be the ruling class in society, and to impose its conditions of existence upon society as an over-riding law. It is unfit to rule, because it is incompetent to assure an existence to its slave within his slavery, because it cannot help letting him sink into such a state that it has to feed him, instead of being fed by him. Society can no longer live under this bourgeoisie; in other words, its existence is no longer compatible with society.

The essential condition for the existence, and for the sway of the bourgeois class, is the formation and augmentation of capital; the condition for capital is wage-labor. Wage-labor rests exclusively on competition between the laborers. The advance of industry, whose involuntary promoter is the bourgeoisie, replaces the isolation of the laborers, due to competition, by their revolutionary combination, due to association. The development of modern industry, therefore, cuts from under its feet the very foundation on which the bourgeoisie produces and appropriates products. What the bourgeoisie therefore produces, above all, are its own grave-diggers. Its fall and the victory of the proletariat are equally inevitable.

The French Revolution of 1848

Economic discontent of the lower classes combined with middle-class dissatisfaction over the corruption of the Orleanist regime and its plutocratic suffrage system led to the revolution of 1848 in France. The uprising itself was triggered by the unpopular minister François Guizot, who attempted to ban a procession and banquet planned by the liberals to protest the Orleanist government. The revolt in Paris lasted only four days. Louis-Philippe abdicated, and romantic liberalism had one of its last flings when the poet-politician Alphonse de Lamartine (1790–1869) proclaimed the republic on February 24. Ruling proved more difficult than oratory and poetry, however, and the republican governments were torn by dissension between moderates and radicals. The "June Days" and the arrival of Louis Napoleon demonstrated that the revolution had gone sour. Some of the romantic spirit and excitement of February is conveyed by Gustave Flaubert (1821–1880) in his partially autobiographical novel Sentimental Education *(1869). Flaubert looked back with realist disenchantment at the enthusiasm of his youth and used the journalist Hussonnet's cynicism as an antidote to the enthusiasm of his hero Frederic.*

Flaubert's *Sentimental Education*

A sudden rattle of musketry made him wake with a start; and, in spite of Rosanette's entreaties, Frederic insisted on going to see what was happening. He followed the sound of the firing down the Champs-Élysées. At the corner of the rue Saint-Honoré he was met by a shout from some workmen in blouses:

'No! Not that way! To the Palais-Royal!'

Frederic followed them. The railings of the Church of the Assumption had been pulled down. Further on he noticed three paving stones torn up in the middle of the road, doubtless the foundation of a barricade — then bits of broken bottles, and bundles of wire, to hamper the cavalry. Suddenly, out of an alley, rushed a tall young man, with black hair hanging over his shoulders and wearing a sort of pea-green singlet. He carried a soldier's long musket; there were slippers on his feet and he was running on tiptoe, as lithe as a tiger, yet with the fixed stare of a sleep-walker. Now and then explosions could be heard.

From Gustave Flaubert, *Sentimental Education,* trans. Anthony Goldsmith (New York: Dutton, Everyman's Library, 1941), pp. 367–73. Reprinted by permission of E. P. Dutton & Co., Inc., and J. M. Dent & Sons Ltd.

The previous evening the public exhibition of a cart containing five bodies from the boulevard des Capucines had changed the temper of the people. At the Tuileries there was a continuous coming and going of equerries; M. Molé, who was constructing a new Cabinet, did not reappear; M. Thiers tried to form another; the king shuffled, hesitated, gave Bugeaud full authority, then prevented him from making use of it. Meanwhile, as though directed by a single hand, the insurrection grew ever stronger and more menacing. Men addressed crowds at street corners with frantic eloquence; others, in the churches, were sounding the tocsin with all their might; lead was melted, cartridges rolled; trees from the boulevards, public urinals, benches, railings, gas jets were torn down or overturned; by morning Paris was filled with barricades. Resistance was not prolonged; everywhere the National Guard intervened; so that by eight o'clock, through force or by consent, the people were in possession of five barracks, nearly all the town halls, and the most important strategic points. No great exertion was necessary; through its own weakness the monarchy was swiftly tottering to its fall. And now the people were attacking the guard post known as the Château-d'Eau, in order to liberate fifty prisoners who were not there.

Frederic was forced to stop at the edge of the square, which was filled with groups of armed men. The rue Saint-Thomas and the rue Fromanteau were occupied by regular soldiers. A huge barricade blocked the rue de Valois. The smoke that hovered about it melted for a moment; men scaled the parapet with wild gestures, and then vanished; the firing began again. The police station replied, although no one could be seen within; the windows were protected by oak shutters, pierced with loopholes; and the monument, with its two tiers and two wings – with the fountain on the first tier and the little door in the middle – began to show the white marks of bullet pocks. Its flight of three steps was empty.

Next to Frederic a man in a smoking cap, with a cartridge pouch under his woollen jacket, was arguing with a woman with a kerchief on her head.

'Come back! Come back, I say!' she was saying.

'Leave me alone!' replied the husband. 'You can look after the door by yourself. Citizen, I ask you, is it fair? I've always done my duty – in '30, in '32, in '34, in '39. They're fighting to-day. I've got to fight! Go away!'

And in the end the porter's wife yielded to his protests, and to those of a National Guard beside them – a man of about forty, whose good-humoured face was fringed all round with a fair beard. He was loading his piece and firing, while he talked to Frederic, as calm in the midst of the fighting as a gardener among his flowers. A boy in a sackcloth apron was trying to persuade him to give him some caps, so that he could use his gun, a fine sporting carbine which 'a gentleman' had given him.

'Take a handful from my back,' said the guard. 'Then make yourself scarce! You'll be getting killed!'

The drums beat the charge. Shrill cries could be heard, and shouts of triumph. The crowd rocked in a continuous surge. Frederic, wedged between two dense masses, stayed where he was. Fascinated, he was enjoying himself hugely. The wounded falling, and the dead lying stretched out, did not look as if they were really wounded or dead. He felt as though he were watching a play.

Above the heads of the swaying multitude could be seen an old man in a black coat, on a white horse with a velvet saddle. He held a green bough in one hand, and a piece of paper in the other, which he shook persistently. At last he gave up hope of making himself heard and withdrew.

The soldiers had disappeared and only the Municipal Guards remained to defend the guard house. A wave of heroes rushed up the steps; they fell; others followed; the door resounded under heavy blows from iron bars; the guards would not surrender. Then a carriage, stuffed with hay and burning like a giant torch, was pushed up against the walls. Quickly they brought up faggots, straw, a barrel of spirits of wine. The fire leaped up the stone wall; the building began to smoke at every point like a volcano; above, great crackling flames burst out through the balustrade that surrounded the roof. The first floor of the Palais-Royal was packed with National Guards. They were shooting from every window; the bullets whistled, the fountain had burst its basin, and the water, mingled with blood, spread over the ground in puddles. People slipped in the mud on coats, shakos, and muskets; Frederic felt something soft under his foot; it was the hand of a sergeant in a grey overcoat, lying face downwards in the gutter. Fresh crowds kept coming up and pushing the fighters towards the guard house. The firing became more intense. The wine merchants' shops were open; from time to time, men went in to smoke a pipe or drink a glass of beer; then returned to the battle. A lost dog was howling. This made the people laugh.

Frederic staggered back under the weight of a man who fell groaning on his shoulder with a ball in his back. This attack, which was perhaps directed against him, made him furious; and he was dashing forward when a National Guard stopped him.

'It's no use. The king has just left. Well, if you don't believe me, go and see!'

This pronouncement calmed Frederic. The place du Carrousel looked peaceful. The Hôtel de Nantes still stood there, tall and solitary. The houses behind, the dome of the Louvre opposite, the long, wooden gallery on the right, and the sort of sloping no man's land that stretched up to the stall keepers' booths — all seemed steeped in the grey tints of the evening; distant murmurs were heard dimly, as if deadened by the mist. But at the other end of the square, through a gap in the clouds, a hard glaring light fell on the front of the Tuileries, making all its windows stand out in white relief. A dead horse lay stretched out by the Arc de Triomphe.

Behind the railings, people were chatting in groups of five or six. The doors of the palace were open, and the servants on the threshold allowed the crowd to go in.

Bowls of coffee were being served in a little room on the ground floor. Some of the visitors sat down to table merrily; others remained standing. A cabman among the latter seized a jar full of soft sugar with both hands, gave an uneasy glance to right and left, and then began to eat voraciously, plunging his nose into the pot. At the foot of the great staircase a man was writing his name in a book. Frederic recognized him from behind.

'Well — Hussonnet!'

'Why, yes,' answered the journalist. 'I'm presenting myself at court. This is a good joke, isn't it?' And they entered the Hall of the Marshals. The protraits of these worthies were intact, except for Bugeaud, who had been pierced through the stomach. The marshals were pictured leaning on their sabres, with gun carriages in the background, in attitudes of menace, little suited to the present juncture. A large clock pointed to twenty past one.

Suddenly the *Marseillaise* rang out. Hussonnet and Frederic leaned over the banisters. It was the people.

The mob surged up the staircase in a swirling stream of bare heads, helmets, caps of liberty, waving bayonets, and heaving shoulders. So violent was their onrush that people vanished in the swarming mass; on and on they climbed, like a springtide sweeping up a river, driven forward by an irresistible impulse, with a continuous roar. At the top they scattered and the singing ceased.

Nothing could be heard but the trampling of feet and the babble of voices. The harmless crowd was content to stare. But from time to time an elbow, cramped for space, burst through a window; sometimes a vase or a statuette rolled off a side table on to the ground. The panelling creaked under the pressure of the throng. Sweat trickled down their red faces in large drops; Hussonnet remarked: 'I don't care much for the smell of heroes.'

'Oh, you annoy me,' said Frederic.

Pushed along helplessly, they entered a room in which a red velvet canopy was stretched across the ceiling. On the throne beneath sat a workman with a black beard, his shirt half open, grinning stupidly, like an ape. Others climbed on to the dais to sit in his place.

'What a legend!' said Hussonnet. 'The sovereignty of the people!'

Outstretched arms lifted the arm-chair and passed it, swaying, right across the room.

'Good Lord! See how it rocks! The ship of state is being tossed in a stormy sea! It's dancing a jig! It's dancing a jig!'

It was taken to a window and thrown out, amid hisses.

'Poor old thing!' said Hussonnet, as he watched it fall into the garden, where it was soon picked up to be carried in procession to the Bastille and afterwards burned.

There followed a burst of frantic joy, as though the throne had been replaced by a future of unlimited happiness; and the people, less out of vengeance than from a desire to assert their mastery, broke and tore down mirrors, curtains, chandeliers, sconces, tables, chairs, stools — everything movable, down to albums of drawings and work baskets. They had conquered, therefore they should celebrate. In mockery, the rabble draped themselves in lace and cashmere. Gold fringes were wound about the sleeves of blouses, hats with ostrich plumes decked the heads of blacksmiths, ribbons of the Legion of Honour made sashes for prostitutes. Each man satisfied his whim; some danced, others drank. In the queen's room a woman was greasing her hair with pomade. Two enthusiasts were playing cards behind a screen; Hussonnet pointed out to Frederic a man leaning on a balcony, smoking his clay pipe; and, amid the general fury, the hall re-echoed to the crash of china and the shattering of glass; and the fragments of crystal tinkled as they fell, like the keys of a harmonica.

Then their frenzy took a darker turn. In obscene curiosity they ransacked the cupboards and closets, and turned out all the drawers. Jailbirds thrust their arms into the princesses' bed and rolled on top of it, as a consolation for not being able to rape them. Sinister characters wandered silently about, searching for something to steal; but the crowd was too numerous. Looking through the doorways, down the long series of rooms, one could see nothing but a dark mass of people in a cloud of dust between the gilded walls. They were all out of breath; the heat became more and more stifling; and the two friends went out, to avoid being suffocated.

In the vestibule, on a pile of clothes, stood a prostitute, posed as a statue of Liberty, motionless, with staring eyes — a figure of terror.

They were only just outside when a troop of Municipal Guards in overcoats came towards them. The guards took off their policemen's caps, revealing their somewhat bald heads, and bowed very low to the people. The ragged victors were enchanted with this sign of respect. Nor were Hussonnet and Frederic entirely displeased by the spectacle.

They were burning with excitement. They went back to the Palais-Royal. At the opening of the rue Fromanteau the corpses of soldiers were piled up on straw. They passed them without emotion, and even took a pride in their imperturbability.

The palace was crammed with people. Seven bonfires were blazing in the inner court. Pianos, chests of drawers, and clocks were being flung out of the windows. Fire-pumps were throwing water up to the roof. Some hooligans tried to cut the hoses with their sabres. Frederic urged an artillery cadet to intervene. The cadet did not understand; he seemed to be half-witted. All round, in the two arcades, the mob, having broken open the cellars, were abandoning themselves to a horrible debauch. Wine flowed in streams and wetted their feet; there were ruffians drinking out of the heels of broken bottles, and shouting as they reeled.

'Let's go,' said Hussonnet. 'I find your friends the people revolting.'

All along the Orleans gallery the wounded were lying on mattresses on the ground, with purple curtains for blankets, while the wives of the local tradesmen brought them soup and clean linen.

'No matter!' said Frederic. 'To my mind, the people are sublime!'

The great hall was filled with an angry swarming crowd; some tried to climb to the higher floors to complete the work of destruction; a few National Guards on the steps struggled to hold them back. The boldest of the guards was a bare-headed rifleman, with tousled hair and tattered belt. His shirt was bulging out between his trousers and his coat, and he fought desperately beside his comrades. Hussonnet, who had very long sight, recognized Arnoux in the distance.

Then they went into the Tuileries garden, where they could breathe more freely. They sank down on a bench; and sat for some minutes with their eyes shut, so dead-beat that they had not the strength to speak. Around them passers-by were meeting and talking. The Duchesse d'Orléans had been nominated regent; it was all over; and every one felt that sense of satisfaction that follows the rapid solution of a crisis. Suddenly servants appeared at all the top-floor windows of the palace; they tore up their liveries as a sign of renunciation. The people booed them. They withdrew.

The two friends' attention was distracted by the sight of a tall youth walking briskly through the trees with a musket on his shoulder. He wore a red tunic with a cartridge belt round his waist; a handkerchief was wound round his forehead, under his cap. He turned his head. It was Dussardier. He flung himself into their arms.

'What happiness, my dear old friends!' he said, and could not utter another word; for he was quite breathless with joy and exhaustion.

He had been on his feet for forty-eight hours. He had worked at the barricades in the Latin quarter, fought in the rue Rambuteau, saved the lives of three dragoons, entered the Tuileries with Dunoyer's column, gone to the Chamber, and afterward to the Hôtel de Ville.

'I'm just back from there. All is well! The people have triumphed. Workmen and shopkeepers are shaking hands! Ah, if you'd seen what I've seen! What wonderful people! How splendid it all is!'

And without noticing that they were unarmed:

'I knew I should find you in the thick of it! Things were warm for a moment — but no matter!'

A drop of blood was trickling down his cheek, and to the others' inquiries he replied:

'It's nothing. A scratch from a bayonet.'

'But you ought to have it seen to.'

'Nonsense! I'm as strong as a horse. What does it matter? The Republic has been proclaimed! We shall be happy now. I heard some journalists talking just now; they said we were going to liberate Poland and Italy. No more kings! Do you understand? The whole world free! The whole world free!'

The Failure of Revolution in Germany

An important turning point of the revolution in Germany came in September, 1848, when the Frankfurt Parliament accepted the Armistice of Malmö between Prussia and Denmark. Both the democrats and the liberals in the Frankfurt Parliament wished to "liberate" Schleswig-Holstein from Denmark, but Prussia, which was assigned this task, was compelled by the Great Powers to desist. The suppression of popular protests against the armistice by the Frankfurt Assembly demonstrated its dependence upon Prussian power in foreign and domestic affairs. While conservatism regained its ground in Austria and Prussia, the Frankfurt Assembly managed to produce a constitution in March, 1849, that was based on a compromise between the democratic forces, who wished a united Germany that included Austria, and the liberals, many of whom wished to offer the imperial crown to Prussia. The liberals agreed to universal suffrage and the democrats to a Germany under Prussian leadership and without Austria. Frederick William IV, however, turned down both the constitution and the crown "from the gutter," and thereafter the days of the Frankfurt Assembly were numbered. Friedrich Engels wrote a searing commentary on the liberal-democratic failure for the New York Tribune *in 1851 and 1852. His articles remain one of the most important analyses of the revolution because of their emphasis on the social aspects of the revolution and the unwillingness of the liberals and democrats to use the power of the lower classes while it remained at their disposal.*

Engels: Revolution and Counterrevolution in Germany

As early as the beginning of April 1848, the revolutionary torrent had found itself stemmed all over the Continent of Europe by the league which those classes of society that had profited by the first victory im-

From *New York Tribune*, March 18, 1852, and July 27, 1852.

mediately formed with the vanquished. In France, the petty trading class and the Republican faction of the bourgeoisie had combined with the Monarchist bourgeoisie against the proletarians; in Germany and Italy, the victorious bourgeoisie had eagerly courted the support of the feudal nobility, the official bureaucracy, and the army, against the mass of the people and the petty traders. Very soon the united Conservative and Counter-Revolutionary parties again regained the ascendant. In England, an untimely and ill-prepared popular demonstration (April 10th) turned out a complete and decisive defeat of the popular party. In France, two similar movements (April 16th and May 15th) were equally defeated. In Italy, King Bomba regained his authority by a single stroke on May 15th. In Germany, the different new bourgeois Governments and their respective constituent Assemblies consolidated themselves, and if the eventful May 15th gave rise, in Vienna, to a popular victory, this was an event of merely secondary importance, and may be considered the last successful flash of popular energy. In Hungary the movement appeared to turn into the quiet channel of perfect legality, and the Polish movement, as we have seen in our last, was stifled in the bud by Prussian bayonets. But as yet nothing was decided as to the eventual turn which things would take, and every inch of ground lost by the Revolutionary parties in the different countries only tended to close their ranks more and more for the decisive action.

The decisive action drew near. It could be fought in France only; for France, as long as England took no part in the revolutionary strife, or as Germany remained divided, was, by its national independence, civilisation, and centralisation, the only country to impart the impulse of a mighty convulsion to the surrounding countries. Accordingly, when, on June 23rd, 1848, the bloody struggle began in Paris, when every succeeding telegraph or mail more clearly exposed the fact to the eyes of Europe, that this struggle was carried on between the mass of the working people on the one hand, and all the other classes of the Parisian population, supported by the army, on the other; when the fighting went on for several days with an exasperation unequalled in the history of modern civil warfare, but without any apparent advantage for either side — then it became evident to every one that this was the great decisive battle which would, if the insurrection were victorious, deluge the whole continent with renewed revolutions, or, if it was suppressed, bring about an at least momentary restoration of counter-revolutionary rule.

The proletarians of Paris were defeated, decimated, crushed with such an effect that even now they have not yet recovered from the blow. And immediately, all over Europe, the new and old Conservatives and Counter-Revolutionists raised their heads with an effrontery that showed how well they understood the importance of the event. The Press was everywhere attacked, the rights of meeting and association were interfered with, every little event in every small provincial town was taken profit of to disarm the people to declare a state of siege, to drill the troops in the new manoeuvres and artifices that Cavaignac had taught them. Besides, for the first time since February, the invincibility of a popular insurrection in a large town had been proved to be a delusion; the honour of the armies had been restored; the troops hitherto always defeated in street battles of importance regained confidence in their efficiency even in this kind of struggle.

From this defeat of the *ouvriers* of Paris may be dated the first positive steps and definite plans of the old feudal bureaucratic party in Germany, to get rid even of their momentary allies, the middle classes, and to restore Germany to the state she was in before the events of March. The army again was the decisive power in the State, and the army belonged not to the middle classes but to themselves. Even in Prussia, where before 1848 a considerable leaning of part of the lower grades of officers towards a Constitutional Government had been observed, the disorder introduced into the army by the Revolution had brought back those reasoning young men to their allegiance; as soon as the private soldier took a few liberties with regard to the officers, the necessity of discipline and passive obedience became at once strikingly evident to them. The vanquished nobles and bureaucrats now began to see their way before them; the army, more united than ever, flushed with victory in minor insurrections and in foreign warfare, jealous of the great success the French soldiers had just attained — this army had only to be kept in constant petty conflicts with the people, and the decisive moment once at hand, it could with one great blow crush the Revolutionists, and set aside the presumptions of the middle-class Parliamentarians. And the proper moment for such a decisive blow arrived soon enough.

We pass over the sometimes curious, but mostly tedious, parliamentary proceedings and local struggles that occupied, in Germany, the different parties during the summer. Suffice it to say that the supporters of the middle-class interest in spite of numerous parliamentary triumphs, not one of which led to any practical result, very generally felt that their position between the extreme parties became daily more untenable, and that, therefore, they were obliged now to seek the alliance of the reactionists, and the next day to court the favour of the more popular factions. This constant vacillation gave the finishing stroke to their character in public opinion, and according to the turn events were taking, the contempt into which they had sunk, profited for the movement principally to the bureaucrats and feudalists.

By the beginning of autumn the relative position of the different parties had become exasperated and critical enough to make a decisive battle inevitable. The first engagements in this war between the democratic and revolutionary masses and the army took place at Frankfort.

Though a mere secondary engagement, it was the first advantage of any note the troops acquired over the insurrection, and had a great moral effect. The fancy Government established by the Frankfort National Assembly had been allowed by Prussia, for very obvious reasons, to conclude an armistice with Denmark, which not only surrendered to Danish vengeance the Germans of Schleswig, but which also entirely disclaimed the more or less revolutionary principles which were generally supposed in the Danish war. This armistice was, by a majority of two or three, rejected in the Frankfort Assembly. A sham ministerial crisis followed this vote, but three days later the Assembly reconsidered their vote, and were actually induced to cancel it and acknowledge the armistice. This disgraceful proceeding roused the indignation of the people. Barricades were erected, but already sufficient troops had been drawn to Frankfort, and after six hours' fighting, the insurrection was suppressed. Similar, but less important, movements connected with this event took place in other parts of Germany (Baden, Cologne), but were equally defeated.

This preliminary engagement gave to the Counter-Revolutionary party the one great advantage, that now the only Government which had entirely — at least in semblance — originated with popular election, the Imperial Government of Frankfort, as well as the National Assembly, was ruined in the eyes of the people. This Government and this Assembly had been obliged to appeal to the bayonets of the troops against the manifestation of the popular will. They were compromised, and what little regard they might have been hitherto enabled to claim, this repudiation of their origin, the dependency upon the anti-popular Governments and their troops, made both the Lieutenant of the Empire, his ministers and his deputies, henceforth to be complete nullities. We shall soon see how first Austria, then Prussia, and later on the smaller States too, treated with contempt every order, every request, every deputation they received from this body of impotent dreamers. . . .

The Left of the Assembly — this *élite* and pride of revolutionary Germany, as it believed itself to be — was entirely intoxicated with the few paltry successes it obtained. . . . Whenever the slightest approximation to their own not very well-defined principles had, in a homoeopathically diluted shape, obtained a sort of sanction by the Frankfort Assembly, these Democrats proclaimed that they had saved the country and the people. These poor, weak-minded men, during the course of their generally very obscure lives, had been so little accustomed to anything like success, that they actually believed their paltry amendments, passed with two or three votes majority, would change the face of Europe. They had, from the beginning of their legislative career, been more imbued than any other faction of the Assembly with that incurable malady *Parliamentary crétinism,* a disorder which penetrates its unfortunate victims with the solemn conviction that the whole world, its history and future, are governed and determined by a majority of votes in that particular representative body which has the honour to count them among its members, and that all and everything going on outside the walls of their house — wars, revolutions, railway-constructing, colonising of whole new continents, California gold discoveries, Central American canals, Russian armies, and whatever else may have some little claim to influence upon the destinies of mankind — is nothing compared with the incommensurable events hinging upon the important question, whatever it may be, just at that moment occupying the attention of their honourable house. Thus it was the Democratic party of the Assembly, by effectually smuggling a few of their nostrums into the "imperial Constitution," first became bound to support it, although in every essential point it flatly contradicted their own oft-proclaimed principles, and at last, when this mongrel work was abandoned, and bequeathed to them by its main authors, accepted the inheritance, and held out for this *Monarchical* Constitution, even in opposition to everybody who *then* proclaimed their own *Republican* principles.

But it must be confessed that in this the contradiction was merely apparent. The indeterminate, self-contradictory, immature character of the Imperial Constitution was the very image of the immature, confused, conflicting political ideas of these Democratic gentlemen. And if their own sayings and writings — as far as they could write — were not sufficient proof of this, their action would furnish such proof; for among sensible people it is a matter of course to judge of a man, not by his professions, but by his actions; not by what he pretends to be, but by what he does, and what he really is; and the deeds of these heroes of German Democracy speak loud enough for themselves, as we shall learn by and by. However, the Imperial Constitution, with all its appendages and paraphernalia, was definitely passed, and on March 28th, the King of Prussia was, by 290 votes against 248 who abstained, and 200 who were absent, elected Emperor of Germany *minus* Austria. The historical irony was complete; the Imperial farce executed in the streets of astonished Berlin, three days after the Revolution of March 18th, 1848, by Frederick William IV, while in a state which elsewhere would come under the Maine Liquor Law — this disgusting farce, just one year afterwards, had been sanctioned by the pretended Representative Assembly of all Germany. That, then, was the result of the German Revolution!

THE REALIST REACTION
Chapter 5

The realism ushered in by the collapse of the revolutions of 1848 pervaded nearly every aspect of human life and was well attuned to the general period of economic upswing and growth that occurred from 1847 to 1873. The conservative leaders who assumed power in the 1850's were less dogmatic than their predecessors, and they were interested more in maintaining the power of the ruling classes than in simply retaining the institutional status quo. Conservatism became more dynamic, realistic, and imaginative. In cultural life, the detachment and realism of Flaubert, the psychological novels of the great Russian writers Leo Tolstoi, Ivan Turgenev, and Feodor Dostoevski, and the satiric caricatures of the French painter Honoré Daumier demonstrated that artists did not need to adhere to the romantic style to produce artistic expressions of great sensitivity and emotional insight.

The period was above all, however, one of scientific progress. In physics, Hermann von Helmholtz formulated the First Law of Thermodynamics in 1847, setting forth the principle of the conservation of energy. James Clerk Maxwell supplied a theoretical framework for electromagnetism in the 1860's. Just as Helmholtz's theoretical work demonstrated the futility of scientists' continuing their efforts to create a perpetual motion machine, so the work of the organic chemists Friedrich Wöhler and Claude Bernard terminated unempirical explanations of organic behavior based on the idea of "vital forces" by synthesizing organic matter and establishing the germ theory of disease. Similarly, Charles Darwin's evolutionary theory of natural selection made it unnecessary for naturalists to continue the "endless disputes whether or not some fifty species of British brambles are true species" because it freed them from the "vain search for the undiscovered and undiscoverable essence of the term species." The new principles established by these scientists enabled their colleagues and future researchers to turn from dead ends to fruitful new areas of scientific research.

The scientists did not always have an easy time gaining acceptance of their ideas. On the one hand, they were attacked by the defenders of antiquated theories within their own ranks. On the other hand, they also ran afoul of religious authority. In Germany, scientists such as Helmholtz who used the empirical inductive method fought an uphill battle against the idealistic school of natural philosophy (*Naturphilosophie*), whose representatives often occupied important chairs in the universities and preached an a priori deductive method. Indeed, during the 1850's and 1860's the German universities were torn with dissension because of this conflict. The debates over Darwin's work are much better known. His theory that man evolved over millions of years from lower forms of life was viewed as an attack upon the story of creation in the Bible and a threat to religious authority. Darwin had never intended this result and, on the contrary, constantly marveled at what he conceived to be the Creator's handiwork, but this did not appease the religious sensibilities of his critics then, just as it does not satisfy fundamentalist opponents of evolution today.

The conflicts over Darwinism served only to intensify the running war between liberalism and religion, especially with the Catholic Church. Even though liberals became more flexible and compromising in political and social matters after 1848, they retained their opposition to the power and authority of the Church almost as an article of faith. Constant political warfare occurred between liberals and ultramontanes in France. The unification of Germany under Protestant Prussia between 1866 and 1871 intensified the long history of conflict between Catholics and Protestants and culminated in the so-called Cultural Struggle (*Kulturkampf*) between the Prussian state and the Catholic Church in the 1870's. The Church lost many rights and privileges, and religious orders were subjected to humiliating demands and actual persecution. Bismarck used the conflict to fight political Catholicism as represented in the Center party rather than religion as such, but the hostility of the liberals, with whom he was then allied, ran much deeper. Pope Pius IX, who reigned from 1846 to 1878, did little to dispel the liberal charges of obscurantism leveled against him. He promulgated the Dogma of the Immaculate Conception in 1854, issued the *Syllabus of Errors* attacking modernity in all its forms in 1864, and used the Vatican Council of 1869 to promulgate the Dogma of Papal Infallibility. For most liberals, this was more than enough to justify their enmity and even intolerance.

Indeed, for many in this period, science became a substitute religion that could solve every conceivable problem. This tendency was epitomized by the founder of modern positivism and of sociology, Auguste Comte (1798–1857), who argued that philosophy could recognize only what could be empirically and scientifically proven. He believed that it was possible to create a body of scientific laws embracing all branches of knowledge and culminating in the science of sciences, Sociology, which would replace its historical predecessors theology and philosophy. Comte's theological-sounding doctrines were too airy to have a direct and immediate influence, but the same cannot be said of the ideas of the Social Darwinists. The most famous Social Darwinist, Herbert Spencer (1820–1903), employed Darwin's theories to buttress the doctrines of classical economics, to extol conflict and competition, and to oppose measures of social amelioration on the grounds that they interfered with the "survival of the fittest." Darwin had no more drawn such implications from his work than he had espoused the imperialist and racist doctrines that became increasingly popular as the century wore on.

Hermann von Helmholtz

Hermann von Helmholtz (1821–1894) was not only a great scientist but also a popularizer of the natural sciences and an academic statesman. The address he gave at the University of Heidelberg in 1862 demonstrates his academic statesmanship. By 1862 the battle between the natural scientists and the Hegelians, in which Helmholtz participated, was being won by the former group. Growing specialization within the university increasingly threatened the traditional notion of the unity of Wissenschaft *(literally, science), which designated all branches of knowledge, not just natural science. Many professors argued that the Philosophical Faculty, which included both the natural and the humanistic branches of knowledge (the other three faculties were Law, Medicine, and Theology), could no longer be maintained as a unit. Though making no concessions to the Hegelians and their vitalistic approach to the natural sciences, Helmholtz nevertheless argued that there were not "two cultures" and that the different branches of knowledge could aid one another. It is difficult to tell from his argument exactly what the natural sciences could learn from the humanistic fields, but the problems he raised still plague us today.*

The Relation of Natural Science to General Science, 1862

One of my strongest motives for discussing to-day the connection of the different sciences is that I am myself a student of natural philosophy; and that it has been made of late a reproach against natural philosophy that

From Hermann von Helmholtz, *Popular Lectures on Scientific Subjects*, trans. E. Atkinson (London: Longmans, Green, 1873), pp. 5–11, 30–32.

it has struck out a path of its own, and has separated itself more and more widely from the other sciences which are united by common philological and historical studies. This opposition has, in fact, been long apparent, and seems to me to have grown up mainly under the influence of the Hegelian philosophy, or, at any rate, to have been brought out into more distinct relief by that philosophy. Certainly, at the end of the last century, when the Kantian philosophy reigned supreme, such a schism had never been proclaimed; on the contrary, Kant's philosophy rested on exactly the same ground as the physical sciences, as is evident from his own scientific works, especially from his 'Cosmogony,' based upon Newton's Law of Gravitation, which afterwards, under the name of Laplace's Nebular Hypothesis, came to be universally recognised. The sole object of Kant's 'Critical Philosophy' was to test the sources and the authority of our knowledge, and to fix a definite scope and standard for the researches of philosophy, as compared with other sciences. According to his teaching, a principle discovered *a priori* by pure thought was a rule applicable to the method of pure thought, and nothing further; it could contain no real, positive knowledge. The 'Philosophy of Identity' [1] was bolder. It started with the hypothesis that not only spiritual phenomena, but even the actual world — nature, that is, and man — were the result of an act of thought on the part of a creative mind, similar, it was supposed, in kind to the human mind. On this hypothesis it seemed competent for the human mind, even without the guidance of external experience, to think over again the thoughts of the Creator, and to rediscover them by its own inner activity. Such was the view with which the 'Philosophy of Identity' set to work to construct *a priori* the results of other sciences. The process might be more or less successful in matters of theology, law, politics, language, art, history, in short, in all sciences, the subject-matter of which really grows out of our moral nature, and which are therefore properly classed together under the name of moral sciences. The state, the church, art, and language, exist in order to satisfy certain moral needs of man. Accordingly, whatever obstacles nature, or chance, or the rivalry of other men may interpose, the efforts of the human mind to satisfy its needs, being systematically directed to one end, must eventually triumph over all such fortuitous hindrances. Under these circumstances, it would not be a downright impossibility for a philosopher, starting from an exact knowledge of the mind, to predict the general course of human development under the above-named conditions, especially if he has before his eyes a basis of observed facts, on which to build his abstractions. Moreover, Hegel was materially assisted, in his attempt to solve this problem, by the profound and philosophical views on historical and scientific subjects, with which the writings of his immediate predecessors, both poets

---

[1] So called because it proclaimed the identity not only of subject and object, but of contradictories, such as existence and non-existence. — Tr.

and philosophers, abound. He had, for the most part, only to collect and combine them, in order to produce a system calculated to impress people by a number of acute and original observations. He thus succeeded in gaining the enthusiastic approval of most of the educated men of his time, and in raising extravagantly sanguine hopes of solving the deepest enigma of human life; all the more sanguine doubtless, as the connection of his system was disguised under a strangely abstract phraseology, and was perhaps really understood by but few of his worshippers.

But even granting that Hegel was more or less successful in constructing, *a priori,* the leading results of the moral sciences, still it was no proof of the correctness of the hypothesis of Identity, with which he started. The facts of nature would have been the crucial test. That in the moral sciences traces of the activity of the human intellect and of the several stages of its development should present themselves, was a matter of course; but surely, if nature really reflected the result of the thought of a creative mind, the system ought, without difficulty, to find a place for her comparatively simple phenomena and processes. It was at this point that Hegel's philosophy, we venture to say, utterly broke down. His system of nature seemed, at least to natural philosophers, absolutely crazy. Of all the distinguished scientific men who were his contemporaries, not one was found to stand up for his ideas. Accordingly, Hegel himself, convinced of the importance of winning for his philosophy in the field of physical science that recognition which had been so freely accorded to it elsewhere, launched out, with unusual vehemence and acrimony, against the natural philosophers, and especially against Sir Isaac Newton, as the first and greatest representative of physical investigation. The philosophers accused the scientific men of narrowness; the scientific men retorted that the philosophers were crazy. And so it came about that men of science began to lay some stress on the banishment of all philosophic influences from their work; while some of them, including men of the greatest acuteness, went so far as to condemn philosophy altogether, not merely as useless, but as mischievous dreaming. Thus, it must be confessed, not only were the illegitimate pretensions of the Hegelian system to subordinate to itself all other studies rejected, but no regard was paid to the rightful claims of philosophy, that is, the criticism of the sources of cognition, and the definition of the functions of the intellect.

In the moral sciences the course of things was different, though it ultimately led to almost the same result. In all branches of those studies, in theology, politics, jurisprudence, aesthetics, philology, there started up enthusiastic Hegelians, who tried to reform their several departments in accordance with the doctrines of their master, and, by the royal road of speculation, to reach at once the promised land and gather in the harvest, which had hitherto only been approached by long and laborious study. And so, for some time, a hard and fast line was drawn between the moral and the physical sciences; in fact, the very name of science was often denied to the latter.

The feud did not long subsist in its original intensity. The physical sciences proved conspicuously, by a brilliant series of discoveries and practical applications, that they contained a healthy germ of extraordinary fertility; it was impossible any longer to withhold from them recognition and respect. And even in other departments of science, conscientious investigators of facts soon protested against the over-bold flights of speculation. Still, it cannot be overlooked that the philosophy of Hegel and Schelling did exercise a beneficial influence; since their time the attention of investigators in the moral sciences had been constantly and more keenly directed to the scope of those sciences, and to their intellectual contents, and therefore the great amount of labour bestowed on those systems has not been entirely thrown away.

We see, then, that in proportion as the experimental investigation of facts has recovered its importance in the moral sciences, the opposition between them and the physical sciences has become less and less marked. Yet we must not forget that, though this opposition was brought out in an unnecessarily exaggerated form by the Hegelian philosophy, it has its foundation in the nature of things, and must, sooner or later, make itself felt. It depends partly on the nature of the intellectual processes the two groups of sciences involve, partly, as their very names imply, on the subjects of which they treat. It is not easy for a scientific man to convey to a scholar or a jurist a clear idea of a complicated process of nature; he must demand of them a certain power of abstraction from the phenomena, as well as a certain skill in the use of geometrical and mechanical conceptions, in which it is difficult for them to follow him. On the other hand an artist or a theologian will perhaps find the natural philosopher too much inclined to mechanical and material explanations, which seem to them commonplace, and chilling to their feeling and enthusiasm. Nor will the scholar or the historian, who have some common ground with the theologian and the jurist, fare better with the natural philosopher. They will find him shockingly indifferent to literary treasures, perhaps even more indifferent than he ought to be to the history of his own science. In short, there is no denying that, while the moral sciences deal directly with the nearest and dearest interests of the human mind, and with the institutions it has brought into being, the natural sciences are concerned with dead, indifferent matter, obviously indispensable for the sake of its practical utility, but apparently without any immediate bearing on the cultivation of the intellect.

It has been shown, then, that the sciences have branched out into countless ramifications, that there has grown up between different groups of them a real and deeply-felt opposition, that finally no single intellect can embrace the whole range, or even a considerable portion of it. Is it still reasonable to keep them together in one place of education? Is the union of the four Faculties to form one University a mere relic of the Middle Ages? Many valid arguments have been adduced for separating them. Why not dismiss the medical faculty to the hospitals of our great towns, the scientific men to the Polytechnic Schools, and form special seminaries for the theologians and jurists? Long may the German universities be preserved from such a fate! Then, indeed, would the connection between the different sciences be finally broken. How essential that connection is, not only from an university point of view, as tending to keep alive the intellectual energy of the country, but also on material grounds, to secure the successful application of that energy, will be evident from a few considerations.

First, then, I would say that union of the different Faculties is necessary to maintain a healthy equilibrium among the intellectual energies of students. Each study tries certain of our intellectual faculties more than the rest, and strengthens them accordingly by constant exercise. But any sort of one-sided development is attended with danger; it disqualifies us for using those faculties that are less exercised, and so renders us less capable of a general view; above all it leads us to overvalue ourselves. Anyone who has found himself much more successful than others in some one department of intellectual labour, is apt to forget that there are many other things which they can do better than he can: a mistake — I would have every student remember — which is the worst enemy of all intellectual activity.

How many men of ability have forgotten to practise that criticism of themselves which is so essential to the student, and so hard to exercise, or have been completely crippled in their progress, because they have thought dry, laborious drudgery beneath them, and have devoted all their energies to the quest of brilliant theories and wonder-working discoveries! How many such men have become bitter misanthropes, and put an end to a melancholy existence, because they have failed to obtain among their fellows that recognition which must be won by labour and results, but which is ever withheld from mere self-conscious genius! And the more isolated a man is, the more liable is he to this danger; while, on the other hand, nothing is more inspiriting than to feel yourself forced to strain every nerve to win the admiration of men whom you, in your turn, must admire. . . .

The sciences have . . . all one common aim, to establish the supremacy of intelligence over the world: while the moral sciences aim directly at making the resources of intellectual life more abundant and more interesting, and seek to separate the pure gold of Truth from alloy, the physical sciences are striving indirectly towards the same goal, inasmuch as they labour to make mankind more and more independent of the material restraints that fetter their activity. Each student works in his own department, he chooses for himself those tasks for which he is best fitted by his abilities and his training. But each one must be convinced that it is only in connection with others that he can further the great work, and that therefore he is bound, not only to investigate, but to do his utmost to make the results of his investigation completely and easily accessible. If he does this, he will derive assistance from others, and will in his turn be able to render them his aid. The annals of science abound in evidence how such mutual services have been exchanged, even between departments of science apparently most remote. Historical chronology is essentially based on astronomical calculations of eclipses, accounts of which are preserved in ancient histories. Conversely, many of the important data of astronomy — for instance, the invariability of the length of the day, and the periods of several comets — rest upon ancient historical notices. Of late years, physiologists, especially Brücke, have actually undertaken to draw up a complete system of all the vocables that can be produced by the organs of speech, and to base upon it propositions for an universal alphabet, adapted to all human languages. Thus physiology has entered the service of comparative philology, and has already succeeded in accounting for many apparently anomalous substitutions, on the ground that they are governed, not as hitherto supposed, by the laws of euphony, but by similarity between the movements of the mouth that produce them. Again, comparative philology gives us information about the rela tionships, the separations and the migrations of tribes in prehistoric times, and of the degree of civilisation which they had reached at the time when they parted. For the names of objects to which they had already learnt to give distinctive appellations reappear as words common to their later languages. So that the study of languages actually gives us historical data for periods respecting which no other historical evidence exists. Yet again I may notice the help which not only the sculptor, but the archaeologist, concerned with the investigation of ancient statues, derives from anatomy. And if I may be permitted to refer to my own most recent studies, I would mention that it is possible, by reference to physical acoustics and to the physiological theory of the sensation of hearing, to account for the elementary principles on which our musical system is constructed, a problem essentially within the sphere of aesthetics. In fact, it is a general principle that the physiology of the organs of sense is most intimately connected with psychology, inasmuch as physiology traces in our sensations the results of mental processes which do not fall within the sphere of conciousness, and must therefore have remained inaccessible to us.

I have been able to quote only some of the most striking instances of this interdependence of different sciences, and such as could be explained in a few words. Naturally, too, I have tried to choose them from the most widely-separated sciences. But far wider is of course the influence which allied sciences exert upon each other. Of that I need not speak, for each of you knows it from his own experience.

In conclusion, I would say, let each of us think of himself, not as a man seeking to gratify his own thirst for knowledge, or to promote his own private advantage, or to shine by his own abilities, but rather as a fellow-labourer in one great common work bearing upon the highest interests of humanity. Then assuredly we shall not fail of our reward in the approval of our own conscience and the esteem of our fellow-citizens. To keep up these relations between all searchers after truth and all branches of knowledge, to animate them all to vigorous co-operation towards their common end, is the great office of the Universities. Therefore is it necessary that the four Faculties should ever go hand in hand, and in this conviction will we strive, so far as in us lies, to press onward to the fulfilment of our great mission.

Charles Darwin

Charles Darwin (1809–1882) did not invent evolution. Evolutionary theories had been popular for some time, particularly among the romantics, but his Origin of Species *did provide the evidence to prove that evolution was a fact. Darwin collected the information for his book while serving as naturalist for the surveying expedition of H.M.S. Beagle from 1831 to 1836. Although he had been convinced of evolution by his observations on the voyage, illness delayed the publication of his findings. His work was influenced by the great geologist Charles Lyell and by the political economist Thomas Malthus. The former provided a new sense of geological time spanning millions of years and the concept of continuing natural change. The latter's description of the struggle for survival inspired Darwin to find in the struggle for existence the mechanism by which natural selection takes place. He extended his theory to include man in* The Descent of Man (1871). *As is obvious from the conclusion of his earlier work, Darwin had no intention of challenging religion, and later in his life he was distressed by the misuse of his ideas by deductive thinkers such as Herbert Spencer. He remained, in short, an empiricist and natural scientist despite the fact that he had revolutionized the traditional conception of man's place among the species by destroying the absolute separation of man from his animal forebears.*

On the Origin of Species, 1859

I have now recapitulated the chief facts and considerations which have thoroughly convinced me that species have changed, and are still slowly changing by the preservation and accumulation of successive slight favourable variations. Why, it may be asked, have all the most eminent living naturalists and geologists rejected this view of the mutability of species? It cannot be asserted that organic beings in a state of nature are subject to no variation; it cannot be proved that the amount of variation in the course of long ages is a limited quantity; no clear distinction has been, or can be, drawn between species and well-marked varieties. It cannot be maintained that species when intercrossed are invariably sterile, and varieties invariably fertile; or that sterility is a special endowment and sign of creation. The belief that species were immutable productions was almost unavoidable as long as the history of the world was thought to be of short duration; and now that we have acquired some idea of the lapse of time, we are too apt to assume, without proof, that the geological record is so perfect that it would have afforded us plain evidence of the mutation of species, if they had undergone mutation.

But the chief cause of our natural unwillingness to admit that one species have given birth to other and distinct species, is that we are always slow in admitting any great change of which we do not see the intermediate steps. The difficulty is the same as that felt by so many geologists, when Lyell first insisted that long lines of inland cliffs had been formed, and great valleys excavated, by the slow action of the coast-waves. The mind cannot possibly grasp the full meaning of the term of a hundred million years; it cannot add up and perceive the full effects of many slight variations, accumulated during an almost infinite number of generations.

Although I am fully convinced of the truth of the views given in this volume under the form of an abstract, I by no means expect to convince experienced naturalists whose minds are stocked with a multitude of facts all viewed, during a long course of years, from a point of view directly opposite to mine. It is so easy to hide our ignorance under such expressions as the "plan of creation," "unity of design," &c., and to think that we give an explanation when we only restate a fact. Any one whose disposition leads him to attach more weight to unexplained difficulties than to the explanation of a certain number of facts will certainly reject my theory. A few naturalists, endowed with much flexibility of mind, and who have already begun to doubt on the immutability of species, may be influenced by this volume; but I look with confidence to the future, to

From Charles Darwin, *On the Origin of Species* (London, 1859), pp. 480–90. Reprinted from the facsimile edition with introduction by Ernst Mayr (© 1964 by the President and Fellows of Harvard College) by permission of Harvard University Press, Cambridge, Mass.

young and rising naturalists, who will be able to view both sides of the question with impartiality. Whoever is led to believe that species are mutable will do good service by conscientiously expressing his conviction; for only thus can the load of prejudice by which this subject is overwhelmed be removed.

Several eminent naturalists have of late published their belief that a multitude of reputed species in each genus are not real species; but that other species are real, that is, have been independently created. This seems to me a strange conclusion to arrive at. They admit that a multitude of forms, which till lately they themselves thought were special creations, and which are still thus looked at by the majority of naturalists, and which consequently have every external characteristic feature of true species, — they admit that these have been produced by variation, but they refuse to extend the same view to other and very slightly different forms. Nevertheless they do not pretend that they can define, or even conjecture, which are the created forms of life, and which are those produced by secondary laws. They admit variation as a *vera causa* in one case, they arbitrarily reject it in another, without assigning any distinction in the two cases. The day will come when this will be given as a curious illustration of the blindness of preconceived opinion. These authors seem no more startled at a miraculous act of creation than at an ordinary birth. But do they really believe that at innumerable periods in the earth's history certain elemental atoms have been commanded suddenly to flash into living tissues? Do they believe that at each supposed act of creation one individual or many were produced? Were all the infinitely numerous kinds of animals and plants created as eggs or seed, or as full grown? and in the case of mammals, were they created bearing the false marks of nourishment from the mother's womb? Although naturalists very properly demand a full explanation of every difficulty from those who believe in the mutability of species, on their own side they ignore the whole subject of the first appearance of species in what they consider reverent silence.

It may be asked how far I extend the doctrine of the modification of species. The question is difficult to answer, because the more distinct the forms are which we may consider, by so much the arguments fall away in force. But some arguments of the greatest weight extend very far. All the members of whole classes can be connected together by chains of affinities, and all can be classified on the same principle, in groups subordinate to groups. Fossil remains sometimes tend to fill up very wide intervals between existing orders. Organs in a rudimentary condition plainly show that an early progenitor had the organ in a fully developed state; and this in some instances necessarily implies an enormous amount of modification in the descendants. Throughout whole classes various structures are formed on the same pattern, and at an embryonic age the species closely resemble each other. Therefore I cannot doubt that the theory of descent with modification embraces all the members of the same class. I believe that animals have descended from at most only four or five progenitors, and plants from an equal or lesser number.

Analogy would lead me one step further, namely, to the belief that all animals and plants have descended from some one prototype. But analogy may be a deceitful guide. Nevertheless all living things have much in common, in their chemical composition, their germinal vesicles, their cellular structure, and their laws of growth and reproduction. We see this even in so trifling a circumstance as that the same poison often similarly affects plants and animals; or that the poison secreted by the gall-fly produces monstrous growths on the wild rose or oak-tree. Therefore I should infer from analogy that probably all the organic beings which have ever lived on this earth have descended from some one primordial form, into which life was first breathed.

When the views entertained in this volume on the origin of species, or when analogous views are generally admitted, we can dimly foresee that there will be a considerable revolution in natural history. Systematists will be able to pursue their labours as at present; but they will not be incessantly haunted by the shadowy doubt whether this or that form be in essence a species. This I feel sure, and I speak after experience, will be no slight relief. The endless disputes whether or not some fifty species of British brambles are true species will cease. Systematists will have only to decide (not that this will be easy) whether any form be sufficiently constant and distinct from other forms, to be capable of definition; and if definable, whether the differences be sufficiently important to deserve a specific name. This latter point will become a far more essential consideration than it is at present; for differences, however slight, between any two forms, if not blended by intermediate gradations, are looked at by most naturalists as sufficient to raise both forms to the rank of species. Hereafter we shall be compelled to acknowledge that the only distinction between species and well-marked varieties is, that the latter are known, or believed, to be connected at the present day by intermediate gradations, whereas species were formerly thus connected. Hence, without quite rejecting the consideration of the present existence of intermediate gradations between any two forms, we shall be led to weigh more carefully and to value higher the actual amount of difference between them. It is quite possible that forms now generally acknowledged to be merely varieties may hereafter be thought worthy of specific names, as with the primrose and cowslip; and in this case scientific and common language will come into accordance. In short, we shall have to treat species in the same manner as those naturalists treat genera, who admit that genera are merely artificial combinations made for convenience. This may not be a cheering prospect; but we shall at least be freed from the vain search for the undiscovered and undiscoverable essence of the term species.

The other and more general departments of natural history will rise greatly in interest. The terms used by naturalists of affinity, relationship, community of type, paternity, morphology, adaptive characters, rudimentary and aborted organs, &c., will cease to be metaphorical, and will have a plain signification. When we no longer look at an organic being as a savage looks at a ship, as at something wholly beyond his comprehension; when we regard every production of nature as one which has had a history; when we contemplate every complex structure and instinct as the summing up of many contrivances, each useful to the possessor, nearly in the same way as when we look at any great mechanical invention as the summing up of the labour, the experience, the reason, and even the blunders of numerous workmen; when we thus view each organic being, how far more interesting, I speak from experience, will the study of natural history become!

A grand and almost untrodden field of inquiry will be opened, on the causes and laws of variation, on correlation of growth, on the effects of use and disuse, on the direct action of external conditions, and so forth. The study of domestic productions will rise immensely in value. A new variety raised by man will be a far more important and interesting subject for study than one more species added to the infinitude of already recorded species. Our classifications will come to be, as far as they can be so made, genealogies; and will then truly give what may be called the plan of creation. The rules for classifying will no doubt become simpler when we have a definite object in view. We possess no pedigrees or armorial bearings; and we have to discover and trace the many diverging lines of descent in our natural genealogies, by characters of any kind which have long been inherited. Rudimentary organs will speak infallibly with respect to the nature of long-lost structures. Species and groups of species, which are called aberrant, and which may fancifully be called living fossils, will aid us in forming a picture of the ancient forms of life. Embryology will reveal to us the structure, in some degree obscured, of the prototypes of each great class.

When we can feel assured that all the individuals of the same species, and all the closely allied species of most genera, have within a not very remote period descended from one parent, and have migrated from some one birthplace; and when we better know the many means of migration, then, by the light which geology now throws, and will continue to throw, on former changes of climate and of the level of the land, we shall surely be enabled to trace in an admirable manner the former migrations of the inhabitants of the whole world. Even at present, by comparing the differences of the inhabitants of the sea on the opposite sides of a continent, and the nature of the various inhabitants of that continent in relation to their apparent means of immigration, some light can be thrown on ancient geography. . . .

Authors of the highest eminence seem to be fully satisfied with the view that each species has been independently created. To my mind it accords better with what we know of the laws impressed on matter by the Creator, that the production and extinction of the past and present inhabitants of the world should have been due to secondary causes, like those determining the birth and death of the individual. When I view all beings not as special creations, but as the lineal descendants of some few beings which lived long before the first bed of the Silurian system was deposited, they seem to me to become ennobled. Judging from the past, we may safely infer that not one living species will transmit its unaltered likeness to a distant futurity. And of the species now living very few will transmit progeny of any kind to a far distant futurity; for the manner in which all organic beings are grouped, shows that the greater number of species of each genus, and all the species of many genera, have left no descendants, but have become utterly extinct. We can so far take a prophetic glance into futurity as to foretel that it will be the common and widely-spread species, belonging to the larger and dominant groups, which will ultimately prevail and procreate new and dominant species. As all the living forms of life are the lineal descendants of those which lived long before the Silurian epoch, we may feel certain that the ordinary succession by generation has never once been broken, and that no cataclysm has desolated the whole world. Hence we may look with some confidence to a secure future of equally inappreciable length. And as natural selection works solely by and for the good of each being, all corporeal and mental endowments will tend to progress towards perfection.

It is interesting to contemplate an entangled bank, clothed with many plants of many kinds, with birds singing on the bushes, with various insects flitting about, and with worms crawling through the damp earth, and to reflect that these elaborately constructed forms, so different from each other, and dependent on each other in so complex a manner, have all been produced by laws acting around us. These laws, taken in the largest sense, being Growth with Reproduction; Inheritance which is almost implied by reproduction; Variability from the indirect and direct action of the external conditions of life, and from use and disuse; a Ratio of Increase so high as to lead to a Struggle for Life, and as a consequence to Natural Selection, entailing Divergence of Character and the Extinction of less-improved forms. Thus, from the war of nature, from famine and death, the most exalted object which we are capable of conceiving, namely, the production of the higher animals, directly follows. There is grandeur in this view of life, with its several powers, having been originally breathed into a few forms or into one; and that, whilst this planet has gone cycling on according to the fixed law of gravity, from so simple a beginning endless forms most beautiful and most wonderful have been, and are being, evolved.

Pope Pius IX

This document of eighty errors, the last of which perhaps sums up the rest with its attack on "progress, liberalism, and modern civilization," is particularly remarkable, for Pius IX was greeted as the "Pope of Progress" after he assumed office in 1846 and initiated various government reforms. The revolutions within the papal territories and his exile from 1848 to 1850 seem to have been decisive in turning him into the open protector of the most ancient and traditional claims of the Church. Pius' attack is largely directed against the secular practices of contemporary governments, liberal doctrines, the scientific approach to religion, and secular ethics. It is also a reassertion of the papal claims to the states lost in the Italian unification of 1860. More important, however, it is a rejection of the liberal forces within the Catholic Church who wished a less dogmatic stand, reconciliation with the secular state, accommodation of some of the new ideas of the age, and greater participation in the decision-making processes of the Church itself. A more accommodating attitude had to await Pius' successor, Leo XIII, who was Pope from 1878 to 1903. The liberal-conservative conflict within the Church continues to this day.

Syllabus of Errors, 1864

SECTION 1. PANTHEISM, NATURALISM, AND RATIONALISM ABSOLUTE

1. There exists no Divine being, perfect in his wisdom and goodness, who is distinct from the universe, and God is of the same nature as things, and consequently subject to change; in effect, God is produced in man and in the world, and all beings are God, and have the same substance as God. God is thus one and the same thing with the world; consequently the mind is the same thing with matter, necessity with liberty, the true with the false, the good with the evil, and the just with the

From *The Vatican Decrees* (London: Bradbury, Agnew, 1870), pp. 13–22.

unjust. — 2. All action of God upon man and upon the world is to be denied. — 3. Human reason, without any regard to God, is the sole arbiter of truth and falsehood, of good and evil; it is a law to itself, and by its natural force it suffices to secure the welfare of men and nations. — 4. All the truths of religion are derived from the inborn strength of human reason; hence it follows that reason is the sovereign rule by which men can and ought to acquire knowledge of all truths of every kind. — 5. Divine revelation is imperfect, and therefore subject to a continual and indefinite progress corresponding with the development of human reason. — 6. Christian faith is in opposition to human reason, and Divine revelation is not only useless but it injures the perfection of man. — 7. The prophecies and the miracles uttered and narrated in the Holy Scriptures are poetic fictions, and the mysteries of the Christian faith are the result of philosophical investigations. In the books of the two Testaments are contained mythical inventions, and Jesus Christ himself is a myth.

SECTION 2. MODERATE RATIONALISM

8. As human reason is on an equality with religion itself, so the theological sciences ought to be treated in the same manner as the philosophical sciences. — 9. All the dogmas of the Christian religion, without distinction, are the object of natural science or philosophy, and human reason, having only an historic culture, can from its own natural strength and principles arrive at a true knowledge of even the most abstruse dogmas, provided that these dogmas have been proposed as a subject for reason. — 10. As the philosopher is one thing and philosophy another, so it is the right and duty of the philosopher to submit himself to the authority which he shall have recognised as true; but philosophy neither can nor ought to submit to any authority. — 11. The Church ought not only never to animadvert upon philosophy, but it ought even to tolerate its errors, leaving to philosophy the care of correcting itself. — 12. The decrees of the Apostolic See and of the Roman Congregation prevent the free progress of science. — 13. The method and principles by which the old scholastic doctors cultivated theology are no longer in harmony with the necessities of the age and the progress of science. — 14. Philosophy must be studied without any account being taken of supernatural revelation. . . .

SECTION 3. INDIFFERENTISM, LATITUDINARIANISM

15. Every man is free to embrace and to profess the religion he shall believe true guided by the light of reason. — 16. Men may find the way of eternal salvation and obtain eternal salvation in any religion. — 17. Men may at least hope for the eternal salvation of those who do not live in the

bosom of the true Church of Christ. — 18. Protestantism is nothing more than another form of the same true Christian religion; a form in which men may be as pleasing to God as in the Catholic Church.

SECTION 4. SOCIALISM, COMMUNISM, SECRET SOCIETIES, BIBLE SOCIETIES, CLERICO-LIBERAL SOCIETIES

Pests of this description are frequently rebuked in the severest terms in the Encyclical, "Qui pluribus" of Nov. 9, 1846; in the Allocution, "Quibus quantisque," of April 20, 1849; in the Encyclical, "Nostris et Nobiscum," of Dec. 8, 1849; in the Allocution, "Singulari quadam," of Dec. 9, 1854; in the Encyclical, "Quanto conficiamur moerore," of August 10, 1863.

SECTION 5. ERRORS CONCERNING THE CHURCH AND HER RIGHTS

19. The Church is not a true and perfect and entirely free society; she does not enjoy peculiar and perpetual rights conferred upon her by her Divine Founder, but it appertains to the civil power to define what are the rights of the Church and in what limits she may exercise them. — 20. The ecclesiastical authority ought not to exercise its prerogative without the permission and assent of the civil Government. — 21. The Church has not the power of defining dogmatically that the religion of the Catholic Church is the only true religion. — 22. The obligation which binds Catholic teachers and writers is limited to things which have been determined by the infallible judgment to be dogmas of faith which ought to be believed by all. — 23. The Roman Pontiffs and Ecumenical Councils have exceeded the limits of their power; they have usurped the rights of princes, and they have even erred in defining matters relating to faith and morals. — 24. The Church has not the right of employing force; she has no temporal power, direct or indirect. — 25. Besides the power inherent in the episcopate, there is a temporal power which has been expressly or tacitly conceded to it by the civil authority, and which is therefore revocable at will by this same authority. — 26. The Church has not the natural and legitimate right of acquisition and possession. — 27. The ministers of the Church and the Roman Pontiffs ought to be excluded from all charge and dominion over temporal affairs. — 28. Bishops have not the right of publishing even their apostolic letters without the permission of the Government. — 29. Dispensations granted by the Roman Pontiff ought to be regarded as null unless they have been requested by the Government. — 30. The immunity of the Church and of ecclesiastical persons derives its origin from the civil power. — 31. Ecclesiastical jurisdiction for temporal causes, whether civil or criminal, of the clergy, ought to be absolutely abolished, without even consulting the Holy See, and without taking

heed to its protests. — 32. The personal immunity by which the clergy are exonerated from military service may be abolished without any violation of equity or natural right. Civil progress requires this abolition, especially in a society constituted on principles of liberal government. — 33. It does not appertain solely to ecclesiastical jurisdiction by any exclusive and inherent right to direct the teaching of theological truths. . . .

SECTION 6. ERRORS RELATING TO CIVIL SOCIETY, CONSIDERED BOTH IN ITSELF AND IN ITS RELATION TO THE CHURCH

39. The State being the origin and source of all rights, enjoys rights which are not circumscribed, by any limits. — 40. The doctrine of the Catholic Church is opposed to the welfare and the interests of human society. — 41. The civil power, even when it is exercised by an infidel sovereign, possesses an indirect and negative power over sacred things. . . . — 42. In case of conflicting laws between the two powers the civil law ought to prevail. — 43. The lay power has the authority to annul, to declare and render void solemn conventions (Concordats) entered into with the Apostolic See relating to the use of rights appertaining to ecclesiastical immunity without the consent of this See, and even in spite of its protest. — 44. Civil authority can interfere in things which regard religion, morals, and spiritual government. Hence it follows that it has control over the instructions published by the pastors of the Church conformably with their mission, for the guidance of consciences: it has even power to decree concerning the administration of the Divine Sacraments, and the necessary dispositions for their reception. — 45. The entire direction of the public schools in which the youth of Christian States is educated, except to a certain extent the episcopal seminaries, may and must appertain to the civil authority in such a manner that no other authority whatsoever shall be recognised as having the right to interfere in the discipline of the schools, the course of the studies, the taking of degrees, or the choice and approval of masters. — 46. Further, even, in clerical seminaries, the method of instruction to be followed must be under the direction of the civil authority. — 47. The best theory of civil society requires that popular schools, which are open to the children of all classes, and generally all public institutions intended for superior instruction in literature and the higher education of youth, should be freed from all ecclesiastical authority, government, and interference, and that they should be entirely under the direction of the civil and political power in conformity with the will of the rulers, and the general opinions of the age. — 48. Catholics can approve of a system of education not in connection with the Catholic faith and the authority of the Church, having for its object, or at least its principal object, only a knowledge of purely natural things

and the social life of this world. — 49. The secular authority can prevent the Bishops and the faithful communicating freely and mutually with each other and with the Roman Pontiff. — 50. The secular authority possesses as inherent in itself the right of presenting Bishops, and may require of them that they take in hand the administration of their dioceses before receiving canonical institution and the Apostolical letters of the Holy See. — 51. Further, the secular power has the right to prevent Bishops exercising their pastoral functions, and is not bound to obey the Roman Pontiff in those things which relate to Bishops' sees and the institution of Bishops. — 52. The Government has of itself the right to change the age prescribed by the Church for the religious profession both of men and women, and it may enjoin upon all religious establishments to admit no person to take solemn vows without its authorisation. — 53. The laws for the protection of religious establishments, their rights and functions, ought to be abolished; further, the civil power may lend its aid to all who desire to quit the religious life they had embraced, and break their solemn vows. It may also abolish religious orders, collegiate churches, and simple benefices, even those belonging to private patronage, and submit their goods and revenues to the administration and disposal of the civil authority. — 54. Kings and princes are not only exempt from the jurisdiction of the Church, but they are even superior to the Church in deciding questions of jurisdiction. — 55. The Church ought to be separated from the State, and the State from the Church.

SECTION 7. ERRORS CONCERNING NATURAL AND CHRISTIAN MORALITY

56. Moral laws do not need the divine sanction, and there is no necessity that human laws should be conformable to the law of nature, or receive from God the power of binding. — 57. Knowledge of philosophical things and morals, as well as civil laws, may and ought to be independent of divine and ecclesiastical authority. — 58. No other forces should be recognised than those which reside in matter, and all moral teaching and moral excellence should consist in accumulating and augmenting riches in every possible way, and in satisfying the passions. — 59. Right consists in material action; all the duties of men are words devoid of sense and all human actions have the force of right. — 60. Authority is nothing else than the result of numbers and material forces. — 61. An unjust action crowned with success is in no way prejudicial to the sanctity of right. — 62. The principle of non-intervention ought to be proclaimed and observed. — 63. It is allowable to refuse obedience to legitimate princes and even to revolt against them. — 64. The violation of an oath, however sacred it may be, and any wicked and shameful action opposed to the eternal law, is not only not blameable, but quite allowable and worthy of the highest praise when it is inspired by patriotism.

SECTION 8. ERRORS CONCERNING CHRISTIAN MARRIAGE

65. There is no proof that Christ raised marriage to the dignity of a sacrament. — 66. The sacrament of marriage is but an accessory to the contract and may be separated from it, and the sacrament itself only consists in the nuptial benediction. — 67. By the law of nature the bond of marriage is not indissoluble, and in certain cases divorce, properly so called, may be sanctioned by the civil authority. — 68. The Church has not the power of laying down what are the impediments fundamentally rendering a marriage void; but this power belongs to the secular authority, by which the existing hindrances may be removed. — 73. A merely civil contract may constitute a true marriage among Christians, and it is false that the contract of marriage between Christians must always be a sacrament, or that the contract is null if the sacrament be excluded. — 74. Matrimonial causes and betrothals belong by their nature to the civil jurisdiction. Here may be placed two other errors: the abolition of the celibacy of the clergy, and the preference due to the state of marriage over that of virginity. . . .

SECTION 9. ERRORS CONCERNING THE TEMPORAL POWER OF THE ROMAN PONTIFF

75. The sons of the Christian and Catholic Church are not agreed upon the compatibility of the temporal sovereignty with the spiritual power. — 76. The abolition of the temporal power of which the Holy See is possessed would conduce greatly to the liberty and happiness of the Church. — 77. Besides these errors explicitly noted several other errors are tacitly condemned by the doctrine which has been declared and maintained concerning the temporal sovereignty of the Roman Pontiff, and which all Catholics are bound most firmly to hold. . . .

SECTION 10. ERRORS HAVING REFERENCE TO MODERN LIBERALISM

77. In the present day it is no longer beneficial for the Catholic Church to be considered as the only religion of the State, to the exclusion of all other forms of worship. — 78. Whence it has been wisely provided by the law in some countries called Catholic, that strangers going to reside there shall enjoy the public exercise of their own forms of worship. — 79. It is false that civil liberty of all forms of worship, and the full power granted to all to manifest openly and publicly all their thoughts and their opinions, leads more easily to the corruption of the morals and minds of the people, and to the spread of the pest of indifferentism. — 80. The Roman Pontiff may and ought to reconcile himself to, and to agree with, progress, liberalism, and modern civilization.

Thomas Henry Huxley

In an age when the proponents of science were almost as fanatical as their clerical opposites, Thomas Henry Huxley (1825–1895) stands apart as a man of remarkable balance and good sense. He was, to be sure, a passionate defender of Charles Darwin and a popularizer of science; he made "Darwinism" a popular word. Yet he suspected that Darwin's theory of natural selection was not completely adequate, and his reservations were well founded since Darwin had not accounted for the phenomenon of mutation. Huxley was a particularly strong critic of the Social Darwinists, among whom was his good friend Herbert Spencer. He accused them of failing to distinguish between the social and natural order, and he insisted that human society represented a qualitative change over the world of nature. Although suspicious of the state, he nevertheless felt that state intervention was necessary to protect society and promote the well-being of its members so that society would not resemble a state of nature and war of all against all. Though he accepted the proposition that nations constantly competed against one another, he argued that better social security for the working man and technical education at government expense were more appropriate than Malthusian solutions and would keep Britain ahead of its commercial competitors.

The Struggle for Existence in Human Society, 1888

The vast and varied procession of events, which we call Nature, affords a sublime spectacle and an inexhaustible wealth of attractive problems to the speculative observer. If we confine our attention to that aspect which engages the attention of the intellect, nature appears a beautiful and harmonious whole, the incarnation of a faultless logical process, from certain premises in the past to an inevitable conclusion in the future. But if it be regarded from a less elevated, though more human, point of view; if our moral sympathies are allowed to influence our judgment, and we permit ourselves to criticise our great mother as we criticise one another; then our verdict, at least so far as sentient nature is concerned, can hardly be so favourable.

In sober truth, to those who have made a study of the phenomena of life as they are exhibited by the higher forms of the animal world, the optimistic dogma, that this is the best of all possible worlds, will seem

From Thomas Henry Huxley, *Evolution and Ethics and Other Essays* (© 1916 by Thomas H. Huxley, renewed 1944) (New York: Appleton-Century-Crofts, 1916), pp. 195–206, 226–29. Reprinted by permission of D. Appleton Century Company.

little better than a libel upon possibility. It is really only another instance to be added to the many extant, of the audacity of *a priori* speculators who, having created God in their own image, find no difficulty in assuming that the Almighty must have been actuated by the same motives as themselves. They are quite sure that, had any other course been practicable, He would no more have made infinite suffering a necessary ingredient of His handiwork than a respectable philosopher would have done the like.

But even the modified optimism of the time-honoured thesis of physico-theology, that the sentient world is, on the whole, regulated by principles of benevolence, does but ill stand the test of impartial confrontation with the facts of the case. No doubt it is quite true that sentient nature affords hosts of examples of subtle contrivances directed towards the production of pleasure or the avoidance of pain; and it may be proper to say that these are evidences of benevolence. But if so, why is it not equally proper to say of the equally numerous arrangements, the no less necessary result of which is the production of pain, that they are evidences of malevolence?

If a vast amount of that which, in a piece of human workmanship, we should call skill, is visible in those parts of the organization of a deer to which it owes its ability to escape from beasts of prey, there is at least equal skill displayed in that bodily mechanism of the wolf which enables him to track, and sooner or later to bring down, the deer. Viewed under the dry light of science, deer and wolf are alike admirable; and, if both were non-sentient automata, there would be nothing to qualify our admiration of the action of the one on the other. But the fact that the deer suffers, while the wolf inflicts suffering, engages our moral sympathies. We should call men like the deer innocent and good, men such as the wolf malignant and bad; we should call those who defended the deer and aided him to escape brave and compassionate, and those who helped the wolf in his bloody work base and cruel. Surely, if we transfer these judgments to nature outside the world of man at all, we must do so impartially. In that case, the goodness of the right hand which helps the deer, and the wickedness of the left hand which eggs on the wolf, will neutralize one another: and the course of nature will appear to be neither moral nor immoral, but non-moral.

This conclusion is thrust upon us by analogous facts in every part of the sentient world; yet, inasmuch as it not only jars upon prevalent prejudices, but arouses the natural dislike to that which is painful, much ingenuity has been exercised in devising an escape from it.

From the theological side, we are told that this is a state of probation, and that the seeming injustices and immoralities of nature will be compensated by and by. But how this compensation is to be effected, in the case of the great majority of sentient things, is not clear. I apprehend that no one is seriously prepared to maintain that the ghosts of all the myriads of generations of herbivorous animals which lived during the millions of years of the earth's duration, before the appearance of man, and which have all that time been tormented and devoured by carnivores, are to be compensated by a perennial existence in clover; while the ghosts of carnivores are to go to some kennel where there is neither a pan of water nor a bone with any meat on it. Besides, from the point of view of morality, the last stage of things would be worse than the first. For the carnivores, however brutal and sanguinary, have only done that which, if there is any evidence of contrivance in the world, they were expressly constructed to do. Moreover, carnivores and herbivores alike have been subject to all the miseries incidental to old age, disease, and over-multiplication, and both might well put in a claim for "compensation" on this score.

On the evolutionist side, on the other hand, we are told to take comfort from the reflection that the terrible struggle for existence tends to final good, and that the suffering of the ancestor is paid for by the increased perfection of the progeny. There would be something in this argument if, in Chinese fashion, the present generation could pay its debts to its ancestors; otherwise it is not clear what compensation the *Eohippus* gets for his sorrows in the fact that, some millions of years afterwards, one of his descendants wins the Derby. And, again, it is an error to imagine that evolution signifies a constant tendency to increased perfection. That process undoubtedly involves a constant remodelling of the organism in adaptation to new conditions; but it depends on the nature of those conditions whether the direction of the modifications effected shall be upward or downward. Retrogressive is as practicable as progressive metamorphosis. If what the physical philosophers tell us, that our globe has been in a state of fusion, and, like the sun, is gradually cooling down, is true; then the time must come when evolution will mean adaptation to an universal winter, and all forms of life will die out, except such low and simple organisms as the Diatom of the arctic and antarctic ice and the Protococcus of the red snow. If our globe is proceeding from a conditon in which it was too hot to support any but the lowest living thing to a condition in which it will be too cold to permit of the existence of any others, the course of life upon its surface must describe a trajectory like that of a ball fired from a mortar; and the sinking half of that course is as much a part of the general process of evolution as the rising.

From the point of view of the moralist the animal world is on about the same level as a gladiator's show. The creatures are fairly well treated, and set to fight — whereby the strongest, the swiftest, and the cunningest live to fight another day. The spectator has no need to turn his thumbs down, as no quarter is given. He must admit that the skill and training displayed are wonderful. But he must shut his eyes if he would not see that more or less enduring suffering is the meed of both vanquished and victor. . . .

But the old Babylonians wisely symbolized Nature by their great goddess Istar, who combined the attributes of Aphrodite with those of Ares. Her terrible aspect is not to be ignored or covered up with shams; but it is not the only one. If the optimism of Leibnitz is a foolish though pleasant dream, the pessimism of Schopenhauer is a nightmare, the more foolish because of its hideousness. Error which is not pleasant is surely the worst form of wrong.

This may not be the best of all possible worlds, but to say that it is the worst is mere petulant nonsense. A worn-out voluptary may find nothing good under the sun, or a vain and inexperienced youth, who cannot get the moon he cries for, may vent his irritation in pessimistic moanings; but there can be no doubt in the mind of any reasonable person that mankind could, would, and in fact do, get on fairly well with vastly less happiness and far more misery than find their way into the lives of nine people out of ten. If each and all of us had been visited by an attack of neuralgia, or of extreme mental depression, for one hour in every twenty-four — a supposition which many tolerably vigorous people know, to their cost, is not extravagant — the burden of life would have been immensely increased without much practical hindrance to its general course. Men with any manhood in them find life quite worth living under worse conditions than these.

There is another sufficiently obvious fact, which renders the hypothesis that the course of sentient nature is dictated by malevolence quite untenable. A vast multitude of pleasures, and these among the purest and the best, are superfluities, bits of good which are to all appearances unnecessary as inducements to live, and are, so to speak, thrown into the bargain of life. To those who experience them, few delights can be more entrancing than such as are afforded by natural beauty, or by the arts, and especially by music; but they are products of, rather than factors in, evolution, and it is probable that they are known, in any considerable degree, to but a very small proportion of mankind.

The conclusion of the whole matter seems to be that, if Ormuzd has not had his way in this world, neither has Ahriman. Pessimism is as little consonant with the facts of sentient existence as optimism. If we desire to present the course of nature in terms of human thought, and assume that it was intended to be that which it is, we must say that its governing principle is intellectual and not moral; that it is a materialized logical process, accompanied by pleasures and pains, the incidence of which, in the majority of cases, has not the slightest reference to moral desert. That the rain falls alike upon the just and the unjust, and that those upon whom the Tower of Siloam fell were no worse than their neighbours, seem to be Oriental modes of expressing the same conclusion.

In the strict sense of the word "nature," it denotes the sum of the phenomenal world, of that which has been, and is, and will be; and soci-

ety, like art, is therefore a part of nature. But it is convenient to distinguish those parts of nature in which man plays the part of immediate
cause, as something apart; and, therefore, society, like art, is usefully to
be considered as distinct from nature. It is the more desirable, and even
necessary, to make this distinction, since society differs from nature in
having a definite moral object; when it comes about that the course
shaped by the ethical man — the member of society or citizen — necessarily runs counter to that which the non-ethical man — the primitive
savage, or man as a mere member of the animal kingdom — tends to
adopt. The latter fights out the struggle for existence to the bitter end,
like any other animal; the former devotes his best energies to the object
of setting limits to the struggle.

In the cycle of phenomena presented by the life of man, the animal,
no more moral end is discernible than in that presented by the lives of
the wolf and of the deer. However imperfect the relics of prehistoric men
may be, the evidence which they afford clearly tends to the conclusion
that, for thousands and thousands of years, before the origin of the oldest
known civilizations, men were savages of a very low type. They strove
with their enemies and their competitors; they preyed upon things weaker
or less cunning than themselves; they were born, multiplied without stint,
and died, for thousands of generations alongside the mammoth, the
urus, the lion, and the hyena, whose lives were spent in the same way;
and they were no more to praised or blamed, on moral grounds, than
their less erect and more hairy compatriots.

As among these, so among primitive men, the weakest and stupidest
went to the wall, while the toughest and shrewdest, those who were best
fitted to cope with their circumstances, but not the best in any other
sense, survived. Life was a continual free fight, and beyond the limited
and temporary relations of the family, the Hobbesian war of each against
all was the normal state of existence. The human species, like others,
plashed and floundered amid the general stream of evolution, keeping its
head above water as it best might, and thinking neither of whence nor
whither.

The history of civilization — that is, of society — on the other hand, is
the record of the attempts which the human race has made to escape from
this position. The first men who substituted the state of mutual peace for
that of mutual war, whatever the motive which impelled them to take
that step, created society. But, in establishing peace, they obviously put a
limit upon the struggle for existence. Between the members of that society, at any rate, it was not to be pursued *à outrance*. And of all the
successive shapes which society has taken, that most nearly approaches
perfection in which the war of individual against individual is most
strictly limited. The primitive savage, tutored by Istar, appropriated
whatever took his fancy, and killed whomsoever opposed him, if he could.

On the contrary, the ideal of the ethical man is to limit his freedom of action to a sphere in which he does not interfere with the freedom of others; he seeks the common weal as much as his own; and, indeed, as an essential part of his own welfare. Peace is both end and means with him; and he founds his life on a more or less complete self-restraint, which is the negation of the unlimited struggle for existence. He tries to escape from his place in the animal kingdom, founded on the free development of the principle of non-moral evolution, and to establish a kingdom of Man, governed upon the principle of moral evolution. For society not only has a moral end, but in its perfection, social life, is embodied morality.

But the effort of ethical man to work towards a moral end by no means abolished, perhaps has hardly modified, the deep-seated organic impulses which impel the natural man to follow his non-moral course. One of the most essential conditions, if not the chief cause, of the struggle for existence, is the tendency to multiply without limit, which man shares with all living things. It is notable that "increase and multiply" is a commandment traditionally much older than the ten; and that it is, perhaps, the only one which has been spontaneously and *ex animo* obeyed by the great majority of the human race. But, in civilized society, the inevitable result of such obedience is the re-establishment, in all its intensity, of that struggle for existence — the war of each against all — the mitigation or abolition of which was the chief end of social organization. . . .

We are here, as in all other questions of social organization, met by two diametrically opposed views. On the one hand, the methods pursued in foreign countries are held up as our example. The State is exhorted to take the matter in hand, and establish a great system of technical education. On the other hand, many economists of the individualist school exhaust the resources of language in condemning and repudiating, not merely the interference of the general government in such matters, but the application of a farthing of the funds raised by local taxation to these purposes. I entertain a strong conviction that, in this country, at any rate, the State had much better leave purely technical and trade instruction alone. But, although my personal leanings are decidedly towards the individualists, I have arrived at that conclusion on merely practical grounds. In fact, my individualism is rather of a sentimental sort, and I sometimes think I should be stronger in the faith if it were less vehemently advocated. I am unable to see that civil society is anything but a corporation established for a moral object only — namely, the good of its members — and therefore that it may take such measures as seem fitting for the attainment of that which the general voice decides to be the general good. That the suffrage of the majority is by no means a scientific test of social good and evil is unfortunately too true; but, in practice, it is the only test we can apply, and the refusal to abide by it means anarchy. The purest despotism that ever existed is as much based upon that will of the majority (which is usually submission to the will of a small minority) as the freest republic. Law is the expression of the opinion of the majority; and it is law, and not mere opinion, because the many are strong enough to enforce it.

I am as strongly convinced as the most pronounced individualist can be, that it is desirable that every man should be free to act in every way which does not limit the corresponding freedom of his fellow-man. But I fail to connect that great induction of political science with the practical corollary which is frequently drawn from it: that the State — that is, the people in their corporate capacity — has no business to meddle with anything but the administration of justice and external defence. It appears to me that the amount of freedom which incorporate society may fitly leave to its members is not a fixed quantity, to be determined *a priori* by deduction from the fiction called "natural rights"; but that it must be determined by, and vary with, circumstances. I conceive it to be demonstrable that the higher and the more complex the organization of the social body, the more closely is the life of each member bound up with that of the whole; and the larger becomes the category of acts which cease to be merely self-regarding, and which interfere with the freedom of others more or less seriously.

If a squatter, living ten miles away from any neighbour, chooses to burn his house down to get rid of vermin, there may be no necessity (in the absence of insurance offices) that the law should interfere with his freedom of action; his act can hurt nobody but himself. But, if the dweller in a street chooses to do the same thing, the State very properly makes such a proceeding a crime, and punishes it as such. He does meddle with his neighbour's freedom, and that seriously. So it might, perhaps, be a tenable doctrine, that it would be needless, and even tyrannous, to make education compulsory in a sparse agricultural population, living in abundance on the produce of its own soil; but, in a densely populated manufacturing country, struggling for existence with competitors, every ignorant person tends to become a burden upon, and, so far, an infringer of the liberty of, his fellows, and an obstacle to their success. Under such circumstances an education rate is, in fact, a war tax, levied for purposes of defence. . . .

THE POLITICS
OF POWER, 1852–1871
Chapter 6

The conservative victory over the revolutions of 1848 did not bring back Metternich. His day was past, and the political leaders who retained power successfully during the two decades following the defeat of the revolutions recognized that they had to come to terms with industrialism, nationalism, and liberalism if the social order they were seeking to preserve was to survive. Napoleon III was a pathfinder in this respect, and he was similar to fascist dictators of a later age in many aspects of his rule. He played upon charismatic symbols and values, above all those connected with his name. He made sure that his power was sanctioned by plebiscite, a direct appeal to the people over the heads of their parliamentary representatives. Napoleon III proved that a democratic suffrage did not have to produce democratic results. For his support he relied upon a preindustrial mass base, especially upon the provincial peasantry, which believed in the Napoleonic legend and resented the liberalism and turmoil emanating from Paris. Although authoritarian in managing the state, particularly before 1860, Napoleon III was liberal in his economic policies, and he encouraged business to use its freedom. He made every effort to suggest the splendor of the new regime, and one of his lasting legacies was the renovation of Paris. Finally, in the manner of modern dictators, Napoleon III promised peace and an active foreign policy, and he tried to use success abroad to pacify discontent at home. This worked for a while, and Paris became the center of European politics when the 1856 peace conference ending the Crimean War was held there. Then Napoleon's policy began to backfire. His influence was decisive in bringing about Italian unity, but irritated Italian feelings by exacting Nice and Savoy as a price and by maintaining French troops in Rome to placate French Catholics. His effort to establish an empire in Mexico under Archduke Maximilian of Austria was a tragic disaster. Worst of all, he allowed Prussia to unify northern Germany in 1866 and then clumsily sought compensations for France. This search for compensations helped bring on the final disaster, the Franco-Prussian War and his downfall in 1871. By then, however, he had already lost much of his grip at home and had replaced the "authoritarian" with the "liberal" empire.

Camillo di Cavour and Otto von Bismarck were less flamboyant and much more effective statesmen in the long run. Cavour was a liberal nobleman with a firm commitment to economic development. He was also a brilliant manipulator, and he used both Napoleon III and the radical nationalist Giuseppe Garibaldi to unite Italy under Piedmontese leadership in 1859 and 1860. Bismarck, however, was by far the greatest statesman of the age. He began his career as an extremely conservative Junker. He was prepared to march his peasants against the Revolution of 1848, and he opposed every one of Frederick William IV's concessions. He even went so far as to welcome the humiliation of Prussia at Olmütz in 1850, which compelled Prussia to renounce its efforts to unite northern Germany under Prussian leadership. While serving as Prussian ambassador to the Diet of the Germanic Confederation, however, Bismarck concluded that cooperation with Austria was impossible without a clear demarcation of spheres of interest and competence in Germany. The old Metternichean policy of joint domination was dead. Bismarck also concluded that Prussia had to expand, connect its separated territories, and dominate northern Germany. To the horror of his conservative friends, he was prepared to do this by employing the forces of liberalism and nationalism if necessary. Eventually he took the momentum away from the liberals and nationalists by achieving many of their basic goals without surrendering the aristocratic-monarchical order to which he remained loyal.

Bismarck's opportunity came in 1862 when he was summoned by King William I to fight liberal efforts to control the military budget. He showed the liberals who had power by ruling for four years without a budget. During this period, in 1864, he conducted a war against Denmark for Schleswig-Holstein and, in 1866, a war against Austria. The latter resulted in the unification of northern Germany under Prussian leadership and the annexation, by Prussia of Hannover, Braunschweig, and part of Saxony. The liberals were tamed and voted an Indemnity Bill legalizing Bismarck's actions. In 1871 he completed the unification of Germany, without Austria, by defeating France and bringing southern Germany into his Confederation. Like Louis Napoleon, and for the same reasons, he introduced universal suffrage, into the constitutions of the North German Confederation and the Second Reich. His hope that the peasantry and provincial areas would vote conservatively was frustrated by the urbanization and industrialization of Germany, and he wanted to abrogate universal suffrage before he left office in 1890. He was much more successful, however, in framing a constitution that left the decisive power in the hands of the king of Prussia, now emperor of

Germany, and changing the political order Bismarck created required a revolution.

Although personalities were especially important in these events, other factors may have been more significant in the broader perspective. Prussia and Piedmont were the most industrialized and the wealthiest states in their respective countries, and it is no accident that both assumed leadership. Since 1834, Prussia had pursued a deliberate policy of using economic superiority to make "moral conquests" in Germany, and the Zollverein became a weapon that Bismarck used effectively to keep the other German states in line and to defeat Austrian ambitions. In comparison with Prussia, Austria was a backward country. Similarly, Piedmont was the wealthiest and most progressive state in Italy. In short, there were material foundations to the brilliant diplomacy and military accomplishments of the period.

Louis Napoleon and the Creation of the Second Empire

Louis Napoleon moved slowly and skillfully to reestablish the empire. He was elected president of the Second French Republic in December, 1848, largely because of his name; his program was a mystery. The vote was in favor of law and order as well, a sentiment expressed even more clearly in the May, 1849, parliamentary elections, which returned a monarchist and conservative legislature. Louis Napoleon, however, had no intention of permitting a restoration of the Bourbon monarchy. He carefully chose and placed his men in the key positions of the army and bureaucracy, and he allowed the conservative legislature to discredit itself by changing the electoral system. He then posed as the champion of universal suffrage, at the same time demanding a revision of the constitution to permit him to serve a second term as president. When the legislature refused, he launched the coup d'état of December 2, 1851, and, after putting down all opposition, conducted a plebiscite on December 21 that empowered him to draw up a new constitution, modeled on that of Napoleon's drawn up in 1799 (Year VIII). Even after the plebiscite, however, Louis Napoleon waited almost a year, until November, 1852, before becoming Napoleon III, and he used this

time to "sell" his system and himself to the parliament and, on tours
through the country, to the people. His object was to create popular
and spontaneous support for a restoration of the empire and to have it
sanctioned by plebiscite.

Speech of the Prince-President to the Chambers, March 29, 1852

Messrs Senators. Messrs Deputies.

The dictatorship which the people confined to me ceases to-day. Things are about to resume their regular course. It is with a feeling of real satisfaction that I come to proclaim here the putting into effect of the constitution; for my constant preoccupation has been not only to re-establish order, but to render it durable by giving France institutions suitable to its needs.

Only a few months ago, you will recall, the more I confined myself within the narrow circle of my attributes, the more it was sought to restrict them, in order to deprive me of movement and action. Often discouraged, I confess, I had thought of abandoning an authority thus disputed. What restrained me was that I saw only one thing to succeed me: anarchy. Everywhere, in fact, ardent passions, incapable of establishing anything, were rising up to destroy. Nowhere was there an institution or a man to whom to attach; nowhere was there an incontestable right, or any organization, or system which could be realized.

So when, thanks to the co-operation of some courageous men, thanks especially to the energetic attitude of the army, all the perils were swept away in a few hours, my first care was to ask the people for institutions. For too long a time society had resembled a pyramid which someone had turned over and sought to make rest upon its apex; I have replaced it upon its base. Universal suffrage, the only source of right in such conjunctures, was immediately re-established, order reconquered its ascendancy; in fine, France adopting the principal provisions of the constitution which I submitted to it, I was permitted to create political bodies whose influence and consideration will be so much greater as their attributes have been wisely regulated.

In fact, among political institutions those alone endure which fix in an equitable manner the limits in which each power must remain. There is no other means of arriving at a useful and beneficent application of liberty; examples are not far from us.

From *The Constitutions and Other Select Documents Illustrative of the History of France, 1789–1907*, ed. Frank Maloy Anderson, 2d ed. (New York: Russell & Russell, 1967), pp. 554–57. Reprinted by permission of Russell & Russell.

Why, in 1814, was the inauguration of a parliamentary régime seen with satisfaction, despite our reverses? It was, I do not fear to avow it, because the Emperor, on account of war, had been led to a too absolute exercise of authority.

Why, on the contrary, in 1851, did France applaud the fall of that same parliamentary régime? It was because the chambers had abused the influence which had been given them, and because, wishing to dominate everything, they were compromising the general equilibrium.

Finally, why has France not risen against the restrictions imposed upon the liberty of the press and personal liberty? It is because one had degenerated into license and the other, instead of being the orderly exercise of the right of each, by odious excesses had menaced the rights of all.

This extreme danger, especially for democracies, of constantly seeing badly defined institutions sacrifice in turn authority or liberty, was perfectly appreciated by our fathers half a century ago, when, upon emerging from the revolutionary turmoil and after vain trial of every kind of system, they proclaimed the constitution of the Year VIII, which has served as the model for that of 1852. Without doubt these do not sanction all those liberties, to the abuses of which we had even become accustomed; but they also consecrate some very real ones. On the morrow of revolutions, the first of the guarantees for a people does not consist in the immoderate use of the tribune and the press; it is in the right to choose the government which is suitable for it. Now the French nation has given to the world, perhaps for the first time, the imposing spectacle of a great people voting in entire liberty the form of its government.

Thus the head of the state whom you have before you is indeed the expression of the popular will; and what do I see before me? two chambers, one elected in virtue of the most liberal law which exists in the world; the other appointed by me, it is true, but independent also, because it is irremovable.

Around me you will notice men of patriotism and of recognized merit, always ready to support me with their counsel and to enlighten me upon the needs of the country.

That constitution which from to-day is going to be in operation is not, then, the work of a vain theory nor of despotism: it is the work of experience and of reason. You will aid, me, gentlemen, to consolidate, extend and improve it.

And now, gentlemen, at the moment in which you are about to associate yourselves patriotically with my labors, I desire to set forth frankly what shall be my conduct.

Seeing me re-establish the institutions and recollections of the Empire, it has been often repeated that I desire to re-establish the Empire itself. If such was my constant preoccupation, that transformation would have been accomplished long since; neither the means nor the occasions were lacking to me.

Thus in 1848, when six million votes elected me, in spite of the *Constituante,* I was not ignorant of the fact that by simple refusal to acquiesce in the constitution, I could have given myself a throne. But an elevation which must necessarily lead to grave disturbances did not seduce me.

On June 13, 1849, it would have been equally easy for me to change the form of the government; I did not wish it.

Finally, on the 2d of December, if personal considerations had outweighed the grave interests of the country, I might have first of all asked the people for a pompous title, which they would not have refused. I was content with what I had.

When, then, I draw examples from the Consulate and the Empire, it is because I find them there especially stamped with nationality and grandeur. Resolved to-day, as before, to do everything for France, and nothing for myself, I shall accept modifications of the present state of things only if I am constrained thereto by evident necessity. Whence can it arise? Only from the conduct of parties. If they are resigned, nothing will be changed. But if by their secret intrigues they seek to undermine the foundations of my government: if, in their blindness, they deny the legitimacy of the result of the popular election; if, in fine, they continue constantly to put in jeopardy the future of the country by their attacks, then, but only then, it may be reasonable to ask the people, in the name of the repose of France, for a new title which shall fix irrevocably upon my head the power with which I am invested. But let us not anticipate difficulties which doubtless have nothing of probability about them. Let us preserve the Republic; it threatens nobody, it can reassure everybody. Under its banner I wish to inaugurate again an era of oblivion and conciliation, and I call upon all, without distinction, who are willing to co-operate freely with me for the public welfare.

Address of the Municipality of Vedennes to Louis Napoleon, October, 1852

The Municipal Council,

Considering that in destroying the hopes and baffling the projects of those perverse men who had dreamed of civil war, anarchy, and the overturning of society, Louis-Napoleon has done for the country and the peace of the entire world more than it has ever been given to any man to do;

From *The Constitutions and Other Select Documents Illustrative of the History of France, 1789–1907,* ed. Frank Maloy Anderson, 2d ed. (New York: Russell & Russell, 1967), pp. 557–58. Reprinted by permission of Russell & Russell.

Considering that by the repression of the anarchical attempts and the re-establishment of the principle of authority, he has rendered to society brilliant services and has merited well of France;

Considering that confidence in the stability of institutions is one of the most essential elements of the strength of states and of public prosperity;

Unanimously expresses the desire that the Empire should be re-established in the person of His Imperial Highness Prince Louis-Napoleon and his descendants, and for that purpose, in conformity with articles 31 and 32 of the constitution, a senatus-consultum should be proposed for the acceptance of the French people.

The Bordeaux Address, October 9, 1852

Gentlemen,

The invitation of the chamber and of the tribunal of commerce of Bordeaux which I have cheerfully accepted furnishes me an opportunity to thank your grand city for its reception so cordial and its hospitality so replete with magnificence, and I am very glad also, towards the end of my tour, to share with you the impressions which it has left upon me.

The purpose of this tour, as you know, was that I might come to know for myself our beautiful provinces of the south, and that I might appreciate their needs. It has, however, given rise to a much more important result.

Indeed, I say it with a candor as far removed from arrogance as from a false modesty, never has a people testified in a manner more direct, spontaneous, and unanimous the desire to be freed from anxieties as to the future by consolidating in the same hands an authority which is in sympathy with them. It is because they know at this hour both the false hopes with which they deluded themselves and the dangers with which they are threatened. They knew that in 1852 society would hasten to its destruction, because each party was consoling itself in advance of the general ship-wreck with the hope of planting its banner upon the ruins which might float on the surface. They are thankful to me for having saved the ship, merely by raising the banner of France.

Disabused of absurd theories, the people have acquired the conviction that the pretended reformers were only dreamers, because there was always inconsistency and disproportion between their means and the results promised.

To-day, France encompasses me with her sympathies, because I am not of the family of the ideologists. In order to secure the welfare of the country, it is not necessary to apply new systems; but, before everything

From *The Constitutions and Other Select Documents Illustrative of the History of France, 1789–1907*, ed. Frank Maloy Anderson, 2d ed. (New York: Russell & Russell, 1967), pp. 558–60. Reprinted by permission of Russell & Russell.

else, to inspire confidence in the present and security for the future. That is why France seems to wish to return to the Empire.

There is, nevertheless, a fear which I must refute. In a spirit of distrust, certain persons declare: The Empire means war. But I say: The Empire means peace.

It means peace, because France desires it, and, when France is satisfied, the world is tranquil. Glory, indeed, is bequeathed by hereditary title, but not war. Did the princes who justly thought themselves honored in being the grandsons of Louis XIV recommence his struggles? War is not made for pleasure, but by necessity; and at these epochs of transition in which everywhere, by the side of so many elements of prosperity, as many causes of death shoot up, it can be said with truth: Woe to him who first should give in Europe the signal of a collision whose consequences would be incalculable!

instead of war, France will modernize

I admit, however, that I, like the Emperor, have indeed conquests to make. I wish, like him, to conquer for conciliation the hostile parties and to bring into the current of the great popular stream the hostile factions which are now ruining themselves without profit to anybody.

I wish to conquer for religion, morality, and comfortable living that part of the population still so numerous, which, in the midst of a country of faith and belief, scarcely knows of the precepts of Christ; which, in the midst of the most fertile land in the world, can scarcely enjoy products of first necessity.

We have enormous uncultivated territories to clear, routes to open, harbors to deepen, rivers to make navigable, canals to finish, and our network of railroads to complete. We have opposite Marseilles an enormous kingdom to assimilate to France. We have to connect all of our great western ports with the American continent by those rapid communications which we still lack. In fine, we have everywhere ruins to raise again, false gods to cast down, and truths to make triumphant.

That is how I shall understand the Empire, if the Empire is to be re-established. Such are the conquests which I meditate, and all of you who surround me, who wish, like myself, the welfare of our fatherland, you are my soldiers.

Senatus-Consultum upon the Empire, November 7, 1852

The Senate has deliberated, in conformity with articles 31 and 32 of the constitution, and voted the senatus-consultum whose tenor follows:

From *The Constitutions and Other Select Documents Illustrative of the History of France, 1789–1907*, ed. Frank Maloy Anderson, 2d ed. (New York: Russell & Russell, 1967), pp. 560–61. Reprinted by permission of Russell & Russell.

1. The imperial dignity is re-established.

Louis-Napoleon Bonaparte is Emperor of the French, under the name of Napoleon III.

2. The imperial dignity is hereditary in the direct and legitimate descendants of Louis-Napoleon Bonaparte, from male to male, by order of primogeniture, and to the perpetual exclusion of women and their descendants. . . .

8. The following proposition shall be presented for the acceptance of the French people in the forms fixed by the decrees of December 2 and 4, 1851.

"The French people wish the re-establishment of the imperial dignity in the person of Louis-Napoleon Bonaparte, with inheritance in his direct descendants, legitimate or adopted, and give to him the right to regulate the order of succession, to the throne within the Bonaparte family, as is provided for by the senatus-consultum of November 7, 1852."

Napoleon III, Cavour,
and Italian Unification

On July 20, 1858, Napoleon III and Cavour met at the resort town of Plombières to plot the war against Austria that unified Italy. Cavour's report to King Victor Emmanuel of Piedmont is a remarkable demonstration of the extent to which Realpolitik had replaced the liberalism and romanticism of men like Cavour's great rival Giuseppe Mazzini (1805–1872) in the fulfillment of national aspirations. Cavour turned his back on Mazzini's republicanism and belief in the capacity of the Italian people to determine their own destiny without outside help. Instead, he chose unification under the aegis of the Piedmontese monarchy and was prepared to make territorial and political compromises in order to secure the French assistance against Austria that he felt was necessary. Napoleon III's motives for the war against Austria were more complex and demonstrated the variety of interests he had to satisfy. Although regarding himself a liberator of nationalities and gravedigger of the treaties of 1815, he also had to consider political, national, and dynastic problems. Thus he insisted that the Pope should control Rome because of his need to pacify French Catholic sentiments. He demanded a reward for French participation in the form of Nice and Savoy, and he wanted his cousin Prince Napoleon to marry the daughter of Victor Emmanuel in order to strengthen the prestige of his house and increase his influence in Italy. In the end, Napoleon only kept part of the

*bargain because he feared Prussian intervention, and he made peace
without securing Venetia as well as Lombardy for Piedmont. Italian unification, however, occurred anyway. Revolts throughout the peninsula
and plebiscites brought about a more complete unification than that
anticipated at Plombières, and Italy later took advantage of Austria's
defeat in 1866 to take Venetia and of France's defeat in 1871 to take
Rome.*

Cavour to Victor Emmanuel, 1858

Baden-Baden, 24 July 1858

To H.M. the King
Sire

The cipher letter which I sent Y.M. from Plombières could give Y.M.
only a very incomplete idea of the long conversations I had with the
Emperor. I believe he will consequently be impatient to receive an exact
and detailed narration of them. . . .

As soon as I was brought to the Emperor's study, he raised the question
which was the purpose of my journey. He began by saying that he had
decided to support Sardinia with all his power in a war against Austria,
provided that the war be undertaken for a non-revolutionary cause, which
could be justified in the eyes of the diplomatic circles, and still more, of
the public opinion of France and of Europe.

Because the search for such a cause presented the main problem we had
to resolve if we were to reach an agreement, I felt obliged to treat that
question before any others. First I suggested that we make use of the
grievances occasioned by Austria's bad faith in not carrying out her commercial treaty with us. To this the Emperor answered: that a commercial
question of piddling importance could not be made the occasion for a
great war which would change the map of Europe.

Then I proposed to revive the issues we had used at the Congress of
Paris as protests against the illegitimate extension of Austrian power in
Italy: that is, the treaty of 1847 between Austria and the Dukes of Parma
and Modena; the prolonged occupation of the Romagna and the Legations; the new fortifications encircling Placentia.

The Emperor did not agree to that proposition. He observed that since
the grievances we put forward in 1856 had not been judged sufficient to
bring French and British intervention in our favor, it would be incom-
prehensible how they now could justify an appeal to arms.

"Besides," he added, "inasmuch as our troops are in Rome, I can hardly demand that Austria withdraw hers from Ancona and Bologna." A reasonable objection. It was therefore necessary to give up my second proposition; I did so reluctantly, for it had a frankness and a boldness about it which went perfectly with the noble and generous character of Your Majesty and the People He governs.

My position became embarrassing, because I had no further clearly defined proposals to make. The Emperor came to my aid, and together we set ourselves to traversing all the States of Italy, seeking those grounds for war; they were hard to find. After we had journeyed through the whole peninsula without success, we arrived almost unawares at Massa and Carrara, and there we discovered what we had been so ardently seeking. After I had given the Emperor an exact description of that unhappy country, of which he already had a clear enough idea anyway, we agreed on getting a petition made from the inhabitants to Your Majesty, asking protection and even beseeching the annexation of the Duchies to Sardinia. This Your Majesty would decline, but he would support the cause of the oppressed populations, by addressing a haughty and menacing note to the Duke of Modena. The Duke, confident of Austrian support, would reply in an impertinent manner. Thereupon Your Majesty would occupy Massa, and the war would begin. As it would be the Duke of Modena who was responsible, the Emperor believes the war would be popular not only in France, but in England as well, and in the rest of Europe, because that Prince is considered, rightly or wrongly, the stalking horse [*bouc émissaire*] of despotism. Besides, since the Duke of Modena has not recognized any sovereign who has ruled in France since 1830, the Emperor has less to be cautious about with him than with any other Prince.

That first question being resolved, the Emperor said to me: "Before going further we must consider two grave difficulties which we shall encounter in Italy: the Pope and the King of Naples. I must deal with them gingerly: the first, so as not stir up French Catholics against me, the second so as to keep for us the sympathies of Russia, who makes it a kind of point of honor to protect King Ferdinand." I answered the Emperor that as for the Pope, it would be easy to maintain him in peaceful possession of Rome by means of the French garrison established there, while letting the provinces of Romagna revolt; that since the Pope had been unwilling to follow the advice he had been given in their regard, he could not complain if those countries took the first favorable occasion to free themselves of the detestable form of government which the Court at Rome had stubbornly refused to reform; and, as for the King of Naples, there was no need to worry about him unless he took up the cause of Austria; but his subjects should be left free to disencumber themselves of his paternal domination if they seized this chance.

This answer satisfied the Emperor, and we passed to the main question: what would be the objective of the war?

The Emperor agreed readily that it was necessary to drive the Austrians out of Italy once and for all, and to leave them without an inch of territory south of the Alps or west of the Isonzo.

But how was Italy to be organized then? After a long discussion, which I spare Your Majesty, we agreed generally to the following principles, recognizing that they were subject to modification by the course the war took. The valley of the Po, the Romagna, and the Legations would be constituted the Kingdom of Upper Italy, under the rule of the House of Savoy. Rome and its immediate surroundings would be left to the Pope. The rest of the Papal States, together with Tuscany, would form the Kingdom of Central Italy. The borders of the Kingdom of Naples would be left unchanged; and the four Italian states would form a confederation on the pattern of the German confederation, the presidency of which would be given to the Pope to console him for the loss of the major part of his estates.

This arrangement seemed to me quite acceptable. For Your Majesty, sovereign in law over the richest and most powerful part of Italy, would be sovereign in fact over the whole peninsula.

The question of what sovereigns would be installed in Florence and in Naples, in the probable event that Your Majesty's uncle and his cousin wisely chose to retire to Austria, was left open; nevertheless the Emperor did not disguise the fact that he could with pleasure see Murat return to the throne of his father;[1] and for my part, I suggested that the Duchess of Parma, at least for the time being, might occupy the Pitti Palace. This last idea pleased the Emperor immensely; he appeared anxious not to be accused of persecuting the Duchess of Parma, because she is a princess of the Bourbon family.

After we had settled the future state of Italy, the Emperor asked me what France would get, and whether Your Majesty would cede Savoy and the County of Nice. I answered that Your Majesty believed in the principle of nationalities and realized accordingly that Savoy ought to be reunited with France; and that consequently he was ready to make this sacrifice, even though it would be terribly painful for him to renounce the country which was the cradle of his family, and the people who had given his ancestors so many proofs of their affection and devotion. And that the question of Nice was different, because the people of Nice leaned in origin, language, and customs closer to Piedmont than to France, and that consequently their incorporation into the Empire would be contrary to that very principle for whose triumph we were taking up arms. Thereupon the Emperor stroked his moustaches several times, and contented himself with the remark that these were for him quite secondary questions which there would be time for later on.

[1] The French general Joachim Murat had been King of Naples under the regime of Napoleon I.

Passing then to examine the means by which a happy outcome to the war might be assured, the Emperor observed that we should try to isolate Austria and so have nobody else to deal with; that was why he deemed it so important that the grounds for war be such as would not alarm the other continental powers, and would be popular in England. The Emperor seemed convinced that what we had adopted fulfilled this double purpose.

The Emperor counts positively on England's neutrality; he advised me to make every effort to influence public opinion in that country to compel the government, which is a slave to public opinion, not to interfere in favor of Austria. He counts too on the antipathy of the Prince of Prussia toward the Austrians to keep Prussia from standing against us.

As for Russia, he has the formal and repeated promise of Alexander not to oppose his Italian projects; unless the Emperor is deluding himself, which I am not inclined to believe after all he told me, the question would be reduced to a war between France and us on one side and Austria on the other.

Still the Emperor believes that even reduced to these proportions, the matter is still of very great importance and still presents immense difficulties. There is no blinking that Austria has enormous military resources. The wars of the Empire were proof of that. Napoleon had to beat upon her a good fifteen years in Italy and in Germany; he had to destroy a great many of her armies, take away her provinces, and subject her to devastating war indemnities. Always he found her back on the battlefield ready to recommence the struggle. And one is bound to recognize that in the last of the wars of the Empire, in the terrible battle of Leipzig, it was still the Austrian battalions which contributed most to the defeat of the French army. Therefore to force Austria to renounce Italy would take more than two or three victorious battles in the valley of the Po or the Tagliamento; it would be necessary to penetrate within the confines of the Empire and place the point of the sword at its heart, which is to say at Vienna itself, to force Austria to make peace on the terms we have resolved on. . . .

Once agreed on the military question, we came to agreement on the financial question, which, I must inform Your Majesty, is what especially preoccupies the Emperor. Nevertheless he is ready to provide us with whatever war materials we need, and to help us negotiate a loan in Paris. As for the contributions of the Italian provinces in money and material, the Emperor believes we should make cautious use of it up to a point.

The questions which I have had the honor to recapitulate for Your Majesty as briefly as possible were the subjects of a conversation with the Emperor which lasted from eleven o'clock in the morning to three o'clock in the afternoon. At three the Emperor dismissed me and engaged me to return at four o'clock to take a drive with him in his carriage. . . .

We had scarcely left the streets of Plombières when the Emperor broached the subject of the marriage of Prince Napoleon and asked what the intentions of Your Majesty might be in that regard. I answered that Your Majesty had been placed in a most embarrassing position . . . and, recalling a certain conversation between Your Majesty and him in Paris in 1855 on the subject of Prince Napoleon and his prospect of marriage with the Duchess of Genoa, he didn't know just how to take it. . . .

I added that Y.M., while attaching great importance to doing what he could to be agreeable, was very reluctant to give his daughter in marriage because of her youth and could not impose an unwelcome choice upon her. That as for Y.M., if the Emperor strongly desired it, Y.M. would not have irremovable objections to the marriage, but wished to leave his daughter entirely free to choose.

The Emperor replied that he was very eager for the marriage of his cousin with Princess Clotilde, that an alliance with the House of Savoy was what he wanted more than anything else. . . .

In my answers to the Emperor I tried not to offend him, while yet avoiding any commitment whatsoever. At the day's end, at the moment when we separated, the Emperor said to me: I understand the King's repugnance at marrying his daughter so young; nor do I insist that the marriage be immediate; I am quite willing to wait a year or more if necessary. All I want to know is what I can count on. So try to beg the King to consult his daughter, and to let me know his intentions definitely. If he consents to the marriage, then let him set the date; I ask no guarantees beyond our mutual word, given and received. With that we parted. Grasping my hand the Emperor dismissed me, saying: have the confidence in me that I have in you.

Y.M. will see that I have faithfully followed his instructions. As the Emperor did not make the marriage of the Princess Clotilde a *sine qua non* condition of the alliance, I did not assume the slightest engagement in that regard, nor did I contract any kind of obligation.

Now I beg Y.M. to let me express to him in a frank and precise manner my opinion on a question upon which may depend the success of the most glorious enterprise, the greatest work undertaken in many years.

The Emperor did not make the marriage of Princess Clotilde with his couson a *sine qua non* condition of the alliance, but he showed clearly that he placed much importance on it. If the marriage does not take place, if Y.M. rejects the propositions of the Emperor without plausible reason, what will happen? Will the alliance be broken? That is possible, but I do not believe it will occur. The alliance will be upheld. But the Emperor will bring to it quite a different spirit from the one which he would have brought if, in exchange for the crown of Italy which he offers Y.M., Y.M. had granted him his daughter's hand for his nearest relative.

If there is one quality which distinguishes the Emperor, it is the persistence of his friendships and his antipathies.

He never forgets a service, just as he never forgives an injury. Now, the rejection to which he has laid himself open would be a blood insult, let us not deceive ourselves. Refusal would have another inconvenience. It would place an implacable enemy in the Imperial Council. Prince Napoleon, still more Corsican than his cousin, would vow deadly hatred against us; and the position he occupies and that to which he can aspire, the affection, I should almost say the weakness the Emperor has for him — these give him numerous ways of satisfying his hatred.

Let us not deceive ourselves; in accepting the proposed alliance, Y.M. and his Nation bind themselves insolubly to the Emperor and to France.

If the consequent war is successful, the Napoleonic dynasty will be consolidated for one or two generations; if it fails, Y.M. and his family run the same grave dangers as their powerful neighbor. But what is certain is that the success of the war and the resulting glorious consequences for Y.M. and his people depend in large part on the good will of the Emperor, and his friendship for Y.M.

If, on the other hand, he nurses in his heart a genuine rancor against Y.M., the most deplorable consequences can follow. I do not hesitate to declare with the profoundest conviction that to accept the alliance and refuse the marriage would be an immense political mistake, which could bring grave misfortunes upon Y.M. and our country.

The Defeat
of German Liberalism

After 1945, many students of German history recognized that Bismarck's defeat of German liberalism in the Prussian constitutional struggle between 1862 and 1866 was as important and fateful for Germany as were his military victories over Denmark, Austria, and France. Bismarck's triumph over the liberals enabled him to unify Germany under a constitutional system different from those in France and England. German ministers were responsible to the crown rather than to parliament, and the crown reserved exclusive control over the army and foreign policy. The fundamental power of parliament was its right to approve the budget, but this right was more negative than positive, for the king's government, not paraliament's, made the budget. Parliament could only accept or refuse the budget, and lack of compromise between par-

*liament and the government meant a complete stalemate. In a parlia-
mentary state, the government would resign and a new government
reflecting the wishes of parliament would take over. In Prussia and in
the German Empire, however, the government was not responsible to
the parliament and remained in office despite disagreements. This state
of affairs could occur no matter how many times the people voted in
elections to support a liberal parliament. The dualism between government and parliament meant that a latent constitutional crisis, a test of
power, was built into German constitutionalism. Between 1862 and
1866 Bismarck demonstrated that when parliament refused to accept
the military budget desired by the king, the government could employ
the "gap" in the constitution and rule without a budget until parliament "came to its senses." Bismarck's speech of January 27, 1863, reflects his refusal to allow Prussia to succumb to parliamentarianism and
civilian control of the army. When the liberals were so impressed with
Bismarck's victory over Austria in 1866 that they recognized the legitimacy of his actions by an Indemnity Act, they accepted a defeat from
which they never recovered.*

Bismarck's Speech to the Reichstag, January 27, 1863

The draft submitted to you by your committee performs an undeniable
service in clarifying our mutual relationships. Less than a year ago (if I
am not mistaken it was during the elections), the contention that the
Landtag was disputing with the King over domination in Prussia was
emphatically rejected. After you have accepted the Address now before
you, this repudiation will no longer be possible. In this Address rights are
claimed for the Lower House which the House does not at all or does not
alone possess. If you, gentlemen, had the exclusive right finally to determine the total amount and the particulars of the budget, if you had the
right to demand of His Majesty the King the dismissal of those ministers
who do not retain your confidence, if you had the right through your
resolutions concerning the budget to determine the strength and organization of the army, if you had the right — as constitutionally you do not
have, although you claim it in the Address — to control the relationship of
the executive power of the government to its officials, then you would in
fact possess the complete governmental power in this country (Prussia).
Your Address is based upon these claims, if it has any basis at all. I be-

From *Europe in the Nineteenth Century: A Documentary Analysis of Change and
Conflict. Volume 1: 1815–1870*, ed. Eugene N. Anderson, Stanley J. Pincetl, Jr., Donald
J. Ziegler, pp. 261–63, 265–67. Copyright © 1961, by Bobbs-Merrill Company, Inc. Re-
printed by permission of the publisher.

lieve, therefore, that its practical significance can be characterized in a
few words: "Through this Address the Royal House of Hohenzollern is
requested to transfer its constitutional governing rights to the majority
of this House."

You clothe the demand in the form of a declaration that the constitution is violated insofar as the Crown and the Upper House do not bow
to your will. You direct the accusation of violation of the constitution
against the ministry, not against the Crown, whose loyalty to the constitution you place beyond all doubt. You know as well as anyone in Prussia
that the ministry acts in Prussia in the name of and on behalf of His
Majesty the King, and that in this sense it has executed those acts in
which you see a violation of the constitution. You know that in this connection a Prussian ministry has a different position from that of the English. An English ministry, call it what you will, is a parliamentary one, a
ministry of the parliamentary majority; but we are ministers of His Majesty
the King. I do not reject the separation of the ministers from the Crown
which is assumed in the Address in order, as was suggested earlier from
the tribune, to make of the Crown a shield behind which the ministry
could be protected. We do not need this protection; we stand firmly on
the ground of our good right. I repudiate the separation because thereby
you are concealing the fact that you are in conflict with the Crown and
not with the ministry for control of the country. You find the constitutional violation specifically in Article 99. Article 99 reads, if I remember
the words correctly: "All income and expenditure of the state must be
estimated each year in advance and brought together into a state budget."

If the article continued that "the latter will be fixed annually by the
Lower House," then you would be completely justified in your complaints in the Address for the constitution would be violated. But the
text of Article 99 continues that the latter, the state household budget,
will be fixed annually by law. Now, Article 62 states with complete clarity
how a law is passed. It says that for the passage of a law, including a
budget law, agreement of the Crown and of both Houses is necessary.
That the Upper House is justified in rejecting a budget approved by the
Lower House but not acceptable to the Upper House, is, moreover, emphasized in the article.

Each of these three concurrent rights is in theory unlimited, one as much
as the other. If agreement among the three powers is not reached, the
constitution is lacking in any stipulation about which one must give
way. In earlier discussions this difficulty was passed over easily; according
to analogy with other countries, whose constitutions and laws, however,
are not published in Prussia and have no validity here, it was assumed
that the difficulty can be settled by the two other parties yielding to the
Lower House, that if agreement over the budget is not reached between
the Crown and the Lower House, the Crown not only submits to the

Lower House and dismisses the ministers who do not have the confidence of the Lower House, but that in case of disagreement with the Lower House the Crown also forces the Upper House by mass appointments to agree with the Lower House. In this way, to be sure, the sovereign and exclusive rule of the Lower House would be established; but such exclusive rule is not constitutional in Prussia. The constitution upholds the balance of the three legislative powers on all questions, including the budget. None of these powers can force the others to give way. The constitution therefore points to understanding by way of compromise. A statesman of constitutional experience has said that all constitutional life is at all times a series of compromises. If the compromise is thwarted by one of the participating parties wishing to enforce its views with doctrinaire absolutism, the series of compromises will be interrupted and in its place will occur conflicts. And since the life of a state cannot remain stationary, conflicts become questions of power. Whoever holds the power prevails, for the life of a state cannot remain immobile even for a moment. You may say that according to this theory the Crown can prevent the passage of a budget as the result of every insignificant difference of opinion. In theory that is indisputable, just as in theory it is indisputable that the deputies can reject the entire budget, in order thereby to cause the discharge of the army or the dissolution of all government agencies. But in practice this does not happen. Such misuse of the undoubted theoretical right of the Crown has not occurred in all these fourteen years [of constitutional government]. In the present situation, we shall hardly agree on who is to blame for not having reached a compromise. I recall, however, that following the dissolution of the preceding Lower House the Crown voluntarily offered substantial concessions. The budget was reduced by several millions; the surtax of twenty-five per cent was voluntarily dropped.

. . . You expect the Crown to give in; we expect you to do so. The Government is convinced that it is your turn to make concessions, and unless you do so, we shall hardly resolve the conflict. The Upper House rejected, and the Royal Government thinks justifiably so, the budget law which you voted as insufficient for the needs of the state. We actually confronted a situation in which no budget came into being, a situation considered impossible. The fact belied the assertion of impossibility. What has occurred unquestionably can be repeated. If the constitutional stipulation that the Crown and the Upper House share equally the right of consent to every law including the budget is not to be completely illusory, then the situation can be repeated. That a gap exists at this point in the constitution is not at all a new discovery. I myself at that time (and I believe that an assertion of mine from this period was cited during my absence) attended the discussions concerning revision of the constitution. For several days we thoroughly examined this possibility, which now for the first time after eighteen [sic] years has become an actuality. It occurred to no one at the time that it was impossible, but we were unable to agree upon the means by which to avert such a situation. I must absolutely and most decidedly reject the assertion that we have acted unconstitutionally, that we have violated the constitution — and I repeat what I said in the committee: Gentlemen, we take our oath and vow to the constitution just as seriously as you do yours. Learn to respect the sincerity of your opponents' convictions and do not be too generous with accusations of constitutional violation and the oath-breaking which that involves. Theories about what is lawful when no budget is passed have been advanced, and I do not intend to evaluate them here. Some say that if no budget is passed the budget of the previous year continues of itself. Others state that in consequence of the *horror vacui* contained in the law, the gap in all cases not covered by the most recent law is filled by supplementing with long-established law, just as we revert to the Joachima [1] when statute law does not suffice, or to customary law and ancient royal ordinances where the Royal Code does not apply. Consequently, the authority of absolute power would again apply if the budget law fails. I do not wish to pursue these theories further. It is sufficient for me to recognize the necessity of state and not pessimistically allow to come to pass a situation in which the treasury is closed. Necessity alone is decisive, and we have taken this necessity into account. You will not demand that we suspend paying interest and salaries of officials. I repudiate absolutely, as I have always done, the idea that the resultant state of affairs is unconstitutional. I also believe that this view [that the government acted unconstitutionally] is shared by no one among the thousands of officials who have sworn allegiance to the constitution. None of the officials has refused to cooperate with the government; none has declared that from the first of January he does not wish to receive his salary. I make no accusations; I merely conclude that the charge of having acted unconstitutionally is not so unassailable; otherwise at least one among the thousands of officials would have had a troubled conscience and would have refused to work under this government.

The situation, moreover, in which we find ourselves is in no way more unconstitutional than the situation which for fourteen years existed during the first four to six months of each year when we were without a budget. You say that the present situation is worsened by your explicit rejection of certain parts of the budget. Pardon my remarking that your resolutions in themselves, as long as they stand alone, carry no force of law whatsoever. Through your individual resolutions you can neither authorize us to make any kind of expenditure, nor in the absence of a budget law can you set a limit for satisfying state needs. It is always neces-

[1] A legal code by which the Elector Joachim I in 1527 introduced Roman law into Brandenburg.

sary to secure the consent of the Upper House and the approval of the Crown in order to make your action legal. As long as this is not the case the law does not exist and the government is not empowered to do anything by your vote alone. I shall not concern myself with reciprocal accusations and recriminations; but from my words I think you will understand our firm conviction that we are not in conflict with the constitution and thereby our resolve to resist strongly and energetically, as long as we retain the confidence of His Majesty, any pressure for an extension of your competence beyond the limits which the constitution approves. Those rights which the constitution grants you shall be completely yours. Any demands beyond this we shall reject, and we shall steadfastly protect the rights of the Crown against your claims.

It is a peculiar coincidence that the discussion of this manifesto which you propose to present to our Royal Master falls exactly on the birthday today of the youngest heir presumptive to the Throne. In this coincidence, gentlemen, we see a double challenge to stand fast for the rights of the monarchy, to stand fast for the rights of the successors to His Majesty. The Prussian monarchy has not yet fulfilled its mission; it is not yet ripe for becoming a purely ornamental decoration of your constitutional edifice, not yet ready to be integrated like a lifeless mechanical part into the mechanism of a parliamentary regime.

The Outbreak of the
Franco-Prussian War

Bismarck's editing of the Ems Dispatch opened the last act of the unification of Germany under Prussian leadership. Bismarck's account in his colorful, if not always truthful, Reflections and Reminiscences should be read with some caution. Recent research has shown that Bismarck took part in instigating the offer of the Spanish throne to a Hohenzollern prince and that Bismarck was quite aware from the start that France would object to having another Hohenzollern prince on French borders. Nevertheless, France's role in bringing on the Franco-Prussian War should not be overlooked. Not only did Napoleon III cause considerable tension in Franco-Prussian relations by demanding compensation as a reward for his neutrality in 1866, but French diplomacy was also particularly tactless in the matter of the Hohenzollern candidature by pressing the issue even after the Prussian king had agreed to back down. In any case, Bismarck and his colleagues, the

Prussian war minister Albrecht von Roon, and the architect of Prussia's military victories, the chief of the general staff, Helmuth von Moltke, were convinced that the time had come for a showdown with France and for the completion of Germany's unification. Bismarck's colorful description of how he brought on the war by editing the Ems Dispatch is a fitting conclusion to the diplomacy of unification begun at Plombières.

Bismarck's Reminiscences

On July 2, 1870, the Spanish ministry decided in favor of the accession to that throne of Leopold, Hereditary Prince of Hohenzollern. This gave the first stimulus in the field of international law to the subsequent military question, but still only in the form of a specifically Spanish matter. It was hard to find in the law of nations a pretext for France to interfere with the freedom of Spain to choose a King; after people in Paris had made up their minds to war with Prussia, this was sought for artificially in the name Hohenzollern, which in itself had nothing more menacing to France than any other German name. On the contrary, it might have been assumed, in Spain as well as in Germany, that Prince Hohenzollern, on account of his personal and family connections in Paris, would be a *persona grata* beyond many another German prince. I remember that on the night after the battle of Sedan I was riding along the road to Donchéry, in thick darkness, with a number of our officers, following the King in his journey round Sedan. In reply to a question from some one in the company I talked about the preliminaries to the war, and mentioned at the same time that I had thought Prince Leopold would be no unwelcome neighbor in Spain to the Emperor Napoleon, and would travel to Madrid *via* Paris, in order to get into touch with the imperial French policy, forming as it did a part of the conditions under which he would have had to govern Spain. I said: "We should have been much more justified in dreading a close understanding between the Spanish and French crowns than in hoping for the restoration of a Spanish-German anti-French constellation after the analogy of Charles V; a king of Spain can only carry out Spanish policy, and the Prince by assuming the crown of the country would become a Spaniard." To my surprise there came from the darkness behind me a vigorous rejoinder from the Prince of Hohenzollern, of whose presence I had not the least idea; he protested strongly against the possibility of presuming any French sympathies in him. This protest in the midst of the battlefield of Sedan was natural for a German officer and

From Otto von Bismarck, *Reflections and Reminiscences*, ed. Theodor S. Hamerow (New York: Harper & Row, Torchbook Edition, 1968), pp. 177–78, 180–89. Reprinted by permission of Harper & Row.

a Hohenzollern Prince, and I could only answer that the Prince, as King of Spain, could have allowed himself to be guided by Spanish interests only, and prominent among these, in view of strengthening his new kingdom, would have been a soothing treatment of his powerful neighbor on the Pyrenees. I made my apology to the Prince for the expression I had uttered while unaware of his presence.

This episode, introduced before its time, affords evidence as to the conception I had formed of the whole question. I regarded it as a Spanish and not as a German one, even though I was delighted at seeing the German name of Hohenzollern active in representing monarchy in Spain, and did not fail to calculate all the possible consequences from the point of view of our interests — a duty which is incumbent on a foreign minister when anything of similar importance occurs in another state. . . .

The first demands of France respecting the candidature for the Spanish throne, and they were unjustifiable, had been presented on July 4, and answered by our Foreign Office evasively, though in accordance with truth, that the *ministry* knew nothing about the matter. This was correct so far, that the question of Prince Leopold's acceptance of his election had been treated by his Majesty simply as a family matter, which in no way concerned either Prussia or the North German Confederation, and which affected solely the personal relations between the Commander in Chief and a German officer, and those between the head of the family and, not the royal family of Prussia, but the entire family of Hohenzollern, or all the bearers of that name.

In France, however, a *casus belli* was being sought against Prussia which should be as free as possible from German national coloring; and it was thought one had been discovered in the dynastic sphere by the accession to the Spanish throne of a candidate bearing the name of Hohenzollern. In this the overrating of the military superiority of France and the underrating of the national feeling in Germany was clearly the chief reason why the tenability of this pretext was not examined either with honesty or judgment. The German national outburst which followed the French declaration, and resembled a stream bursting its sluices, was a surprise to French politicians. They lived, calculated, and acted on recollections of the Confederation of the Rhine, supported by the attitude of certain West German ministers; also by ultramontane influences, in the hope that the conquests of France, "gesta Dei per Francos," would make it easier in Germany to draw further consequences from the Vatican council, with the support of an alliance with Catholic Austria. The ultramontane tendencies of French policy were favorable to it in Germany and disadvantageous in Italy; the alliance with the latter being finally wrecked by the refusal of France to evacuate Rome. In the belief that the French army was superior, the pretext for war was lugged out, as one may say, by the hair; and instead of making Spain responsible for its reputed anti-French election of a king, they attacked the German Prince who had not refused to relieve the need of the Spaniards, in the way they themselves wished, by the appointment of a useful king, and one who would presumably be regarded as *persona grata* in Paris; and the King of Prussia, whom nothing beyond his family name and his position as a German fellow countryman had brought into connection with this Spanish affair. In the very fact that the French cabinet ventured to call Prussian policy to account respecting the acceptance of the election, and to do so in a form which, in the interpretation put upon it by the French papers, became a public threat, lay a piece of international impudence which, in my opinion, rendered it impossible for us to draw back one single inch. The insulting character of the French demand was enhanced, not only by the threatening challenges of the French press, but also by the discussions in parliament and the attitude taken by the ministry of Gramont and Ollivier upon these manifestations. The utterance of Gramont in the session of the "Corps Législatif" of July 6:

> We do not believe that respect for the rights of a neighboring people binds us to suffer a foreign power to set one of its princes on the throne of Charles V. . . . This event will not come to pass, of that we are quite certain. . . . Should it prove otherwise we shall know how to fulfil our duty without shrinking and without weakness.

this utterance was itself an official international threat, with the hand on the sword hilt. The phrase, *La Prusse cane* (Prussia climbs down), served in the press to illustrate the range of the parliamentary proceedings of July 6 and 7; which, in my feeling, rendered all compliances incompatible with our sense of national honor.

On July 12 I decided to hurry off from Varzin to Ems to discuss with his Majesty about summoning the Reichstag for the purpose of the mobilization. As I passed through Wussow my friend Mulert, the old clergyman, stood before the parsonage door and warmly greeted me; my answer from the open carriage was a thrust in carte and tierce in the air, and he clearly understood that I believed I was going to war. As I entered the courtyard of my house at Berlin, and before leaving the carriage, I received telegrams from which it appeared that the King was continuing to treat with Benedetti, even after the French threats and outrages in parliament and in the press, and not referring him with calm reserve to his ministers. During dinner, at which Moltke and Roon were present, the announcement arrived from the embassy in Paris that the Prince of Hohenzollern had renounced his candidature in order to prevent the war with which France threatened us. My first idea was to retire from the service, because, after all the insolent challenges which had gone before, I perceived in this extorted submission a humiliation of Germany for which I did not desire to be responsible. This impression of a wound to our sense of national honor by the compulsory withdrawal so dominated me that I had already decided to announce my retirement at Ems. I considered this humiliation before France and her swaggering demonstrations as worse than that of Olmütz, for which the previous history on both sides, and our want of preparation for war at the time, will always be a valid excuse. I took it for granted that France would lay the Prince's renunciation to her account as a satisfactory success, with the feeling that a threat of war, even though it had taken the form of international insult and mockery, and though the pretext for war against Prussia had been dragged in by the head and shoulders, was enough to compel her to draw back, even in a just cause; and that even the North German Confederation did not feel strong enough to protect the national honor and independence again French arrogance. I was very much depressed, for I saw no means of repairing the corroding injury I dreaded to our national position from a timorous policy, unless by picking quarrels clumsily and seeking them artificially. I saw by that time that war was a necessity, which we could no longer avoid with honor. I telegraphed to my people at Varzin not to pack up or start, for I should be back again in a few days. I now believed in peace; but as I would not represent the attitude by which this peace had been purchased, I gave up the journey to Ems and asked Count Eulenburg to go thither and represent my opinion to his Majesty. In the same sense I conversed with the Minister of War, von Roon: we had got our slap in the face from France, and had been reduced, by our complaisance, to look like seekers of a quarrel if we entered upon war, the only way in which we could wipe away the stain. My position was now untenable, solely because, during his course at the baths, the King, under pressure of threats, had given audience to the French ambassador for four consecutive days, and had exposed his royal person to insolent treatment from this foreign agent without ministerial assistance. Through this inclination to take state business upon himself in person and alone, the King had been forced into a position which I could not defend; in my judgment his Majesty while at Ems ought to have refused every business communication from the French negotiator, who was not on the same footing with him, and to have referred him to the department in Berlin. The department would then have had to obtain his Majesty's decision by a representation at Ems, or, if dilatory treatment were considered useful, by a report in writing. But his Majesty, however careful in his usual respect for departmental relations, was too fond not indeed of deciding important questions personally, but, at all events, of discussing them, to make a proper use of the shelter with which the sovereign is purposely surrounded against importunities and inconvenient questionings and demands. That the King, considering the consciousness of his supreme dignity which he possessed in so high a degree, did not withdraw at the very beginning from Benedetti's importunity was to be attributed for the most part to the influence exercised upon him by the Queen, who was at Coblenz close by. He was seventy-three years old, a lover of peace, and disinclined to risk the laurels of 1866 in a fresh struggle; but when he was free from the feminine influence, the sense of honor of the heir of Frederick the Great and of a Prussian officer always remained paramount. Against the opposition of his consort, due to her natural feminine timidity and lack of national feeling, the King's power of resistance was weakened by his knightly regard for the lady and his kingly consideration for a Queen, and especially for his own Queen. I have been told that Queen Augusta implored her husband with tears, before his departure from Ems to Berlin, to bear in mind Jena and Tilsit and avert war. I consider the statement authentic, even to the tears.

Having decided to resign, in spite of the remonstrances which Roon made against it, I invited him and Moltke to dine with me alone on the 13th, and communicated to them at table my views and projects for doing so. Both were greatly depressed, and reproached me indirectly with selfishly availing myself of my greater facility for withdrawing from service. I maintained the position that I could not offer up my sense of honor to politics, that both of them, being professional soldiers and consequently without freedom of choice, need not take the same point of view as a responsible Foreign Minister. During our conversation I was informed that a telegram from Ems . . . was being deciphered. When the copy was handed to me it showed that Abeken had drawn up and signed the telegram at his Majesty's command, and I read it out to my guests,[1] whose dejection was so great that they turned away from food and drink. On a repeated examination of the document I lingered upon the authorization of his Majesty, which included a command, immediately to communicate Benedetti's fresh demand and its rejection both to our ambassadors and to the press. I put a few questions to Moltke as to the extent of his confidence in the state of our preparations, especially as to

---

[1] The telegram handed in at Ems on July 13, 1870, at 3.50 P.M. and received in Berlin at 6.9, ran as deciphered:

"His Majesty writes to me: 'Count Benedetti spoke to me on the promenade, in order to demand from me, finally in a very importunate manner, that I should authorize him to telegraph at once that I bound myself for all future time never again to give my consent if the Hohenzollerns should renew their candidature. I refused at last somewhat sternly, as it is neither right nor possible to undertake engagements of this kind à tout jamais. Naturally I told him that I had as yet received no news, and as he was earlier informed about Paris and Madrid than myself, he could clearly see that my government once more had no hand in the matter.' His Majesty has since received a letter from the Prince. His Majesty having told Count Benedetti that he was awaiting news from the Prince, has decided, with reference to the above demand, upon the representation of Count Eulenburg and myself, not to receive Count Benedetti again, but only to let him be informed through an aide-de-camp: That his Majesty had now received from the Prince confirmation of the news which Benedetti had already received from Paris, and had nothing further to say to the ambassador. His Majesty leaves it to your Excellency whether Benedetti's fresh demand and its rejection should not be at once communicated both to our ambassadors and to the press."

the time they would still require in order to meet this sudden risk of war. He answered that if there was to be war he expected no advantage to us by deferring its outbreak; and even if we should not be strong enough at first to protect all the territories on the left bank of the Rhine against French invasion, our preparations would nevertheless soon overtake those of the French, while at a later period this advantage would be diminished; he regarded a rapid outbreak as, on the whole, more favorable to us than delay.

In view of the attitude of France, our national sense of honor compelled us, in my opinion, to go to war; and if we did not act according to the demands of this feeling, we should lose, when on the way to its completion, the entire impetus towards our national development won in 1866, while the German national feeling south of the Main, aroused by our military successes in 1866, and shown by the readiness of the southern states to enter the alliances, would have to grow cold again. The German feeling, which in the southern states lived long with the individual and dynastic state feeling, had, up to 1866, silenced its political conscience to a certain degree with the fiction of a collective Germany under the leadership of Austria, partly from South German preference for the old imperial state, partly in the belief of her military superiority to Prussia. After events had shown the incorrectness of that calculation, the very helplessness in which the South German states had been left by Austria at the conclusion of peace was a motive for the political Damascus that lay between Varnbültr's "Vae victis" and the willing conclusion of the offensive and defensive alliance with Prussia. It was confidence in the Germanic power developed by means of Prussia, and the attraction which is inherent in a brave and resolute policy if it is successful, and then proceeds within reasonable and honorable limits. This nimbus had been won by Prussia; it would have been lost irrevocably, or at all events for a long time, if in a question of national honor the opinion gained ground among the people that the French insult, *La Prusse cane,* had a foundation in fact. . . .

. . . Under this conviction I made use of the royal authorization communicated to me through Abeken, to publish the contents of the telegram; and in the presence of my two guests I reduced the telegram by striking out words, but without adding or altering, to the following form: "After the news of the renunciation of the hereditary Prince of Hohenzollern had been officially communicated to the imperial government of France by the royal government of Spain, the French ambassador at Ems further demanded of his Majesty the King that he would authorize him to telegraph to Paris that his Majesty the King bound himself for all future time never again to give his consent if the Hohenzollerns should renew their candidature. His Majesty the King thereupon decided not to receive the French ambassador again, and sent to tell him through the aide-de-camp on duty that his Majesty had nothing further to communicate to the ambassador." The difference in the effect of the abbreviated text of the Ems telegram as compared with that produced by the original was not the result of stronger words but of the form, which made this announcement appear decisive, while Abeken's version would only have been regarded as a fragment of negotiation still pending, and to be continued at Berlin.

After I had read out the concentrated edition to my two guests, Moltke remarked: "Now it has a different ring; it sounded before like a parley; now it is like a flourish in answer to a challenge." I went on to explain: "If in execution of his Majesty's order I at once communicate this text, which contains no alteration in or addition to the telegram, not only to the newspapers, but also by telegraph to all our embassies, it will be known in Paris before midnight, and not only on account of its contents, but also on account of the manner of its distribution, will have the effect of a red rag upon the Gallic bull. Fight we must if we do not want to act the part of the vanquished without a battle. Success, however, essentially depends upon the impression which the origination of the war makes upon us and others; it is important that we should be the party attacked, and this Gallic overweening and touchiness will make us if we announce in the face of Europe, so far as we can without the speaking tube of the Reichstag, that we fearlessly meet the public threats of France."

This explanation brought about in the two generals a revulsion to a more joyous mood, the liveliness of which surprised me. They had suddenly recovered their pleasure in eating and drinking and spoke in a more cheerful vein. Roon said: "Our God of old lives still and will not let us perish in disgrace." Moltke so far relinquished his passive equanimity that, glancing up joyously towards the ceiling and abandoning his usual punctiliousness of speech, he smote his hand upon his breast and said: "If I may but live to lead our armies in such a war, then the devil may come directly afterwards and fetch away the 'old carcass.'" He was less robust at that time than afterwards, and doubted whether he would survive the harships of the campaign.

THE SPREAD
OF MODERN INDUSTRY
Chapter 7

Between 1850 and 1914 the industrial revolution that had begun in Britain spread across much of the European continent and to the United States as well. Indeed, by the end of the period Britain had lost its lead to the German Empire and the United States. Time showed that Britain did not have the resources of a continental power such as the United States and that its early start in industrializing meant that its industrial plant quickly became antiquated in comparison with a late starter such as Germany. German industrialization was particularly notable for its employment of the latest technological methods, and its rapid pace required huge amounts of capital and encouraged concentration and rationalization. After 1890, Russia too began to industrialize at a rapid pace, and its industries were usually large in scale and geographically concentrated. Although these late industrializers were important, Britain remained the greatest financial power in the world until World War I. France, slower in economic growth and more agriculturally oriented than England and Germany, was a major exporter of capital and was Russia's chief source of funds for economic and military development.

The industrialization of Europe would have been impossible without a close relationship between the laboratory and the factory. Furthermore, the connection and interaction between scientific research and technological innovation accelerated rapidly as time passed. The most important technological innovations took place between 1856 and 1878 in heavy industry with the development of the Bessemer, Siemens-Martin, and Thomas-Gilchrist processes for producing large quantities of cheap steel. The availability of steel hastened the transportation revolution begun by the railroad and steamship and also permitted a phenomenal expansion in the quantity and quality of manufactured goods. The development of the chemical and electro-technical industries later in the nineteenth century, often called the Second Industrial Revolution, was closely linked to scientific discoveries, particularly the development of synthetic dyestuffs and the invention of the dynamo. Germany became particularly outstanding.in developing these newer industries.

Industrialization, however, did not take place as smoothly as might be inferred from this bare sketch of technological innovation and progress. One of the consequences of industrialization was the creation of world economy whose parts were increasingly interdependent and susceptible to each other's troubles. The depression of 1857 was the first worldwide economic crisis and thus marked a turning point in economic history. Industrial development required and was encouraged by the establishment of investment banks and joint stock companies based on limited liability, but these institutions often functioned in an irresponsible manner, frequently encouraging wild speculation and exacerbating the depressions that followed booms. Between 1850 and 1873 these institutions were permitted to operate with little restraint, until the crash of 1873 ushered in a downswing that lasted until 1896. This period was important for economic development, but low prices and periodic depressions encouraged businessmen to be more sober in their practices, to cut costs through technological and organizational innovation, and to seek government protection. Indeed, one of the chief characteristics of this period was a retreat from laissez faire and a search for security and protection through association, reduction of competition, and government intervention. Businessmen organized to promote their interests, forming cartels and syndicates to reduce competition by partitioning markets and maintaining prices. They also asked government to create tariffs to protect them from foreign competition, to lower freight rates, and to keep labor at bay. Britain remained a free trading nation until the end of the period, but the United States, France, and Germany chose protectionism. Bismarck's decision to embark on a protectionist course in 1879 was particularly important in solidifying the social structure on which the empire was based. The agrarian Junkers, once free traders, by 1879 were calling for protection against the competition of American and Russian grains, and German businessmen wanted protection from foreign textiles and iron. Bismarck conceded to the wishes of both groups, and often used their coalition to maintain the political system and fight the demands of labor. Economic conditions improved markedly in the 1890's, and the period between 1896 and 1914 was one of general prosperity, rising prices, and rapid economic development. An organized capitalism based on trusts and cartels and often in a state of warfare with an increasingly powerful labor movement was triumphant.

The rise of the labor movement was a socioeconomic as well as a political phenomenon. On the one hand, it was an effort to raise the economic and social status of the workers through self-help and the organized representation of labor's needs. On the other hand, it often had the purpose of integrating the workers into the state and society by giving them an effective political voice. This last purpose was particularly relevant to the severely persecuted English Chartist movement in the 1830's and 1840's, which called for universal suffrage and the secret ballot. Although most of this movement's demands were eventually realized, the English trade union movement that developed after 1850 was most concerned with bread-and-butter issues. By 1913 it had a membership of four million. Trade unionism was more ideological on the Continent. French trade unionism suffered from the relative lack of industrial concentration and from the ideological conflicts within French socialism. As a result, it was weak and tended toward syndicalism. German trade unionism, in contrast, was highly organized and well disciplined, and the Socialist unions had two million members by 1913 despite the unwillingness of the leading employers to recognize them. Although formally committed to a Marxist program and closely tied to the Social Democratic Party, the trade unions in Germany devoted much attention to the practical work of organization and improving worker conditions.

Technology
and the Entrepreneur

The combination of invention, science, and business acumen in the development of the most advanced industries is almost classically illustrated by Werner von Siemens (1816–1892), the founder of a firm that bears his name and is still a leading producer of electrical equipment. Siemens began a career in the Prussian army before starting his business, and military interest in the telegraph and the use of electricity provided one of the main sources of contracts for his firm. In a manner typical of most liberal German businessmen, Siemens applauded Bismarck's solution to the German question and readily relinquished the political activity that had taken some of his time before 1866. Thereafter, he devoted almost all his time to invention and to running his business, which had important branches in Russia and England and which made such significant contributions to modern life as the streetcar. The development of the dynamo, one of the major breakthroughs in utilization of electrical power, owes much to Siemens. His memoirs reveal his passionate interest in science and his personal contact with

*the leading Berlin physicists. They also illustrate the confidence and
sense of accomplishment of one of the most successful entrepreneurs of
the age.*

Siemens' Memoirs

As in the past two years I have come here to Harzburg at the end of
June, in order to devote a few weeks to recording these reminiscences,
and do not intend to leave before I have come to the end of them. I
have repeatedly tried in Charlottenburg to continue my task, but there,
where everything is pressing forward, I have not succeeded in persistently looking backward. For it is habit which puts the strongest shackles
on us. I have never been able entirely to put aside the thoughts and
plans which were just then occupying my mind, and this has frequently
spoiled my enjoyment of the present, to which I could never wholly devote myself except in passing moments. But on the other hand such a
mental life, partly spent in dreamy speculations, partly in strenuous aspirations, also affords great enjoyment. It sometimes even perhaps brings
us the purest and sublimest joys of which man is capable. When a law
of nature, hitherto hovering darkly before the mind, all at once clearly
emerges from the enveloping mist, when the key is found to a mechanical
combination long sought in vain, when the missing link of a chain of
thought is happily inserted, this affords the discoverer the elevating feeling of a mental victory achieved, which alone richly compensates him for
all the pains of the struggle and exalts him for the moment to a higher
stage of existence. Certainly the ecstasy does not generally last long. Self-
criticism usually soon discovers a dark spot in the discovery, which renders its truth dubious or at least narrowly restricts it. It exposes a fallacy
in which one has been entangled or, as is unfortunately almost the rule,
it leads to the perception that only an old friend has been met with in a
new dress. Only when strict examination has left a sound kernel does the
regular hard labour begin of elaborating and completing the invention,
and then the struggle for its introduction into scientific or technical life,
in which most men are ultimately ruined. Discovering and inventing
therefore brings hours of supreme delight, but also hours of the greatest
disappointment, and of hard fruitless work. The public commonly notices
only the few cases in which successful inventors have hit, almost accidentally, upon a useful idea, and by making the most of it, have attained
without much labour to fame and affluence, or the class of acquisitive in-
vention-hunters, who make it their life's work to seek for technical appli-

From *Inventor and Entrepreneur: Recollections of Werner von Siemens*, 2d English
ed. (London: Lund, Humphries; Munich: Prestel-Verlag, 1966), pp. 226–31, 275–77. Reprinted by permission of Percy Lund, Humphries & Co. Ltd.

cations of well-known things and to secure the benefit of them by patents. But these are not the inventors who open new paths for the development of mankind, which will presumably conduct it to more perfect and happier conditions of life, but those who — either in the quiet of scholarly seclusion, or in the bustle of technical activity — devote their whole being and thought to this development for its own sake. Whether, by correct judgment and use of the opportunities of practical life, inventions lead to the accumulation of wealth or not, frequently depends on chance. Unfortunately however the instances of success possess great attraction and have called forth a host of inventors, who plunge into discovery and invention without the necessary knowledge and without self-criticism and thus are mostly ruined. I have ever regarded it as a duty to turn such deluded inventors from the dangerous path which they had entered upon, and this has always cost me much time and trouble. Unhappily my efforts have rarely been attended with success, and only complete failure and the bitterest self-inflicted distress occasionally brings these inventors to a perception of their errors. . . .

After these digressions I resume the thread of my narrative with my retirement from political activity.

The war of 1866 had removed the obstacles which opposed the longed-for unity of Germany, and had at the same time restored internal peace in Prussia. A new support was thereby given to the idea of nationhood, and the hitherto vague, as it were tentative, efforts of German patriots now obtained a firm foundation and definite direction. It is true, the Main boundary still divided Germany into a northern and a southern half, but no one doubted that its removal was only a question of time, if it was not rigidly fixed by external force. That France would make that attempt appeared certain, but there was a growing confidence that Germany would successfully stand this trial also. As a consequence of this great revolution of popular sentiment there resulted the general endeavour to consolidate quickly what had been attained, to strengthen the feeling of solidarity of North and South despite the Main boundary and to prepare for the coming struggle.

This buoyant feeling was evidenced by increased activity in all departments of life, nor did it fail to react on our business affairs. Magneto-electric mine-exploders, electric range-finders, electric apparatus for steering unmanned boats, furnished with explosives, against hostile ships, as well as numerous improvements of military telegraphy, were the offspring of this stirring time.

I will here only give a detailed account of a non-military invention of this time, as it has become the foundation of a new and important branch of industry, and has exerted and still continues to exert a stimulating and transforming influence in all departments of the industrial arts; I refer to the invention of the dynamo-electric machine.

As early as the autumn of 1866, when I was intent on perfecting electric exploding apparatus with the help of my cylindrical inductor, the question occupied my mind, whether it would not be possible by suitable employment of the so-called extra-current, to intensify considerably the induction-current. It became clear to me that an electro-magnetic machine, whose working power is very much enfeebled by the induced currents arising in its coils, because these induced currents considerably diminish the energy of the galvanic battery, might conversely strengthen the power of the latter, if it were forcibly turned in the opposite direction by an external force. This could not fail to be the case, because the direction of the induced currents was at the same time reversed by the reversed movement. In fact, experiments confirmed this theory, and it appeared that there always remains sufficient magnetism in the fixed electro-magnets of a suitably contrived electromagnetic machine to produce the most surprising effects by gradually strengthening the current generated by the reversed rotation.

This was the discovery and first application of the dynamo-electric principle underlying all dynamo-electric machines. The first problem, which was thereby practically solved, was the construction of an effective electric exploding apparatus without steel magnets, and such exploding apparatus is still in general use at the present day. The Berlin physicists, among them Magnus, Dove, Riess, Du Bois-Reymond, were extremely surprised when I laid before them in December 1866 such an exploding inductor, and showed that a small electromagnetic machine without battery and permanent magnets, which could be turned in one direction without effort and with any velocity, offered an almost insuperable resistance when turned in the opposite direction, and at the same time produced an electric current of such strength, that its wire-coils became quickly heated. Professor Magnus immediately offered to lay a description of my invention before the Berlin Academy of Sciences, but, on account of the Christmas holidays, this could only be done in the following year, on the 17th of January 1867.

The priority of my application of the dynamo-electric principle was afterwards impugned in various quarters, when its enormous importance came to be seen during its further development. At first, Professor Wheatstone was almost universally recognised in England as simultaneous inventor, because at a sitting of the Royal Society on the 15th of February 1867, at which my brother William produced my apparatus, he immediately exhibited a similar apparatus, which was only distinguishable from mine by the wire-coils of the fixed electromagnet being differently disposed in their relation to those of the rotating cylindrical magnet. Next, Mr. Varley came forward with the assertion, that already in the early part of the autumn of 1866 he had given orders to a mechanician for just such an apparatus, and also subsequently handed in a 'provisional specification' of the same. My first complete theoretical establishment of the principle in the printed Transactions of the Berlin Academy, and its previous practical elucidation, have however finally been taken to be decisive in my favour. The name given by me to the apparatus, 'dynamo-electric machine,' has also become general, although frequently corrupted in practice into 'the dynamo.'

Already in my communication to the Berlin Academy, I had pointed out that the industrial arts were now in possession of appliances capable of producing electric currents of any desired tension and strength by the expenditure of energy, and that this would prove of great importance for many of its branches. In fact large machines of the kind were immediately constructed by my firm, one of which was exhibited at the Paris Universal Exhibition of 1867, whilst a second was employed in the summer of the same year by the military authorities for electric lighting experiments in Berlin. These experiments indeed proved quite satisfactory, with the drawback, however, that the wire-coils of the armatures rapidly became so hot, that the electric light produced could only be allowed without interruption for a short time. The machine exhibited in Paris was never actually put to the test, as there were no appliances for the transmission of power in the space allotted to my firm, and the jury, to which I myself belonged, did not subject the exhibits of their members, which were *hors concours,* to any trial. All the greater was the sensation caused by an imitation of my machine exhibited by an English mechanician, which produced from time to time a small electric light. It was considered a sufficient recognition that the order of the Legion of Honour was awarded to me at the close of the exhibition.

When at a later time the dynamo-machine, after considerable improvement, especially by the introduction of Pacinotti's ring and Hefner's coiling system, had received the most extensive application in practice, and both mathematicians and engineers had developed its theory, it seemed almost self-evident and hardly to be called an invention, that one should arrive at the dynamo-electric machine by merely reversing the rotation of an electromagnetic machine. Against this it may be said that the most obvious inventions, of primary importance, are commonly made very late, and in the most round-about way. For the rest it would not have been easy to have arrived by accident at the discovery of the dynamo-electric principle, because electromagnetic machines only 'excite,' i.e. continuously and spontaneously strengthen their electromagnetism, on reversing the rotation, when their dimensions and the disposition of the coils are perfectly correct.

To this period also belongs my invention of the alcoholmeter, which very successfully solved an extremely difficult problem, and accordingly excited much attention at the time. The problem consisted in constructing an apparatus to register continuously and automatically the quantity of absolute alcohol contained in the spirit flowing through it. My apparatus solved this problem so completely, that it indicated the quantity of alcohol, reduced to the customary normal temperature, as accurately as could be determined by the most exact scientific measurements. The Russian Government has employed this apparatus for almost a quarter of a century in levying the high tax which is imposed on the production of spirit, and many other European states have also subsequently adopted it for the same purpose. Apart from a few important practical improvements due to my cousin Louis Siemens, the apparatus is still supplied in the original form as a regular article of manufacture by a factory specially erected for the purpose in Charlottenburg. No imitation has hitherto been successful anywhere, although the apparatus is unprotected by a patent. . . .

When at its close I survey my life, and search for the determining causes and impelling forces, which carried me over all hindrances and dangers to a position which brought me outward recognition and inward satisfaction, and superabundantly provided me with the material blessings of life, there I indeed am bound to admit that many fortunate circumstances have co-operated and that altogether I owe a large debt to fortune. It was a lucky coincidence that my early years were passed in a time of rapid progress of natural sciences, and that I devoted myself especially to electrical engineering, when it was still quite undeveloped and therefore formed a very fertile ground for inventions and improvements. On the other hand however I have also frequently had to contend with very unusual misfortune. This continual struggle with altogether unexpected difficulties and unlucky accidents, which as a rule in the beginning hampered my undertakings, but which I mostly by good hap succeeded in overcoming, William Meyer, the dear friend of my youth and faithful companion, very forcibly described in students' slang as: *Sau beim Pech* (bad luck coupled with astonishing flukes). I must admit the correctness of this view, but still do not believe that it was only blind fate, when the wavelike line of happiness and unhappiness, on which our life moves, carried me so frequently to the desired goals. Success and failure, victory and defeat, often depend in human life entirely on the timely and right use of the opportunities offered. The quality of quickly making up one's mind in critical moments, and of doing the right thing without long reflection, has remained tolerably faithful to me during my whole existence, in spite of the somewhat dreamy meditative life in which I frequently, I might almost say usually, was plunged. In innumerable cases this quality has preserved me from harm and rightly guided me in difficult situations. Undoubtedly a certain stimulus was always necessary to give me full control of my mental qualities. I needed it, not only to be snatched from my own meditative life, but also as a protection against my own weaknesses. Among these I especially reckon an excessive benignness, which made it uncommonly hard for me to refuse a request, not to fulfill a known wish, nay in general to say or do anything to anybody that would be unpleasant or painful to him. To my good fortune, this quality, very inconvenient especially for a businessman and master over many people, was neutralized by another, that of being easily provoked and excited to anger. This anger, which was always easily aroused when my good intentions were misunderstood or abused, was ever a relief and outlet for my feelings, and I have often declared that anybody, with whom I had unpleasant dealings, could never do me a greater service than by giving me cause to be angry. For the rest this irascibility was usually only a form of mental excitement, which never got beyond my control. Although in younger years I was often nicknamed by my friends 'curly head,' wherewith they would hint at a certain connection between my curly hair and 'curly' mind, yet my easily roused anger has never led me to actions which I had afterwards to regret. For a manager of great undertakings I was also in other respects but inadequately suited. I lacked the good memory, the orderly sense, and consistent, unbending strictness. If notwithstanding I have founded large business concerns and managed them with unusual success, this is a proof that industry coupled with energy often overcomes our weaknesses or renders them less harmful. At the same time I can say on my own behalf that it was not desire of gain which impelled me to devote my working power and my mind in so great a degree to technical undertakings. In the first place it was generally the interest for technical science which led me to my task. A business friend quizzed me once with the assertion that I always let myself be guided in my undertakings by the public benefit they would bring, but that ultimately I always found my account thereby. I admit this remark to be correct within certain limits, for such undertakings as further the public welfare command a general interest, and thereby present greater prospects of being successfully carried through. However I will not undervalue the powerful influence which success and the consciousness arising from it of doing something useful, and at the same time of giving their bread to thousands of industrious workers, exerts on mankind. This gratifying consciousness has a stimulating effect on our mental qualities and is doubtless the foundation of the otherwise somewhat paradoxical German proverb: "To whom God giveth an office, He also giveth understanding therefor."

A main reason of the rapid growth of our factories is, in my opinion, that the products of our manufacture were in large part results of our own inventions. Though these were in most cases not protected by patents, yet they always gave us a start on our competitors, which usually lasted until we gained a fresh start by new improvements. This could certainly only have lasting effect in consequence of the reputation for great solidity and excellence, which our products enjoyed throughout the world.

Besides this public recognition of my technical achievements marks of honour have been so abundantly conferred upon me personally both by the rulers of the larger states of Europe and by universities, academies, scientific and technical institutes and societies, that hardly anything remains for me to desire.

I began the writing of my recollections with the biblical aphorism 'The days of our life are threescore years and ten, or even by reason of strength fourscore years,' and I think I have shown that also the close of the sentence, 'yet is their pride but labour and sorrow,' has held good in my case. For my life was beautiful, because it essentially consisted of successful labour and useful work, and if I finally give expression to the regret that it is approaching its end, I am only urged thereto by the pain that I must be parted from my dear ones, and that it is not permitted me to continue to labour for the full development of the Age of Science.

The World Economy and
the Economic Crisis of 1857

One of the most disturbing features of industrialization was the recurrent cycle of boom and bust. Great Britain, Europe's principal industrial power and exporter of capital, was particularly sensitive to such cyclical developments. In 1847 Parliament established a Select Committee on Commercial Distress to investigate the reasons for the depression at that time. A similar committee investigated the economic crisis of 1857, felt throughout the world. The committee's report is particularly interesting because it reveals the growing interrelationship of the various national economies and the increasing sophistication of international economic relations. It demonstrates that the European economic boom beginning in 1849 was started by the discovery of gold in California and Australia. England benefited particularly because of British free trade policies. The boom gave a decisive impetus to the triumph of joint stock banks and a vigorous lending policy not only within England but also abroad. The impulse for the crash of 1857 also came from America, and it was quickly felt throughout Europe. Furthermore, it soon became evident that abuse of credit, encouraged by good economic conditions and the excessively liberal policies of the joint stock banks, helped intensify the distress. In the long run, such crashes had a salutary economic effect by terminating excessive speculation and liquidating economically inefficient ventures. Needless to say, they were not so viewed by their victims. Even worse, the lessons learned were quickly forgotten. The crash of 1873 was even more severe than its predecessor.

Report of the Select Committee on Commercial Distress

1. The ten years which have elapsed since the last Committee sat under the same Order of Reference, *viz.,* the Committee on Commercial Distress, which reported in 1848, have been marked by many circumstances of peculiar interest and importance. The foreign trade of the United Kingdom has in that period increased with a development unprecedented, perhaps, by any other instance in the history of the world. The exports, which before 1848 had never exceeded £60,110,000 — the amount which they attained in 1845 — have risen with little variation and with great rapidity; and in 1857, notwithstanding the severe commercial pressure which marked the latter portion of that year, they stood at £122,155,000.

2. In the year 1849, the newly discovered mines of California began to add perceptibly to the arrivals of gold; and in 1851, the supply was increased by the still more fertile discoveries in Australia. The figures [on the facing page], for which your Committee are indebted to the authorities of the Bank, will show how important an addition appears to have been made to the circulating medium of the world from these new sources of supply.

3. The remission of duties upon articles of necessity, and upon the raw materials of industry, and the great increase of trade to which your Committee have referred, were naturally attended by a very remarkable improvement in the comforts and consuming power of the people, as exhibited in the imports; and especially in the vast increase in the clearances of those articles which enter most materially into the consumption of the working classes. It is probable that to this cause ought chiefly to be attributed the great increase which is believed to have taken place in the circulating medium of the United Kingdom. Mr. Weguelin, a Member of the Committee, and the Governor of the Bank, stated to the Committee of 1857, that this increase was estimated by those in whose judgment the Bank Directors placed the greatest reliance, at 30 per cent. in the six years then last elapsed. . . .

4. With regard to bank notes, it is interesting here to observe, that in the smaller denominations, those, namely, which enter most into the retail transactions of the country, the number has considerably increased,

From *Parliamentary Papers,* vol. 5 (1857–1858), pp. iii–xvi. Reprinted by permission of Her Majesty's Stationery Office.

ESTIMATED INCREASE OF THE EUROPEAN STOCK
OF BULLION IN SEVEN YEARS 1851–1856

	Imports from producing countries		Exports to the East from Great Britain and Mediterranean	
	Gold	Silver	Gold	Silver
	£	£	£	£
1851	8,654,000	4,076,000	102,000	1,716,000
1852	15,194,000	4,712,000	922,000	2,630,000
1853	22,435,000	4,355,000	974,000	5,559,000
1854	22,077,000	4,199,000	1,222,000	4,583,000
1855	19,875,000	3,717,000	1,192,000	7,934,000
1856	21,275,000	4,761,000	479,000	14,108,000
1857	21,366,000	4,050,000	529,000	20,146,000
	£130,876,000	29,870,000	5,420,000	56,676,000

GOLD

	£
The total import of gold in seven years has been, say	130,000,000
The exports of gold bullion and British gold coin to India, China, Australia, the Cape, Brazils, the West Indies, United States, &c., may be taken at	22,500,000
Which would leave as the increase to the European Stock of Gold	107,500,000

SILVER

The exports of silver to India and China have been	£56,676,000	
The imports from the producing countries	£29,870,000	
Making the amount of silver abstracted from the European stock		26,800,000
And the estimated increase in the European stock of bullion		£80,700,000

concurrently with the increase of the gold circulation above referred to. The £5 and £10 notes of the Bank of England, which in 1851 were £9,362,000, had risen in 1856 to £10,680,000. . . .

7. While this expansion of trade was in progress, and the precious metals received this remarkable addition, a new feature in the banking business of the country was observable. The joint stock banks in London entered more and more into competition with the private banks, and by their practice of allowing interest on deposits, began to accumulate vast amounts. . . .

8. Meanwhile the joint stock banks of London, now nine in number, have increased their deposits from £8,850,774 in 1847 to £43,100,724 in 1867, as shown in their published accounts. The evidence given to your Committee leads to the inference that of this vast amount, a large part has been derived from sources not heretofore made available for this purpose; and that the practice of opening accounts and depositing money with bankers has extended to numerous classes who did not formerly employ their capital in that way. It is stated by Mr. Rodwell, the chairman

of the Association of Private Country Bankers, and delegated by them to give evidence to your Committee, that in the neighbourhood of Ipswich this practice has lately increased fourfold among the farmers and shop-keepers of that district; that almost every farmer, even those paying only £50 per annum rent, now keep deposits with bankers. The aggregate of these deposits of course finds its way to the employments of trade, and especially gravitates to London, the centre of commercial activity, where it is employed first in the discount of bills, or in other advances to the customers of the London bankers. That large portion, however, for which the bankers themselves have no immediate demand passes into the hands of the bill-brokers, who give to tł ꞏ banker in return commercial bills already discounted by them for pers ⸍ns in London and in different parts of the country, as a security for the sum advanced by the banker. The bill-broker is responsible to the banker for payment of this money at call; and such is the magnitude of these transactions, that Mr. Neave, the present Governor of the Bank, stated in evidence, "We know that one broker had 5 millions, and we were led to believe that another had between 8 and 10 millions; there was one with 4, another with 3½, and a third above 8. I speak of deposits with the brokers."

9. It thus appears that since 1847 three most important circumstances have arisen, affecting the question referred to your Committee, *viz.:*

1. An unprecedented extension of our foreign trade.
2. An importation of gold and silver on a scale unknown in history since the period which immediately succeeded the first discovery of America; and,
3. A most remarkable development of the economy afforded by the practice of banking for the use and distribution of capital.

10. In the years which immediately succeeded the great commercial crisis of 1847–8, the natural effect of such a crisis on the minds of persons engaged in trade was exhibited, and for a time prudence and caution were the marked characteristics of the commercial world. . . .

14. In the earlier part of the autumn of last year, the trade of the United Kingdom was generally considered to be in a sound and healthy state. . . .

15. In this state of things, the bullion standing at £10,606,000, the reserve at £6,296,000, and the minimum rate of discount at 5½ per cent., the Bank, on the 17th of August 1857, commenced a negotiation with the East India Company, which ended in a shipment of £1,000,000 in specie for the East. The general aspect of affairs continued without change until the 15th September, when the first tidings arrived of the great depreciation of railway securities in the United States, and immediately afterwards of the failure of a very important corporation, called the Ohio Life and Trust Company. Before 8th October the tidings from America

had become very serious; news of the suspension of cash payments by the banks in Philadelphia and Baltimore were received; cotton bills were reduced to par, and bankers' drafts to 105; railroad securities were depreciated from 10 to 20 per cent.; the artisans were getting out of employment; and discounts ranged from 18 to 24 per cent. The transactions between America and England are so intimate, and so large, the declared value of British and Irish produce exported in 1856 to the United States having been £21,918,000, while the amount of securities held by English capitalists in America was by some persons estimated at £80,000,000, that this serious state of commercial disorder there could not but produce in this country great alarm.

16. In New York, 62 out of 63 banks suspended their cash payments. In Boston, Philadelphia, and Baltimore, the banks generally did the same. The effect of the American calamity fell with the greatest weight upon the persons engaged in trade with that country, and Liverpool, Glasgow, and London naturally exhibited the first evidences of pressure. On the 27th October the Borough Bank of Liverpool closed its doors, and on the 7th November the great commercial house of Messrs. Dennistoun & Co. suspended payment. The Western Bank of Scotland failed on the 9th November, and on the 11th the City of Glasgow Bank suspended its payments, which it has since resumed. The Northumberland and Durham District Bank failed on the 26th, and on the 17th the Wolverhampton Bank for a time suspended payment.

17. Great alarm naturally prevailed in London, the centre of all the monetary transactions of the world. Vast sums deposited with the joint stock banks, at interests, and employed directly by themselves, or by the bill brokers, in addition to other monies deposited by their other customers, were chiefly held at call; and the bill brokers are stated to have carried on their enormous transactions without any cash reserve; relying on the run off of their bills falling due, or in extremity, on the power of obtaining advances from the Bank of England. . . .

33. During the month of October there was a very great gloom in Glasgow, occasioned by the commercial panic in America, Glasgow being very intimately connected in trade with America, with New York particularly. Towards the end of October that feeling was much increased, from its being well known that the Western Bank were in difficulties from their connexion with the three houses which have been above referred to. The bank closed on the 9th November, at two o'clock. The Western Bank and the City of Glasgow Bank had establishments open at night for the purpose of receiving the savings of small depositors. During the evening of the 9th November, the Monday, there was a demand for gold by the savings bank depositors at the branches of the City Bank. On the Tuesday morning, when the doors of the banks were opened, a great number of parties appeared with deposit receipts, demanding gold; one witness,

speaking of his own bank, says "The office of our own establishment was quite filled with parties within a quarter of an hour of the opening of the doors; I think at half-past nine." This run or panic increased, and the continued refusal of the notes of the Western Bank added very much to the excitement. These people who came for money would not take the notes of any bank; it did not matter what bank it was; they refused everything but gold. Two of the banks sent a deputation of the directors to Edinburgh to confer with the managers of the Edinburgh banks on the subject, and to induce them to rescind a decision at which they had arrived, not to take the notes of the Western Bank. They failed in that; the notes of the Western Bank were refused the whole day on the Tuesday. The streets of Glasgow were in a very excited state; crowds were walking about going from one bank to another to see what was going on; there was an immense crowd of people. At the National Securities Savings Bank the run was very great indeed. The National Savings Bank paid in notes, and then the depositors, having received their deposits in notes, went with those notes to the banks that had issued them to demand gold. The City of Glasgow Bank did not open on Wednesday the 11th. Troops were sent for by the authorities, who were afraid of some disturbance. The magistrates issued a proclamation either on the Tuesday night or on the Wednesday morning, and it was circulated very extensively, advising the people not to press upon the banks for payment, and to take the notes of all banks. . . .

38. Your Committee have before them the particulars of 30 houses which failed in 1857. The aggregate liability of these houses is £9,080,000, of this sum the liabilities which other parties ought to provide for amount to £5,215,000, and the estimated assets £2,317,000. Besides the failures which arose from the suspension of American remittances, another class of failures is disclosed. The nature of these transactions was the system of open credits which were granted; that is, by granting to persons abroad liberty to draw upon the house in England to such extent as had been agreed upon between them; those drafts were then negotiated upon the foreign exchanges, and found their way to England, with the understanding that they were to be provided for at maturity. They were principally provided for, not by staple commodities, but by other bills that were sent to take them up. There was no real basis to the transaction, but the whole affair was a means of raising a temporary command of capital for the convenience of the individuals concerned, merely a bare commission hanging upon it; a banker's commission was all that the houses in England got upon those transactions, with the exception of receiving the consignments probably of goods from certain parties, which brought them a merchant's commission upon them; but they formed a very small amount in comparison with the amount of credits which were granted. One house at the time of its suspension was under obligation to the world to the extent of about £900,000, its capital at the last time of taking stock

was under £10,000. Its business was chiefly the granting of open credits, *i.e.*, the house permitted itself to be drawn upon by foreign houses without any remittance previously or contemporaneously made, but with an engagement that it should be made before the acceptance arrived at maturity. In these cases the inducement to give the acceptance is a commission, varying from ½ to 1½ per cent. The acceptances are rendered available by being discounted, as will appear hereafter, when the affairs of the banks which failed come under our notice. . . .

40. This practice appears to have grown up of late, and to be principally connected with the trade of Sweden, Denmark and other countries in the north of Europe. One house at Newcastle is described as conducting before 1854 a regular trade in the Baltic. They were not great people, but were respectable people, and were doing a moderately profitable trade. They unfortunately entered upon this system of granting credits; and in the course of three years the following result ensued; *viz.* in 1854 their capital was between £2,000 and £3,000; in 1857 they failed for £100,000, with the prospect of paying about 2s. in the pound.

41. For other instances of this abuse of credit, your Committee refer to the evidence, concurring entirely in the opinions expressed by the witnesses, that the great abuse of credit is a feature common to the two years 1847 and 1857, and has been, in their judgement, the principal cause of the failures that took place in those years.

Mr. Coleman says,

Speaking generally with regard to 1847, of which your experience is now complete, are you prepared to say that the failures which occurred in that year were owing to any imperfection of the law by which the facilities for obtaining credit were unduly curtailed? No.

With regard to the year 1857, what would your answer be to the same question? That every house which applied and deserved assistance received it.

The Troubled Path
to Labor Organization

The organization of the workers for the collective defense of their interests was slow and difficult. Opposition did not come from the employers alone. It took time for the workers themselves to realize their collective strength and to overcome their inertia and fear. When the workers did organize, they were harsh toward those of their fellows who refused to do so. Social conservatives and even liberals sympathetic with the problems of labor often thought there was a solution better than trade unionism. One of these liberals was the great English novelist Charles Dickens (1812–1870), whose Hard Times *(1854) condemned the mechanistic utilitarianism and dehumanization of industrial England. The country was symbolized by the city of Coketown and its leading characters, the manufacturer Josiah Bounderby, the merchant Thomas Gradgrind, and the teacher Mr. M'Choakumchild. Dickens was too intelligent to believe that industrialization could be reversed, but he did believe that it could be humanized and that the isolation and spiritual poverty of employers and workers could be remedied by humane education that would encourage mutual cooperation. It was from this perspective that he expressed his suspicion of the union organizer Slackbridge and identified himself with Stephen Blackpool, an "honest, hard-working power-loom weaver in Mr. Bounderby's factory," who was unwilling to accept the narrow struggle for class interests represented by trade unionism. However dubious Dickens' conception of the purpose and actual consequences of labor organization is, he does present an unforgettable picture, based on his own attendance at organizing meetings, of what it was like.*

Dickens' *Hard Times*

"Oh my friends, the down-trodden operatives of Coketown! Oh my friends and fellow-countrymen, the slaves of an iron-handed and a grinding despotism! Oh my friends and fellow-sufferers, and fellow-workmen, and fellow-men! I tell you that the hour is come, when we must rally round one another as One united power, and crumble into dust the oppressors that too long have battened upon the plunder of our families, upon the sweat of our brows, upon the labour of our hands, upon the sweat of our sinews, upon the God-created glorious rights of Humanity, and upon the holy and eternal privileges of Brotherhood!"

"Good!" "Hear, hear, hear!" "Hurrah!" and other cries, arose in many voices from various parts of the densely crowded and suffocatingly close Hall, in which the orator, perched on a stage, delivered himself of this and what other froth and fume he had in him. He had declaimed himself into a violent heat, and was as hoarse as he was hot. By dint of roaring at the top of his voice under a flaring gaslight, clenching his fists, knitting his brows, setting his teeth, and pounding with his arms, he had taken so much out of himself by this time, that he was brought to a stop, and called for a glass of water.

As he stood there, trying to quench his fiery face with his drink of water, the comparison between the orator and the crowd of attentive

From Charles Dickens, *Hard Times* (London: Bradbury and Evans, 1854), pp. 63–71.

faces turned towards him, was extremely to his disadvantage. Judging him by Nature's evidence, he was above the mass in very little but the stage on which he stood. In many great respects he was essentially below them. He was not so honest, he was not so manly, he was not so good-humoured; he substituted cunning for their simplicity, and passion for their safe solid sense. An ill-made, high-shouldered man, with lowering brows, and his features crushed into an habitually sour expression, he contrasted most unfavourably, even in his mongrel dress, with the great body of his hearers in their plain working clothes. Strange as it always is to consider any assembly in the act of submissively resigning itself to the dreariness of some complacent person, lord or commoner, whom three-fourths of it could, by no human means, raise out of the slough of inanity to their own intellectual level, it was particularly strange, and it was even particularly affecting, to see this crowd of earnest faces, whose honesty in the main no competent observer free from bias could doubt, so agitated by such a leader.

Good! Hear, hear! Hurrah! The eagerness both of attention and intention, exhibited in all the countenances, made them a most impressive sight. There was no carelessness, no languor, no idle curiosity; none of the many shades of indifference to be seen in all other assemblies, visible for one moment there. That every man felt his condition to be, somehow or other, worse than it might be; that every man considered it incumbent on him to join the rest, towards the making of it better; that every man felt his only hope to be in his allying himself to the comrades by whom he was surrounded; and that in this belief, right or wrong (unhappily wrong then), the whole of that crowd were gravely, deeply, faithfully in earnest; must have been as plain to any one who chose to see what was there, as the bare beams of the roof and the whitened brick walls. Nor could any such spectator fail to know in his own breast, that these men, through their very delusions, showed great qualities, susceptible of being turned to the happiest and best account; and that to pretend (on the strength of sweeping axioms, howsoever cut and dried) that they went astray wholly without cause, and of their own irrational wills, was to pretend that there could be smoke without fire, death without birth, harvest without seed, anything or everything produced from nothing.

The orator having refreshed himself, wiped his corrugated forehead from left to right several times with his handkerchief folded into a pad, and concentrated all his revived forces, in a sneer of great disdain and bitterness.

"But, oh my friends and brothers! Oh men and Englishmen, the down-trodden operatives of Coketown! What shall we say of that man — that working-man, that I should find it necessary so to libel the glorious name — who, being practically and well acquainted with the grievances and wrongs of you, the injured pith and marrow of this land, and having heard you, with a noble and majestic unanimity that will make Tyrants tremble, resolve for to subscribe to the funds of the United Aggregate Tribunal, and to abide by the injunctions issued by that body for your benefit, whatever they may be — what, I ask you, will you say of that working-man, since such I must acknowledge him to be, who, at such a time, deserts his post, and sells his flag; who, at such a time, turns a traitor and a craven and a recreant; who, at such a time, is not ashamed to make to you the dastardly and humiliating avowal that he will hold himself aloof, and will *not* be one of those associated in the gallant stand for Freedom and for Right?"

The assembly was divided at this point. There were some groans and hisses, but the general sense of honour was much too strong for the condemnation of a man unheard. "Be sure you're right, Slackbridge!" "Put him up!" "Let's hear him!" Such things were said on many sides. Finally, one strong voice called out, "Is the man heer? If the man's heer, Slackbridge, let's hear the man himseln, 'stead o' yo." Which was received with a round of applause.

Slackbridge, the orator, looked about him with a withering smile; and, holding out his right hand at arm's length (as the manner of all Slackbridges is), to still the thundering sea, waited until there was a profound silence.

"Oh my friends and fellow-men!" said Slackbridge then, shaking his head with violent scorn, "I do not wonder that you, the prostrate sons of labour, are incredulous of the existence of such a man. But he who sold his birthright for a mess of pottage existed, and Judas Iscariot existed, and Castlereagh existed, and this man exists!"

Here, a brief press and confusion near the stage, ended in the man himself standing at the orator's side before the concourse. He was pale and a little moved in the face — his lips especially showed it; but he stood quiet, with his left hand at his chin, waiting to be heard. There was a chairman to regulate the proceedings, and this functionary now took the case into his own hands.

"My friends," said he, "by virtue o' my office as your president, I ashes o' our friend Slackbridge, who may be a little over hetter in this business, to take his seat, whiles this man Stephen Blackpool is heern. You all know this man Stephen Blackpool. You know him awlung o' his misfort'ns, and his good name."

With that, the chairman shook him frankly by the hand, and sat down again. Slackbridge likewise sat down, wiping his hot forehead — always from left to right, and never the reverse way.

"My friends," Stephen began, in the midst of a dead calm; "I ha' hed what's been spok'n o' me, and 'tis lickly that I shan't mend it. But I'd liefer you'd hearn the truth concernin myseln, fro my lips than fro onny other man's, though I never cud'n speak afore so monny, wi'out being moydert and muddled."

Slackbridge shook his head as if he would shake it off, in his bitterness.

"I'm th' one single Hand in Bounderby's mill, o' a' the men theer, as don't coom in wi' th' proposed reg'lations. I canna' coom in wi' 'em. My friends, I doubt their doin' yo onny good. Licker they'll do yo hurt."

Slackbridge laughed, folded his arms, and frowned sarcastically.

"But 't an't sommuch for that as I stands out. If that were aw, I'd coom in wi' th' rest. But I ha' my reasons — mine, yo see — for being hindered; not on'y now, but awlus — awlus — life long!"

Slackbridge jumped up and stood beside him, gnashing and tearing. "Oh my friends, what but this did I tell you? Oh my fellow-countrymen, what warning but this did I give you? And how shows this recreant conduct in a man on whom unequal laws are known to have fallen heavy? Oh you Englishmen, I ask you how does this subornation show in one of yourselves, who is thus consenting to his own undoing and to yours, and to your children's and your children's children's?"

There was some applause, and some crying of Shame upon the man; but the greater part of the audience were quiet. They looked at Stephen's worn face, rendered more pathetic by the homely emotions it evinced; and, in the kindness of their nature, they were more sorry than indignant.

"'Tis this Delegate's trade for t' speak," said Stephen, "an' he's paid for 't, an' he knows his work. Let him keep to 't. Let him give no heed to what I ha' had'n to bear. That's not for him. That's not for nobbody but me."

There was a propriety, not to say a dignity in these words, that made the hearers yet more quiet and attentive. The same strong voice called out, "Slackbridge, let the man be heern, and howd thee tongue!" Then the place was wonderfully still.

"My brothers," said Stephen, whose low voice was distinctly heard, "and my fellow-workmen — for that yo are to me, though not, as I knows on, to this delegate here — I ha' but a word to sen, and I could sen nommore if I was to speak till strike o' day. I know weel, aw what's afore me. I know weel that yo 'aw resolve to ha' nommore ado wi' a man who is not wi' yo in this matther. I know weel that if I was a lyin parisht i' th' road, yo'd feel it right to pass me by, as a forrenner and stranger. What I ha' getn, I mun mak th' best on."

"Stephen Blackpool," said the chairman, rising, "think on 't agen. Think on 't once agen, lad, afore thou'rt shunned by aw owd friends."

There was an universal murmur to the same effect, though no man articulated a word. Every eye was fixed on Stephen's face. To repent of his determination, would be to take a load from all their minds. He looked around him, and knew that it was so. Not a grain of anger with them was in his heart; he knew them, far below their surface weaknesses and misconceptions, as no one but their fellow-labourer could.

"I ha' thowt on't, above a bit, Sir. I simply canna coom in. I mun go th' way as lays afore me. I mun tak my leave o' aw heer."

He made a sort of reverence to them by holding up his arms, and stood for the moment in that attitude; not speaking until they slowly dropped at his sides.

"Monny's the pleasant word as soom heer has spok'n wi' me; monny's the face I see heer, as I first seen when I were young and lighter heart'n than now. I ha' never had no fratch afore, sin ever I were born, wi' any o' my like; Gonnows I ha' none now that's o' my makin'. Yo'll ca' me traitor and that — yo I mean t' say," addressing Slackbridge, "but 'tis easier to ca' than mak' out. So let be."

He had moved away a pace or two to come down from the platform, when he remembered something he had not said, and returned again.

"Haply," he said, turning his furrowed face slowly about, that he might as it were individually address the whole audience, those both near and distant; "haply, when this question has been tak'n up and discoosed, there'll be a threat to turn out if I'm let to work among yo. I hope I shall die ere ever such a time cooms, and I shall work solitary among yo unless it cooms — truly, I mun do't, my friends; not to brave yo, but to live. I ha' nobbut work to live by; and wheerever can I go, I who ha' worked sin I were no heighth at aw, in Coketown heer? I mak' no complaints o' bein turned to the wa', o' being outcasten and overlooken fro this time forrard, but hope I shall be let to work. If there is any right for me at aw, my friends, I think 'tis that."

Not a word was spoken. Not a sound was audible in the building, but the slight rustle of men moving a little apart, all along the centre of the room, to open a means of passing out, to the man with whom they had all bound themselves to renounce companionship. Looking at no one, and going his way with a lowly steadiness upon him that asserted nothing and sought nothing, Old Stephen, with all his troubles on his head, left the scene.

Then Slackbridge, who had kept his oratorical arm extended during the going out, as if he were repressing with infinite solicitude and by a wonderful moral power the vehement passions of the multitude, applied himself to raising their spirits. Had not the Roman Brutus, oh my British countrymen, condemned his son to death; and had not the Spartan mothers, oh my soon to be victorious friends, driven their flying children on the points of their enemies' swords. Then was it not the sacred duty of the men of Coketown, with forefathers before them, an admiring world in company with them, and a posterity to come after them, to hurl out traitors from the tents they had pitched in a sacred and a Godlike cause? The winds of heaven answered Yes; and bore Yes, east, west, north, and south. And consequently three cheers for the United Aggregate Tribunal!

Slackbridge acted as fugleman, and gave the time. The multitude of doubtful faces (a little conscience-stricken) brightened at the sound, and took it up. Private feeling must yield to the common cause. Hurrah! The roof yet vibrated with the cheering, when the assembly dispersed.

Thus easily did Stephen Blackpool fall into the loneliest of lives, the life of solitude among a familiar crowd. The stranger in the land who looks into ten thousand faces for some answering look and never finds it, is in cheering society as compared with him who passes ten averted faces daily, that were once the countenances of friends. Such experience was to be Stephen's now, in every waking moment of his life; at his work, on his way to it and from it, at his door, at his window, everywhere. By general consent, they even avoided that side of the street on which he habitually walked; and left it, of all the working men, to him only.

He had been for many years, a quiet silent man, associating but little with other men, and used to companionship with his own thoughts. He had never known before the strength of the want in his heart for the frequent recognition of a nod, a look, a word; or the immense amount of relief that had been poured into it by drops through such small means. It was even harder than he could have believed possible, to separate in his own conscience his abandonment by all his fellows from a baseless sense of shame and disgrace.

Ferdinand Lassalle
and the German Labor Movement

By 1914, the German Socialist party and its affiliated trade union organizations composed the most powerful labor movement in Europe. Officially, they were committed to a Marxist ideoloy; in practice, they were reformist and sought to gain power within the existing order. They looked to the state to improve the conditions of the working class. The strong reformist and statist tradition of the party owed much to the founder of Germany's first significant socialist organization, Ferdinand Lassalle (1825–1864), who created the General Association of German Workers in 1863. Lassalle rejected both capitalism and Marxism, and he hoped that universal suffrage would enable the workers to take power in the state and then use the state to defeat capitalism and assist the workers in organizing industry into "productive associations." From Lassalle's standpoint, the liberals were the chief enemies of the workers, and Bismarck briefly flirted with the idea of an alliance against the liberals during a series of discussions he held with Lassalle. In 1864, Lassalle was killed in a duel, but his ideas formed the basis of the socialist program established at the Gotha Congress of 1875. Subsequently, the Marxist wing of the party won, and its program was adopted at the Erfurt Congress of 1891. Nevertheless, the Lassallean strain remained of great practical importance in the history of the party. Lassalle's open letter to the Central Committee on the calling of a General German Workers' Congress in Leipzig demonstrates Lassalle's rejection of both classical and Marxist economic solutions. He did accept classical economic theory, however, and argued that only the state could turn Ricardo's iron law of wages to the advantage of the workers.

Lassalle's Letter to the Central Committee on the Calling of a General Workers' Congress

The iron law of economics, which determines the wages of labour under the present conditions, under the dominance of supply and demand for labour, is this: That the average wage is always reduced to the minimum level necessary to maintain the habitual subsistence and propagation of a people. This is the point around which the real wage always fluctuates, without ever being able to rise far above, or fall far below it. It cannot remain for long above it — otherwise the easier, better conditions would lead to an increase in the marriages and births among the working classes, and these would lead to an increase in the supply of hands, which would reduce wages to and below their former levels.

Equally, wages cannot for long fall below the necessary subsistence level, for then we should have emigration, abstention from marriage and from procreation and finally diminished numbers caused by misery, which would reduce the supply of labour and thus raise wages to their former levels.

Real wages therefore fluctuate constantly around their point of gravity, at times above it (prosperity in some or all industries) at times a little below (periods of more or less general depression and crisis).

The limitation of the average wage to the minimum level necessary for subsistence and procreation habitual to a people — this is, I repeat, the iron and cruel law determining the wages of labour under present conditions.

This law cannot be disputed by anyone. I can bring you as many witnesses for it as there are great and famous names in economic science, from the liberal school of economics itself, for it was this school which discovered and found the proof for this law. . . .

There is, even in the Liberal school, not a single economist of stature who denies it. Adam Smith and Say, Ricardo and Malthus, Bastiat and John Stuart Mill acknowledge it unanimously. . . .

From *Documents of European Economic History. Volume 1: The Process of Industrialization, 1750–1870*, ed. S. Pollard and C. Holmes (London: Edward Arnold, 1968), pp. 556–61. Reprinted by permission of Edward Arnold Ltd.

Let us look for a moment more closely on the effect and nature of this law. . . .

From the total produce of labour, that part is deducted and distributed among the workers which is necessary for their subsistence (the wages of labour). The whole surplus of the produce goes to the entrepreneur.

It is therefore a consequence of this iron and cruel law that you . . . are necessarily excluded from the increased productivity caused by the progress of civilisation, i.e. from the increased produce, from the increased efficiency of your own labour! For you forever the minimum subsistence, for the entrepreneur always everything beyond it.

But since, by the rapid progress in productivity [the efficiency of labour], many industrial products fall to very low prices at the same time, it may happen that . . . you gain for a time a certain indirect advantage from the increased productivity of labour. This advantage does not accrue to you as producer, it does not alter your quota of the total produce of labour, it merely affects you as consumer, equally with the entrepreneur and even those not taking part in the productive process at all, whose position as consumers is improved in even greater measure than your own.

And even this advantage, accruing to you as men, not as workers, will disappear again according to this iron and cruel law, which always depresses the wages of labour in the long run to the consumption level of minimum necessary subsistence.

If now, further, such an increase in productivity of labour and the resultant extreme cheapness of several products occur suddenly, and if they occur at the same time as a prolonged increase in the demand for labour — then these disproportionately cheapened products may be absorbed into the concept of the habitual necessary minimum of subsistence. . . .

Thus, if various periods are compared with each other, the condition of the working classes in the later century or in the later generation may have improved *vis-à-vis* the condition of the working classes of an earlier century or an earlier generation, in so far as the minimum of the habitual necessary subsistence has meanwhile been raised a little. . . .

Whether you are better off than the worker of 80 or 200 years ago (if that should be the case) because the minimum habitual subsistence has been raised in the meantime — what value has this question for you, and what satisfaction can you derive from it? As little as the equally undisputed fact that you are better off than Hottentots and cannibals.

All human satisfaction depends always on the relation of the available consumption goods to the subsistence needs habitually established in any age, or, what amounts to the same thing, on the surplus of the available consumption goods over the lowest margin of the minimum necessary subsistence at any given time. An increase in the necessary minimum cre-

ates misery and want unknown in earlier ages. What want has the Hot-
tentot for soap, what want has the cannibal for a decent overcoat, what
want had the worker for tobacco, before the discovery of America, what
want had the worker for a useful book before the invention of printing?

All human suffering and want therefore depends solely on the relation
of consumption goods to the needs and habits existing at any given time.
All human suffering and want and all human satisfaction, in other words
every human situation, must be measured against the condition in which
other men are placed at the same time in relation to habitual needs.
Every situation of a class must therefore be measured solely in relation
to the condition of other classes at the same time.

Even if it could be proved that the level of necessary subsistence conditions had been raised in various periods, that satisfactions previously
unknown have become habitual needs and by the very development
wants and sufferings previously unknown have been caused — your human
situation has remained the same throughout that period; it is always this:
to fluctuate around the lowest margin of the currently valid minimum
subsistence level, being at times just above, and at times just below it.

Your human condition has therefore remained the same, for the human condition cannot be measured in relation to the condition of animals in the jungle, or of negroes in Africa, or of serfs in the Middle Ages,
or of workers 200 or 80 years ago, but must be measured in relation to the
situation of your contemporaries, the condition of other classes at the
same time. . . .

To make the working class into its own employer — this is the means by
which, and by which alone — as you will see in a moment — the iron and
cruel law can be removed which determines the wages of labour.

If the working class becomes its own employer, all distinctions between
wages and profits disappear, and with them, wages as such also, and in
their place we have the return to labour of the whole produce of labour.

The abolition of profit by the most peaceful and simple method, by the
organisation of the working classes into its own employer through voluntary associations, which alone can abolish that law which under present
conditions distributes only the minimum necessary for subsistence to the
worker as wage, and leaves all the surplus to the employer, that is the
only true, the only just, the only non-visionary improvement of the condition of the working classes.

But how? Cast a glance at the railways, the engineering works, the ship-
yards, the cotton spinning mills, the weaving sheds, etc., and at the millions required for them, and then look into your empty pockets, and ask
yourselves where you could obtain the massive capital sums required for
the former, and how you could ever be able to run large-scale industry on
your own account?

And it is true that nothing is more certain than that you will never accomplish this, as long as you remain solely and exclusively reduced to your isolated efforts as individuals.

For this reason it is the task of the State to enable you to do it, to take in hand the great issue of the free individual association of the working classes in a positive and helpful manner, and to make it its sacred duty to provide you with the means and opportunity for your self-organisation and self-association.

And do not be misled by the shouts of those who will tell you that every such intervention by the State destroys social self-help.

It is not true that I prevent someone from climbing a tower if I hand him ladder and rope for it. It is not true that the State prevents our children from educating themselves if it provides teachers, schools and libraries. It is not true that I prevent someone from ploughing his field on his own if I provide him with a plough. It is not true that I prevent someone from defeating a hostile army by his own hand if I give him the weapons to do it with. . . .

The true improvement of the condition of labour and of the working class as such, which it demands with justice, can be achieved only with the assistance of the State.

And equally, do not be misled by the shouts of those who begin to speak of Socialism or Communism and try to oppose you with such cheap slogans. Be convinced that they only want to mislead you or do not know themselves what they are talking about. Nothing is further from this so-called Socialism or Communism than this demand, under which the workers will, as today, keep their individual freedom, individual style of life and individual wages and will stand in no other relationship to the State than that of having received from it the necessary capital or credit for their association. But this is precisely the great historical role of the State, to facilitate and set in train the major steps in the progress of civilised humanity. This is its function. This is its purpose; it always has been and had to be. I want to give you a single example, in the place of the hundreds of examples which I could give you — the canals, high roads, mail services, steam packet lines, telegraphs, mortgage banks, agricultural improvements, the introduction of new industries, etc. — a single example, but one that is worth hundreds of others, and is a particularly close parallel: when the railways had to be built, in all the German States — and likewise in most countries abroad — with the exception of a few very small and scattered lines, it was the State that had to intervene in one form or another, mostly by at least guaranteeing the interest on the shares, and in many countries by far more drastic action.

The interest guarantee represented, in addition, the following favourable contract of the entrepreneurs — the rich shareholders — with the State: 'If the new enterprises are unprofitable, the burden falls on the State, i.e. on all the taxpayers, which is particularly on you, the large class of the propertyless! But if, on the contrary, the new enterprises are profitable, then the advantage — the high dividends — shall belong to us, the rich shareholders.' This is not invalidated by the fact that in some countries, as e.g. in Prussia, the State bargained for certain, and at the time very doubtful, advantages for the very, very distant future, advantages which could be more than matched by those that would arise from the support of associations of workmen.

Without this State intervention of which, as noted, the interest-guarantee was the mildest expression, we might even today be without railways on the continent!

At any rate, it is certain that the State had to take this action, that even the interest-guarantee alone represented an extremely active form of State intervention, that this intervention favoured the rich and propertied classes, which in any case dispose of all capital and credit and which therefore could have much more easily done without State intervention than you, and that this intervention was demanded by the whole of the bourgeoisie.

Why was there no campaign then against the interest-guarantee as an 'inadmissible intervention by the State?' Why was it not said then that the interest-guarantee threatened the 'social self-help' of the wealthy entrepreneurs of those joint-stock companies? Why was the interest guarantee not libelled as 'Socialism and Communism'?

But of course, that form of State intervention was in favour of the rich and propertied classes of society, and in that case it was quite permissible, and always was so! It is only in the case of an intervention in favour of the needy, the vast majority — only then does it become 'Socialism and Communism'! . . .

Moreover, however great the progress of civilization caused by the railways, it is minute compared with the enormous step forward in human progress which would be caused by the association of the working classes. For what good are all hoarded treasures and all the fruits of civilization, if they are to be available only to the few, and the rest of limitless humanity as a whole remains forever like Tantalus, snatching in vain at these fruits? Worse than Tantalus, for he, at least, did not himself produce the fruit, for which his parched palate was doomed to yearn in vain.

If ever the helpful intervention of the State was justified, it was in the case of this, the largest step in the progress of civilization known to history.

DEMOCRATIC REFORM
AND SOCIAL STRIFE, 1871–1914

Chapter 8

Domestic politics in western Europe between 1871 and 1914 presented an ambivalent picture. During that time, the forces of parliamentarianism and political democracy seemed to be growing stronger. Yet social conflict also intensified, and many thought it had reached dangerous levels by 1914.

Great Britain moved forward fairly steadily toward universal suffrage, although the final step was not taken until 1918. Nevertheless, the majority of urban workers received the vote in the Reform Act of 1867, and rural laborers received it in the Reform Act of 1884. In 1872 the secret ballot was introduced. Democratization was largely completed by David Lloyd George, who borrowed a tactic from the Whigs of 1832 and threatened to pack the House of Lords unless it accepted his Budget Bill of 1911. The House of Lords surrendered its veto power over the budget, agreed to a provision for general elections at least once every five years, and accepted a provision establishing payment for members of the House of Commons. Liberal leaders, especially William Gladstone and David Lloyd George, were responsible for many of the great political and social reforms of the age, but credit must also be given to Tory leaders. Benjamin Disraeli, Gladstone's great rival, for example, was responsible for the introduction of the Reform Bill of 1867, although Gladstone supported it and undertook major administrative reforms during his tenure as prime minister from 1874 to 1880.

Despite these considerable achievements, British liberalism was in trouble in the years immediately before World War I. The Irish problem proved particularly difficult. Reforms undertaken by Gladstone corrected many abuses, but his political career ended with the failure of his proposal for home rule in 1893. The Liberal Home Rule Bill of 1912 was strongly resisted by the Ulster Protestants and the English landlords. It finally passed in 1914 but did not take effect until after the war and was passed too late to prevent civil war in Ireland. Political life was also disoriented by the unconventional and disruptive activities of the suffragettes and the severe strikes of 1911 and 1912. The fear was growing that the Triple Industrial Alliance of transport workers, railwaymen, and miners could and would paralyze the country. The association between liberalism and labor was breaking down, and the rising power of the Independent Labour Party at the expense of the Liberals presaged a development that occurred rapidly after 1918.

Political life in the Third Republic was more unsettled than in Great Britain. It began with the bloody suppression of the Paris Commune in 1871 and then faced opposition from the monarchists. The Republic was saved from the monarchists only because they could not agree, first on a candidate and then on whether to accept the flag of the Revolution. Nevertheless, the Third Republic still suffered from the often virulent opposition of monarchists and clericals, who were joined by proto-fascists such as Charles Maurras, Léon Daudet, and Maurice Barrès. These elements capitalized on the desire for revenge against Germany and the recovery of Alsace-Lorraine, and they took constant advantage of the financial and personal scandals to which the republican parties seemed particularly prone. Fortunately for the Republic, the conservative forces had some remarkable mishaps of their own. When they thought they had found their "man on horseback" in General Georges Boulanger, he proved too cowardly to make a bid for power in 1889 when a coup d'état seemed imminent and fled to his mistress instead. The Dreyfus Affair, which dragged on from 1894 to 1906, proved even more disastrous to the conservatives than the loss of Boulanger's leadership in the long run. They formed the backbone of the anti-Dreyfusard forces, who supported the trumped up treason charges against Jewish Captain Alfred Dreyfus, whose supporters proved him innocent after years of trials and domestic disturbances. The pro-republican forces used the situation to separate church and state in 1905 and to undertake other anticlerical measures. Although republicans such as Georges Clemenceau and socialists such as Jean Jaurès were able to collaborate in the struggle for Dreyfus and against the church, they were unable to agree on the best means of handling the epidemic of strikes and syndicalist disturbances that began in 1906. This social unrest and the dangerous international situation combined to give rightist forces a new lease on life and to move the republican parties in a more conservative direction.

In Germany, the impasse was both political and social. Bismarck sought to deal with labor by a mixture of the carrot and the stick. He introduced the most progressive social legislation in the Europe of his time while persecuting the socialists with his Anti-Socialist Law of 1878. Bismarck's domestic policy was a failure. During his years as chancellor of the empire, from 1870 to 1890, Germany was transformed from a largely rural and agrarian economy into an urban, industrialized society. Universal suffrage worked in favor of the Socialist party, contrary to Bismarck's calculations. The Reichstag refused to renew the Anti-Socialist Law in 1890 and the new emperor, William II, turned down Bismarck's plan to abrogate universal suffrage and instead dismissed Bismarck. Neither William II nor his chancellors, however, proved equal to the task of running the country. They felt compelled to rest their power on a coalition of Junkers and big industrialists, but they also tried to pacify the more progressive sections of the bourgeoisie and to pay some heed to the demands of the workers. As a result, spurts of social reform alternated with periods of reaction. By 1912, the socialists were the strongest party in the Reichstag and seemed willing to play a more reformist role if the government and ruling classes would make some concessions. The latter, however, blocked reform of the plutocratic suffrage system in Prussia, Germany's largest state, and refused to recognize the trade unions. The stalemate was finally broken by war and military collapse.

The English Reform Bill
of 1867

William Gladstone (1809–1898), who personified British liberalism with its commitment to reform, free trade, and anti-imperialism, began his political career as a Tory but converted to liberalism as a consequence of the Corn Law struggle. Gladstone was a fine classical scholar and a man of deep religious commitments as well as a remarkable financier and administrator. Between 1868 and 1894, he served as prime minister four times and undertook major reforms of the British administrative and educational system. Gladstone was a member of the House of Commons for more than sixty years and was one of its most effective debaters. He was particularly skilled at marshaling a vast array of facts to support his case, and his argument for the Reform Bill in a speech on April 12, 1866, is a good illustration of his style as well as of the moral, religious, and political considerations that induced him to support the extension of the suffrage to the urban working man. Despite his efforts, it took another year before the measure was passed.

Gladstone's Speech in Parliament

. . . The House will remember that on a former occasion I ventured to refer to the state of the constituency at the present moment as compared with what it was in 1832; and I endeavoured to show . . . that the proportion of the working classes included in the present constituency, although to our great satisfaction we had found it to be larger than we had supposed, yet was smaller than it had been in the year 1832. That statement has not been impugned in this House, and I do not think it can be impugned successfully. I do not think that any Gentleman who has examined the figures will venture to question my statement that at the present moment the quantitative proportion of the working men in the town constituencies is less than it was in 1832. But in order to obtain a full view of the importance of this fact, neither must the House forget that since 1832 every kind of beneficial change has been in operation in favour of the working classes. There never was a period in which religious influences were more active than in the period I now name. It is hardly an exaggeration to say that within that time the civilizing and training powers of education have for all practical purposes been not so much improved as, I might almost say, brought into existence as far as the mass of the people is concerned. As regards the press, an emancipation and an extension have taken place to which it would be difficult to find a parallel. I will not believe that the mass of Gentlemen opposite are really insensible to the enormous benefit that has been effected by that emancipation of the press, when for the humble sum of a penny, or for even less, newspapers are circulated from day to day by the million rather than by the thousand, in numbers almost defying the powers of statistics to follow, and carrying home to all classes of our fellow-countrymen accounts of public affairs, enabling them to feel a new interest in the transaction of those affairs, and containing articles which, I must say, are written in a spirit, with an ability, with a sound moral sense, and with a refinement, that have made the penny press of England the worthy companion — I may indeed say the worthy rival — of those dearer and older papers which have long secured for British journalism a renown perhaps without parallel in the world. By external and material, as well as by higher means, by measures relating to labour, to police, and to sanitary arrangements, Parliament has been labouring, has been striving to raise the level of the working community, and has been so striving with admitted success. And there is not a call which has been made upon the self-improving powers of the working community which has not been fully answered. Take, for instance, the Working Men's Free Libraries and Institutes throughout the country; take, as an example of the class, Liverpool; who are the fre-

From *Hansard's Parliamentary Debates*, vol. 182, 3d series, pp. 1131–42. Reprinted by permission of Her Majesty's Stationery Office.

quenters of that institution? I believe that the majority of the careful, honest, painstaking students who crowd that library are men belonging to the working classes, a large number of whom cannot attend without making some considerable sacrifice. Then again, Sir, we called upon them to be provident, we instituted for them Post Office savings banks, which may now be said to have been in full operation for four years; and what has been the result? During these four years we have received these names at the rate of thousands by the week, and there are now 650,000 depositors in those savings banks. This, then, is the way in which Parliament has been acting towards the working classes. But what is the meaning of all this? Parliament has been striving to make the working classes progressively fitter and fitter for the franchise; and can anything be more unwise, not to say more senseless, than to persevere from year to year in this plan, and then blindly to refuse to recognize its legitimate upshot — namely, the increased fitness of the working classes for the exercise of political power? The proper exercise of that power depends upon the fitness of those who are to receive it. That fitness you increase from day to day, and yet you decline, when the growing fitness is admitted, to give the power. ("No, no!" from the back Opposition Benches.) You decline to give the working classes political power by lowering the borough franchise. ("No, no!" from the back Opposition Benches.) I do not complain of the interruption — in fact, I am very glad to hear it. (Cheers and laughter.) I wish it were universal, I wish it came from the front Opposition Benches, and from my noble Friend behind me; for if our opponents were so prepared to proceed in what seems their natural sense, we should have little matter for controversy on the subject of this Bill. But I fear it is not so. I fear the intention is to resist the consummation of the process, of which the earlier stages have been favoured and approved. This course appears about as rational as the process of a man who incessantly pours water into a jug or bason, and wonders and complains that at last it overflows.

Now, what are the arguments that the busy brain of man has framed in opposition to this measure? It is one favourite plea for our opponents that we ought not to hand over the power to govern to those who do not pay the charges of Government. . . . But is this the thing that we are really going to do? Are we, indeed, going to hand over the power to those who do not pay the charges of Government? I will not at this moment go into the first portion of the proposition, although I say distinctly we are not going to hand over the power at all; but is it true that the working classes do not contribute fairly, fully, largely, to the expenses of Government? This question was put to me two days ago, in consequence of my statement that, according to the best estimate I could form, the working classes were possessed of an income forming not less than five-twelfths — that is, not very far short of one-half — of the entire income of the country. . . . Now, on the very showing of our antagonists, and putting aside altogether the question how far the human elements itself may weigh, apart from money, is not such a state of things absolutely unjust? (Loud cheers.) Perhaps I shall be told that I have based my estimates upon the income and not upon the property of the working classes. Probably that may be the answer to my statement. Yes, I hear a cheer. I admit I have spoken in reference to income, and not in reference to property. Well, anyone so inclined may take it on that ground if he chooses; but he must also take the consequence of having made that choice, and he must be prepared to change the whole system of your taxation. We now lay upon income the great bulk of your taxes, and to these taxes the working classes contribute, perhaps a larger proportion, looking at the amount of their earnings, than is paid by the proudest noble in the land. I, therefore, say to those Gentlemen who argue that the working classes are not entitled to the franchise because they do not possess property, but they must be prepared . . . instead of raising a fourteenth part of the revenue, or some such proportion, as we now do, from property and the rest from income, we must raise a fourteenth part from income and the rest from property.

Again it is said, at least I believe it has been so said, that where the working classes have a majority they vote together as a class. Now, is there any shade or shadow, any rag of proof that such is the fact? I am going to trespass upon the patience of the House by reading a letter which I received to-day from a working man, and which I shall venture to read for the especial benefit of the Gentlemen opposite. I believe the statements it contains to be perfectly true, and it is my sincere opinion that the writer's arguments are typical of the class to which he belongs. In any case their nature is such that I am confident hon. Gentlemen will not be sorry to hear them.

> Dear Sir (I do not know him personally, but he thus kindly addresses me) —
> My motive in writing this is to remind you of the Tories who belong to the
> working classes, as you cannot think perhaps all you wish at the right time.
> We all know that there are the same variety of principles and opinions in all
> classes of society, I am a working man, and have an opportunity of knowing
> that the Tories in principle, especially the artizan class, who are very nu-
> merous, who are not now in possession of the franchise. The new Reform Bill,
> I think, will do about as much for the Tories as for the Liberals. It would for
> all we know. The love of country and constitution is confined to no particular
> class. A Liberal is as loyal as a Tory. Is there any evidence to show that these
> men which the Reform Bill or Franchise Bill would enfranchise are not fit to
> be trusted? They know well that the welfare and prosperity of the country
> and their masters is at the same time their welfare and prosperity. Please not
> to make my name public.

Well, Sir, in my opinion, the letter presents a true view of the question. There is in it that latent concentrated good sense which often comes from the mind, from the mouth, and from the pen of an uneducated man with a peculiar free meaning, perhaps because he is in a certain sense, as I may say, without any reproach or disparagement to education, so much nearer to the point at which nature originally placed him than are men with minds more refined and cultivated. Now, Sir, I maintain that there is no proof whatever that the working classes, if enfranchised, would act together as a class. Perhaps you ask for proofs to the contrary. It is exceedingly difficult to give a direct proof of that which has not happened: although in my opinion ample proof, substantial, even if indirect, of the correctness of my statement does exist. For example, I take this point. Municipal franchises are in a predominant degree working men's franchises. Those franchises, if they do not quite come up to universal suffrage, at all events nearly approach household suffrage. What has been the system followed by the working classes in municipal elections? In order to institute a comparison between the municipal and Parliamentary franchises we must select those towns in which the municipal and Parliamentary boundaries are the same. There are 346,000 municipal voters in that portion of the towns of this country, and, computing as well as the information in our hands will permit, I find that there are 163,000 of them on the Parliamentary register. I deduct from that number one-fourth or 41,000 as representing the maximum portion of working men, and the result is that there remain 122,000 as the number of non-working men in the municipal constituency. Thus the working men number 224,000. Is not this a dreadful state of things? Yet there has been no explosion, no antagonism between classes, no question has been raised about property, nor indeed has any, even the slightest attempt, been made to give a political character to municipal institutions. ("Oh, oh!") Yes, but when the municipal franchise was discussed in 1835 the party who occupied the seats of hon. Gentlemen opposite . . . prophesied that great danger and mischief would spring from the municipal franchise, because it would give a political character to municipal elections, and imbue all our corporations with a similar spirit. That being the case, I think I am perfectly justified in standing upon an important and strictly relevant fact, that, as far as I am aware, we are not able to adduce a single instance in which this majority composed from the working class majority has given a democratic — I will not say a disloyal, but a democratic character — a character distinct from that which they bore under the influence of the middle classes to our municipal institutions. . . .

But there is a much broader ground, to which, I think, no reference has yet been made, and that is the case of the boroughs which had open constituencies containing large majorities of the working classes before the Reform Act — constituencies much more popular than those of the present day. Upon examining the probable operation of the new Bill, I find that, according to our very large definitions of the working classes — a definition which I have employed rather for argument's sake, I mean in order to avoid contention, than because it was strictly and literally accurate — I find this as the result, that in sixty boroughs, returning 101 Members, the working classes will or may have majorities. In these sixty boroughs the electors form 8.4 per cent of the population. Now, let us compare with this state of things the state of things that existed in the popular boroughs before the Reform Act. Before 1830 there were sixty-five boroughs of a strictly popular character; more popular, indeed, than the sixty boroughs that are likely to have a majority of the labouring classes under the Bill now on the table, for the electors in them instead of being 8.4 per cent of the population, numbered nearly 10 per cent, and furthermore, the sixty-five boroughs returned Members for 130 seats. If it be true that the majority of the working classes in a constituency give the control of the seat, which, however, I entirely deny, you cannot show that, under our Bill, there would be more than 101 such seats; while, under the old Parliamentary system, that system which so scandalizes my right hon. Friend the Member for Calne, . . . they numbered 130. We now, therefore, stand, to a certain extent, upon the firm ground of history and experience for the purpose of comparison. Was there among those 130 Members at any period of our history developed a character in any degree dangerous to the institutions of the country? I doubt if any Gentleman will be found ready to affirm that there was.

. . . It is constantly alleged, and the argument is employed with confidence, that, if we would only let the matter take its course, the enfranchisement of the working classes is actually in course of being effected by a natural process, whereas we are endeavouring to stimulate and force onwards this enfranchisement by artificial means. This is a matter upon which I should be extremely slow to dogmatize; because it does not admit of being brought to a test with such precision as to warrant confidence. But I must say that the whole of the argument upon such facts as are known to us in the other way, and that I wait with anxiety, but without expectation, for the proof of this enlargement, of this natural and spontaneous enlargement, with which it is said we are rashly intermeddling. The number of working men on the register is, I think, undeniably less at present than it was in 1832; but, of course, there is the fact that since 1832 the working men belonging to the class of freemen have somewhat diminished. I do not think that the diminution in this direction is numerically of much importance, but there has been a great diminution in the scot and lot voters who are working men. This class is not, indeed, yet extinct; and therefore, in our computations respecting the future, we must allow for a continuance of this dwindling process, until the whole number of scot and lot voters in existence at the time of the Reform Bill has disappeared. It is said, however, that there is a rapid growth of the working classes among the £10 householders. But where is the proof of this assertion? I believe it to be undeniable that the rate of progress in the aggregate number of £10 householders has been very much less of late years than in the first few years after the passing of the Reform Bill. From 1832 to 1851, while the population increased at the rate of 43 per cent, the constituency grew more than twice as fast, but from 1851 to 1866 the constituency grew only 50 per cent faster than the aggregate population, thus showing a great slackening as compared with the earlier period. This, however, can in some degree be accounted for. There were persons not belonging to the working classes who were classed under other denominations at the time of the Reform Act, but whose successors, as they died off, have subsequently appeared as £10 householders. But it is a mistake, I believe, to imagine that some very extraordinary growth has taken place among the £10 householders; and a still greater mistake to imagine that such growth, as may have occurred, has taken place in the working portion of the population. Let us look at the economical facts of the case. If we take the case of the towns, we find that the increase of the constituencies since 1832 has been nearly the same for the entire period as that of the population. In the population it has been 79 per cent, and in the franchise 82 per cent; a variation so slight that it may be practically disregarded. It is said that there is a growth in the wealth of the working classes more than proportionate to that of the classes above them; but no attempt has been made to prove this. In my firm opinion, the largest share of the recent increase of wealth has taken place among the middle classes of the country. To put it shortly and intelligibly, the capital of the country has grown in a far greater degree than the income of the working classes. But other circumstances must be taken into view. We must not assume that the improvement in the dwellings of the artizans in towns has kept pace with the increase of their income, nor even that they are in as great a degree as formerly the occupiers of houses so as to obtain the franchise. Again, we must remember that in the large towns, where the area is limited, the growth in the value of land and rents has been much more rapid than the growth of wealth. If we inquire what is the value of land in the City of London, and compare it with what it was twenty years ago, we shall find that its growth is entirely out of proportion to the growth in the wealth of the City, great as that has been. This constant pressure of growing rents and limitation of area may drive the working man into lodgings, or may send him to such a dwelling beyond the limits of a represented town instead of within them. I shall not be going too far if I assert — in fact, I may say that it is notorious — that there are large masses of the labouring people, especially in London, who, as compared with their position twenty years ago, are better clothed and better fed, but who live in worse houses than they did, although enjoying a larger income. And this arises from the fact that there is not the same limitation in the supply of food and clothing as exists in the supply of houses, because of the contraction of area. I state my own opinions with the reserve that the nature of the question requires; but I must say that I have heard no good argument to the contrary. And I stand finally upon this general statement of the case. For a man to occupy a house of £10 clear annual value, setting aside only the class of men who receive lodgers into their houses, he must, all things considered, have an income from £90 to £100 a year. That clear annual value is minus rates and taxes, and it is minus the cost and the depreciation of furniture also. It is vain then to stand in the face of your working population and say, "We have a law which will enfranchise all the careful, diligent, and respectable men among you; but no working man is intelligent, or industrious, or respectable unless he can earn 35s. a week." That is too severe a test; and my general statement of the facts is enough, therefore, to show that it is vain to speak of a £10 franchise, taking the country all over, as one which is capable of admitting, by the natural or spontaneous process which has been set up in argument against us, all the industrious and diligent among the lower class.

The Dreyfus Affair

It was rare for a Jew to be a member of the French general staff, or any general staff for that matter, during the nineteenth century, and when it was discovered that secrets had been passed to the Germans, Dreyfus quickly came under suspicion. In reality, the documents in question had been transmitted to the Germans by Major Esterhazy, and the documents on which Dreyfus was convicted, degraded, and sent to Devil's Island were forgeries. High-ranking officers were involved in the forgeries and misrepresentations that led to Dreyfus' conviction and were used to sustain it after the controversy began. Some of the truth was discovered by the head of military intelligence, Lieutenant-Colonel Piquart, who was dismissed when he tried to expose the truth. The case, however, was then picked up by members of parliament, among them the socialist leader Jaurès, and given publicity by the famous naturalist author, Émile Zola (1840–1902), whose "J'Accuse" ("I Accuse") was published in Clemenceau's newspaper Aurore *in 1898. Zola's letter to the French president, the conclusion of which follows, was a ringing denunciation of those responsible for the injustice done to Dreyfus. Zola was convicted of libel, but only after he divided France between the Dreyfusards and the anti-Dreyfusards. Many of the latter were prepared to argue that even if Dreyfus were innocent, it was wrong and dangerous to impugn the honor of the army. Dreyfus was tried again in 1899, convicted with "extenuating circumstances," and then pardoned.*

His supporters remained adamant, however, and Dreyfus was retried
and found innocent in 1906, after which he was reinstated in the army.
Many of France's greatest artists and intellects became involved in the
affair. One of these, the novelist Anatole France (1844–1924), dealt with
the case in his satirical history of France, Penguin Island. *Pyrot (Drey-*
fus) is accused of selling eight thousand bales of hay meant for the Pen-
guin cavalry to their enemies, the Porpoises. He is persecuted by the
war minister, Greatauk, and the chief of staff, General Panther. Colom-
ban (Zola) exposes the case. His trial is followed by a battle between
the Pyrotists and Anti-Pyrotists. Although it is clear on which side the
author is, his satire spares neither side and is an important commentary
on the foibles of the political groups in France and on the social groups
that supported them.

Zola's "J'accuse"

. . . Moreover, I do not in the least despair of victory. I repeat with a
feeling of vehement certainty: truth is on the march and nothing can
stop it. It is only now that the Affair is beginning, because only now are
men assuming clear positions: on one hand, the guilty, who do not wish
justice to be done; on the other, the adherents of justice, who will give
their lives so that justice may triumph. When you drive truth under-
ground, it grows and gathers so great an explosive force that, when it
finally does burst forth, it carries everything before it. Indeed, we shall
see whether there has not already been prepared — for a future date — the
most shocking of disasters.

But this letter has grown long, Mr. President, and it is time to conclude.

I accuse Lieutenant Colonel du Paty de Clam of having been the dia-
bolical author of the judicial wrong — unconsciously, I am ready to believe — and of having then for three years defended his pernicious work
by the most absurd and culpable machinations.

I accuse General Mercier of having rendered himself the accomplice, at
least by want of firmness, of one of the greatest iniquities of the century.

I accuse General Billot of having had in his hands certain proofs of
Dreyfus' innocence and of having hushed them up, of having rendered
himself guilty of the crime of *lèse-humanité* and *lèse-justice* with a political object and in order to screen the compromised General Staff.

I accuse General de Boisdeffre and General Gonse of having made

From *The Dreyfus Case by the Man — Alfred Dreyfus and His Son — Pierre Dreyfus,*
ed. Donald C. McKay (New Haven: Yale University Press, 1937), pp. 118–19. Reprinted
by permission of Mrs. Pierre Dreyfus.

themselves accomplices of the same crime — the one, doubtless, through clerical prejudice, the other, perhaps, from the *esprit de corps* which makes the War Office a sacred, unassailable ark.

I accuse General de Pellieux and Major Ravary of having made an infamous inquiry — I mean by that an inquiry of monstrous partiality — of which their report is an imperishable monument of naïve audacity.

I accuse the three experts, *Sieurs* Belhomme, Varinard and Couard, of having made a false and fraudulent report, unless a medical examination should find them to be suffering from defective vision and diseased judgment.

I accuse the War Office of having carried on in the press, particularly in the *Éclair* and the *Écho de Paris,* an abominable campaign, in order to screen their mistake and mislead the public.

Lastly, I accuse the first Court-Martial of having violated the law by condemning an accused man on the basis of a secret document, and I accuse the second Court-Martial of having, in obedience to orders, screened that illegality by committing in its turn the judicial crime of knowingly acquitting a guilty man.

In preferring these charges, I am aware that I bring myself under Articles 30 and 31 of the Press Law of July 29, 1881, which punishes defamation. And I do so voluntarily.

As to the men I accuse, I do not know them, I have never seen them, I have no resentment or animosity toward them. They are for me merely entities, spirits of social maleficence. And the act which I perform here is only a revolutionary means of hastening the revelation of truth and justice.

I have but one passion — that of light. This I crave for the sake of humanity, which has suffered so much, and which is entitled to happiness. My passionate protest is merely the cry of my soul. Let them venture then to bring me before the Court of Assize and let an inquiry be made in broad daylight!

I wait.

France's *Penguin Island*

PYROT

All Penguinia heard with horror of Pyrot's crime; at the same time there was a sort of satisfaction that this embezzlement combined with treachery and even bordering on sacrilege, had been committed by a Jew. In order

From Anatole France, *Penguin Island* (© 1909 by Dodd, Mead & Company; renewed 1937) (New York: Random House, Modern Library edition, 1933), pp. 177–80, 204–09. Reprinted by permission of Dodd, Mead & Company and The Bodley Head.

to understand this feeling it is necessary to be acquainted with the state of the public opinion regarding the Jews both great and small. As we have had occasion to say in this history, the universally detested and all powerful financial caste was composed of Christians and of Jews. The Jews who formed part of it and on whom the people poured all their hatred were the upper-class Jews. They possessed immense riches and, it was said, held more than a fifth part of the total property of Penguinia. Outside this formidable caste there was a multitude of Jews of a mediocre condition, who were not more loved than the others and who were feared much less. In every ordered State, wealth is a sacred thing: in democracies it is the only sacred thing. Now the Penguin State was democratic. Three or four financial companies exercised a more extensive, and above all, more effective and continuous power, than that of the Ministers of the Republic. The latter were puppets whom the companies ruled in secret, whom they compelled by intimidation or corruption to favour themselves at the expense of the State, and whom they ruined by calumnies in the press if they remained honest. In spite of the secrecy of the Exchequer, enough appeared to make the country indignant, but the middle-class Penguins had, from the greatest to the last of them, been brought up to hold money in great reverence, and as they all had property, either much or little, they were strongly impressed with the solidarity of capital and understood that a small fortune is not safe unless a big one is protected. For these reasons they conceived a religious respect for the Jews' millions, and self-interest being stronger with them than aversion, they were as much afraid as they were of death to touch a single hair of one of the rich Jews whom they detested. Towards the poorer Jews they felt less ceremonious and when they saw any of them down they trampled on them. That is why the entire nation learnt with thorough satisfaction that the traitor was a Jew. They could take vengeance on all Israel in his person without any fear of compromising the public credit.

That Pyrot had stolen the eighty thousand trusses of hay nobody hesitated for a moment to believe. No one doubted because the general ignorance in which everybody was concerning the affair did not allow of doubt, for doubt is a thing that demands motives. People do not doubt without reasons in the same way that people believe without reasons. The thing was not doubted because it was repeated everywhere and, with the public, to repeat is to prove. It was not doubted because people wished to believe Pyrot guilty and one believes what one wishes to believe. Finally, it was not doubted because the faculty of doubt is rare among men; very few minds carry in them its germs and these are not developed without cultivation. Doubt is singular, exquisite, philosophic, immoral, transcendent, monstrous, full of malignity, injurious to persons and to property, contrary to the good order of governments, and to the prosperity of empires, fatal to humanity, destructive of the gods, held in horror by heaven and earth. The mass of the Penguins were ignorant of doubt: it believed in Pyrot's guilt and this conviction immediately became one of its chief national beliefs and an essential truth in its patriotic creed.

Pyrot was tried secretly and condemned.

General Panther immediately went to the Minister of War to tell him the result.

"Luckily," said he, "the judges were certain, for they had no proofs."

"Proofs," muttered Greatauk, "proofs, what do they prove? There is only one certain, irrefragable proof — the confession of the guilty person. Has Pyrot confessed?"

"No, General."

"He will confess, he ought to. Panther, we must induce him; tell him it is to his interest. Promise him that, if he confesses, he will obtain favours, a reduction of his sentence, full pardon; promise him that if he confesses his innocence will be admitted, that he will be decorated. Appeal to his good feelings. Let him confess from patriotism, for the flag, for the sake of order, from respect for the hierarchy, at the special command of the Minister of War militarily. . . . But tell me, Panther, has he not confessed already? There are tacit confessions; silence is a confession."

"But, General, he is not silent; he keeps on squealing like a pig that he is innocent."

"Panther, the confessions of a guilty man sometimes result from the vehemence of his denials. To deny desperately is to confess. Pyrot has confessed; we must have witnesses of his confessions, justice requires them."

There was in Western Penguinia a seaport called La Cirque, formed of three small bays and formerly greatly frequented by ships, but now solitary and deserted. Gloomy lagoons stretched along its low coasts exhaling a pestilent odour, while fever hovered over its sleepy waters. Here, on the borders of the sea, there was built a high square tower, like the old Campanile at Venice, from the side of which, close to the summit, hung an open cage which was fastened by a chain to a transverse beam. In the times of the Draconides the Inquisitors of Alca used to put heretical clergy into this cage. It had been empty for three hundred years, but now Pyrot was imprisoned in it under the guard of sixty warders, who lived in the tower and did not lose sight of him night or day, spying on him for confessions that they might afterwards report to the Minister of War. For Greatauk, careful and prudent, desired confessions and still further confessions. Greatauk, who was looked upon as a fool, was in reality a man of great ability and full of rare foresight.

In the mean time Pyrot, burnt by the sun, eaten by mosquitoes, soaked in the rain, hail and snow, frozen by the cold, tossed about terribly by the wind, beset by the sinister croaking of the ravens that perched upon his cage, kept writing down his innocence on pieces torn off his shirt with a toothpick dipped in blood. These rags were lost in the sea or fell into the hands of the gaolers. Some of them, however, came under the eyes of the public. But Pyrot's protests moved nobody because his confessions had been published. . . .

THE COLOMBAN TRIAL

When the Colomban trial began, the Pyrotists were not many more than thirty thousand, but they were everywhere and might be found even among the priests and millionaires. What injured them most was the sympathy of the rich Jews. On the other hand they derived valuable advantages from their feeble number. In the first place there were among them fewer fools than among their opponents, who were over-burdened with them. Comprising but a feeble minority they co-operated easily, acted with harmony, and had no temptation to divide and thus counteract one another's efforts. Each of them felt the necessity of doing the best possible and was the more careful of his conduct as he found himself more in the public eye. Finally, they had every reason to hope that they would gain fresh adherents, while their opponents, having had everybody with them at the beginning, could only decrease.

Summoned before the judges at a public sitting, Colomban immediately perceived that his judges were not anxious to discover the truth. As soon as he opened his mouth the President ordered him to be silent in the superior interests of the State. For the same reason, which is the supreme reason, the witnesses for the defence were not heard. General Panther, the Chief of the Staff, appeared in the witness-box, in full uniform and decorated with all his orders. He deposed as follows:

"The infamous Colomban states that we have no proofs against Pyrot. He lies; we have them. I have in my archives seven hundred and thirty-two square yards of them which at five hundred pounds each make three hundred and sixty-six thousand pounds weight."

That superior officer afterwards gave, with elegance and ease, a summary of those proofs.

"They are of all colours and all shades," said he in substance, "they are of every form — pot, crown, sovereign, grape, dove-cot, grand eagle, etc. The smallest is less than the hundredth part of a square inch, the largest measures seventy yards long by ninety yards broad."

At this revelation the audience shuddered with horror.

Greatauk came to give evidence in his turn. Simpler, and perhaps greater, he wore a grey tunic and held his hands joined behind his back.

"I leave," said he calmly and in a slightly raised voice, "I leave to M. Colomban the responsibility for an act that has brought our country to the brink of ruin. The Pyrot affair is secret; it ought to remain secret. If it were divulged the cruelest ills, wars, pillages, depredations, fires, massacres, and epidemics would immediately burst upon Penguinia. I should consider myself guilty of high treason if I uttered another word."

Some persons known for their political experience, among others M. Bigourd, considered the evidence of the Minister of War as abler and of greater weight than that of his Chief of Staff.

The evidence of Colonel de Boisjoli made a great impression.

"One evening at the Ministry of War," said that officer, "the attaché of a neighbouring Power told me that while visiting his sovereign's stables he had once admired some soft and fragrant hay, of a pretty green colour, the finest hay he had ever seen! 'Where did it come from?' I asked him. He did not answer, but there seemed to me no doubt about its origin. It was the hay Pyrot had stolen. Those qualities of verdure, softness, and aroma, are those of our national hay. The forage of the neighbouring Power is grey and brittle; it sounds under the fork and smells of dust. One can draw one's own conclusions."

Lieutenant-Colonel Hastaing said in the witness-box, amid hisses, that he did not believe Pyrot guilty. He was immediately seized by the police and thrown into the bottom of a dungeon where, amid vipers, toads, and broken glass, he remained insensible both to promises and threats.

The usher called:

"Count Pierre Maubec de la Dentdulynx."

There was deep silence, and a stately but ill-dressed nobleman, whose moustaches pointed to the skies and whose dark eyes shot forth flashing glances, was seen advancing toward the witness-box.

He approached Colomban and casting upon him a look of ineffable disdain:

"My evidence," said he, "here it is: you excrement!"

At these words the entire hall burst into enthusiastic applause and jumped up, moved by one of those transports that stir men's hearts and rouse them to extraordinary actions. Without another word Count Maubec de la Dentdulynx withdrew.

All those present left the court and formed a procession behind him. Prostrate at his feet, Princess des Boscénos held his legs in a close embrace, but he went on, stern and impassive, beneath a shower of handkerchiefs and flowers. Viscountess Olive, clinging to his neck, could not be removed, and the calm hero bore her along with him, floating on his breast like a light scarf.

When the court resumed its sitting, which it had been compelled to suspend, the President called the experts.

Vermillard, the famous expert in handwriting, gave the results of his researches.

"Having carefully studied," said he, "the papers found in Pyrot's house, in particular his account book and his laundry books, I noticed that, though apparently not out of the common, they formed an impenetrable cryptogram, the key to which, however, I discovered. The traitor's infamy is to be seen in every line. In this system of writing the words 'Three glasses of beer and twenty francs for Adèle,' mean 'I have delivered thirty thousand trusses of hay to a neighbouring Power.' From these documents I have even been able to establish the composition of the hay delivered by this officer. The words waistcoat, drawers, pocket handkerchief, collars, drink, tobacco, cigars, mean clover, meadowgrass, lucern, burnet, oats, ryegrass, vernal-grass, and common cat's tail grass. And these are precisely the constituents of the hay furnished by Count Maubec to the Penguin cavalry. In this way Pyrot mentioned his crimes in a language that he believed would always remain indecipherable. One is confounded by so much astuteness and so great a want of conscience."

Colomban, pronounced guilty without any extenuating circumstances, was condemned to the severest penalty. The judges immediately signed a warrant consigning him to solitary confinement.

In the Place du Palais on the sides of a river whose banks had during the course of twelve centuries seen so great a history, fifty thousand persons were tumultuously awaiting the result of the trial. Here were the heads of the Anti-Pyrotist Association, among whom might be seen Prince des Boscénos, Count Cléna, Viscount Olive, and M. de La Trumelle; here crowded the Reverend Father Agaric and the teachers of St. Maël College with their pupils; here the monk Douillard and General Caraguel, embracing each other, formed a sublime group. The market women and laundry women with spits, shovels, tongs, beetles, and kettles full of water might be seen running across the Pont-Vieux. On the steps in front of the bronze gates were assembled all the defenders of Pyrot in Alca, professors, publicists, workmen, some conservatives, others Radicals or Revolutionaries, and by their negligent dress and fierce aspect could be recognised comrades Phoenix, Larrivée, Lapersonne, Dagobert, and Varambille. Squeezed in his funereal frock-coat and wearing his hat of ceremony, Bidault-Coquille invoked the sentimental mathematics on behalf of Colomban and Colonel Hastaing. Maniflore shone smiling and resplendent on the topmost step, anxious, like Leaena, to deserve a glorious monument, or to be given, like Epicharis, the praises of history.

The seven hundred Pyrotists disguised as lemonade sellers, gutter-merchants, collectors of odds and ends, or as Anti-Pyrotists, wandered round the vast building.

When Colomban appeared, so great an uproar burst forth that, struck by the commotion of air and water, birds fell from the trees and fishes floated on the surface of the stream.

On all sides there were yells:

"Duck Colomban, duck him, duck him!"

There were some cries of "Justice and truth!" and a voice was even heard shouting:

"Down with the Army!"

This was the signal for a terrible struggle. The combatants fell in thousands, and their bodies formed howling and moving mounds on top of which fresh champions gripped each other by the throats. Women, eager, pale, and dishevelled, with clenched teeth and frantic nails, rushed on the man, in transports that, in the brilliant light of the public square, gave to their faces expressions unsurpassed even in the shade of curtains and in the hollows of pillows. They were going to seize Colomban, to bite him, to strangle, dismember and rend him, when Maniflore, tall and dignified in her red tunic, stood forth, serene and terrible, confronting these furies who recoiled from before her in terror. Colomban seemed to be saved; his partisans succeeded in clearing a passage for him through the Place du Palais and in putting him into a cab stationed at the corner of the Pont-Vieux. The horse was already in full trot when Prince des Boscénos, Count Cléna, and M. de La Trumelle knocked the driver off his seat. Then, making the animal back and pushing the spokes of the wheels, they ran the vehicle on to the parapet of the bridge, whence they overturned it into the river amid the cheers of the delirious crowd. With a resounding splash a jet of water rose upwards, and then nothing but a slight eddy was to be seen on the surface of the stream.

Almost immediately comrades Dagobert and Varambille, with the help of the seven hundred disguised Pyrotists, sent Prince des Boscénos head foremost into a river-laundry in which he was lamentably swallowed up.

Serene night descended over the Place du Palais and shed silence and peace upon the frightful ruins with which it was strewed. In the mean time, Colomban, three hundred yards down the stream, cowering beside a lame old horse on a bridge, was meditating on the ignorance and injustice of crowds.

"The business," said he to himself, "is even more troublesome than I believed. I foresee fresh difficulties."

He got up and approached the unhappy animal.

"What have you, poor friend, done to them?" said he. "It is on my account they have used you so cruelly."

He embraced the unfortunate beast and kissed the white star on his forehead. Then he took him by the bridle and led him, both of them limping, through the sleeping city to his house, where sleep soon allowed them to forget mankind.

The Problem
of Labor Unrest

Georges Clemenceau (1841–1929), who relentlessly drove France to victory as prime minister in 1917 and 1918, dominated the radical republican party. An ardent patriot, anticlerical, and individualist, Clemenceau was passionately dedicated to the Republic and its preservation. He was as willing to ally with the left to fight monarchism and the church as he was willing to ally with the right to fight internal disorder and defeatism. The syndicalist strikes that disturbed France in 1906 outraged Minister of the Interior Clemenceau, who felt betrayed by their violent character, particularly since he had made a number of efforts to deal with them. His use of troops and police to put down the disturbances outraged the socialists, whose position was defended by their leader, Jean Jaurès (1859–1914). Jaurès was critical of the syndicalists, but he defended picketing and resistance to strikebreaking and accused the army and police of brutality. Clemenceau replied with an address in the Chamber of Deputies on June 18 and 19, 1906, in which he defended his actions, upheld the right to work, and urged the socialists to adopt a reformist, nonrevolutionary course.

Clemenceau's Speech in the Chamber of Deputies, 1906

M. CLEMENCEAU: Having been personally and directly challenged by the Honorable M. Jaurès, I wish at the outset to render full homage to the noble passion for social justice so gloriously animating his eloquence. With an irresistible impulse of idealism he wishes the happiness of all humanity, and we are witnesses that he would spare no effort to assure this happiness. . . .

Alas! While this magnificent mirage unfolds before the charmed eyes of the new creator, I, vacillating mortal that I am, labor miserably in the plain and in the depths of the valley, struggling with an ungrateful soil which yields me a niggardly harvest. Hence the difference between our points of view which his good will has so much difficulty forgiving me for. [Laughter and applause from the Left and the Center.] . . .

I argue, I struggle, I revolt, and when M. Jaurès tells me that he has

From *Europe in the Nineteenth Century: A Documentary Analysis of Change and Conflict. Volume 2: 1870–1914*, ed. Eugene Anderson, Stanley J. Pincetl, Jr., Donald J. Ziegler, pp. 269–72, 275–76, 287–91, 301–03. Copyright © 1961, by Bobbs-Merrill Company, Inc. Reprinted by permission of the publisher.

conceived a most unfavorable opinion of my policy, I appeal from this judgment to a superior judge, to this Chamber, exponent of a republican country.

Of what am I accused? M. Jaurès reproaches me in harsh words for having rejected and repressed the working class. . . .

Where then did I meet the working class? Was it among those panic-stricken unfortunates who were going to pillage and destroy, ravage the homes of their comrades from the mines? Certainly not. I have met miners; but were they in these acts the legitimate representatives of the working class? Were they at this moment committing acts which you who question me could defend? Certainly not.

I know well — and you have done me the favor of agreeing with me — that I would have considered an armed encounter between the troops and the workers on strike as the worst possible disaster. Surely, if you do not do justice to me in this, I shall do it to myself, and that is enough for me. [Applause from the Left.]

I have done everything in the world to avert this catastrophe. Through difficulties such as no other government has met — I speak of those governments with which you compare me so lightly — through these difficulties, by my presence not only in the strikes of the North and the Pas-de-Calais, but in Paris itself (and I will tell you what I have done in Paris), have you not seen that I have striven to show that not for a moment was I of those governmerts which allowed the panic-stricken unfortunates to take their chance and walk to their death?

No, I wanted to take a personal part insofar as I could do so. . . .

I arrived at Lens as soon as the strike was called because I had something to say to the strikers which I wanted to say myself. In a hundred articles I have always maintained that the government should not send troops preventively on the strike scene before violence has taken place.

I borrowed the argument from Gambetta, who said: "When the troops arrive after a strike is called, it is first the employer who feels supported."

And Gambetta observed that the impartiality of the government thus found itself compromised in the eyes of the workers. . . . It is this conception of Gambetta's which I wished to apply, and it seemed to me that I should first go to explain it to the workers. I arrived at Lens, where the greatest tranquillity reigned everywhere. I went to the town hall of Lens, and had the honor of being received by M. Basly, mayor of Lens, and by his friends. He was in conflict with the anarchists' syndicate; naturally, he advised me against going to the House of the People, which was the meeting place of the anarchists. I went there all the same; it was to speak to them that I had come, and I said to them — not as M. Vaillant makes me say, with a levity which from him astounds me — that no matter what they did they would not see troops in the city of Lens. It would have been simple folly if I had spoken thus I said to them: "Do you want to have a strike without soldiers? Well! That depends upon you. Nothing is easier; you have only to respect order; you have only not to violate the law." And they answered me: "The presence of soldiers is a provocation; that is what has always brought trouble." Well! I told them: "There will be no soldiers . . . unless by acts of violence you oblige me to repress unlawful acts." And I went farther, adding: "However, as there might be certain ones who are interested in trouble-making, during the night I am going to have soldiers brought in who will be installed in the pits, so that there will be no surprise by violence there; they will not go into the streets but will prevent any violence on the part of the ill-disposed; if the machines were to be damaged, it would mean a loss of several months' work for you when you went back to work."

We agreed on this point, and some of the men told me that if there was any damage done to the machinery in the mines, it would be only at the instigation of the companies.

I left with that, and in leaving I said to the prefect: "There will perhaps be a critical hour. If this hour arrives, call me and I will come again. I will again have something to say to the strikers, though it will be for the last time.

This hour came the day when I received a telephone call from the prefect of the Pas-de-Calais, who told me: "The general and I are surrounded in the Lens railroad station. What is to be done?"

The word "surrounded" was not exact, as M. Basly observed immediately; the truth is that without troops, with only a squad or half a squad, the general and the prefect of the Pas-de-Calais found themselves attacked on the railroad line by a considerable mob of strikers.

I left, and while I was en route the troop commanded by Colonel Schwartz, with an admirable stoicism to which I have already rendered homage, undertook to release the prefect of the Pas-de-Calais and the general shut in the station. . . .

Ask the Parisian strikers if they have learned the path to the Minister of the Interior. There is not a trade union, there is not a group of strikers who have not been received when they have asked to see me. My door has always been as open, also, to the employers as to the workers.

I received them all, I listened to them all. I held discussions with everyone. I had the disputing parties brought together for talks. At the time of the diggers' strike, which could have resulted in difficulties for the municipal administration in the construction of the subway, I called into my office the prefect of the Seine and his directors, the president of the municipal council, the chairman, all those who could negotiate with the strikers. I must say that after the negotiations, which lasted sometimes until midnight, it happened that strikers, perhaps at the end of their arguments — I do not want to insist on that — left, slamming the door and saying disagreeable things to us. But until that time they had not stopped telling us: "At least we thank you for having received us and having listened to us."

Are those, I repeat, the acts of a man who represses the working class?

You have said to me, M. Jaurès, using a bit of psychological fakery, that I must have become angry when comparing my helplessness to construct the new city with the power of idealistic construction of which you have given proof ["Very good!" and laughter from Left, Center and Right], and that this anger decided me to send the troops against the strikers.

I assure you that I acknowledge myself beaten on this point. I yield before it. Certainly your power of construction goes much beyond even the power of destruction with which you have so well reproached me. ["Very good!" and laughter from the same benches.] No, I did not get angry; I sent the troops only gradually, according to need.

When the outbursts started, I sent a greater number of soldiers, in such a way that the troops were everywhere in possession of the ground which they occupied and were not in danger of being overcome.

I sent some more; and the more I sent, the more it proved that they were necessary and that I should send still more until the riot was broken. [Applause from the Left, Center, and Right.]

While the strike was following its course in Paris, other conflicts broke out at many points, and my attention was focused upon various places where there were disturbances. There was not a single one of these disturbances reported and personally investigated on which a contradictory report was not presented to me either by the plaintiff or by the prefecture of police.

Often I recognized that a striker was right; sometimes the policemen were punished. . . .

M. Révelin, . . . in *Humanité,* reproached us for having governed France as Russia was governed before the Duma. . . . And to crown all, the same M. Révelin as a supreme insult reproached us for being prejudiced in favor of order.

This prejudice I have. Here is a point of conflict on which it is possible to reason. I fear no idea, I retreat before no proposition, if it is open to reason; but I say that (especially if you who interrupt us have conceived the ambitious projects which you revealed the other day) you have no less need for order than ourselves, for nothing may take place in any society if legal order is not maintained. [Lively applause from a great number of benches.]

I believe that I have demonstrated the inanity of the reproaches which were addressed to me by the Honorable M. Jaurès concerning the acts of my administration with respect to the strikes. . . .

It remains for me to show the contradiction of ideas which has dictated our evaluations of the two sides.

First of all, concerning the strikes themselves, I find myself in opposition to the Honorable M. Jaurès on a fundamental point.

I am of the opinion that any man who needs to work and who finds work has the right to work. [Applause from the Left, Center, and Right.] I am of the opinion that society and the public authority have the duty of assuring him the exercise of this right.

Eighteen months or two years ago I had a discussion on this point in the press with M. Jaurès, and this is how I know the singular opinion which he holds. M. Jaurès denies this right without any ambiguity. He wrote: "I admit that I am stupified when suddenly M. Clemenceau invokes the supposed right of workers to replace other workers on strike as a form of the right of livelihood."

And continuing his demonstration, my adversary observes that while I seek to assure the worker's right to a living, I put obstacles in the way of the strikers' exercise of the right to a living. That is certainly your argument, my dear colleague.

I take the liberty of answering that the comparison is not an exact one. First of all, I do not pretend to suppress vital competition with universal laws. I believe that vital competition is a phenomenon which should be regulated by social laws. I believe that as much as possible we should attempt to correct through law the fundamental evil in nature, but I believe at the same time that this is possible only if we establish our social organization on the only solid basis, the inalienable rights of all men.

The situation between the two competitors is not equal. It is inexact to say that both fight for the right to livelihood. The worker who demands work, who seeks it and finds it, fights for a living, to assure his own life and that of his family. But we cannot say that the worker who abandons his position for a higher wage fights for his life. . . .

If you refuse the right of the employers to replace the workers on strike and the right of the free workers to present themselves for hire, as M. Jaurès clearly did in his thesis, what will you do with the women and children whom you will deprive of nourishment? That is the question which is asked; I await the answer and well believe that I shall wait for it a long time. [Laughter and applause from the Left and the Center.]

It is unnecessary to say that in his answer the Honorable M. Jaurès has explained to me that this conflict will not exist in his future society; he has indicated to me in broad outline, as he usually does, under what conditions the conflict may be alleviated. I do not disagree, but as we still need six months to know the conditions of the future city, I demand that I be told today how to resolve the conflict which confronts me in the present social plight.

I have naturally tried to inform myself about this matter through the election programs of the Socialist party. I have here a great number of manifestos — all very interesting, incidentally, some demanding reforms which I would be prepared to adopt for my own — but I addressed myself especially to the program of the Socialist party. The Socialist party published a program for the use of all its candidates, as is perfectly natural. . . .

Here is what I find in the manifesto. First of all, a statement of doctrine: "The only way of freeing yourselves is to substitute collective property for capitalistic property." The consequences of this affirmation are not reasoned out; the means of bringing this substitution about are not proposed. But at least the affirmation of the principle is contained in the declaration.

What reforms are to result from this affirmation of principle?

Here they are:

Limitation of the working day to eight hours.

Extension of the right to organize to all the employees of the state, the department, and the commune.

Social insurance against all the risks of unemployment and sickness.

Progressive tax on income and inheritance.

Return to the nation of the monopolies which capital has made its greatest fortresses.

Voting by list with proportional representation.

This is very bourgeois. [Laughter and applause from the Left and the Center. Noise from the extreme Left.] And when, after explaining his program, M. Jaurès asked me what mine is, I had some difficulty resisting the temptation to answer: "You know my program very well — it is in your pocket, you have taken it from me."

M. Jaurès: Very good. We take note of it.

M. Clemenceau: What! Really! You take note of the fact that I support the eight-hour day in principle!

From the Extreme Left: In principle.

M. Clemenceau: Naturally in principle. I do not believe that any among you can run the risk of economic catastrophe by suddenly replacing the eleven-hour day with the eight-hour day. As for myself, I would not be ready for it now, but I am ready to orient myself as soon as possible and even immediately toward this final result, the eight-hour day. . . .

It was not only the Catholic Pope who was vanquished at the last elections; it was the spirit of oppression, the spirit of dogmatism, in all walks of life. The dogmatic spirit was driven from the purely intellectual domain, and it is not we who will seek to reestablish it in the economic dogma. . . .

Even in your party, men are found who have my point of view; one of those here, M. Varenne, an integral Socialist, I believe, has recently written in the *Lanterne* an article from which I take the following passage: "As to the social transformation which doubtless is the long-range" — he does not ask for six months — "but unchanging aim in our platform, it is not enough to announce it and to erect the image in the foreground like a kind of scarecrow. The essential thing is to prepare for it by education and organization."

That is the whole program of the Radical party.

My answer is: "If this education comes in its own time when the proletariat is enlightened and disciplined enough . . ." — that is what I said myself when I said that it was not enlightened or disciplined enough at the present time to find a place in the organization which you have conceived — "when the proletariat is enlightened and disciplined enough to assume the responsibility for directing production, the transformation, matured by long evolution, will take place without violence and almost without effort. Political democracy will develop freely into social democracy. By universal suffrage, which consecrates the political sovereignty of the citizens, the workers will have conquered economic sovereignty."

I have, incidentally, another authority to cite which is no less important. It is perhaps yet more important than yours; it is from a man whom you know well, M. Edouard Bernstein.

M. Bernstein, in a book entitled *Socialism théorique et la social démocratie pratique,* has written the following:

What social democracy will have to do for a long time yet instead of speculating on the great catastrophe of Karl Marx, the revolution, is to organize politically and prepare the working class for democracy. It must fight for all the reforms in the state suitable for raising the working class and for transforming the institution of the state in a democratic sense. . . .

["Very good! Very good!" from the extreme Left.]

There is nothing there which is not simply a statement of the republican doctrine.

And as I am absolutely convinced that it is impossible to skip the periods important in the evolution of peoples, I attach the greatest significance to the present duty of social democracy, to the struggle for the political rights of the workers, to the political activity of the workers in the interest of their class, as well as to the work of their economic organization. It is in this sense that I once wrote that for me the movement is everything and that what we usually call the final aim of socialism is nothing.

Here we are in full agreement. The final aim of socialism is nothing, and the movement in the direction of social justice is everything. It is one of your own who said it. It is the program of the Radical party, and I believe that I may say that it is even the program of the Government.

We do not need you to recall our program to us; we do not need you to ask us whether we mean to apply it. Our only reason for being on these benches is action, action which dispels uncertainty, which does away with weakness, which rules and disciplines the will of the strong.

By action we have overcome the oppression of the Church. By action we shall suppress the economic oppression of existing privileges. We have delivered the soul, and we shall deliver the body. . . .

If you are willing to work with us, here is our hand outstretched to you and your electors.

If not, let each follow his own destiny. Without you we shall try to be adequate to the task. We shall bravely carry the day's responsibilities, and for the rest we place ourselves before the enlightened impartiality of the Chamber and the republican country. [Lively and prolonged applause from a great number of benches on the Left and in the Center.]

Evolutionary Socialism

Clemenceau's reference to Éduard Bernstein (1850–1932) reveals the influence that Bernstein's revisionist doctrine was having throughout Europe. Although Bernstein was condemned by his own German Social Democratic party, his theory was much closer to the reality of German socialist politics than the party's leadership cared to admit. Socialists were cooperating in bourgeois governments in southern Germany, and the trade unions were pursuing reform rather than violent revolution. In Bernstein's essay of 1899, "The Preconditions of Socialism and the Tasks of Social Democracy," he attempted to explain why reformism was winning. Contrary to expectations, the anticipated great crisis of capitalism with its immiserization of the workers and polarization of classes failed to materialize. Instead, the condition of the workers was visibly improving, and they had demonstrated that the increasing democratization of political life could serve their advantage. For Bernstein, however, this did not mean that they should surrender the goal of socialism. In his view, socialism had supreme ethical value because it would secure the quality and justice of human existence in industrial society. It was, therefore, the ultimate goal to be attained, not by revolution, but by political and social action. Bernstein set down some of the basic themes of his work in a letter to the Social Democratic party meeting at Stuttgart in 1898. Portions of this statement follow.

Bernstein's Revisionism

It has been maintained in a certain quarter that the practical deductions from my treatises would be the abandonment of the conquest of political power by the proletariat organised politically and economically. That is quite an arbitrary deduction, the accuracy of which I altogether deny.

I set myself against the notion that we have to expect shortly a collapse of the bourgeois economy, and that social democracy should be induced by the prospect of such an imminent, great, social catastrophe to adapt its tactics to that assumption. That I maintain most emphatically.

The adherents of this theory of a catastrophe; base it especially on the conclusions of the *Communist Manifesto*. This is a mistake in every respect.

The theory which the *Communist Manifesto* sets forth of the evolution of modern society was correct as far as it characterised the general tendencies of that evolution. But it was mistaken in several special deductions, above all in the estimate of the *time* the evolution would take. The last has been unreservedly acknowledged by Friedrich Engels, the joint author with Marx of the *Manifesto,* in his preface to the *Class War in France.* But it is evident that if social evolution takes a much greater period of time than was assumed, it must also take upon itself *forms* and lead to forms that were not foreseen and could not be foreseen then.

Social conditions have not developed to such an acute opposition of things and classes as is depicted in the *Manifesto*. It is not only useless, it is the greatest folly to attempt to conceal this from ourselves. The number of members of the possessing classes is to-day not smaller but larger. The enormous increase of social wealth is not accompanied by a decreasing number of large capitalists but by an increasing number of capitalists of all degrees. The middle classes change their character but they do not disappear from the social scale.

The concentration in productive industry is not being accomplished even to-day in all its departments with equal thoroughness and at an equal rate. In a great many branches of production it certainly justifies the forecasts of the socialist critic of society; but in other branches it lags even to-day behind them. The process of concentration in agriculture proceeds still more slowly. Trade statistics show an extraordinarily elaborated graduation of enterprises in regard to size. No rung of the ladder is disappearing from it. The significant changes in the inner structure of these enterprises and their inter-relationship cannot do away with this fact.

Éduard Bernstein, *Evolutionary Socialism: A Criticism and Affirmation,* trans. Edith C. Harvey (New York: Huebsch, 1909), pp. x–xvi.

In all advanced countries we see the privileges of the capitalist bourgeoisie yielding step by step to democratic organisations. Under the influence of this, and driven by the movement of the working classes which is daily becoming stronger, a social reaction has set in against the exploiting tendencies of capital, a counteraction which, although it still proceeds timidly and feebly, yet does exist, and is always drawing more departments of economic life under its influence. Factory legislation, the democratising of local government, and the extension of its area of work; the freeing of trade unions and systems of co-operative trading from legal restrictions, the consideration of standard conditions of labour in the work undertaken by public authorities — all these characterise this phase of the evolution.

But the more the political organisations of modern nations are democratised the more the needs and opportunities of great political catastrophes are diminished. He who holds firmly to the catastrophic theory of evolution must, with all his power, withstand and hinder the evolution described above, which, indeed, the logical defenders of that theory formerly did. But is the conquest of political power by the proletariat simply to be by a political catastrophe? Is it to be the appropriation and utilisation of the power of the State by the proletariat exclusively against the whole nonproletarian world?

He who replies in the affirmative must be reminded of two things. In 1872 Marx and Engels announced in the preface to the new edition of the *Communist Manifesto* that the Paris Commune had exhibited a proof that "the working classes cannot simply take possession of the ready-made State machine and set it in motion for their own aims." And in 1895 Friedrich Engels stated in detail in the preface to *War of the Classes* that the time of political surprises, of the "revolutions of small conscious minorities at the head of unconscious masses" was to-day at an end, that a collision on a large scale with the military would be the means of checking the steady growth of social democracy and of even throwing it back for a time — in short, that social democracy would flourish far better by lawful than by unlawful means and by violent revolution. And he points out in conformity with this opinion that the next task of the party should be "to work for an uninterrupted increase of its votes" or to carry on a slow *propaganda of parliamentary activity*.

Thus Engels, who, nevertheless, as his numerical examples show, still somewhat overestimated the rate of process of the evolution! Shall we be told that he abandoned the conquest of political power by the working classes, because he wished to avoid the steady growth of social democracy secured by lawful means being interrupted by a political revolution?

If not, and if one subscribes to his conclusions, one cannot reasonably take any offence if it is declared that for a long time yet the task of social democracy is, instead of speculating on a great economic crash, "to organise the working classes politically and develop them as a democracy and to fight for all reforms in the State which are adapted to raise the working classes and transform the State in the direction of democracy."

That is what I have said in my impugned article and what I still maintain in its full import. As far as concerns the question propounded above it is equivalent to Engels' dictum, for democracy is, at any given time, as much government by the working classes as these are capable of practising according to their intellectual ripeness and the degree of social development they have attained. Engels, indeed, refers at the place just mentioned to the fact that the *Communist Manifesto* has "proclaimed the conquest of the democracy as one of the first and important tasks of the fighting proletariat."

In short, Engels is so thoroughly convinced that the tactics based on the presumption of a catastrophe have had their day, that he even considers a revision of them necessary in the Latin countries where tradition is much more favourable to them than in Germany. "If the conditions of war between nations have altered," he writes, "no less have those for the war between classes." Has this already been forgotten?

No one has questioned the necessity for the working classes to gain the control of government. The point at issue is between the theory of a social cataclysm and the question whether with the given social development in Germany and the present advanced state of its working classes in the towns and the country, a sudden catastrophe would be desirable in the interest of the social democracy. I have denied it and deny it again, because in my judgment a greater security for lasting success lies in a steady advance than in the possibilities offered by a catastrophic crash.

And as I am firmly convinced that important periods in the develop ment of nations cannot be leapt over I lay the greatest value on the next tasks of social democracy, on the struggle for the political rights of the working man, on the political activity of working men in town and country for the interests of their class, as well as on the work of the industrial organisation of the workers.

In this sense I wrote the sentence that the movement means everything for me and that what is *usually* called "the final aim of socialism" is nothing; and in this sense I write it down again to-day. Even if the word "usually" had not shown that the proposition was only to be understood conditionally, it was obvious that it *could* not express indifference concerning the final carrying out of socialist principles, but only indifference — or, as it would be better expressed, carelessness — as to the form of the final arrangement of things. I have at no time had an excessive interest in the future, beyond general principles; I have not been able to read to the end any picture of the future. My thoughts and efforts are concerned with the duties of the present and the nearest future, and I only busy myself with the perspectives beyond so far as they give me a line of conduct for suitable action now.

The conquest of political power by the working classes, the expropriation of capitalists, are no ends in themselves but only means for the accomplishment of certain aims and endeavours. As such they are demands in the programme of social democracy and are not attacked by me. Nothing can be said beforehand as to the circumstances of their accomplishment; we can only fight for their realisation. But the conquest of political power necessitates the possession of political *rights;* and the most important problem of tactics which German social democracy has at the present time to solve, appears to me to be to devise the best ways for the extension of the political and economic rights of the German working classes.

THREE ARCHAIC EMPIRES
Chapter 9

World War I proved that the Russian, Austro-Hungarian, and Ottoman empires were too archaic to withstand the ultimate test of a state, a major war. Although Germany collapsed also, it did not disintegrate, and considerable continuity remained between prewar and postwar Germany. The same cannot be said for the other three empires. The disintegration of the Ottoman Empire began well before the war. Austria-Hungary had always suffered from chronic instability, and the Central Powers went to war in 1914 to save it from complete disintegration. The Russian Empire, though possibly the best candidate of the three for survival, was racked by revolutionary movements and political discontent throughout the last half of the nineteenth century.

Russia's dilemma was that although the nation's status as a great power with imperialist ambitions required modernization and reform, the maintenance of the autocracy made a consistently progressive policy utterly impossible. Thus it was no accident that the most important bursts of reform in Russia came almost immediately after military defeat. After the loss of the Crimean War, Alexander II (1855–1881) abandoned his father's reactionary policies and undertook fundamental reforms. He emancipated the peasants in 1861, created a measure of local self-government with the Zemstvo Law of 1864, and undertook military and judicial reforms. His reforms were only partial, however, and Russia's problems became more complicated. Intead of creating a truly free landowning peasantry, emancipation left the peasants with little or no land and tied them to the village commune (*mir*). Bureaucratic control from St. Petersburg made a mockery of much local initiative. Most important, radical activity quickly led the tsar to abandon reform, and his assassination by revolutionaries in 1881 was followed by the reactionary rules of Alexander III (1881–1894) and Nicholas II (1894–1917).

This is not to say that there was no modernization in Russia under these rulers. After 1890, Russian industrialization made great strides, but it also added new problems to the old. Industry and a working class concentrated in large cities developed rapidly, but the government did little to prevent the alienation of the workers. Indeed, where previously the revolutionaries had been either populists who sought to preserve the agrarian character of Russia and win over the peasantry by "going to the people" in the countryside, or nihilists who threatened to eliminate the existing order by assassination and terrorism, now they were often Marxists. Russia's defeat in the Russo-Japanese War of 1905 led to a revolution by soldiers, workers, and peasants that was a rehearsal for 1917. Nicholas II tried to pacify the discontent with his October Manifesto, making Russia a constitutional monarchy, but he demonstrated his bad faith as soon as the opportunity arose, and the gap between state and society widened. Russian liberalism remained embryonic, and the potential of the revolutionary forces was only heightened by increasing industrialization within an autocratic context.

The problems of Austria-Hungary were largely dictated by its attempt to maintain a multinational empire on an inadequate foundation in an age of nationalism. The expulsion of Austria from Germany in 1866 threatened the Hapsburg Empire with disintegration unless it pacified the Hungarians, the most powerful of its non-German nationalities. The *Ausgleich,* or Compromise of 1867, an arrangement between the two dominant nationalities, often worked at the expense of the others. Throughout its history, the Hungarian portion of the Dual Monarchy was ruled by an oligarchic clique of Magyar landowners who oppressed the lower classes, especially the Slavs. A variety of methods of rule were used in the Austrian half of the monarchy. Until 1879, the Germans dominated political life, much to the chagrin of the other nationalities, especially the Czechs. Then, under Count Taafe, the government bureaucracy tried to rule in collaboration with the other nationalities against the German liberals. Taafe fell in 1893, and with him went the regime's relative stability. Nationalist agitation by both Slavs and Germans and the rise of the powerful Social Democratic party made political life chaotic. The introduction of universal suffrage in 1907 did not solve the problem. At the same time, the rapid disintegration of the Ottoman Empire and the increasing Pan-Slavic agitation centered in Serbia and encouraged by Russia on the Dual Monarchy's southern borders created an insoluble dilemma. If the Dual Monarchy incorporated new Slavic populations, then its nationalities would exacerbate its problem unless it discovered some more equitable foundation — a trialistic solution — for the monarchy. This solution, however, would alienate Hungary. If the Dual Monarchy stood by and did nothing, then the stability of the monarchy would continue to be undermined anyway, and Austrian ambitions in the

Balkans would go unrealized. It is thus comprehensible that the occupation of Bosnia-Herzegovina in 1878 and its annexation in 1908 led to the Dual Monarchy's greatest crisis and ultimate dissolution.

The Ottoman Empire was more archaic than Russia and more disturbed by nationality problems than Austria-Hungary. Internal reform efforts did not save it from either Russian aggression or the total loss of its European possessions by 1913. Its survival was due largely to the mutual suspicions of the great powers, who found it difficult to agree on the terms of partition, but who were willing to invest in the empire and train its armed forces in order to exploit its resources and establish a foothold in the event of its collapse. The Young Turk Revolution of 1908, which led to the granting of a constitution, only accelerated the rebellion of the European portions of the empire. The reformers, however, helped build some of the foundations of modern Turkey.

Russia: Emancipation, Reaction, and Revolutionary Terrorism

When the edict of March 3, 1861, emancipated the serfs, few serious defenders of serfdom remained in Russia. The social and economic foundations of serfdom had deteriorated. Serf labor was economically inefficient, and the development of a money economy and new agricultural methods was eroding the traditional relationships between landlords and serfs. Indeed, even the secret police criticized serfdom because rebellions and escapes created serious police problems, and the army had discovered that serfs made poor soldiers in the Crimean War. Last, great moral revulsion against serfdom was felt among educated Russians. Although the emancipation was not the total surrender to landowner interests that modern Soviet historians argue, it was not a satisfactory solution to the agrarian problem either. The emancipation of the Russian peasant with land was a progressive approach that required sacrifices on the part of the gentry, but the system of redemption payments to the state proved unworkable over the long run and had to be abolished in 1905. More important, the perpetuation of the commune and the continued restrictions on the legal status and rights of the peasantry encouraged the perpetuation of an anachronistic agricultural system. Ultimately, the emancipation served the cause of Russian industrialization because it was a necessary precondition for the creation of a labor force.

As Alexander II moved in the direction of actual constitutional reform, resistance grew in conservative Russian circles. Their chief and most influential representative was Konstantin Petrovich Pobedonostsev (1827–1907), who served as procurator of the Holy Synod (lay head of the Orthodox Church) from 1880 to 1905 and was chief adviser to Alexander III and Nicholas II. A pious reactionary who was nevertheless well read in the literature of the West, Pobedonostsev considered constitutional and parliamentary government a fraud. He presented his views in his Reflections. *Alexander II, however, nearly surrendered to his proconstitutionalist adviser Count Michael Loris-Melikov and had actually signed a proposal creating a consultative elective body on the day of his assassination, March 13, 1881. His assassins, members of the "Will of the People" group, believed that Russia's centralization meant that the assassination of the tsar was the most effective means of forcing change. If their explanation to Alexander III had any effect, it was strictly negative.*

The Emancipation Edict, 1863

We, Alexander II, by the grace of God Tsar and Autocrat of all the Russias, King of Poland, Grand Duke of Finland, etc., make known to all our faithful subjects:

Summoned to the throne of our ancestors by Divine Providence and the sacred law of heredity, we have promised ourselves with heartfelt sincerity to extend our affection and imperial solicitude to all our faithful subjects, whatever their rank or condition, from the soldier who nobly bears arms in the defense of his country to the humble artisan who faithfully carries on his industry; from the functionary who occupies a high office in the State to the laborer whose plow furrows the fields.

As we consider the various classes of which the State is composed, we are convinced that the laws of our empire which have wisely provided for the upper and middle classes, and have fixed with precision their rights and obligations, have not reached the same degree of success in relation to the peasants bound to the soil, who, either through ancient laws or custom, have been hereditarily subjected to the authority of the landlords. Indeed, the rights of landowners over their serfs have hitherto been very extensive and very imperfectly defined by the laws, which have been supplemented by tradition, custom, and the good will of the landlords.

From *Readings in Modern European History,* vol. 2, ed. James Harvey Robinson and Charles A. Beard (Boston: Ginn, 1909), pp. 348–52.

This system has at best established patriarchal relations based upon the fairness and benevolence of the landowners and an affectionate docility on the part of the peasants; but as manners have lost their simplicity, the paternal ties between the landlords and the peasants have been weakened. Furthermore, as the seigniorial authority falls into the hands of those exclusively intent on their own selfish advantage, those relations of mutual good will have tended to give way and open the door to arbitrariness, burdensome to the peasants and hostile to their prosperity. This has served to develop in them an indifference to all progress.

These facts did not fail to impress our predecessors of glorious memory, and they took measures to improve the lot of the peasants; but these measures have had little effect, since they were either dependent for their execution on the individual initiative of such landlords as might be animated by a liberal spirit or were merely local in their scope, or adopted as an experiment.

We became convinced, therefore, that the work of fundamentally ameliorating the condition of the peasant was for us a sacred heritage from our ancestors, a mission which in the course of events Divine Providence had called us to fulfill. We have commenced this work by demonstrating our imperial confidence in the nobility of Russia, who have given us so many proofs of their devotion and their constant disposition to make sacrifices for the well-being of the country. It was to the nobility themselves that, in conformity to their own wishes, we reserved the right of formulating the provisions for the organization of the peasants — provisions which involve the necessity of limiting their own rights over the peasants, and of accepting the responsibilities of a reform which could only be accomplished with some material losses to them. Our confidence has not been deceived. We have found the nobility, united in committees in the various governments, ready to make, through agents who enjoyed their confidence, the voluntary sacrifices of their rights so far as the personal servitude of the peasants is concerned.

The propositions of the local committees of the nobility — which varied greatly, as might be expected from the nature of the problem — have been collated, compared, and reduced to a regular system, then adjusted and supplemented by a higher committee appointed for the purpose. The new provisions thus formulated relative to the peasants and the domestic serfs of the landholders have been submitted to the Council of the Empire. After having invoked divine assistance we have resolved to carry out the work according to the regulations thus drawn up.

The peasants now bound to the soil shall, within the term fixed by the law, be vested with the full rights of freemen. The landed proprietors, while they shall retain all the rights of ownership over all the lands now belonging to them, shall transfer to the peasants, in return for a rent

peasant pay rent

fixed by law, the full enjoyment of their cottages, farm buildings, and gardens. Furthermore, in order to assure to the peasants their subsistence and enable them to meet their obligations toward the State, the landlords shall turn over to the peasants a quantity of arable and other land provided for in the regulations above mentioned. In return for these allotments the peasant families shall be required to pay rent to the landlords, as fixed by the provisions of the law. Under these conditions, which are temporary, the peasants shall be designated as "temporarily bound."

At the same time the peasants are granted the right of purchasing their cottages and gardens, and, with the consent of the landlords, they may acquire in complete ownership the arable lands and other lands allotted to them as a permanent holding. By the acquisition of a complete title to the land assigned them, the peasants [1] shall be freed from their obligations toward the landlords for land thus purchased, and thus enter definitively into the class of free peasants and landowners.

Since the new organization, owing to the unavoidable complexity of the changes which it involves, cannot immediately be put into execution, a lapse of time is necessary, which cannot be less than two years or thereabouts; to avoid all misunderstanding and to protect public and private interests during this interval, the system actually existing on the estates of landowners will be maintained up to the moment when the new system shall have been instituted by the completion of the required preparatory measures.

Aware of all the difficulties of the reform we have undertaken, we place our trust in the goodness of Divine Providence, who watches over the destinies of Russia. We also count upon the generous devotion of our faithful nobility, and we are happy to testify to that body the gratitude it has deserved from us, as well as from the country, for the disinterested support it has given to the accomplishment of our designs. Russia will not forget that the nobility, actuated solely by its respect for the dignity of man and its love for its neighbor, has spontaneously renounced the rights it enjoyed in virtue of the system of serfdom now abolished, and has laid the foundation of a new future for the peasants. We also entertain the firm hope that it will also direct its further efforts to carry out the new regulation by maintaining good order, in a spirit of peace and benevolence.

In order to render the transactions between the landlords and the peasants easier, so that the latter may acquire in full proprietorship their houses and the adjacent lands and buildings, the government will grant them assistance, according to a special regulation, through loans of money or a transfer of mortgages encumbering an estate.

gov't will assist peasants

1 This does not mean the *individual* peasants, but the village community, which was perpetuated under the new law.

When the first rumors of this great reform contemplated by the government spread among the country people who were scarcely prepared for it, it gave rise in some instances to misunderstandings among individuals more intent upon liberty than mindful of the duties which liberty imposes. But generally the good sense of the country has asserted itself. It has been understood that the landlords would not be deprived of rights legally acquired, except for a fit and sufficient indemnity, or by a voluntary concession on their part; that it would be contrary to all equity for the peasants to accept the enjoyment of the lands conceded by the landlords without at the same time accepting equivalent charges.

And now we confidently hope that the freed serfs, in the presence of the new future which is opened before them, will appreciate and recognize the considerable sacrifices which the nobility has made on their behalf. They will understand that the blessing of an existence based upon full ownership of their property, as well as the greater liberty in the administration of their possessions, entails upon them, with new duties towards society and themselves, the obligation of justifying the new laws by a loyal and judicious use of the rights which are now accorded them. For if men do not themselves endeavor to insure their own well-being under the aegis of laws, the best of those laws cannot guarantee it to them. Only by assiduous labor, a rational expenditure of their strength and resources, a strict economy, and, above all, by an upright life — a life constantly inspired by the fear of the Lord — can they hope for prosperity and progress.

And now, my orthodox and faithful people, make the holy sign of the cross and join thy prayers to ours, invoking the blessing of the Most High upon thy first free labors, for this alone is a sure pledge of private well-being and the public weal.

Given at St. Petersburg, the nineteenth day of February [March 3, new style], of the year of grace 1861 and the seventh of our reign.

Alexander

Pobedonostsev: "The Great Falsehood of Our Time"

That which is founded on falsehood cannot be right. Institutions founded on false principles cannot be other than false themselves. This truth has been demonstrated by the bitter experience of ages and generations.

From Konstantin P. Pobedonostsev, *Reflections of a Russian Statesman*, trans. Robert Crozier Long (Ann Arbor: University of Michigan Press, 1965), pp. 32–34, 43–44. Copyright by Grant Richards 1898. Reprinted by permission of The University of Michigan Press.

Among the falsest of political principles is the principle of the sovereignty of the people, the principle that all power issues from the people, and is based upon the national will — a principle which has unhappily become more firmly established since the time of the French Revolution. Thence proceeds the theory of Parliamentarism, which, up to the present day, has deluded much of the so-called "intelligence" and unhappily infatuated certain foolish Russians. It continues to maintain its hold on many minds with the obstinacy of a narrow fanaticism, although every day its falsehood is exposed more clearly to the world.

In what does the theory of Parliamentarism consist? It is supposed that the people in its assemblies makes its own laws, and elects responsible officers to execute its will. Such is the ideal conception. Its immediate realisation is impossible. The historical development of society necessitates that local communities increase in numbers and complexity; that separate races be assimilated, or, retaining their polities and languages, unite under a single flag, that territory extend indefinitely: under such conditions direct government by the people is impracticable. The people must, therefore, delegate its right of power to its representatives, and invest them with administrative autonomy. These representatives in turn cannot govern immediately, but are compelled to elect a still smaller number of trustworthy persons — ministers — to whom they entrust the preparation and execution of the laws, the apportionment and collection of taxes, the appointment of subordinate officials, and the disposition of the militant forces.

In the abstract this mechanism is quite symmetrical: for its proper operation many conditions are essential. The working of the political machine is based on impersonal forces constantly acting and completely balanced. It may act successfully only when the delegates of the people abdicate their personalities; when on the benches of Parliament sit mechanical fulfillers of the people's behests; when the ministers of State remain impersonal, absolute executors of the will of the majority; when the elected representatives of the people are capable of understanding precisely, and executing conscientiously, the programme of activity, mathematically expressed, which has been delivered to them. Given such conditions the machine would work exactly, and would accomplish its purpose. The law would actually embody the will of the people; administrative measures would actually emanate from Parliament; the pillars of the State would rest actually on the elective assemblies, and each citizen would directly and consciously participate in the management of public affairs.

Such is the theory. Let us look at the practice. Even in the classic countries of Parliamentarism it would satisfy not one of the conditions enumerated. The elections in no way express the will of the electors. The popular representatives are in no way restricted by the opinions of their constituents, but are guided by their own views and considerations, modified by the tactics of their opponents. In reality, ministers are autocratic, and they rule, rather than are ruled by, Parliament. They attain power, and lose power, not by virtue of the will of the people, but through immense personal influence, or the influence of a strong party which places them in power, or drives them from it. They dispose of the force and resources of the nation at will, they grant immunities and favours, they maintain a multitude of idlers at the expense of the people, and they fear no censure while they enjoy the support in Parliament of a majority which they maintain by the distribution of bounties from the rich tables which the State has put at their disposal. In reality, the ministers are as irresponsible as the representatives of the people. Mistakes, abuse of power, and arbitrary acts, are of daily occurrence, yet how often do we hear of the grave responsibility of a minister? It may be once in fifty years a minister is tried for his crimes, with a result contemptible when compared with the celebrity gained by the solemn procedure. . . .

Such is the complicated mechanism of the Parliamentary farce; such is the great political lie which dominates our age. By the theory of Parliamentarism, the rational majority must rule; in practice, the party is ruled by five or six of its leaders who exercise all power. In theory, decisions are controlled by clear arguments in the course of Parliamentary debates; in practice, they in no wise depend from debates, but are determined by the wills of the leaders and the promptings of personal interest. In theory, the representatives of the people consider only the public welfare; in practice, their first consideration is their own advancement, and the interests of their friends. In theory, they must be the best citizens; in practice, they are the most ambitious and impudent. In theory, the elector gives his vote for his candidate because he knows him and trust him; in practice, the elector gives his vote for a man whom he seldom knows, but who has been forced on him by the speeches of an interested party. In theory, Parliamentary business is directed by experience, good sense, and unselfishness; in practice, the chief motive powers are a firm will, egoism, and eloquence.

Such is the Parliamentary institution, exalted as the summit and crown of the edifice of State. It is sad to think that even in Russia there are men who aspire to the establishment of this falsehood among us; that our professors glorify to their young pupils representative government as the ideal of political science; that our newspapers pursue it in their articles and feuilletons, under the name of justice and order, without troubling to examine without prejudice the working of the parliamentary machine. Yet even where centuries have sanctified its existence, faith already decays; the Liberal intelligence exalts it, but the people groans under its despotism, and recognises its falsehood. We may not see, but our children and grandchildren assuredly will see, the overthrow of this idol, which contemporary thought in its vanity continues still to worship.

The Executive Committee of "Will of the People" to Alexander III, March 10, 1881

Your Majesty:

Although the Executive Committee understands fully the grief that you must experience at this moment, it believes that it has no right to yield to the feeling of natural delicacy which would perhaps dictate the postponement of the following explanation to another time. There is something higher than the most legitimate human feeling, and that is, duty to one's country — the duty for which a citizen must sacrifice himself and his own feelings, and even the feelings of others. In obedience to this all-powerful duty we have decided to address you at once, waiting for nothing, as will wait for nothing the historical process that threatens us with rivers of blood and the most terrible convulsions. . . .

You are aware, your Majesty, that the government of the late Tsar could not be reproached with a lack of energy. It hanged the innocent and the guilty, and filled prisons and remote provinces with exiles. Scores of so-called "leaders" were captured and hanged, and died with the courage and tranquillity of martyrs; but the movement did not cease — on the contrary it grew and strengthened. The revolutionary movement, your Majesty, is not dependent upon any particular individuals; it is a process of the social organism; and the scaffolds raised for its more energetic exponents are as powerless to save the outgrown order of things as the cross that was erected for the Redeemer was powerless to save the ancient world from the triumph of Christianity. The government, of course, may yet capture and hang an immense number of separate individuals, it may break up a great number of separate revolutionary groups; but all this will not change, in the slightest degree, the condition of affairs. . . .

A dispassionate glance at the grievous decade through which we have just passed will enable us to forecast accurately the future progress of the revolutionary movement, provided the policy of the government does not change. The movement will continue to grow and extend; deeds of a terroristic nature will increase in frequency and intensity. Meanwhile the number of the discontented in the country will grow larger and larger; confidence in the government, on the part of the people, will decline; and the idea of revolution — of its possibility and inevitability — will establish itself in Russia more and more firmly. A terrible explosion, a bloody chaos, a revolutionary earthquake throughout Russia, will complete the destruction of the old order of things. Do not mistake this for a mere phrase. We understand better than any one else can how lamentable is the waste of so much talent and energy — the loss, in bloody skirmishes and in the work of destruction, of so much strength which, under other

From *Readings in Modern European History*, vol. 2, ed. James Harvey Robinson and Charles Beard (Boston: Ginn, 1909), pp. 364–67.

conditions, might have been expended in creative labor and in the development of the intelligence, the welfare, and the civil life of the Russian people. Whence proceeds this lamentable necessity for bloody conflict?

It arises, your Majesty, from the lack in Russia of a real government in the true sense of that word. A government, in the very nature of things, should only give outward form to the aspirations of the people and effect to the people's will. But with us — excuse the expression — the government has degenerated into a mere coterie, and deserves the name of a usurping "gang" much more than does the Executive Committee.

Whatever may be the *intentions* of the Tsar, the *actions* of the government have nothing in common with the popular welfare or popular aspirations. The government has brought Russia to such a pass that, at the present time, the masses of the people are in a state of pauperism and ruin; are subjected to the most humiliating surveillance, even at their own domestic hearths; and are powerless even to regulate their own communal and social affairs. The protection of the law and of the government is enjoyed only by the extortionist and the exploiter, and the most exasperating robbery goes unpunished. But, on the other hand, what a terrible fate awaits the man who sincerely considers the general good! You know very well, your Majesty, that it is not only socialists who are exiled and prosecuted.

These are the reasons why the Russian government exerts no moral influence and has no support among the people. These are the reasons why Russia brings forth so many revolutionists. These are the reasons why even such a deed as killing a Tsar excites in the minds of a majority of the people only gladness and sympathy. Yes, your Majesty! Do not be deceived by the reports of flatterers and sycophants; Tsaricide is popular in Russia.

From such a state of affairs there can be only two modes of escape: either a revolution — absolutely inevitable and not to be averted by any punishments; or a voluntary turning of the supreme power to the people. In the interest of our native land, in the hope of preventing the useless waste of energy, in the hope of averting the terrible miseries that always accompany revolution, the Executive Committee approaches your Majesty with the advice to take the second course. Be assured, so soon as the supreme power ceases to rule arbitrarily, so soon as it firmly resolves to accede to the demands of the people's conscience and consciousness, you may, without fear, discharge the spies that disgrace the administration, send your guards back to their barracks, and burn the scaffolds that are demoralizing the people. The Executive Committee will voluntarily terminate its own existence, and the organizations formed about it will disperse, in order that their members may devote themselves to the work of promoting culture among the people of their native land.

We address your Majesty as those who have discarded all prejudices, and who have suppressed the distrust of you created by the actions of the government throughout a century. We forget that you are the representative of the authority that has so often deceived and that has so injured the people. We address you as a citizen and as an honest man. We hope that the feeling of personal exasperation will not extinguish in your mind your consciousness of your duties and your desire to know the truth. *We* also might feel exasperation. You have lost your father. We have lost not only our fathers, but our brothers, our wives, our children, and our dearest friends. We are nevertheless ready to suppress personal feeling if it be demanded by the welfare of Russia. We expect the same from you.

We set no conditions for you; do not let our proposition irritate you. The conditions that are prerequisite to a change from revolutionary activity to peaceful labor are created, not by us, but by history. These conditions are, in our opinion, two.

1. A general amnesty to cover all past political crimes; for the reason that they were not crimes but fulfillments of civil duty.

2. The summoning of representatives of the whole Russian people to examine the existing framework of social and governmental life, and to remodel it in accordance with the people's wishes.

We regard it as necessary, however, to remind you that the legalization of the supreme power, by the representatives of the people, can be valid only in case the elections are perfectly free. We declare solemnly, before the people of our native land and before the whole world, that our party will submit unconditionally to the decisions of a National Assembly elected in the manner above indicated, and that we will not allow ourselves, in future, to offer violent resistance to any government that the National Assembly may sanction.

And now, your Majesty, decide! Before you are two courses, and you are to make your choice between them. We can only trust that your intelligence and conscience may suggest to you the only decision that is compatible with the welfare of Russia, with your own dignity, and with your duty to your native land.

Russia After 1905:
Limited Constitutionalism

The Revolution of 1905 compelled Nicholas II to make some concessions to constitutionalism. Consequently, he paid heed to the advice of Count Sergei Witte, who, as finance minister from 1892 to 1902, had made major contributions to the encouragement of foreign investment in Russia and to Russian industrialization. Witte had suggested that the tsar issue the August, 1905, manifesto summoning a first Duma and laying the groundwork for constitutional government in Russia. The concession was, in fact, quite modest since the powers of the Duma were purely consultative, but as with his efforts to modernize the Russian economy, so now in his efforts to deal with the political situation, Witte faced constant opposition from the reactionary court and the foolish and suspicious tsar. Witte's memoirs portray some feeling for these difficulties as well as for the penchant of the reactionaries to employ anti-Semitic violence to deflect attention from the real problems of Russian society. The effort to mobilize the so-called Black Hundreds in the cause of reaction and the pogroms thus unleashed had a distinctly protofascist character. Witte was dismissed in April, 1906, and the first Duma was dissolved for its refractory behavior in July. Subsequent Dumas were able to do little to break through the power of the reactionary circle surrounding the tsar or Nicholas' own absolutist proclivities.

Nicholas' Manifesto of August, 1905

The empire of Russia is formed and strengthened by the indestructible union of the Tsar with the people and the people with the Tsar. This concord and union of the Tsar and the people is the great moral force which has created Russia in the course of centuries by protecting her from all misfortunes and all attacks, and has constituted up to the present time a pledge of unity, independence, integrity, material well-being, and intellectual development in the present and in the future.

In our manifesto of February 26, 1903, we summoned all faithful sons of the fatherland in order to perfect, through mutual understanding, the organization of the State, founding it securely on public order and private welfare. We devoted ourselves to the task of coördinating local elective bodies [*zemstvos*] with the central authorities, and removing the disagreements existing between them, which so disturbed the normal course of the national life. Autocratic Tsars, our ancestors, have had this aim constantly in view, and the time has now come to follow out their good intentions and to summon elected representatives from the whole of Russia to take a constant and active part in the elaboration of laws, adding for this purpose to the higher State institutions a special consultative body intrusted with the preliminary elaboration and discussion of measures and with the examination of the State Budget. It is for this reason that, while preserving the fundamental law regarding autocratic power, we have deemed it well to form a *Gosoudarstvennaia Duma* (i.e. State Council) and to approve regulations for elections to this Duma, extend-

From *Readings in Modern European History,* vol. 2, ed. James Harvey Robinson and Charles Beard (Boston: Ginn, 1909), pp. 375–77.

ing these laws to the whole territory of the empire, with such exceptions only as may be considered necessary in the case of some regions in which special conditions obtain. . . .

We have ordered the Minister of the Interior to submit immediately for our approbation regulations for elections to the Duma, so that deputies from fifty governments, and the military province of the Don, may be able to assemble not later than the middle of January, 1906. We reserve to ourselves exclusively the care of perfecting the organization of the *Gosoudarstvennaia Duma,* and when the course of events has demonstrated the necessity of changes corresponding to the needs of the times and the welfare of the empire, we shall not fail to give the matter our attention at the proper moment.

We are convinced that those who are elected by the confidence of the whole people, and who are called upon to take part in the legislative work of the government, will show themselves in the eyes of all Russia worthy of the imperial trust in virtue of which they have been invited to coöperate in this great work; and that in perfect harmony with the other institutions and authorities of the State, established by us, they will contribute profitably and zealously to our labors for the well-being of our common mother, Russia, and for the strengthening of the unity, security, and greatness of the empire, as well as for the tranquillity and prosperity of the people.

In invoking the blessing of the Lord on the labors of the new assembly which we are establishing, and with unshakable confidence in the grace of God and in the assurance of the great historical destinies reserved by Divine Providence for our beloved fatherland, we firmly hope that Russia, with the help of God Almighty, and with the combined efforts of all her sons, will emerge triumphant from the trying ordeals through which she is now passing, and will renew her strength in the greatness and glory of her history extending over a thousand years.

Given at Peterhof on the nineteenth day of August, in the year of grace 1905, and the eleventh year of our reign.

Witte's Memoirs

At the conference with His Majesty which preceded the publication of the constitutional manifesto, I was exceedingly cautious in the expression of my opinions. True, I stated my convictions, which were later embodied in my report to His Majesty, without the slightest equivocation. I did not

From *The Memoirs of Count Witte,* ed. and trans. Abraham Yarmolinsky (London: Heinemann, 1921), pp. 316–18, 325–27, 328–30. Reprinted by permission of Abraham Yarmolinsky.

hesitate to draw his attention to the fact that should, God forbid, anything fatal happen to him, the dynasty would be represented by the baby Emperor and the regent, Mikhail Alexandrovich, who is completely un-- prepared for the task of ruling the Empire — a situation fraught with grave dangers for both the dynasty and the country, especially at a time of mighty revolutionary upheaval. It was therefore, necessary, I argued, to seek support for the political régime in the people, however deficient and unreliable the social consciousness of the uncultured masses may be. It was painful for me thus to speak to my Monarch, whom I had known since the days of his youth, whom I had served since the very beginning of his reign and who was the son of a man and ruler I had literally worshipped. Yet, had I failed to tell the Emperor the whole truth as I understood it, I would consider myself remiss of my direct moral duty.

While I was thus quite outspoken, nevertheless, I repeatedly told the Emperor that I might be in the wrong, and I urged him to take counsel with other statesmen in whom he had faith. It goes without saying that I did not advise him to do it on the sly, nor did I intimate that he should seek light from either such nonentities as Goremykin or from the court flunkeys. I did not conceal from His Majesty that, in my opinion, the situation was fraught with great difficulties and dangers. Seeing that he was bent upon placing the burden of power on my shoulders, I made use on one occasion of an allegory, in order to present to him the situation as I saw it. I likened His Majesty to a man who must cross a stretch of heavy sea. Several routes are urged upon him, I said, and several ships offered by different seamen. No matter what route is selected and what ship is boarded some danger and much injury is inevitable. I believed, I asserted, that both my route and my boat were the least dangerous and the most advisable from the standpoint of Russia's future. But should His Majesty accept my route and boat, this is what would happen. No sooner will he put to sea than the boat will begin to pitch and roll; later storms may come and probably damage the boat. It is then that wise counsellors could intimate that His Majesty ought to have chosen another route and trusted his own destiny and that of the country to another vessel. Hence doubts, hesitations, and plotting would arise and greatly endanger the public cause.

His Majesty protested and assured me of his unqualified confidence. I had, however, no illusions as to my Monarch's character. I knew that, devoid of either will or statesmanlike purpose, he was the plaything of all manner of evil influences, and that his personal peculiarities would add to the difficulties of the situation. I saw clearly that the near future held many bitter experiences in store for me and that in the end I would have to part with His Majesty without having accomplished my appointed task. The history of my brief premiership (October 20, 1905–April 20, 1906) fully bears out my predictions and justifies my apprehensions.

I found myself at the helm, essentially against my own will. His Majesty was forced to resort to me for the simple reason that his favourites, such as Goremykin, General Ignatyev and General Trepov, were scared by the revolutionary terrorists and lost themselves in the chaos of contradictory measures, for which they themselves were responsible.

Immediately upon my nomination as President of the Imperial Council I made it clear that the Procurator of the Holy Synod Pobiedonostzev, could not remain in office, for he definitely represented the past. His participation in my ministry, I argued, was incompatible with the inauguration of the new régime and out of keeping with the spirit of the times. . . .

Before proceeding with my task of forming a Cabinet of Ministers, I decided to call a conference of public leaders, including Shipov, a well-known zemstvo worker; Guchkov, now leader of the Octobrist Party in the Imperial Duma; M. A. Stakhovich, Prince Urusov, and Prince Trubetzkoi, Professor of the University of Moscow, later member of the Imperial Council. I had previously been authorized, as a matter of principle, to offer some of the portfolios to prominent public men, should I find that their prestige might help allay the unrest. The conference was a failure, and further acquaintance with these men convinced me that they were not fit for the responsible ministerial posts, in spite of the fact that some of them were persons of excellent character and eminent abilities. Thus, for several weeks after my appointment, I was unable to form a Cabinet which would be in sympathy with the principles set forth in the constitutional manifesto or which would at least recognize its historic inevitability. As a result, for some time I ruled the country, a huge Empire in a state of profound upheaval, singlehandedly, with the vast and intricate machinery of government practically out of commission. . . .

Some two weeks after my appointment, General Trepov, Governor-General of St. Petersburg, Commander of the garrison of that city, and Assistant Minister of the Interior, formally tendered his resignation. I informed him over the telephone that I accepted it. The next morning I met him on board the government ship which was taking me to Peterhof for my daily report to His Majesty. He informed me that he had been appointed Court Commandant. . . .

Trepov is a central figure in our revolution and must be dealt with at considerable length. Prince Urusov speaking before the first Duma characterized him as "a quartermaster by education and a pogrom-maker by conviction." While it is impossible to squeeze a human being with all its complexities into a narrow word formula, nevertheless Prince Urusov's phrase succeeds in bringing out one essential feature of Trepov's personality. He was indeed "a quarter-master by education," and therein lay his own and Russia's misfortune. In his youth he attended a military school (the Corps of Pages), yet whatever education he had he received in the barracks of the Cavalry Guards, and in the Officers' Club. He probably never in his life read a single serious book. It cannot be denied, however, that he was a smart, thoroughly trained, and conscientious officer.

"Pogrom-maker by conviction" — that is not altogether accurate. Trepov did not love the art of pogrom-making for its own sake. He merely did not hesitate to resort to pogroms whenever he considered them necessary for the protection of the vital interests of the State, as he saw them. Only his attitude toward anti-Jewish pogroms was rather light-hearted, but in this respect he resembled Plehve, Count Ignatyev, and many other high officials to whom the bloody game of pogrom-making was a mere political amusement. And did not the Emperor himself call on all of us to rally under the banners of the Union of Russians, which political party openly advocates the annihilation of the Jews? . . .

During the revolutionary days General Trepov became a house divided against itself, and exhibited a complete confusion of mind. Unassisted by either political education or vision, he expressed simultaneously the most opposed views and passed from one extreme to another. An advocate of absolute autocracy, he expressed the most radical opinions in discussing Bulygin's project of a consultative Duma. In October, 1905, he issued the famous order of the day instructing the troops "not to spare cartridges," i.e., in dealing with the revolutionists. Several days later he spoke in favour of a most liberal political amnesty. On one hand, in the Committee of Ministers he insisted on the most stringent measures against both the students and the teaching staff of the institutions of higher learning; on the other hand, he originated and carried the plan of granting to these institutions a broad and vaguely defined autonomy, a measure which was instrumental in precipitating the revolution.

It must be admitted, nevertheless, that whatever this sorry statesman did was done in good faith and in the spirit of absolute loyalty to the Emperor and the man in the monarch. It is noteworthy that toward the end of his life the General fell into disfavour with His Majesty, and the latter was going to get rid of Trepov when he died a natural death. I am certain that no one will suspect me of being partial to General Trepov. He was practically my archenemy, and it was he who, more than any one else, made my position as Prime Minister unbearable. I feel, therefore, at liberty to assert, that, when all is said, Trepov was a man of good faith and political decency.

While Trepov held the ostensibly modest and nonpolitical office of Court Commandant, in reality he was a cross between an irresponsible dictator and an Asiatic eunuch day and night attached to the person of his Master. A man of a resolute and martial air, he wielded an overwhelming influence over the weak-willed Emperor. It was in Trepov's hands that lay His Majesty's safety, inasmuch as he was in charge of both the open and secret defence of the Monarch's person. He was at liberty to advise His Majesty at all times, and he acted as a middleman between

the Czar and the authors of various confidential memoirs and secret reports, which were addressed to the Emperor. He had the power to smother
a document or bring it emphatically to the Monarch's attention. Naturally enough, the numerous people who in their efforts to rise rely on
other means than sheer merit and who make their careers in society bou-
doirs — those people began to seek by hook or crook to gain access to
Trepov's reception room in the palaces of Tsarskoye-Selo and Peterhof.
It was also natural for the Court clique to choose Trepov as the instrument of reaction, which followed upon the confusion and panic of the
revolution.

Trepov's influence over His Majesty was by far greater than mine. In
fact, he was the irresponsible head of the Government, while I wielded
little power and bore all the responsibility. This circumstance greatly
hindered my activities and was the chief reason why I gave up my post
several days before the opening of the Imperial Duma.

The Dissolution of the First Duma, July, 1906

We summoned the representatives of the nation by our will to the
work of productive legislation. Confiding firmly in divine clemency and
believing in the great and brilliant future of our people, we confidently
anticipated benefits for the country from their labors. We proposed great
reforms in all departments of the national life. We have always devoted
our greatest care to the removal of the ignorance of the people by the
light of instruction, and to the removal of their burdens by improving
the conditions of agricultural work.

A cruel disappointment has befallen our expectations. The representatives of the nation, instead of applying themselves to the work of productive legislation, have strayed into spheres beyond their competence, and
have been making inquiries into the acts of local authorities established by
ourselves, and have been making comments upon the imperfections of
the fundamental laws, which can only be modified by our imperial will.
In short, the representatives of the nation have undertaken really illegal
acts, such as the appeal by the Duma to the nation.

The peasants, disturbed by such anomalies, and seeing no hope of the
amelioration of their lot, have resorted in a number of districts to open
pillage and the destruction of other people's property, and to disobedi-
ence of the law and of the legal authorities. But our subjects ought to remember that an improvement in the lot of the people is only possible
under conditions of perfect order and tranquillity. We shall not permit

From *Readings in Modern European History,* vol. 2, ed. James Harvey Robinson and
Charles Beard (Boston: Ginn, 1909), pp. 377–78.

arbitrary or illegal acts, and we shall impose our imperial will on the disobedient by all the power of the State.

We appeal to all well-disposed Russians to combine for the maintenance of legal authority and the restoration of peace in our dear fatherland. May calm be reëstablished once more in Russia, and may God help us to accomplish the chiefest of our tasks, the improvement of the lot of the peasant. Our will on this point is unalterable. The Russian husbandman, in case his land is too small to maintain him, shall be supplied, without prejudice to the property of others, with legitimate and honest means for enlarging his holdings. The representatives of the other classes will, at our request, devote all their efforts to the promotion of this great undertaking which will be given a definitely legal form by a future Duma.

In dissolving the Duma we confirm our immutable intention of maintaining this institution, and in conformity with this intention we fix March 5, 1907, as the date of the convocation of a new Duma by a ukase addressed to the Senate. With unshakable faith in divine clemency and in the good sense of the Russian people, we shall expect from the new Duma the realization of our efforts and their promotion of legislation in accordance with the requirements of a regenerated Russia.

Faithful sons of Russia, your Tsar calls upon you as a father upon his children to unite with him for the regeneration of our holy fatherland. We believe that giants in thought and action will appear, and that, thanks to their assiduous efforts, the glory of Russia will continue to shine.

Nicholas

The Politics
of the Dual Monarchy

In 1866, with its expulsion from Germany, the Hapsburg Empire obviously faced dissolution unless it accommodated the Hungarians. Russian assistance had been necessary to quell their powerful military uprising in 1848, and Bismarck was prepared to encourage a Hungarian revolution if Austria did not surrender quickly in 1866. The Ausgleich *was made at the expense of the other peoples of the empire. While some concessions were made to the Slavs in the Austrian half of the monarchy, Hungary and its dominant landowning class were to remain disproportionately powerful to the end. Although the suffrage system outlined in the* Ausgleich *was reformed, first by the creation of a class voting system and then by the granting of virtual universal suffrage,*

Austrian political life was plagued by peculiarities that became of more than passing importance. The report on the elections of 1907 from the Fortnightly Review *gives some idea of the role played by clerical, national, and social interests in the empire's politics. The agrarian and relatively backward character of much of the monarchy's economy was of great importance in these elections. The comments on Vienna are particularly interesting. Most Austrian industry was owned by Jews, and the result in a backward and nationally mixed state was a great deal of anti-Semitism. In Vienna this was often combined with Pan-Germanism, and Mayor Lueger was one of the representatives of this lower-middle-class combination of social resentment, racism, and German nationalism. One of the men most influenced by the political life of Vienna during these years was Adolf Hitler, who identified the Jews with both capitalism and socialism.*

The *Ausgleich,* 1867

Law of December 21, 1867, concerning the matters common to all the countries of the Austrian monarchy and the manner of treating them.

ART. I. The following affairs are declared common to the realms and countries represented in the *Reichsrath,* and to the countries under the crown of Hungary:

(*a*) Foreign affairs, comprising the diplomatic and commercial representation in foreign countries as well as measures relating to international treaties, reserving the right of the ratification of the said treaties by the bodies representing each of the two halves of the empire (i.e. the Austrian *Reichsrath* and the Hungarian *Reichstag*), in so far as this approbation is constitutionally required.

(*b*) Military affairs, including the navy but excluding the determination of the quotas of troops and legislation regulating the military service.

(*c*) Finances, relating to those expenses for which it is necessary to provide in common.

ART. II. The following matters are not to be treated in common, but are, from time to time, to be settled on the same basis by joint agreements.

1. Commercial matters, particularly tariff legislation.

2. Legislation on indirect taxes closely connected with industrial production.

3. The regulation of the monetary system and the system of coinage.

4. Arrangements affecting railway lines which concern both portions of the empire.

From *Readings in Modern European History,* vol. 2, ed. James Harvey Robinson and Charles Beard (Boston: Ginn, 1909), pp. 165–68.

5. The establishment of a system of defense for the country.

ART. III. The common expenses are to be met by the two parts of the monarchy according to a ratio fixed by periodical agreements between the respective parliaments of the two parts of the empire, and approved by the emperor. The ways and means of raising the portion charged to each of the two parts of the empire remain the exclusive affair of each. . . .

ART. V. The administration of the common affairs shall be vested in a joint responsible ministry, which is prohibited from managing, during the same period, the affairs peculiar to either of the two parts of the empire.

Arrangements concerning the management, conduct, and internal organization of the entire army belong exclusively to the emperor.

ART. VI. The parliaments of the two portions of the empire [to wit, the Austrian Reichsrath and the Hungarian Reichstag] shall exercise their legislative powers, which relate to common matters, through Delegations.

ART. VII. The Delegation of the Reichsrath numbers sixty members, one third to be chosen from the House of Lords, two thirds from the lower house.[1]

ART. VIII. The House of Lords shall choose from its own body, by absolute majority vote, the twenty members of the Delegation whom it has a right to elect.

The forty members left to the choice of the lower house shall be elected by the deputies of the various provincial diets, either from their own number or from the entire Chamber, by an absolute majority of votes. . . .

ART. X. The choice of delegates and their alternates shall be renewed each year by the two chambers of the Reichsrath. Members of the Delegation are reeligible.

ART. XI. The Delegations shall be convoked each year by the emperor, who fixes the place of meeting. . . .

ART. XIII. The authority of the Delegations shall extend to all matters concerning common affairs. All other subjects are beyond this sphere of action.

ART. XIV. The proposals of the government shall be transmitted by the common ministry to each of the two Delegations separately.

Each Delegation shall have an equal right to present projects with reference to matters within its jurisdiction.

ART. XV. For the passage of every law within the powers of the two Delegations, the approval of both is necessary, or, in case of disagreement, a vote of the two bodies assembled in joint session; in both cases the approval of the emperor is necessary. . . .

ART. XIX. Each Delegation acts, deliberates, and decides in separate session on matters which concern it. . . .

[1] The Delegation of the Hungarian Reichstag, numbering sixty, is also chosen by the two chambers composing that body.

ART. XXX. The two Delegations shall communicate their decisions to each and, whenever it is necessary, the motives for these decisions.

This communication shall be made in writing in the German language on the part of the Delegation from the Richsrath, and in the Hungarian language on the part of the Delegation from the Reichstag; in each case there shall be annexed to the text an authentic translation into the language of the other Delegation.

ART. XXXI. Each Delegation has the right to propose that a question shall be decided by a vote taken in common, and that proposition cannot be rejected by the other Delegation after there has been an exchange of three written communications which have produced no result.

The two presidents shall fix by mutual agreement the time and place of a joint session for taking the common vote.

Report on the Elections of 1907

The result of the elections of May 14, which has, it is true, been considerably modified by the supplementary elections, was very startling. Overwhelming successes of the socialist candidates were reported from all parts of the country. If we turn first to Bohemia, the most important part of the western division of the monarchy and at all times the cockpit of Austrian political warfare, we find that the discomfiture of the Young Czech party was the most important feature of the first pollings. . . . There seems little doubt that on May 14 many electors in Bohemia who were not socialists gave their votes to the socialist candidates, moved by a general feeling of discontent caused by the unjust treatment of Bohemia in the electoral bill to which most of the Young Czechs had given their assent. The elections of May 23 in Bohemia, as in other parts of the empire, witnessed the rally of the nonsocialist parties; as already mentioned, a considerable number of the members of the formerly dominant Young Czech party now obtained seats, as well as some men belonging to the more ancient, more conservative party known as the Old Czechs. A few seats were also won by the Radical party, whose platform included the reëstablishment — in a modified form — of the ancient Bohemian constitution.

The party, however, that achieved the greatest success at the elections of May 23 was that known as the "agrarians," and it is to this party that the largest number of the representatives of Bohemia in the new parliament of Vienna will belong. Land is overtaxed in Austria to an almost incredible degree, and the peasants have succeeded in returning a consid-

From *Readings in Modern European History*, vol. 2, ed. James Harvey Robinson and Charles Beard (Boston: Ginn, 1909), pp. 171–74.

erable number of members specially pledged to protect the interests of landowners. The fate of the German deputies of Bohemia was yet more disastrous; their places were almost everywhere taken by socialists. An interesting feature of the election was the complete discomfiture of the so-called "Pan-Germanic" party, most of whose representatives were returned by the Germans of Bohemia. These men had attempted to establish, in a manner they were never able clearly to define, a closer connection between Austria and Germany. They had rendered themselves ridiculous by their abject devotion to Germania, who somewhat contemptuously rejected the wooing of her uncouth lovers. . . .

The "sister lands" of Bohemia — that is, Moravia and Silesia, both countries which have a mainly Slavic population — voted in a manner not dissimilar from that of Bohemia. It should, however, be noted that in Moravia a considerable number of the clericals were elected — a fact that may not inconsiderably influence the state of parties in the new parliament.

As regards the German parts of Austria, the elections of Vienna, the capital of the empire, of course attract the most attention. That city had formerly held liberal views, but gradually became clerical through the almost unlimited influence which Dr. Karl Lueger acquired over the Viennese. This somewhat second-rate Cleon began life as a Liberal, but soon became a Jew-baiter or Anti-Semite. Through the indomitable energy of Lueger, his party, which afterward assumed the name of Christian Socialists — though it is really conservative or rather clerical — widely extended its influence and power. As one of its leaders stated at a recent public meeting, this party now has "adherents among all Germany from the Lake of Constance to the Bukovina!" At the Vienna elections the Christian Socialists were successful, but hardly to so great an extent as had been anticipated. The liberals indeed only secured three seats, but the Christian Socialists, to whom the absence of Dr. Lueger through illness was very harmful, found more dangerous antagonists in the members of the socialist party. That party has been very ably organized by Dr. Adler, a man of exceptional talent, and one of the many brilliant leaders whom, from the time of Lassalle downward, the Semitic race has given to the socialists. Besides winning many seats in Vienna, the socialists have also won seats in provincial towns of Lower Austria, while they have won a seat even at Innsbruck and have captured the entire parliamentary representation of Linz, the capitol of Upper Austria, and of Trieste, the great seaport of the empire. The former German Liberal party has been long split up into various factions, and has at the election lost largely both to the clericals and to the socialists. . . .

The Slovenes, who inhabit parts of Styria, Carinthia, and Carniola, have mainly elected representatives who, though favorable to the claims of the Slavic populations which they represent, will consider it their principal duty to further the clerical policy which finds favor among the agricultural populations of the districts which elected them. In Galicia, which sends about a hundred representatives to the parliament of Vienna, the elections have only just ended. As already mentioned, the new electoral law greatly favored the Polish majority of the population at the expense of the Ruthenian minority. The Poles were therefore, on the whole, successful, though a certain number of Ruthenians obtained seats in the new parliament. Two Zionists elected by the Galician Jews will be members of the new parliament of Vienna.

Hardly ever, perhaps, in the annals of parliamentary government, have elections resulted in so complete a surprise as did those just held in Austria. The recent defeat of the socialists in Germany led even experienced statesmen to believe that they would be far more unsuccessful in Austria, which, rightly or wrongly, has always been considered a very conservative country. The extreme moderation hitherto displayed by the socialists largely contributed to their victory. It is a proof of the universal veneration with which all Austrians look on their sovereign, that not a single disloyal cry was heard during the recent elections — and the socialists formed no exception in this respect.

The Sick Men of Europe
and Balkan Nationalism

As the Ottoman Empire disintegrated, the Dual Monarchy inherited its ills. The tension in Bosnia-Herzegovina was the most fateful of these. Both provinces had rebelled against the Turks in 1875, and the Dual Monarchy had occupied them in 1878 at the mandate of the great powers. The object of the occupation was to maintain order in the area, restrict the growth of Serbia, and check Russian ambitions. Legally, they remained parts of the Ottoman Empire. At the time, Russian foreign minister Gorchakov prophetically remarked that Austria-Hungary had put on the Shirt of Nessus. In 1908, the Dual Monarchy decided to clarify its position in the provinces in order to forestall potential threats from Serb nationalists and Ottoman reformers. Francis Joseph annexed the provinces. The ensuing crisis foreshadowed World War I in many respects. It drastically increased tension with Russia, and it infuriated the Serbs. Secret societies such as the Society of National Defense (Narodna Odbrana) established programs for the liberation of the Slavs and carried on subversive activities from bases in Serbia.

A member of such a society was responsible for the murder of Archduke Ferdinand of Austria on June 28, 1914, in the Bosnian city of Sarajevo.

Francis Joseph's Annexation of Bosnia-Herzegovina, 1908

We, Francis Joseph, Emperor of Austria, King of Bohemia, and Apostolic King of Hungary, to the inhabitants of Bosnia and Herzegovina:

When a generation ago our troops crossed the borders of your lands, you were assured that they came not as foes, but as friends, with the firm determination to remedy the evils from which your fatherland had suffered so grievously for many years. This promise given at a serious moment has been honestly kept. It has been the constant endeavor of our government to guide the country by patient and systematic activity to a happier future.

To our great joy we can say that the seed then scattered in the furrows of a troubled soil has richly thrived. You yourselves must feel it a boon that order and security have replaced violence and oppression, that trade and traffic are constantly extending, that the elevating influence of education has been brought to bear in your country, and that under the shield of an orderly administration every man may enjoy the fruits of his labors.

It is the duty of us all to advance steadily along this path. With this goal before our eyes, we deem the moment come to give the inhabitants of the two lands a new proof of our trust in their political maturity. In order to raise Bosnia and Herzegovina to a higher level of political life we have resolved to grant both of those lands constitutional governments that are suited to the prevailing conditions and general interests, so as to create a legal basis for the representation of their wishes and needs. You shall henceforth have a voice when decisions are made concerning your domestic affairs, which, as hitherto, will have a separate administration. But the necessary premise for the introduction of this provincial constitution is the creation of a clear and unambiguous legal status for the two lands.

For this reason, and also remembering the ties that existed of yore between our glorious ancestors on the Hungarian throne and these lands, we extend our suzerainty over Bosnia and Herzegovina, and it is our will that the order of succession of our House be extended to these lands also. The inhabitants of the two lands thus share all the benefits which a lasting confirmation of the present relation can offer. The new order of

From *Readings in Modern European History*, vol. 2, ed. James Harvey Robinson and Charles Beard (Boston: Ginn, 1909), pp. 171–74.

things will be a guarantee that civilization and prosperity will find a sure footing in your home.

Inhabitants of Bosnia and Herzegovina:

Among the many cares of our throne, solicitude for your material and spiritual welfare shall not be the last. The exalted idea of equal rights for all before the law, a share in the legislation and administration of the provincial affairs, equal protection for all religious creeds, languages, and racial differences, all these high possessions you shall enjoy in full measure. The freedom of the individual and the welfare of the whole will be the aim of our government in the two lands. You will surely show yourselves worthy of the trust placed in you, by attachment and loyalty to us and to our House. And thus we hope that the noble harmony between the prince and the people, that dearest pledge of all social progress, will ever accompany us on our common path.

Program of the Society of National Defense, 1911

I. THE RISE AND ACTIVITY OF THE FIRST
NARODNA ODBRANA

The Serbian people has endured during its existence many difficult and bitter days. Among these days is September 24, 1908, when Austria-Hungary illegally annexed Bosnia and Herzegovina. This day can be compared to the worst days of our past. It was especially painful for the Serbian people in that it came at a time when more fortunate peoples had already completed their national unification and had created large states, and when culture and freedom were presumed to be at their peak.

At such a time Austria-Hungary oppressed along with other peoples several million Serbs, whom she penalizes and seeks to alienate from us. They may not openly call themselves Serbs, and may not adorn their homes with the Serbian flag; they may not trade freely, cultivate their soil, erect Serbian schools, openly celebrate the feast of the patron saint [Slava], and may not sing of Kossowo or of Prince Marko and Milosch Obilitsch. Only such a state, only an Austria-Hungary, could carry through such an annexation.

1. RISE OF THE ORGANIZATION AND ITS PROGRAM

The annexation of Bosnia and Herzegovina not only aroused Serbia and Montenegro; it aroused all Serbs, and one can say all of Europe as well.

From *Europe in the Nineteenth Century: A Documentary Analysis of Change and Conflict. Volume 2: 1870–1914,* ed. Eugene N. Anderson, Stanley J. Pincetl, Jr., Donald J. Ziegler, pp. 304–06, 333–35. Copyright © 1961, by Bobbs-Merrill Company, Inc. Reprinted by permission of the publisher.

After the proclamation of annexation the situation was such that it appeared impossible for the matter to end peacefully. The continual rolling of drums, the shrilling of trumpets, and the daily proclamations and excited telegrams indicated war. Our land was in feverish excitement, meetings were held everywhere, and the people demanded war. In these serious times and under these conditions the *Narodna Odbrana* [Society of National Defense] was founded. The aroused nationalistic masses asked that words be translated into deeds, that all necessary preparations for war be made, that the great national will to sacrifice be organized. Overnight, simultaneously in various cities, through the will and determination of the national masses, the *Narodna Odbrana* was created. Urged on by the will of the people, the leading citizens came together in Schabatz, Nisch, and other places to found committees of defense. Such a committee was chosen also in Belgrade early in October, 1908, at a meeting of leading citizens assembled at the City Hall. Because it was for the defense and protection of the people, the committee was called the Society of National Defense, or *Narodna Odbrana,* as in the previously mentioned cities.

The full committee was set up at the session of October 8, when the program which had been worked out by the provisional committee was adopted. In accordance with this program the *Narodna Odbrana* accepted the duty of:

1. arousing national consciousness, spurring it on, and strengthening it;
2. taking up the registration and acceptance of volunteers;
3. building volunteer branches and preparing for armed action;
4. collecting voluntary gifts of money and supplies in kind for the realization of the goals;
5. organizing free corps for special and independent guerrilla warfare, arming and training these groups;
6. carrying out defensive action for the Serbian people in every direction.

Even before the *Narodna Odbrana* was organized, similar committees had grown up in the interior of the country. Therefore, in order better to carry out its purpose, the *Narodna Odbrana* proceeded to get in touch with the others and to found more groups wherever they did not yet exist. The founding and the program of this committee were so enthusiastically greeted by the people that within three weeks the entire country was organized like one group under the slogan: "All for the Serbian people and the fatherland!"

The enthusiasm was so great that committees were founded in places where no one had expected it. In less than a month, 223 committees and almost as many branch committees were set up in cities and villages. Committees were founded even abroad. In part this was done on the initiative

of the Belgrade committee; but even without it, in a good many places
outside Serbia either committees or branch committees were founded to
work for the goals of national defense. . . .

XIII. TWO IMPORTANT TASKS

In conclusion, we want to mention two more important tasks of the
Narodna Odbrana, and with them we will close the part of our pamphlet
setting forth our program.

The *Narodna Odbrana* maintains that the annexation of Bosnia and
Herzegovina is clearly an invasion of our country from the north; thus it
regards Austria as our principal and greatest enemy and so represents it
to our people. The exposition of this idea is in no way fanaticism or
chauvinism but a healthy and entirely understandable task, an elementary duty, a need exactly like that to impress the fact that two times two
makes four.

The Serbs have never hated for the mere sake of hating, but they have
always loved freedom and independence. We have already said in another place that, just as once the Turks from the south pressed upon us,
now the Austrians from the north are coming. If the *Narodna Odbrana*
is preaching the need for a struggle with Austria, it is but proclaiming
the sacred truth which arises out of our national position. If hate and
fanaticism develop, they are but natural phenomena which come as results and not as an end. For us the goal is our existence, our freedom. If
hate against Austria breaks out, we are not the ones who have sown it;
Austria is the sower of the hate, through her action against us which
forces us to struggle until she is destroyed.

Today everywhere a new concept of nationalism has become prevalent.
Nationalism (the feeling of nationality) is no longer a historical or poeti-
cal feeling, but the true practical expression of life. Among the French,
Germans, and English, and among all other civilized peoples, nationalism
has grown into something quite new; in it lies the concept of bread,
space, air, commerce, competition in everything. Only among us is it still
in the old form; that is, it is the fruit of spiritual suffering rather than of
reasonable understanding and national advantage. If we speak of freedom
and union, we parade far too much the phrases "breaking our chains"
and "freeing the slaves"; we call far too much upon our former Serbian
glory and think too little of the fact that the freeing of subjected areas
and their union with Serbia are necessary to our citizens, our merchants,
and our peasants on the grounds of the most elementary needs of culture
and trade, of food and space. If one were to explain to our sharp-eyed
people our national task as one closely connected with the needs of every-
day life, our people would take up the work in a greater spirit of sacrifice
than is today the case. We must tell our people that the freedom of Bos-

nia is necessary, not just because of their feeling of sympathy with their brothers who suffer there, but also because of commerce and its connection with the sea; national union is necessary because of the stronger development of a common culture. The Italians welcome the conquest of Tripoli not just because of the glory to be won by the success of their arms, but especially because of the advantage they hope to gain by annexing Tripoli. Our people must adopt a more realistic attitude toward politics. We must show them how we would stand culturally and economically if we were united into one state and were in as favorable a position commercially as that of Timok in relation to the Adriatic. . . .

Along with the task of explaining to our people the danger threatening us from Austria, the *Narodna Odbrana* has also the other important tasks of explaining to them, while preserving our holy national memories, this new, healthy, fruitful conception of nationalism, and of convincing them to work for national freedom and unity.

XIV. CONCLUSION

The old *Narodna Odbrana* was called into being on account of the annexation. When we saw that there would be no war, the organization ceased its original activity relating to the crisis of annexation and turned to the new activity demanded by its holy mission as national defender. The lesson that had been learned from the annexation was that we must prepare ourselves as thoroughly as possible, with all the strength and persistence we can command. The state is to prepare its forces administratively; and parallel with its effort, private initiative is to prepare itself by means of its voluntary strength. Let us prepare, let us prepare unceasingly for the struggle which the annexation foreshadows. To activate these private efforts, to assemble and to concentrate them is what the *Narodna Odbrana* has undertaken; it will rouse them where they have become weak, plant them where they are lacking, conciliate them where they are feuding. The preparation and strengthening of Serbia in all fields of national life and of national effort is our working program. The *Narodna Odbrana* is the same as it was in the annexation period, adapting its work to the changing times and situations while maintaining all its previous ties. It still is a source of protection and is national in scope. Around its banner the citizens of Serbia gather today as they did during the annexation. Then we called for war, but now we call for work. Then we wanted meetings, demonstrations, volunteers, guerrillas, rifles, and bombs; today we want quiet, fanatical, untiring effort and responsibility as a preparation for the struggle which will come with guns and cannons.

The change which took place in Serbia after the annexation is in great part due to the efforts of the *Narodna Odbrana*. As a true national defender, our organization will endure to the end; and if the end comes, if a situation obtains like that at the time of the annexation, thanks to its present activity the *Narodna Odbrana* will face the task which it will have to fulfill then with a tenfold greater ability than it had at the time of the annexation. Through its present activity it is preparing itself and the country for the real function for which it has come into being.

All in all, the *Narodna Odbrana* aims through its work to advance upon the enemy on the day of reckoning with a sound, nationally conscious, and internally reconciled Serbian people, a nation of Sokols, rifle clubs, heroes — in fact, the fear and terror of the enemy — reliant front-rank fighters and executors of Serbia's holy cause.

If this succeeds, all will be well for us; woe to us if we fail.

THE REVIVAL
OF WESTERN IMPERIALISM

Chapter 10

The last great outburst of European imperialism, which occurred between 1870 and 1914, continues to arouse both historical controversy
and political passion. No explanation of the phenomenon seems to be
totally satisfactory. The classic economic explanations by the liberal
British opponent of imperialism John Hobson and the Marxist V. I.
Lenin interpreted imperialism as a response to the malfunctioning of
capitalism that involved the need to search for outlets for surplus capital
and surplus production. Certainly many imperialists *believed* they
needed such outlets, but two problems with this economic argument are
that the greatest migration of English capital took place before the great
imperialist upsurge and that much of the investment of European capitalists was made in noncolonial areas — for example, the United States.
Furthermore, many colonial enterprises were demonstrably unsuited
for any substantial export of capital, production, or population, although the European powers engaged in them anyway. Italy's "collection of deserts" is an example.

Another interpretation, that of the economist Joseph Schumpeter,
treated imperialism as a "social atavism," a return to premodern forms
of aggression and domination resulting from the continued power of
warlike precapitalistic classes in European society. Schumpeter's theory
is useful for considering many aspects of imperialist rivalry and competition, but it is based on a rather narrow definition of imperialism
and fails to explain the more informal types of empire and domination
that are attracting much attention from historians today. Nor would
historians find fully satisfactory a more intellectual interpretation explaining imperialism as either a humanitarian movement in which
Europe took up the "white man's burden" or a product of Social Darwinism. It is clear from the evidence, however, that both humanitarian
ideals and Social Darwinist ideas were significant components of imperialism and must be taken into account. Needless to say, arguments
about the motives for imperialism are closely connected with conflicts

over the consequences of imperialism. No responsible person would deny that there were cases of egregious brutality and exploitation, the most notorious of which perhaps is Leopold III's Belgian Congo, but a difference of opinion is apparent between those who would argue that in the balance colonialism benefited subject peoples by bringing them the material and spiritual rewards of Western civilization and those who would argue that the West's intrusion was too culturally disruptive and economically exploitative to have had positive results.

Discussions of imperialism have tended to concentrate on Great Britain for the obvious reason that it was the most important of the imperialist powers. Much of the hostility in the rivalry among the European powers was directed against Britain because it was so often ahead of its competitors. The British Empire antedated the colonial scramble that began in the 1880's. British control of India, New Zealand, Australia, Gibraltar, and certain other areas constituted an early formal empire, alongside which stood an informal empire based on investments and special treaty relationships in Asia, Africa, South America, and the Middle East. It has often been argued that Britain developed her great empire after 1880 in a "fit of absence of mind." Thus the instability of Egypt threatened Britain's vital interest in the Suez Canal and compelled it to occupy that country, which in turn led to military incursions in the Sudan and a growing interest in the direct control of the areas of Africa vital to the security of Egypt. A less charitable though not entirely dissimilar interpretation has been advanced by J. Gallagher and R. Robinson, who argue that Britain established a formal empire because the absence of adequate governments in certain colonial areas, coupled with increasing European competition, frightened the British into assuming direct control. Whatever the truth, imperialist politicians such as Benjamin Disraeli and Joseph Chamberlain and adventurers such as Cecil Rhodes consciously and deliberately stirred up imperialist sentiment and involved Britain in colonial adventures.

France was another European country with an old colonial tradition. It had conquered Algeria in 1830 and had important interests in Tunisia and Morocco that led to the occupation of these countries in 1881 and 1911 respectively. France was unquestionably Britain's most important rival in Africa, and the conflict between the two powers was particularly tense from 1882 when Britain occupied Egypt until the showdown at Fashoda in 1898 when France backed away from the contest. Germany, of course, was a latecomer as a colonial power because it was a latecomer as a nation. Bismarck was never overly enthusiastic about colonies, and he actually encouraged France to build up its colonial empire in the hope that this would distract it from Alsace-Lorraine. Ironically, however, it was Bismarck who created the German colonial

empire in Africa in 1884 and 1885, after he became convinced that colonies would be useful to the economy and would help him in domestic
politics, and he gave way to the pressure for colonies from the Colonial
League and adventurers such as Dr. Carl Peters. Bismarck's successors
talked much more and accomplished much less. William II demanded
a "place in the sun" for Germany, and his foreign office tried to force
Britain and France to make concessions to Germany in Africa by a
combination of bombast and blackmail. The results were small in territory and disastrous to Germany's international position.

Much of the imperialism of this period was promoted by the weakness and decay of great empires. The scramble for concessions in China
would not have been possible if China had been capable of fighting
back. The rivalry between Britain and Russia in Asia might have led
to grave consequences, but Britain found in Japan an ally capable of
checking Russian expansion and of proving what an Asian power could
achieve if it modernized. Perhaps the most dangerous areas of European rivalry in the end were the Balkans and the Ottoman Empire,
and it was becoming clear well before the war that imperialist rivalry
on the continent of Europe posed a major threat to peace. The history
of Russia's expansion was over land rather than overseas, and just as
Russian ambitions in central Asia and Manchuria had led to conflict
with Britain, so Russian ambitions in the Balkans and Ottoman Empire were creating conflicts with Austria-Hungary and Germany. Germany, in particular, was coming to the conclusion that the only way to
force the other parties to make concessions overseas was by establishing a great continental sphere of influence in central Europe, the Balkans, and the Ottoman Empire.

British Imperialism
in Egypt and Africa:
The Confrontation with France

*The settlement of the Egyptian question marks the turning point in
Britain's transition from informal to formal empire. The Egyptian khe-
dive (ruler) was nominally a subject of the Ottoman Sultan, but he
was independent in practice. Even before the completion of the Suez
Canal in 1869, they had contracted huge debts to the European powers.
The completion of the canal made Egypt an area of basic strategic im-*

portance, and in 1875 Disraeli succeeded in getting the khedive to sell his canal stock to Great Britain. In 1876, Egyptian finances deteriorated once again, and Britain and France established de facto control over the Egyptian government in the interests of its European creditors. Nevertheless, Britain considered its position in Egypt a special one and was concerned more with the stability of the regime than with the interests of the other powers. If necessary, it was prepared to take control directly. In 1882, a group of nationalistic Egyptian officers revolted against the foreign domination of their country. Britain responded by bombarding Alexandria and occupying Egypt. Britain promised to get out as soon as conditions stabilized but instead became more involved in Egyptian affairs, particularly in a lengthy war against the rebellious Sudan. At the same time, Britain became fearful that France might try to reassert the French position in Egypt and expand its African empire by reaching the headwaters of the Nile in Abyssinia. There was veritable panic at the thought that the Nile River could be diverted by French engineers. In 1895, foreign secretary Sir Edward Grey warned France that an advance to the Nile would be viewed as an "unfriendly act." The crisis came in 1898 when General Kitchener advanced up the Nile after capturing Khartoum with instructions to keep the French out. His meeting with the French expedition of Colonel Marchand created a tense crisis, resolved when France, torn by the Dreyfus Affair and lacking Russian support, backed down.

Foreign Secretary Lord Salisbury to Sir Edward Malet, the British Agent in Cairo, October 16, 1879

As you will shortly proceed to Egypt to take up the appointment of Her Majesty's Agent and Consul-General in that country, I think it right to address to you some observations as to the principles by which your conduct should be guided.

The leading aim of our policy in Egypt is the maintenance of the neutrality of that country, that is to say, the maintenance of such a state of things that no great Power shall be more powerful there than England.

This purpose might, of course, be secured by the predominance of England itself, or even by the establishment of the Queen's authority in the country. Circumstances may be conceived in which this would be the only way of attaining the object; but it would not be the best method. It would not in the present state of affairs confer any other advantages

From J. C. Hurewitz, *Diplomacy in the Near and Middle East: A Documentary Record, 1535–1914*, vol. 1 (Princeton: Van Nostrand, 1956), pp. 191–94. Reprinted by permission of J. C. Hurewitz.

than opportunities of employing English people and introducing English capital; and these would be outweighed by the responsibilities, military and financial, it would entail. The only justification of such a policy would consist in its being the only available mode of assuring the neutrality of Egypt towards us.

With this object in view it is obvious that we can have no jealousy of Native rule in itself. On the contrary, its continuance is, for us, the easiest solution of the problem. But it must not degenerate into anarchy, or perpetuate the oppression of recent years. Egypt is too much in view of the whole world, and there are too many interests attaching to it, to be suffered to relapse into the barbarous administration which in Persia and Burmah has resulted in misery so acute as to produce depopulation. An opinion would grow up in Europe in favour of intervention, which, in this case, would mean occupation; and if England could not satisfy it, she would not be able to prevent some other Power from doing so.

For this reason there is a value in the present relations between Egypt and the Porte, however anomalous they may appear to be. In case of extreme misgovernment, they furnish a machinery for changing the ruler, without any violation of Treaties or breach of diplomatic comity. They enable us to exercise a general control without taking over the government.

We have no present reason, therefore, for wishing any formal change in the position or institutions of Egypt; and the only change in the present, or rather the recent, practice which we desire is, that these institutions shall be worked with tolerable honesty, and with economy and humanity. Thus worked, they furnish what we want — an Egyptian neutrality which has a fair chance of permanence. Our Representatives in Egypt should, therefore, do all in their power to sustain the Native Government in its efforts to govern the country well; and this, for the present, must be an object with which no other should be allowed to interfere. So long as the country is formally independent, the Natives only can govern it. If they cannot do it, no one else can do it — without military occupation. It has been sufficiently proved that the Mussulmans will not willingly obey a Government which is nominally European, or of which the prevailing and most conspicuous elements are European. Their reluctance can only be overcome by force; and force the Europeans do not possess without military occupation.

It becomes, therefore, matter of great moment to make the Native Government succeed. For this purpose it should, in its own interest, employ Europeans largely, and should be pressed to do so, if insensible to its own interest in that respect; but they must be kept as much in the background as possible. They should not be used in sufficient numbers to destroy the apparent authority of the Native Government; and the employments to which they are named should be selected rather with a view to the effective exercise of power, than to the possession of conspicuous official rank. The posts which confer the greatest influence, and excite the least jealousy, are the posts which should be sought for Europeans.

In the performance of their duty as counsellors of the Egyptian Government, the Representatives of Her Majesty will be distinguished by one peculiar mark from those of any other Power. The policy they counsel will not be shaped by the interests of any particular class of creditors. It is their duty to do what they properly can to secure any rights Englishmen may possess in the country; they will not exclude English creditors from the benefit of this rule; and, for the sake of Egypt herself, they will wish that she should pay her debts. If, therefore, it shall appear that any particular claim, or class of claims in which Englishmen are largely interested, is being unfairly treated by reason of the diplomatic support given to competing creditors of other nationalities, the English Agent cannot refuse to interfere. But the protection of the private interests of creditors or others will be an object of a merely secondary kind, and will not compete with the important political aims which it is their chief duty to secure. . . .

What I have said refers to the present order of things; it serves the interest of England better than any that apparently could be substituted for it, and the efforts of Her Majesty's Agent must be chiefly directed to insure that it shall work efficiently, and thus continue to exist.

But the contingency of a failure in these efforts must be contemplated. The character of the present Khedive gives ground for hope; on the other hand, the character and capacity of the men by whom he is surrounded, and from whom his Ministers must be chosen, justify apprehension as to the future. It may be that the causes of decay which at present threaten all the Mahommedan countries of the world will prove incurable in Egypt also. Such an issue is, however, in any case, probably distant, and the conditions under which it may take place cannot be foreseen now. But the possibility of it must be borne in mind. When it comes, if it is to come, it must find England as strong as any other country in substantial influence.

If any tendency betrays itself so to arrange the European appointments that a preponderance either in importance or number is assigned to other European nations, a state of things is being created which in the case of a collapse of Egypt would be dangerous to English interests. Her Majesty's Agent should, therefore, watch these appointments with vigilance, and interpose on any symptom of a hostile inclination on the part of the Government in this respect. I should be disposed to attach less importance to the distribution of Native appointments. In all Oriental countries where Embassies are powerful, the Native competitors for place are very ready to enrol themselves as clients of one Power or the other. But their friendship is not trustworthy, and their success of little real value to the Power of whom they are nominally partisans. Foreign Representatives in supporting them are apt to allow their exertions to degenerate into a race for small diplomatic victories, and in the struggle the object of appointing the best man is entirely forgotten. To us, whose chief interest in Egypt is that the Government should last and work well, it is much more important that the best men should be employed than that the partisans of England should be promoted. This principle, however, must not be stretched so far as to sanction the abandonment of Native statesmen or officials who, by listening to the advice of England, had exposed themselves to the resentment either of some other Agency, or of the Native authorities.

It should further be borne in mind that if the Ottoman Empire were to fall to pieces, and Egypt become independent, the part of Egypt which interests England is the sea-coast, including the railway and other communications across the Isthmus. If it should happen that Egypt were divided, and the sea-coast and communications remained under the dominant influence of England, while the interior were to be otherwise disposed of — supposing the stability of such an arrangement could be guaranteed — England would have no reason to be dissatisfied with it.

In the disposal, therefore, of European appointments, it is of primary importance to keep in English hands, as far as may be possible, the harbours, customs, lighthouses, and the communications by land and water from sea to sea. It is only of course to a limited extent that this can be done; and the necessity is not sufficiently urgent at present to justify steps which would awaken the jealousy of other Powers. But the extension and consolidation of English influence upon these points is the object which, as regards the future, must be kept in view. Whether it shall be pursued slowly or energetically must depend upon the circumstances of the moment.

Foreign Secretary Lord Salisbury to Lord Cromer in Egypt, August 2, 1898

It is desirable that you should be placed in possession of the views of Her Majesty's Government in respect to the line of action to be followed in the event of Khartoum being occupied at an early date by the forces now operating in the Soudan under the command of Sir Herbert Kitchener.

In view of the substantial military and financial co-operation which has recently been afforded by Her Majesty's Government to the Government

From *Foundations of British Foreign Policy*, ed. Harold Temperley and Lillian M. Penson (Cambridge: Cambridge University Press, 1938), pp. 507–09. Reprinted by permission of Cambridge University Press.

of the Khedive, Her Majesty's Government have decided that at Khartoum the British and Egyptian flags should be hoisted side by side. This decision will have no reference to the manner in which the occupied countries are to be administered in the future. It is not necessary at present to define their political status with any great precision. These matters can be considered at a later period. You will, however, explain to the Khedive and to his Ministers that the procedure I have indicated is intended to emphasise the fact that Her Majesty's Government consider that they have a predominant voice in all matters connected with the Soudan, and that they expect that any advice which they may think fit to tender to the Egyptian Government, in respect to Soudan affairs, will be followed.

Her Majesty's Government do not contemplate that after the occupation of Khartoum any further military operations on a large scale, or involving any considerable expense, will be undertaken for the occupation of the provinces to the south; but the Sirdar is authorised to send two flotillas, one up the White and the other up the Blue Nile.

You are authorised to settle the composition of these two forces in consultation with the Sirdar.

Sir Herbert Kitchener should in person command the White Nile Flotilla as far as Fashoda, and may take with him a small body of British troops, should you concur with him in thinking such a course desirable.

The officer in command of the Blue Nile Flotilla is authorised to go as far as the foot of the cataract, which is believed to commence about Roseires. He is not to land troops with a view to marching beyond the point on the river navigable for steamers. Should he, before reaching Roseires, encounter any Abyssinian outposts, he is to halt, report the circumstances, and wait for further instructions.

There are two points to which Sir Herbert Kitchener's attention should be specially directed.

The first of these is that in dealing with any French or Abyssinian authorities who may be encountered, nothing should be said or done which would in any way imply a recognition on behalf of Her Majesty's Government of a title to possession on behalf of France or Abyssinia to any portion of the Nile Valley.

As regards France, the following extract from a note addressed by Sir Edmund Monson to M. Hanotaux on the 10th December, 1897, sets forth the view held by Her Majesty's Government on this subject —

"Her majesty's Government," Sir Edmund Monson said, "must not be understood to admit that any other European Power than Great Britain has any claim to occupy any part of the Valley of the Nile. The views of the British Government upon this matter were plainly stated in Parliament by Sir Edward Grey some years ago, during the administration of the Earl of Rosebery, and were formally communicated to the French Government at the time. Her

Majesty's present Government entirely adhere to the language that was on this occasion employed by their predecessors."

The second point, which you should press strongly on the attention of Sir Herbert Kitchener, is the necessity of avoiding, by all possible means, any collision with the forces of the Emperor Menelek.

It is possible that a French force may be found in occupation of some portion of the Nile Valley. Should this contingency arise, the course of action to be pursued must depend so much on local circumstances that it is neither necessary nor desirable to furnish Sir Herbert Kitchener with detailed instructions. Her Majesty's Government entertain full confidence in Sir Herbert Kitchener's judgment and discretion. They feel assured that he will endeavour to convince the Commander of any French force with which he may come in contact that the presence of the latter in the Nile Valley is an infringement of the rights both of Great Britain and of the Khedive. . . .

It is scarcely necessary for me to add that, in the execution of the difficult and important work which now lies before him, Sir Herbert Kitchener may rely on the full and cordial support of Her Majesty's Government.

Rennell Rodd, British Representative in Cairo, to Lord Salisbury, September 25, 1898

I have just received the following telegram this morning from Sir Herbert Kitchener:

"I have just returned here from Fashoda where I found Captain Marchand, accompanied by eight officers and 120 men, located in the old Government buildings, over which they had hoisted the French flag; I sent a letter announcing my approach the day before my arrival at Fashoda. A small rowboat carrying the French flag brought me a reply from Captain Marchand on the following morning, the 19th September, stating that he had reached Fashoda on the 10th July, his Government having given him instructions to occupy the Bahr-el-Ghazal as far as the confluence of the Bahf-el-Jebel, as well as the Shilluk country on the left bank of the White Nile as far as Fashoda. He stated that he had concluded a Treaty with the protection of France, and that he had sent this Treaty to his Government for ratification by way of Abyssinia, as well as by the Bahr-el-Ghazal. Captain Marchand described the fight which he had had with the Dervishes on the 25th August, and said that, in anticipation of a second and more

From *The Imperialism Reader: Documents and Readings on Modern Expansionism*, ed. Louis L. Snyder (Princeton: Van Nostrand, 1962), pp. 342–43. Reprinted by permission of Van Nostrand Reinhold Company.

severe attack, he had sent his steamer south for reinforcements, but our arrival had averted this danger.

"When we arrived at Fashoda, Captain Marchand and M. Germain came on board, and I at once stated that the presence of a French force at Fashoda and in the Valley of the Nile was regarded as a direct infringement of the rights of the Egyptian Government and that of Great Britain, and I protested in the strongest terms against their occupation of Fashoda and their hoisting of the French flag in the dominions of His Highness the Khedive. In reply, Captain Marchand stated that he had precise orders to occupy the country and to hoist the French flag over the Government buildings at Fashoda, and that it was impossible for him to retire without receiving orders from his Government to that effect, but he did not expect that these orders would be delayed. On my pressing him to say whether, seeing that I had a preponderating force, he was prepared to resist the hoisting of the Egyptian flag at Fashoda, he hesitated and replied that resistance was impossible. I then caused the flag to be hoisted on a ruined bastion of the old Egyptian fortifications about 500 yards south of the French flag, and on the only road which leads to the interior from the French position, which is surrounded by impassable marshes on all sides. Before leaving for the south, I handed to Captain Marchand a formal protest in writing, on behalf of the British and Egyptian Governments, against any occupation by France of any part of the Nile Valley, such occupation being an infringement of the rights of these Governments which I could not recognise.

"I appointed Major Jackson to be Commandant of the Fashoda district, where I left a garrison consisting of one Soudanese battalion; four guns, and a gun-boat, after which I proceeded to the Sobat, where, on the 20th September, a post was established and the flag hoisted. . . . On my way north, as I passed Fashoda, I sent a letter to Captain Marchand, stating that all transport of war material on the Nile was absolutely prohibited, as the country was under military law. The Shilluk Chief, with a large following, has come into Major Jackson's camp; the whole tribe are delighted to return to their allegiance to us, and the Chief absolutely denies having made any Treaty with the French.

"The position in which Captain Marchand finds himself at Fashoda is as impossible as it is absurd. He is cut off from the interior, and his water transport is quite inadequate; he is, moreover, short of ammunition and supplies, which must take months to reach him; he has no following in the country, and nothing could have saved him and his expedition from being annihilated by the Dervishes had we been a fortnight later in crushing the Khalifa.

"The futility of all their efforts is fully realised by Captain Marchand himself, and he seems quite as anxious to return as we are to facilitate his departure. In his present position he is powerless, but I hope that Her

Majesty's Government will take the necessary steps for his removal as soon as possible, as the presence of a French force and flag on the Nile is manifestly extremely undesirable.

"Captain Marchand only lost four natives on the journey, and his expedition is all well.

"I am sending a complete despatch by Lord Edward Cecil, who is leaving with it for Cairo at once."

Spokesmen for Imperialism

British poet and writer Rudyard Kipling (1865–1936) wrote his poem "White Man's Burden" in 1899 following America's victory in the Spanish-American War. The poem was a clarion call to the Anglo-Saxon powers to fulfill their mission and bring "civilization" to the non-Western world. It is a good illustration of how humanitarian and missionary zeal could be combined with a Social Darwinist sense of racial superiority. The arguments of the French colonialist statesman, Jules Ferry (1832–1893) are quite similar to those of Kipling, but, as one might expect, he adds some of a more sober variety. Like Bismarck, who encouraged him, Ferry was convinced that the age of free trade was over and that colonialism was an economic as well as a political and military necessity. Under Ferry's two premierships, France occupied Tunis and Indochina. His policy was unpopular with the extreme left for ideological reasons and was also disliked by many nationalists because they feared it would divert France from the German danger.

Kipling: "White Man's Burden"

Take up the White Man's burden —
Send forth the best ye breed —
Go bind your sons to exile
To serve your captives' need;
To wait in heavy harness,
On fluttered folk and wild —
Your new caught, sullen peoples,
Half-devil and half-child.

From *Rudyard Kipling's Verse*, definitive edition (New York: Doubleday, 1940), and Rudyard Kipling, *The Five Nations* (London: Methuen, n.d.). Reprinted by permission of Mrs. George Bambridge, Doubleday and Company, Inc., Methuen & Co., and Macmillan Co. of Canada.

Take up the White Man's burden —
In patience to abide,
To veil the threat of terror
And check the show of pride;
By open speech and simple,
An hundred times made plain
To seek another's profit,
And work another's gain.

Take up the White Man's burden —
The savage wars of peace —
Fill full the mouth of Famine
And bid the sickness cease;
And when your goal is nearest
The end for others sought,
Watch sloth and heathen Folly
Bring all your hopes to nought.

Take up the White Man's burden —
No tawdry rule of kings,
But toil of serf and sweeper —
The tale of common things.
The ports ye shall not enter,
The roads ye shall not tread,
Go make them with your living,
And mark them with your dead.

Take up the White Man's burden —
And reap his old reward:
The blame of those ye better,
The hate of those ye guard —
The cry of hosts ye humour
(Ah, slowly!) toward the light: —
"Why brought he us from bondage,
Our loved Egyptian night?"

Take up the White Man's burden —
Ye dare not stoop to less —
Nor call too loud on Freedom
To cloke your weariness;
By all ye cry or whisper,
By all ye leave or do,
The silent, sullen peoples
Shall weigh your Gods and you.

Take up the White Man's burden —
Have done with childish days —
The lightly proferred laurel,
The easy, ungrudged praise.
Comes now, to search your manhood
Through all the thankless years,
Cold, edged with dear-bought wisdom,
The judgment of your peers!

Ferry's Speech to the French National Assembly, July 28, 1883

M. JULES FERRY. Gentlemen, it embarrasses me to make such a prolonged demand upon the gracious attention of the Chamber, but I believe that the duty I am fulfilling upon this platform is not a useless one: It is as strenuous for me as for you, but I believe that there is some benefit in summarizing and condensing, in the form of arguments, the principles, the motives, and the various interests by which a policy of colonial expansion may be justified; it goes without saying that I will try to remain reasonable, moderate, and never lose sight of the major continental interests which are the primary concern of this country. What I wish to say, to support this proposition, is that in fact, just as in word, the policy of colonial expansion is a political and economic system; I wish to say that one can relate this system to three orders of ideas: economic ideas, ideas of civilization in its highest sense, and ideas of politics and patriotism.

In the area of economics, I will allow myself to place before you, with the support of some figures, the considerations which justify a policy of colonial expansion from the point of view of that need, felt more and more strongly by the industrial populations of Europe and particularly those of our own rich and hard working country: the need for export markets. Is this some kind of chimera? Is this a view of the future or is it not rather a pressing need, and, we could say, the cry of our industrial population? I will formulate only in a general way what each of you, in the different parts of France, is in a position to confirm. Yes, what is lacking for our great industry, drawn irrevocably on to the path of exportation by the [free trade] treaties of 1860, what it lacks more and more is export markets. Why? Because next door to us Germany is surrounded by barriers, because beyond the ocean, the United States of America has

From *Modern Imperialism: Western Overseas Expansion and Its Aftermath*, ed. Ralph A. Austen (Lexington, Mass.: Heath, 1969), pp. 70–73.

become protectionist, protectionist in the most extreme sense, because not only have these great markets, I will not say closed but shrunk, and thus become more difficult of access for our industrial products, but also these great states are beginning to pour products not seen heretofore onto our own markets. . . . It is not necessary to pursue this demonstration any farther. . . .

Gentlemen, there is a second point, a second order of ideas to which I have to give equal attention, but as quickly as possible, believe me; it is the humanitarian and civilizing side of the question. On this point the honorable M. Camille Pellatan has jeered in his own refined and clever manner; he jeers, he condemns, and he says "What is this civilization which you impose with cannon-balls? What is it but another form of barbarism? Don't these populations, these inferior races, have the same rights as you? Aren't they masters of their own houses? Have they called upon you? You come to them against their will, you offer them violence, but not civilization." There, gentlemen, is the thesis; I do not hesitate to say that this is not politics, nor is it history: it is political metaphysics. ["Ah, Ah" *on far left*].

. . . Gentlemen, I must speak from a higher and more truthful plane. It must be stated openly that, in effect, superior races have rights over inferior races. [*Movement on many benches on the far left.*]

M. JULES MAIGNE. Oh! You dare to say this in the country which has proclaimed the rights of man!

M. DE GUILLOUTET. This is a justification of slavery and the slave trade!

M. JULES FERRY. If M. Maigne is right, if the declaration of the rights of man was written for the blacks of equatorial Africa, then by what right do you impose regular commerce upon them? They have not called upon you.

M. RAOUL DUVAL. We do not want to impose anything upon them. It is you who wish to do so!

M. JULES MAIGNE. To propose and to impose are two different things!

M. GEORGES PERIN. In any case, you cannot bring about commerce by force.

M. JULES FERRY. I repeat that superior races have a right, because they have a duty. They have the duty to civilize inferior races. . . . [*Approbation from the left. New interruptions from the extreme left and from the right.*] . . .

Gentlemen, there are certain considerations which merit the attention of all patriots. The conditions of naval warfare have been profoundly altered. ["Very true! Very true!"]

At this time, as you know, a warship cannot carry more than fourteen days' worth of coal, no matter how perfectly it is organized, and a ship which is out of coal is a derelict on the surface of the sea, abandoned to the first person who comes along. Thence the necessity of having on the oceans provision stations, shelters, ports for defense and revictualling. [*Applause at the center and left. Various interruptions.*] And it is for this that we needed Tunisia, for this that we needed Saigon and the Mekong Delta, for this that we need Madagascar, that we are at Diégo-Suarez and Vohemar [two Madagascar ports] and will never leave them! [*Applause from a great number of benches.*] Gentlemen, in Europe as it is today, in this competition of so many rivals which we see growing around us, some by perfecting their military or maritime forces, others by the prodigious development of an ever growing population; in a Europe, or rather in a universe of this sort, a policy of peaceful seclusion or abstention is simply the highway to decadence! Nations are great in our times only by means of the activities which they develop; it is not simply "by the peaceful shining forth of institutions" [*Interruptions on the extreme left and right*] that they are great at this hour . . .

As for me, I am astounded to find the monarchist parties becoming indignant over the fact that the Republic of France is following a policy which does not confine itself to that ideal of modesty, of reserve, and, if you will allow me the expression, of bread and butter [*Interruptions and laughter on the left*] which the representatives of fallen monarchies wish to impose upon France. [*Applause at the center.*]

. . . [The Republican Party] has shown that it is quite aware that one cannot impose upon France a political ideal conforming to that of nations like independent Belgium and the Swiss Republic; that something else is needed for France: that she cannot be merely a free country, that she must also be a great country, exercizing all of her rightful influence over the destiny of Europe, that she ought to propagate this influence throughout the world and carry everywhere that she can her language, her customs, her flag, her arms, and her genius. [*Applause at center and left.*]

Russian Expansion in Asia

Feodor Dostoevsky (1821–1881) is far better known for his brilliant psychological novels than for his support of Russian imperialism in Asia. Yet he was a strong supporter of tsarism and Russian orthodoxy, and he opposed Westernizing tendencies in Russia. His celebration of General Skobelev's capture of the Turkoman central Asian fortress of Geok-Tepe in December, 1880, shows that Dostoevsky believed that the continuous expansion of Russian frontiers in Asia would give the tsar-

*ist empire new strength and opportunities and would prepare it to
complete its Pan-Slavic mission in the Balkans and at the Straits. He
was prepared to risk confrontation with Britain in the east, as were
many of the military men in central Asia who often advanced without
orders from their superiors. In 1885 war did almost erupt with Britain
over the Afghanistan frontier. In 1891 Russia began building the
Trans-Siberian Railroad, and its expansion in the Far East was only
checked by the Russo-Japanese War of 1904.*

Dostoevsky: What Is Asia to Us?

Geok-Tepe is captured. The Turkomans are defeated, and although
they are not yet quite pacified, our victory is indubitable. Society and the
press are jubilant. But was it long ago that society, and partly also the
press, took a most indifferent attitude toward this affair? . . . "Why
should we go there? What is Asia to us? So much money has been expended, whereas we have a famine, diphtheria, we have no schools, etc."
Yes, such opinions were expressed; we heard them. Not everybody shared
them — far from it. Even so, one has to admit that, of late, many people
began to adopt a hostile attitude toward our aggressive policy in Asia.
True, the lack of information concerning the expedition undertaken was
a contributing factor to this mood. Only quite recently news began to
slip into Russia from the foreign press, whereas Skobelev's telegrams
were printed throughout Russia when the undertaking was practically all
over. Nevertheless, one can hardly maintain that our society has a clear
conception of our mission in Asia — what specifically she means to us now
and in the future. Generally speaking, our whole Russian Asia, including
Siberia, still exists to Russia merely in the form of some kind of an ap-
pendix in which European Russia has no desire to take any interest. "We
are Europe," it is implied. "What is our business in Asia!" There even
sounded very harsh voices: "Oh, this Russian Asia of ours! We are even
unable to establish order and settle properly in Europe, and here we have
to meddle with Asia! Why, Asia is quite superfluous to us! How can we
get rid of her!" Even in our day such opinions are expressed by our wiseacres — of course, out of their great wisdom.

Skobelev's victory resounded all over Asia to her remotest corners:
"Another fierce and proud orthodox people bowed before the White
Czar!" And let this rumor echo and re-echo. Let the conviction of the
invincibility of the White Czar and of his sword grow and spread among

From Feodor Dostoevsky, *Diary of a Writer* (© 1949 by Charles Scribner's Sons), vol.
2, trans. Boris Brasol (New York: Scribner's, 1949), pp. 1043–52. Reprinted by permission of Charles Scribner's Sons.

the millions of those peoples — to the very borders of India and in India herself. . . .

What for? What future? What is the need of the future seizure of Asia? What's our business there?

This is necessary because Russia is not only in Europe but also in Asia; because the Russian is not only a European but also an Asiatic. Moreover, Asia, perhaps, holds out greater promises to us than Europe. In our future destinies Asia is, perhaps, our main outlet!

I anticipate the indignation with which this reactionary suggestion of mine will be read. To me, however, it is an axiom. Yes, if there is one of the major roots which has to be rendered healthy, it is precisely our opinion of Asia. We must banish the slavish fear that Europe will call us Asiatic barbarians, and that it will be said that we are more Asiatics than Europeans. This fear that Europe might regard us as Asiatics has been haunting us for almost two centuries. It has particularly increased during the present nineteenth century, reaching almost the point of panic. . . . This erroneous fright of ours, this mistaken view of ourselves solely as Europeans, and not Asiatics — which we have never ceased to be — this shame and this faulty opinion have cost us a good deal in the course of the last two centuries, and the price we have had to pay has consisted of the loss of our spiritual independence, of our unsuccessful policies in Europe, and finally of money — God only knows how much money — which we spent in order to prove to Europe that we were Europeans and not Asiatics. . . .

Europe, however, for once, at least, did not believe our Russian Europeans. On the contrary, in this matter her inferences coincide with those of our Slavophiles, although she knows them not — at best she might have merely heard something about them. The coincidence is precisely that Europe believes, much as the Slavophiles believe, that we have an "idea" of our own — a peculiar, not a European idea; that Russia can have, is capable of possessing, an idea. Of course, as yet, Europe knows nothing about the essence of our idea, since did she know it she would forthwith be pacified and even gladdened. But some day she will unfailingly come to know this idea, precisely when the critical moment in her destiny arrives. At present, however, she does not believe: admitting the fact that we possess an idea, she is afraid of it. Finally, she is quite disgusted with us, even though, at times, she is polite to us. For instance, they readily admit that Russian science can already point to several remarkable workers; that it has to its credit several good works which have even rendered service to European science. But under no circumstance will Europe now believe that not only scientific workers (even though very talented) may be born in Russia, but men of genius, leaders of mankind, such as a Bacon, Kant or Aristotle. This they will never believe, since they do not believe in our civilization, while, as yet, they do not know our future idea. In truth, they are right: we shall have no Bacon, no Newton, no Aristotle so long as we fail to stand on our own road and be spiritually independent. The same is true of all other things — of art and industry: Europe is ready to praise us, to stroke our heads, but she does not recognize us as hers, she despises us, whether secretly or openly: she considers us an inferior race. At times, she feels aversion to us, especially when we fling ourselves on her neck with brotherly embraces.

However, it is difficult to turn away from "the window to Europe"; here is predestination. Meanwhile Asia may be, in truth, our future outlet! I reiterate this exclamation. And if we could only take cognizance of this idea, even though partially, what a root would be rendered whole! Asia, our Asiatic Russia — why, this is also our sick root, which has to be not only refreshed but resurrected and transformed! A principle, a new principle, a new vision of the matter — this is what we need. . . .

"What for? What for?" irritated voices will sound. "Our Asiatic affairs even now continually require from us troops and unproductive expenditures. And what is Asia's industry? What is her merchandise? Where shall we find there consumers of our goods? And you suggest, no one knows why, that we should forever turn away from Europe!"

"Not forever," I continue to insist, "for the time being, and not altogether: hard as we may try we shall never completely tear ourselves away from Europe. We should not abandon Europe completely. Nor is this necessary. She is a 'land of holy miracles'; this was uttered by a most ardent Slavophile. Europe, even as Russia, is our mother, our second mother. We have taken much from her; we shall again take, and we shall not wish to be ungrateful to her. Last year, at the Pushkin festivities in Moscow, I said a few words about the future great mission of the Russian people in Europe (in which I believe), and much mud was thrown at me, I was scolded, by everybody — even by those who had then embraced me — as though I had perpetrated an abomination, a nasty deed, having then uttered my word.

"However, perhaps, my word will not be forgotten. But enough has been said about this. Even so, we have the right to take care of our reeducation and of our exodus from Egypt, since we ourselves created out of Europe something on the order of our spiritual Egypt."

"Wait" — I shall be interrupted — "in what way will Asia contribute to our independence? There, we'll fall asleep in an Asiatic fashion, but we shall not become independent!"

"You see" — I continue — "when we turn to Asia, with our new vision of her, in Russia there may occur something akin to what happened in Europe when America was discovered. Since, in truth, to us Asia is like the then undiscovered America. With our aspiration for Asia, our spirit and forces will be regenerated. The moment we become independent, we shall find what to do, whereas during the two centuries with Europe we lost the habit of any work; we became chatterers and idlers."

"Well, how are you going to arouse us for the Asiatic venture, if we are idlers? Who's going to be aroused first even if it were proved, as by two times two, that our happiness lies there?"

"In Europe we were hangers-on and slaves, whereas we shall go to Asia as masters. In Europe we were Asiatics, whereas in Asia we, too, are Europeans. Our civilizing mission in Asia will bribe our spirit and drive us thither. It is only necessary that the movement should start. Build only two railroads: begin with the one to Siberia, and then — to Central Asia — and at once you will see the consequences."

"Indeed, yours is a modest desire!" people will tell me laughingly. "Where are the funds? And what shall we get in return? — Nothing but a loss to us!"

"First, had we in the last twenty-five years set aside only three million rubles annually (and three million rubles, at times, simply slip through our fingers), by now we should have built seventy-five million rubles' worth of Asiatic roads, *i.e.*, over one thousand versts, no matter how you reckon. Then you speak about losses. Oh, if instead of us Englishmen or Americans inhabited Russia, they would show you what losses mean! They would certainly discover our America! Do you know that in Asia there are lands which are less explored than the interior of Africa? And do we know what riches are concealed in the bosom of these boundless lands? Oh, they would get at everything — metals and minerals, innumerable coal fields; they would find and discover everything — and they would know how to use these materials. They would summon science to their aid; they would compel the earth to yield fifty grains to one — that same earth about which we here still think that it is nothing but a steppe naked as our palm. Corn would attract people; production, industry, would come into existence. Don't you worry: consumers would be found, and the road to them would be discovered; they would be found in the depths of Asia, where millions of them are slumbering now; to reach them new roads would be constructed!" . . .

. . . A new Russia will arise which in due time will regenerate and resurrect the old one and will show the latter the road which she has to follow. This, however, requires a new principle and a turn. These would necessitate the least destruction and commotion. Let it be only slightly fathomed (but fathomed) that Asia is our future outlet, that our riches are there, that there is our ocean; that when in Europe, because of the overcrowded condition alone, inevitable and humiliating communism is established, communism which Europe herself will loathe; when whole throngs will crowd around one hearth, and gradually individual economies will be ruined, while families will forsake their homes and will start living in collective communes; when children (three quarters of them foundlings) will be brought up in foundling institutions — then we shall still have wide expanses, meadows and forests, and our children will grow up in their parents' homes, not in stone barracks — amidst gardens and sowed fields, beholding above them clear, blue skies.

"Yes, Asia holds out to us many a promise, many an opportunity, the full scale of which we here cannot clearly conceive. . . .

"Wait" — I hear a voice — "you said something about Gambetta. But we are in no position to brush everything aside. Take, to begin with, the Eastern question: it remains pending. How are we going to evade it?"

"On the Eastern question at this time I would say: At this minute, in our political spheres there is, perhaps, not even one political mind which would consider it common sense that Constantinople must be ours (save in some remote, enigmatic future). If so, what is there to wait for? At this minute the essence of the Eastern problem comes down to an alliance of Germany with Austria, plus the Austrian seizures in Turkey which are encouraged by Prince Bismarck. We can and, of course, will protest only in some extreme cases. However, so long as these two nations are united, what can we do without incurring very grave risks? Please observe that the Allies are waiting only until, at length, we should grow angry. However, as heretofore, we may love the Slavic nations, encourage them at times, even extend our help to them. Besides, they will not perish within a short time. And the term is likely to expire very soon. Let it suffice to say that we shall make it appear that we do not intend to meddle with European affairs, as heretofore; bereft of us, they will quarrel among themselves all the sooner. Indeed, Austria will never believe that Germany fell in love with her solely because of her beautiful eyes: Austria knows only too well that in the long run Germany must incorporate the Austrian Germans into the German union. But for no price will Austria cede her Germans — not even if Constantinople were offered her for them — so highly she values them. Therefore pretexts for discords are present there. And, on top of that, Germany is faced with the same insoluble French problem which, to her, has now become an eternal problem. Besides, Germany's unification itself appears to be incomplete and is apt to be undermined. It also appears that European socialism not only is not dead but continues to constitute a very grave menace.

"In a word, let us only wait and refrain from meddling — even if we are invited to meddle. Just as soon as their discord comes to a crash, 'political equilibrium' will crack, and then the Eastern question will at once be solved. We should only have to choose the opportune moment, even as at the time of the Franco-Prussian slaughter, and we should suddenly declare, as we then declared concerning the Black Sea: 'We do not wish to recognize any Austrian seizures in Turkey!' — and all seizures will instantly vanish, perhaps, together with Austria herself. In this way we shall catch up with everything which ostensibly, for the time being, we let slip."

"What about England? You overlook England. When she observes our Asiatic aspirations, she will instantly grow alarmed."

"Paraphrasing the proverb, I retort: 'If one fears England one should sit at home and move nowhere.' Besides, nothing new is going to alarm her since she is also alarmed with the same old thing at present. On the contrary, now we are holding her in confusion and ignorance concerning the future, and she is expecting from us the worst things. When, however, she comes to understand the true character of all our moves in Asia, perhaps some of her apprehensions will be toned down. . . . Well, I concede: she will not tone them down; she is too far from this frame of mind. Still, I repeat: 'If one fears England, one should sit at home and move nowhere!' Therefore, let me exclaim once more: 'Long live the Geok-Tepe victory! Long live Skobelev and his good soldiers!' Eternal memory to those valiant knights who 'were eliminated from the rolls.' We shall record them on our rolls."

Europeans in China
and Germany's Search
for a "Place in the Sun"

In 1894 the old rivalry between China and Japan erupted into war. China's defeat led to a scramble for concessions among the European powers, and the greed of one inevitably led to a demand for compensations by another. Germany had no intention of being left out of the act. The Germans had difficulty determining exactly what they should take in China. Finally, they fixed on Kiaochow on the Shantung peninsula, and they used the murder of two German missionaries in that part of China as an excuse to send part of the German fleet to occupy Kiaochow. William II, who had longed to engage in a "world policy," took the occasion of the fleet's departure to make one of his many ill-considered speeches. His reference to the "mailed fist" was a prelude to an even more notorious address he delivered in 1900, when German troops were sent to put down the Boxer uprising in China. At that time, he urged them to behave like "Huns." The appellation was picked up by the Allies in World War I and was thereafter used when speaking of the German army.

Chancellor Hohenlohe's Memorandum to Emperor William II, March 19, 1895

Apropos the telegram submitted to Your Majesty in which the Emperor of China has sought Your Majesty's support in bringing about peace with Japan, I beg Your Imperial and Royal Majesty's permission to present the following regarding our position relative to the Chinese-Japanese conflict:

Conformable to the previous decision of Your Majesty our attitude hitherto was one of strict neutrality. Even before it came to real hostilities Your Majesty's representatives in Peking and Tokio were empowered to join in the common efforts of the other Great Powers for the peaceful settlement of differences, and later after the outbreak of hostilities we declared ourselves ready to coöperate in common measures of the Powers insofar as these were restricted to the protection of persons and property.

On the other hand, the repeated requests from England and also from China that we participate in intervention were rejected on the ground that such a step seemed premature.

The following were the essential considerations: England and Russia are especially interested in the development of things in the Far East to the extent that the former would like to see China maintained as far as possible unweakened as a buffer state to protect India against the advance of Russia and the latter does not wish to see its possible claims upon Korea, or at least upon portions of that country, prejudiced by further Japanese progress. But Germany, for the present at any rate, has not at stake any interests of like importance in Eastern Asia. German commerce especially has not suffered noticeably under war conditions. On the contrary, our manufacturers, merchants, and ship owners have had a good opportunity to make profit by supplying and transporting war materials. With our participation in the intervention undertaken by England and Russia merely for the restoration of peace, we would serve the interests of those States and indeed probably with considerable sacrifice for us, for it is obvious that against a victorious Japan only an armed intervention or at least the display of preponderant forces upon the theater of war would offer prospect of success.

It already follows from these considerations that our attitude would be altered if there were a prospect of special advantages as compensation for the sacrifices on our part. And indeed the gaining of several places on the Chinese coast might be considered as such an advantage of first rate importance, which could serve as points of support for the navy and for our

From *The Imperialism Reader: Documents and Readings on Modern Expansionism*, ed. Louis L. Snyder (Princeton: Van Nostrand, 1962), pp. 297–301. Reprinted by permission of Van Nostrand Reinhold Company.

commerce, a need which has already been felt for some decades. [*Kaiser's note: "Right."*]

Naturally it cannot be the affair of Germany, relatively the least directly interested, to come forward with claims of this sort and thereby give a signal to a certain extent for the first partition of the Chinese Empire. Rather we should have to wait until other powers set about to realize similar purposes.

Whether or not it comes to this will depend on the peace negotiations. Japan holds back for the time being the conditions which it will set up and appears to be willing to reveal its final demands only gradually. There are in the meantime indications that these will be very hard for China. The Japanese Ambassador here spoke a few days ago in strictest confidence and with the request for secrecy of an exchange of views between the Russians and his Government at the end of last month whereby Japan would acquiesce in the Russian demand for the complete independence of Korea and in return Russia will accord its benevolent support in the peace negotiations in the sense of procuring war indemnity, surrender of territory, and new regulations of commercial relations between Japan and China. In harmony with this is the fact that according to the announcement of Your Majesty's Ambassador in London, Russia and England have agreed that the independence of Korea is to be maintained.

Mr. Aoki added the confidential communication that Japanese military men consider the cession of Port Arthur with a part of the hinterland as indispensable while in their eyes the surrender of an island, for example Formosa, would be only of lesser significance. [*Kaiser's note: "We might claim that then."*]

Now, in my opinion, Port Arthur in Japanese hands would signify the domination of the Gulf of Chili and hence a standing menace to the Chinese capital. It may be assumed therefore that the Chinese will resist such a cession to the utmost.

To be sure, China's position in a military way is almost hopeless. Your Majesty's minister in Peking answered to questions sent by telegraph to the effect that he did not believe that the Chinese forces could hold the enemy back from Peking; that the capture of the capital would not necessarily result in the dissolution of the existing political order; but that nevertheless Le-Hung-Chang considers the withdrawal of the Court from Peking as no longer possible. On the other hand, Baron von Gutschmid telegraphs from Tokio that Japan can continue the war till next winter without fearing exhaustion of man power, financial means or materials of war. Moreover, that the war enthusiasm of the Japanese nation was undiminished.

Likewise, it seems not impossible that the disposition which has thus far prevailed among Chinese statesmen to deceive themselves regarding the true situation reaches even to the extent of renewing the unequal struggle if Japan will not let drop its demand regarding Port Arthur and be satisfied possibly with Formosa.

In this case it might indeed come to an intervention of the powers in spite of existing differences of interests among them and so precipitate for us as well the Chinese question.

In this situation it follows in my humble opinion as a criterion of our policy that on the one hand we must avoid allowing ourselves to be drawn prematurely into action to serve primarily foreign interests, but on the other hand we must hold open to ourselves the participation in such undertakings as could lead to dislocations in the relative strength of the great European powers in Eastern Asia. [*Kaiser's note: "Right."*]

I ask Your Majesty, accordingly, to authorize me to direct the Imperial Ambassador in London, who is for the time being generally informed regarding the above-mentioned viewpoint, to give the Government there to understand at this time orally and without committing ourselves that Your Majesty's Government is not essentially opposed to the idea of a common intervention, and indeed would not hesitate, in the face of essential alterations in the situation in Eastern Asia, to take an emphatic stand for German [*Kaiser's note: "Yes, but not Chinese"*] interests.

England seems urgently to desire our participation to have at least a counterweight against France and Russia, judging from the utterances thus far of the statesmen there, and will undoubtedly meet our wishes to a certain extent at any rate. [*Kaiser's note: "But we must sell ourselves very dearly."*]

What and how much we shall ask for our coöperation can scarcely at this time be determined and will depend among other things upon what the other powers claim. In this connection there is the statement of the English Ambassador, Sir F. Lascelles, at Petersburg, and reported by Your Majesty's Ambassador there, indicating that England would have no objections to Russia's annexing a part of Northern China on account of her railway and perhaps a harbor in Korea. What England would take for herself is not known. [*Kaiser's note: "Shanghai!"*] Past experience suggests among other possibilities the Island of Chusan opposite Ningpo, which was once occupied by her.

In the meantime I have asked the Secretary of State for the Imperial Navy for a statement as to which points in Eastern Asia might perhaps be desirable for Germany in the interest of her Navy. I still await this statement.

In this connection, the Island of Formosa could hardly be considered. Among other things, Baron von Richthofen, the Professor at the University here and a distinguished authority on China, warns against the acquisition of this place. So far as is known, it has no harbors suitable for large vessels on account of its relatively dense and wild population it is unsuited for colonization; and on account of its extent it is hard to defend. [*Kaiser's note: "Not quite pertinent."*] An effort to secure Formosa would bring us into conflict not only with Japan but probably also with France who has herself asserted claims to it since 1885. [*Kaiser's note: "Formosa must be considered again."*] On the other hand, it would not be disadvantageous to us if Japan with England's and Russia's support would make claims to Formosa because in that way France would be brought into a certain opposition to Russia.

Finally, as regards the Chinese Emperor's telegram, mentioned at the beginning, I humbly ask permission to say to the Chinese envoy that Your Majesty has taken cognizance thereof and authorized him to report to his Imperial Master that Your Majesty has the most complete sympathy with his and his Empire's hard lot and also that Your Majesty's most fervent wishes are directed to the early success of the approaching peace negotiations. Your Majesty is ready and glad to have renewed expression of these wishes given to the Japanese Government. [*Kaiser's note: "Yes"; and to the whole note: "Agreed."*]

William II Addresses His Fleet, 1897

The voyage on which you are starting and the task you have to perform have nothing essentially novel about them. They are the logical consequences of the political labours of my late grandfather and his great Chancellor, and of our noble father's achievements with the sword on the battlefield. They are nothing more than the first effort of the reunited and reëstablished German Empire to perform its duties across the seas. In the astonishing development of its commercial interests the empire has attained such dimensions that it is my duty to follow the new German Hansa, and to afford it the protection it has a right to demand from the empire and the emperor. Our German brethren in holy orders, who have gone out to work in peace, and who have not shrunk from risking their lives in order to carry our religion to foreign soil and among foreign nations, have placed themselves under my protection, and we have now to give permanent support and safety to these brethren, who have been repeatedly harassed and often hard pressed.

For this reason, the enterprise which I have entrusted to you, and which you will have to carry out conjointly with the comrades and the ships already on the spot, is essentially of a defensive and not of an offensive nature. Under the protecting banner of our German war flag, the rights we are justified in claiming are to be secured to German commerce, German merchants, and German ships — the same rights that are accorded by

From *The Imperialism Reader: Documents and Readings on Modern Expansionism*, ed. Louis L. Snyder (Princeton: Van Nostrand, 1962), pp. 301–03. Reprinted by permission of Van Nostrand Reinhold Company.

foreigners to all other nations. Our commerce is not new, for the Hansa was, in old times, one of the mightiest enterprises the world has ever seen, and the German towns were able to fit out fleets such as the broad expanse of the sea had hardly ever borne before.

The Hansa decayed, however, and could not but decay, for the one condition, namely imperial protection, was wanting. Now things are altered. As the first preliminary condition, the German Empire has been created. As the second preliminary condition, German commerce is flourishing and developing, and it can develop and prosper securely only if it feels safe under the power of the empire. Imperial power means naval power, and they are so mutually dependent that the one cannot exist without the other.

As a sign of imperial and of naval power, the squadron, strengthened by your division, will now have to act in close intercourse and good friendship with all the comrades of the foreign fleets out there, for the protection of our home interests against everybody who tries to injure Germany. That is your vocation and your task. May it be clear to every European out there, to the German merchant, and, above all, to the foreigner whose soil we may be on, and with whom we shall have to deal, that the German Michael has planted his shield, adorned with the eagle of the empire, firmly on that soil, in order, once for all, to afford protection to those who apply to him for it. May our countrymen abroad, whether priests or merchants or of any other calling, be firmly convinced that the protection of the German Empire, as represented by the imperial ships, will be constantly afforded them. Should, however, any one attempt to affront us, or to infringe on our good rights, then strike out with mailed fist, and, if God will, weave round your young brow the laurel which nobody in the whole German Empire will begrudge you.

EUROPEAN CULTURE AND SOCIETY: THE END OF THE GOLDEN AGE

Chapter 11

Although historians customarily use 1914 as a division between the nineteenth and the twentieth centuries, this probably is a somewhat misleading form of periodization for the cultural and intellectual historian. The artistic, intellectual, and scientific styles that are identified with the twentieth century were clearly evident in the years before the war, and there was much cultural and intellectual continuity between the prewar and the postwar periods. By the end of the nineteenth century, some of the most sensitive and intellectually powerful personalities on the European cultural scene were frightened by the development of mass society as well as highly critical of the hypocrisy and philistinism of bourgeois society. Yet the consequences that these individuals drew from their perceptions were often remarkably dissimilar. Poet and essayist Matthew Arnold, philosopher Friedrich Nietzsche, and poets William Butler Yeats and Stefan George rejected bourgeois culture vehemently, and the last three called for the creation of a new aristocracy of the spirit to overcome the leveling and mediocrity encouraged by modern mass industrial society. Fascists often found in these writers much that was congenial, although the fascists frequently were precisely the philistines and mass men these writers detested. Other cultural critics, however, such as playwright George Bernard Shaw, poet and essayist William Morris, and novelist Romain Rolland turned to pacifism and socialism or social reform in the hope that the values they cherished could be rescued by making industrial society more humane and just.

By the end of the nineteenth century writers and thinkers rejected both realism and positivism, revolutionizing the arts and sciences. Symbolism dominated poetry, and interest in the psychological became almost universal in the novel and the theater. The impressionists tried to use the science of optics to explore color and light, and expressionists such as Vincent Van Gogh, Edvard Munch, Emil Nolde, and Vasily

Kandinsky turned inward and used color to explore and convey emotion. Indeed, many of the most important artists, architects, and composers of the post-1918 period were already productive and doing some of their most significant work before 1914. There was, in fact, a remarkable willingness to experiment and break through traditions. In Italy, Filippo Tommaso Marinetti founded the Futurist Movement, which outraged the public with its cult of youth and its worship of the machine and fascination with speed, the automobile, and the airplane. Futurism, which was to influence Dadaism and Surrealism in the arts and fascism in politics, demonstrated that it was possible to combine modern technology and science with a high degree of irrationality and vitalism.

The combination of engineering, violence, and myth-making took political form in Georges Sorel's syndicalist doctrines, which, like Futurism, strongly influenced fascism. In philosophy, the new emphasis on will and intuition received sanction in the philosophy of the Frenchman Henri Bergson. The most revolutionary and far-reaching concern with the emotions and invisible forces determining human behavior, however, was expressed by Sigmund Freud. Freud's discovery of the subconscious determinants of human behavior was a revolution in science comparable in its implications to those of the discoveries of Galileo and Darwin. Freud himself pointed out that just as Galileo had shown that the earth was not the center of the universe and Darwin had closed the gap between man and animal, so he had proven that man was not the autonomous master of his own fate that he believed himself to be. This is not to say that Freud was an irrationalist. On the contrary, he was firmly convinced that behavior could be explained in rational terms, and he was not as far from the positivists in his attitude as is sometimes argued. In sociology also a revolution took place in man's understanding of social structures and processes. Max Weber, like Freud, believed that it was possible to understand behavior rationally and objectively no matter how irrational or complex that behavior might be. His studies of the role of Protestantism in the development of the spirit of capitalism and his investigation of the phenomenon of bureaucratization are still basic to contemporary work in the social sciences.

In contrast to the Romantic revolt against science and the Enlightenment, the reaction against positivism was not really a rejection of science or of the scientific method. If anything, the scientific method became more sophisticated and compelling, and Western man emerged with a more profound and deeper understanding of the universe and the world about him than ever before. This was made necessary and possible by the breakdown of the Newtonian world view upon which the work of positivist physicists such as Hermann von Helmholtz had largely been based. The investigations of physicists Max Planck, Niels Bohr, and Albert Einstein and Einstein's theories of relativity published between 1905 and 1915 demonstrated that the Newtonian world view with its strict divisions between matter and force and between time and space was useful only for a limited range of phenomena and that the universe could not be explained in terms of strict causal relationships. Probability replaced certainty, and physicists were compelled to take a more sober attitude toward their theories. Although physicists now are less certain of the ultimate validity of their constructs, they are able to accomplish remarkable things on the basis of their hypotheses. Thus the great discoveries in the various sciences before World War I all took the same direction. They shattered the easy optimism, confidence, and certainties of the bourgeois nineteenth century.

Cultural Anxiety

Anxiety over the growing democratization of life and culture and fear that mass society would drown humanistic values were quite widespread late in nineteenth-century Europe. Matthew Arnold (1822–1888), a Victorian essayist and poet, was one of the most impressive critics of the philistinism of the English middle class, and he was very fearful that democratization would destroy culture. These feelings were intensified by a lecture tour in the United States. In general, Arnold sought to preserve culture by promoting classical and humanistic education, but he gave more pessimistic expression to his perceptions in his poem "Dover Beach." Friedrich Nietzsche (1844–1900) was more pessimistic and far less balanced than Arnold, and his epigrammatic style and frequently violent use of language have made him one of the most misunderstood philosophers of all time. The Nazis tried to appropriate him for a while, but the only way they could make him congenial was by quoting him out of context. Basically, Nietzsche viewed Christianity, democracy, and socialism as various expressions of a common "slave-morality" that was destroying everything fine and noble. In contrast to Herbert Spencer and other Social Darwinists, Nietzsche thought that evolution promoted the survival of the mediocre rather than of the best. If this process was to be checked, then the development of a new morality, "beyond good and evil," that would make room for the self-expression of men who were aristocrats in their actions and thought was necessary. In his view, society had to live for the exceptional, rather than the exceptional for the good of society, and the level of mankind would be raised if it served the strong instead of the weak. Nietzsche did not confuse the strong with the successful statesmen and business-men of his time, and he detested nationalist and racist agitation. His concerns were primarily moral and esthetic, although his ideas have been abused by those who have tried to apply them to political and social purposes.

Arnold: "Dover Beach"

The sea is calm to-night.
The tide is full, the moon lies fair
Upon the straits; — on the French coast the light
Gleams and is gone; the cliffs of England stand,
Glimmering and vast, out in the tranquil bay.
Come to the window, sweet is the night-air!
Only, from the long line of spray
Where the sea meets the moon-blanch'd land,
Listen! you hear the grating roar
Of pebbles which the waves draw back, and fling,
At their return, up the high strand,
Begin, and cease, and then again begin,
With tremulous cadence slow, and bring
The eternal note of sadness in.

Sophocles long ago
Heard it on the Aegaean, and it brought
Into his mind the turbid ebb and flow
Of human misery; we
Find also in the sound a thought,
Hearing it by this distant northern sea.

   The sea of faith
Was once, too, at the full, and round earth's shore
Lay like the folds of a bright girdle furl'd.
But now I only hear
Its melancholy, long, withdrawing roar,
Retreating, to the breath
Of the night-wind, down the vast edges drear
And naked shingles of the world.

Ah, love, let us be true
To one another! for the world, which seems
To lie before us like a land of dreams,
So various, so beautiful, so new,
Hath really neither joy, nor love, nor light,
Nor certitude, nor peace, nor help for pain;
And we are here as on a darkling plain
Swept with confused alarms of struggle and flight,
Where ignorant armies clash by night.

Nietzsche's *Beyond Good and Evil*

257

Every elevation of the type "man," has hitherto been the work of an aristocratic society — and so will it always be — a society believing in a long scale of gradations of rank and differences of worth among human beings, and requiring slavery in some form or other. Without the *pathos of distance,* such as grows out of the incarnated difference of classes, out of the constant outlooking and downlooking of the ruling caste on subordinates and instruments, and out of their equally constant practice of obeying and commanding, of keeping down and keeping at a distance — that other more mysterious pathos could never have arisen, the longing for an ever new widening of distance within the soul itself, the formation of ever higher, rarer, further, more extended, more comprehensive states, in short, just the elevation of the type "man," the continued "self-surmounting of man," to use a moral formula in a supermoral sense. To be sure, one must not resign oneself to any humanitarian illusions about the history of the origin of an aristocratic society (that is to say, of the preliminary condition for the elevation of the type "man"): the truth is hard. Let us acknowledge unprejudicedly how every higher civilisation hitherto has *originated!* Men with a still natural nature, barbarians in every terrible sense of the word, men of prey, still in possession of unbroken strength of will and desire for power, threw themselves upon weaker, more moral, more peaceful races (perhaps trading or cattle-rearing communities), or upon old mellow civilisations in which the final vital force was flickering out in brilliant fireworks of wit and depravity. At the commencement, the noble caste was always the barbarian caste: their superiority did not consist first of all in their physical, but in their psychical power — they were more *complete* men (which at every point also implies the same as "more complete beasts").

From Friedrich Nietzsche, *Beyond Good and Evil: Prelude to a Philosophy of the Future,* trans. Helen Zimmern (New York: Russell & Russell, 1964), pp. 223–32. Reprinted by permission of Russell & Russell and George Allen & Unwin Ltd.

258

Corruption — as the indication that anarchy threatens to break out among the instincts, and that the foundation of the emotions, called "life," is convulsed — is something radically different according to the organisation in which it manifests itself. When, for instance, an aristocracy like that of France at the beginning of the Revolution, flung away its privileges with sublime disgust and sacrificed itself to an excess of its moral sentiments, it was corruption: — it was really only the closing act of the corruption which had existed for centuries, by virtue of which that aristocracy had abdicated step by step its lordly prerogatives and lowered itself to a *function* of royalty (in the end even to its decoration and parade-dress). The essential thing, however, in a good and healthy aristocracy is that it should *not* regard itself as a function either of the kingship or the commonwealth, but as the *significance* and highest justification thereof — that it should therefore accept with a good conscience the sacrifice of a legion of individuals, who, *for its sake,* must be suppressed and reduced to imperfect men, to slaves and instruments. Its fundamental belief must be precisely that society is *not* allowed to exist for its own sake, but only as a foundation and scaffolding, by means of which a select class of beings may be able to elevate themselves to their higher duties, and in general to a higher *existence:* like those sun-seeking climbing plants in Java — they are called *Sipo Matador,* — which encircle an oak so long and so often with their arms, until at last, high above it, but supported by it, they can unfold their tops in the open light, and exhibit their happiness.

259

To refrain mutually from injury, from violence, from exploitation, and put one's will on a par with that of others: this may result in a certain rough sense in good conduct among individuals when the necessary conditions are given (namely, the actual similarity of the individuals in amount of force and degree of worth, and their co-relation within one organisation). As soon, however, as one wished to take this principle more generally, and if possible even as *the fundamental principle of society,* it would immediately disclose what it really is — namely, a Will to the *denial* of life, a principle of dissolution and decay. Here one must think profoundly to the very basis and resist all sentimental weakness: life itself is *essentially* appropriation, injury, conquest of the strange and weak, suppression, severity, obtrusion of peculiar forms, incorporation, and at the least, putting it mildest, exploitation; but why should one for ever use precisely these words on which for ages a disparaging purpose has been stamped? Even the organisation within which, as was previously supposed, the individuals treat each other as equal — it takes place in every

healthy aristocracy — must itself, if it be a living and not a dying organisation, do all that towards other bodies, which the individuals within it refrain from doing to each other: it will have to be the incarnated Will to
Power, it will endeavour to grow, to gain ground, attract to itself and
acquire ascendency — not owing to any morality or immorality, but because it *lives,* and because life *is* precisely Will to Power. On no point,
however, is the ordinary consciousness of Europeans more unwilling to be
corrected than on this matter; people now rave everywhere, even under
the guise of science, about coming conditions of society in which "the
exploiting character" is to be absent: that sounds to my ears as if they
promised to invent a mode of life which should refrain from all organic
functions. "Exploitation" does not belong to a depraved, or imperfect and
primitive society: it belongs to the *nature* of the living being as a primary
organic function; it is a consequence of the intrinsic Will to Power, which
is precisely the Will to Life. Granting that as a theory this is a novelty —
as a reality it is the *fundamental fact* of all history: let us be so far honest
towards ourselves!

260

In a tour through the many finer and coarser moralities which have
hitherto prevailed or still prevail on the earth, I found certain traits recurring regularly together and connected with one another, until finally
two primary types revealed themselves to me, and a radical distinction
was brought to light. There is *master-morality* and *slave-morality;* I
would at once add, however, that in all higher and mixed civilisations,
there are also attempts at the reconciliation of the two moralities; but one
finds still oftener the confusion and mutual misunderstanding of them,
indeed, sometimes their close juxtaposition — even in the same man,
within one soul. The distinctions of moral values have either originated
in a ruling caste, pleasantly conscious of being different from the ruled
— or among the ruled class, the slaves and dependents of all sorts. In the
first case, when it is the rulers who determine the conception "good," it
is the exalted, proud disposition which is regarded as the distinguishing
feature, and that which determines the order of rank. The noble type of
man separates from himself the beings in whom the opposite of this exalted, proud disposition displays itself: he despises them. Let it at once
be noted that in this first kind of morality the antithesis "good" and
"bad" means practically the same as "noble" and "despicable"; the antithesis "good" and *"evil"* is of a different origin. The cowardly, the timid,
the insignificant, and those thinking merely of narrow utility are despised; moreover, also, the distrustful, with their constrained glances, the
self-abasing, the dog-like kind of men who let themselves be abused, the
mendicant flatterers, and above all the liars: it is a fundamental belief of

all aristocrats that the common people are untruthful. "We truthful ones" — the nobility in ancient Greece called themselves. It is obvious that everywhere the designations of moral value were at first applied to *men,* and were only derivatively and at a later period applied to *actions;* it is a gross mistake, therefore, when historians of morals start with questions like, "Why have sympathetic actions been praised?" The noble type of man regards *himself* as a determiner of values; he does not require to be approved of; he passes the judgment: "What is injurious to me is injurious in itself"; he knows that it is he himself only who confers honour on things; he is a *creator of values.* He honours whatever he recognises in himself: such morality is self-glorification. In the foreground there is the feeling of plenitude, of power, which seeks to overflow, the happiness of high tension, the consciousness of a wealth which would fain give and bestow: the noble man also helps the unfortunate, but not — or scarcely — out of pity, but rather from an impulse generated by the superabundance of power. The noble man honours in himself the powerful one, him also who has power over himself, who knows how to speak and how to keep silence, who takes pleasure in subjecting himself to severity and hardness, and has reverence for all that is severe and hard. "Wotan placed a hard heart in my breast," says an old Scandinavian Saga: it is thus rightly expressed from the soul of a proud Viking. Such a type of man is even proud of *not* being made for sympathy; the hero of the Saga therefore adds warningly: "He who has not a hard heart when young, will never have one." The noble and brave who think thus are the furthest removed from the morality which sees precisely in sympathy, or in acting for the good of others, or in *désintéressement,* the characteristic of the moral; faith in oneself, pride in oneself, a radical enmity and irony towards "selflessness," belong as definitely to noble morality, as do a careless scorn and precaution in presence of sympathy and the "warm heart." It is the powerful who *know* how to honour, it is their art, their domain for invention. The profound reverence for age and tradition — all law rests on this double reverence — the belief and prejudice in favour of ancestors and unfavourable to newcomers, is typical in the morality of the powerful; and if, reversely, men of "modern ideas" believe almost instinctively in "progress" and the "future," and are more and more lacking in respect for old age, the ignoble origin of these "ideas" has complacently betrayed itself thereby. A morality of the ruling class, however, is more especially foreign and irritating to present-day taste in the sternness of its principle that one has duties only to one's equals; that one may act towards beings of a lower rank, towards all that is foreign, just as seems good to one, or "as the heart desires," and in any case "beyond good and evil": it is here that sympathy and similar sentiments can have a place. The ability and obligation to exercise prolonged gratitude and prolonged revenge — both only within the circle of equals — artfulness in retaliation, *raffinement* of the idea in friendship, a certain necessity to have enemies (as outlets for the emotions of envy, quarrelsomeness, arrogance — in fact, in order to be a good *friend*): all these are typical characteristics of the noble morality, which, as has been pointed out, is not the morality of "modern ideas," and is therefore at present difficult to realise, and also to unearth and disclose. It is otherwise with the second type of morality, *slave-morality*. Supposing that the abused, the oppressed, the suffering, the unemancipated, the weary, and those uncertain of themselves, should moralise, what will be the common element in their moral estimates? Probably a pessimistic suspicion with regard to the entire situation of man will find expression, perhaps a condemnation of man, together with his situation. The slave has an unfavourable eye for the virtues of the powerful; he has a scepticism and distrust, a *refinement* of distrust of everything "good" that is there honoured — he would fain persuade himself that the very happiness there is not genuine. On the other hand, *those* qualities which serve to alleviate the existence of sufferers are brought into prominence and flooded with light; it is here that sympathy, the kind, helping hand, the warm heart, patience, diligence, humility, and friendliness attain to honour; for here these are the most useful qualities, and almost the only means of supporting the burden of existence. Slave-morality is essentially the morality of utility. Here is the seat of the origin of the famous antithesis "good" and *"evil"*: power and dangerousness are assumed to reside in the evil, a certain dreadfulness, subtlety, and strength, which do not admit of being despised. According to slave-morality, therefore, the "evil" man arouses fear; according to master-morality, it is precisely the "good" man who arouses fear and seeks to arouse it, while the bad man is regarded as the despicable being. The contrast attains its maximum when, in accordance with the logical consequences of slave-morality, a shade of depreciation — it may be slight and well-intentioned — at last attaches itself even to the "good" man of this morality; because, according to the servile mode of thought, the good man must in any case be the *safe* man: he is good-natured, easily deceived, perhaps a little stupid, *un bonhomme*. Everywhere that slave-morality gains the ascendency, language shows a tendency to approximate the significations of the words "good" and "stupid." A last fundamental difference: the desire for *freedom,* the instinct for happiness and the refinements of the feeling of liberty belong as necessarily to slave-morals and morality, as artifice and enthusiasm in reverence and devotion are the regular symptoms of an aristocratic mode of thinking and estimating. Hence we can understand without further detail why love *as a passion* — it is our European speciality — must absolutely be of noble origin; as is well known, its invention is due to the Provençal poet-cavaliers, those brilliant ingenious men of the *"gai saber,"* to whom Europe owes so much, and almost owes itself.

William Morris

The disgust of William Morris (1834–1896) at the cheapening of art and life in modern industrial civilization led him to conclusions very different from those of Arnold and Nietzsche. Morris was concerned with restoring wholeness to man by reestablishing a connection between man and the products of his labor. He idealized the medieval craftsman, and he found in English reformist socialism an answer to the problem of how to eliminate the exploitation and commercialization he identified with industrial capitalism and restore the sense of craftsmanship and the combination of functionality and decorativeness he identified with the products of medieval enterprise. Although he did not reject the machine, Morris insisted that the machine be made to serve man and not the reverse. His desire to reintroduce the artistic and decorative into the objects of daily life has had a major influence on architecture and other arts in the twentieth century.

The Aim of Art

. . . The Aim of Art is to increase the happiness of men, by giving them beauty and interest of incident to amuse their leisure, and prevent them wearying even of rest, and by giving them hope and bodily pleasure in their work; or, shortly, to make man's work happy and his rest fruitful. Consequently, genuine art is an unmixed blessing to the race of man.

But as the word "genuine" is a large qualification, I must ask leave to attempt to draw some practical conclusions from this assertion of the Aims of Art, which will, I suppose, or indeed hope, lead us into some controversy on the subject; because it is futile indeed to expect any one to speak about art, except in the most superficial way, without encountering those social problems which all serious men are thinking of; since art is and must be, either in its abundance or its barrenness, in its sincerity or its hollowness, the expression of the society amongst which it exists.

First, then, it is clear to me that, at the present time, those who look widest at things and deepest into them are quite dissatisfied with the present state of the arts, as they are also with the present condition of society. This I say in the teeth of the supposed revivification of art which has taken place of late years: in fact, that very excitement about the arts amongst a part of the cultivated people of to-day does but show on how

From *The Collected Works of William Morris* (London: Longmans, Green, 1915), pp. 84–90.

firm a basis the dissatisfaction above mentioned rests. Forty years ago there was much less talk about art, much less practice of it, than there is now; and that is specially true of the architectural arts, which I shall mostly have to speak about now. People have consciously striven to raise the dead in art since that time, and with some superficial success. Nevertheless, in spite of this conscious effort, I must tell you that England, to a person who can feel and understand beauty, was a less grievous place to live in then than it is now; and we who feel what art means know well, though we do not often dare to say so, that forty years hence it will be a more grievous place to us than it is now if we still follow up the road we are on. Less than forty years ago — about thirty — I first saw the city of Rouen, then still in its outward aspect a piece of the Middle Ages: no words can tell you how its mingled beauty, history, and romance took hold on me; I can only say that, looking back on my past life, I find it was the greatest pleasure I have ever had: and now it is a pleasure which no one can ever have again: it is lost to the world for ever. At that time I was an undergraduate of Oxford. Though not so astounding, so romantic, or at first sight so mediaeval as the Norman city, Oxford in those days still kept a great deal of its earlier loveliness: and the memory of its grey streets as they then were has been an abiding influence and pleasure in my life, and would be greater still if I could only forget what they are now — a matter of far more importance than the so-called learning of the place could have been to me in any case, but which, as it was, no one tried to teach me, and I did not try to learn. Since then the guardians of this beauty and romance so fertile of education, though professedly engaged in "the higher education" (as the futile system of compromises which they follow is nick-named), have ignored it utterly, have made its preservation give way to the pressure of commercial exigencies, and are determined apparently to destroy it altogether. There is another pleasure for the world gone down the wind; here, again, the beauty and romance have been uselessly, causelessly, most foolishly thrown away.

These two cases are given simply because they have been fixed in my mind; they are but types of what is going on everywhere throughout civilization: the world is everywhere growing uglier and more commonplace, in spite of the conscious and very strenuous efforts of a small group of people towards the revival of art, which are so obviously out of joint with the tendency of the age that, while the uncultivated have not even heard of them, the mass of the cultivated look upon them as a joke, and even that they are now beginning to get tired of.

Now, if it be true, as I have asserted, that genuine art is an unmixed blessing to the world, this is a serious matter; for at first sight it seems to show that there will soon be no art at all in the world, which will thus lose an unmixed blessing; it can ill afford to do that, I think.

For art, if it has to die, has worn itself out, and its aim will be a thing forgotten; and its aim was to make work happy and rest fruitful. Is all work to be unhappy, all rest unfruitful, then? Indeed, if art is to perish, that will be the case, unless something is to take its place — something at present unnamed, undreamed of.

I do not think that anything will take the place of art; not that I doubt the ingenuity of man, which seems to be boundless in the direction of making himself unhappy, but because I believe the springs of art in the human mind to be deathless, and also because it seems to me easy to see the causes of the present obliteration of the arts.

For we civilized people have not given them up consciously, or of our free will; we have been *forced* to give them up. Perhaps I can illustrate that by the detail of the application of machinery to the production of things in which artistic form of some sort is possible. Why does a reasonable man use a machine? Surely to save his labour. There are some things which a machine can do as well as a man's hand, *plus* a tool, can do them. He need not, for instance, grind his corn in a hand-quern; a little trickle of water, a wheel, and a few simple contrivances will do it all perfectly well, and leave him free to smoke his pipe and think, or to carve the handle of his knife. That, so far, is unmixed gain in the use of a machine — always, mind you, supposing equality of condition among men; no art is lost, leisure or time for more pleasurable work is gained. Perhaps a perfectly reasonable and free man would stop there in his dealings with machinery; but such reason and freedom are too much to expect, so let us follow our machine-inventor a step farther. He has to weave plain cloth, and finds doing so dullish on the one hand, and on the other that a power-loom will weave the cloth nearly as well as a hand-loom: so, in order to gain more leisure or time for more pleasurable work, he uses a power-loom, and foregoes the small advantage of the little extra art in the cloth. But so doing, as far as the art is concerned, he has not got a pure gain; he has made a bargain between art and labour, and got a makeshift as a consequence. I do not say that he may not be right in so doing, but that he has lost as well as gained. Now, this is as far as a man who values art and is reasonable would go in the matter of machinery *as long as he was free* — that is, was not *forced* to work for another man's profit; so long as he was living in a society *that had accepted equality of condition.* Carry the machine used for art a step farther, and he becomes an unreasonable man, if he values art and is free. To avoid misunderstanding, I must say that I am thinking of the modern machine, which is as it were alive, and to which the man is auxiliary, and not of the old machine, the improved tool, which is auxiliary to the man, and only works as long as his hand is thinking; though I will remark, that even this elementary form of machine has to be dropped when we come to the higher and more intricate forms of art. Well, as to the machine proper used for art, when it gets to the stage above dealing with a necessary production that has accidentally some beauty about it, a reasonable man with a feeling for art will only use it when he is *forced* to. If he thinks he would like ornament, for instance, and knows that the machine cannot do it properly, and does not care to spend the time to do it properly, why should he do it at all? He will not diminish his leisure for the sake of making something he does not want unless some man or band of men force him to it; so he will either go without the ornament, or sacrifice some of his leisure to have it genuine. That will be a sign that he wants it very much, and that it will be worth his trouble: in which case, again, his labour on it will not be mere trouble, but will interest and please him by satisfying the needs of his mood of energy.

This, I say, is how a reasonable man would act if he were free from man's compulsion; not being free, he acts very differently. He has long passed the stage at which machines are only used for doing work repulsive to an average man, or for doing what could be as well done by a machine as a man, and he instinctively expects a machine to be invented whenever any product of industry becomes sought after. He is the slave to machinery; the new machine *must* be invented, and when invented he *must* — I will not say use it, but be used by it, whether he likes it or not.

But why is he the slave to machinery? Because he is the slave to the system for whose existence the invention of machinery was necessary.

And now I must drop, or rather have dropped, the assumption of the equality of condition, and remind you that, though in a sense we are all the slaves of machinery, yet that some men are so directly without any metaphor at all, and that these are just those on whom the great body of the arts depends — the workmen. It is necessary for the system which keeps them in their position as an inferior class that they should either be themselves machines or be the servants to machines, in no case having any interest in the work which they turn out. To their employers they are, so far as they are workmen, a part of the machinery of the workshop or the factory; to themselves they are proletarians, human beings working to live that they may live to work: their part of craftsmen, of makers of things by their own free will, is played out.

At the risk of being accused of sentimentality, I will say that since this is so, since the work which produces the things that should be matters of art is but a burden and a slavery, I exult in this at least, that it cannot produce art; that all it can do lies between stark utilitarianism and idiotic sham.

Or indeed is that merely sentimental? Rather, I think, we who have learned to see the connection between industrial slavery and the degradation of the arts have learned also to hope for a future for those arts; since the day will certainly come when men will shake off the yoke, and refuse to accept the mere artificial compulsion of the gambling-market to waste their lives in ceaseless and hopeless toil; and when it does come, their instincts for beauty and imagination set free along with them, will produce such art as they need; and who can say that it will not as far surpass the art of past ages as that does the poor relics of it left us by the age of commerce?

A word or two on an objection which has often been made to me when I have been talking on this subject. It may be said, and is often, You regret the art of the Middle Ages (as indeed I do), but those who produced it were not free; they were serfs, or gild-craftsmen surrounded by brazen walls of trade restrictions; they had no political rights, and were exploited by their masters, the noble caste, most grievously. Well, I quite admit that the oppression and violence of the Middle Ages had its effect on the art of those days, its shortcomings are traceable to them; they repressed art in certain directions, I do not doubt that; and for that reason I say, that when we shake off the present oppression as we shook off the old, we may expect the art of the days of real freedom to rise above that of those old violent days. But I do say that it was possible then to have social, organic, hopeful progressive art; whereas now such poor scraps of it as are left are the result of individual and wasteful struggle, are retrospective and pessimistic. And this hopeful art was possible amidst all the oppression of those days, because the instruments of that oppression were grossly obvious, and were external to the work of the craftsman. They were laws and customs obviously intended to rob him, and open violence of the highway-robbery kind. In short, industrial production was not the instrument used for robbing the "lower classes"; it is now the main instrument used in the honourable profession. The mediaeval craftsman was free in his work, therefore he made it as amusing to himself as he could; and it was his pleasure and not his pain that made all things beautiful that were made, and lavished treasures of human hope and thought on everything that man made, from a cathedral to a porridge-pot. Come, let us put it in the way least respectful to the mediaeval craftsman, most polite to the modern "hand": the poor devil of the fourteenth century, his work was of so little value that he was allowed to waste it by the hour in pleasing himself — and others; but our highly-strung mechanic, his minutes are too rich with the burden of perpetual profit for him to be allowed to waste one of them on art; the present system will not allow him — cannot allow him — to produce works of art.

Georges Sorel

The history of the twentieth century demonstrates that, for all their differences, many common denominators can be found between the extreme Left and the extreme Right. One of the most important of these is violence, and it is no accident that Georges Sorel (1847–1922) identified himself with both the Left and the Right at various times. Until 1892 Sorel was one of France's most distinguished engineers, serving the government in positions of prestige and responsibility. Then he turned to writing and published his Reflections on Violence, *a work that extolled the principles of syndicalist socialism and its chief weapon, the general strike. Sorel rejected the evolutionary or reformist socialism of the Webbs in England, Bernstein in Germany, and Jaurès in France. At the same time, he was critical of Marx's claim to be scientific. Instead, Sorel sought the solution in action and myth. The two, used together, would create the future order desired by the syndicalists and would save the workers from the passivity imposed by the belief that it would be possible to substitute evolution for revolution or that one must wait for the revolutionary moment to come before acting. The influence of vitalist thought, especially that of Bergson, was very strong on Sorel. Clearly, however, both action and myth could be used to serve any cause, and in the end the fascists learned more from Sorel than did the socialists.*

Reflections on Violence

Every time that we attempt to obtain an exact conception of the ideas behind proletarian violence we are forced to go back to the notion of the general strike; and this same conception may render many other services, and throw an unexpected light on all the obscure parts of Socialism. In the last pages of the first chapter I compared the general strike to the Napoleonic battle which definitely crushes an adversary; this comparison will help us to understand the part played by the general strike in the world of ideas.

Military writers of to-day, when discussing the new methods of war necessitated by the employment of troops infinitely more numerous than those of Napoleon, equipped with arms much more deadly than those of his time, do not for all that imagine that wars will be decided in any other way than that of the Napoleonic battle. The new tactics proposed

From Georges Sorel, *Reflections on Violence* (© 1950 by The Free Press, a corporation), trans. T. E. Hulme and J. Roth (Glencoe, Ill.: Free Press, 1950), pp. 136–47. Reprinted by permission of The Macmillan Company.

must fit into the drama Napoleon had conceived; the detailed development of the combat will doubtless be quite different from what it used to
be, but the end must always be the catastrophic defeat of the enemy. The
methods of military instruction are intended to prepare the soldier for
this great and terrible action, in which everybody must be ready to take
part at the first signal. From the highest to the lowest, the members of a
really solid army have always in mind this catastrophic issue of international conflicts.

The revolutionary Syndicates argue about Socialist action exactly in
the same manner as military writers argue about war; they restrict the
whole of Socialism to the general strike; they look upon every combination as one that should culminate in this catastrophe; they see in each
strike a reduced facsimile, an essay, a preparation for the great final upheaval.

The *new school,* which calls itself Marxist, Syndicalist, and revolutionary, declared in favour of the idea of the general strike as soon as it became clearly conscious of the true sense of its own doctrine, of the consequences of its activity, and of its own originality. It was thus led to leave
the old official, Utopian, and political tabernacles, which hold the general
strike in horror, and to launch itself into the true current of the proletarian revolutionary movement; for a long time past the proletariat had
made adherence to the principle of the general strike the *test* by means
of which the Socialism of the workers was distinguished from that of the
amateur revolutionaries.

Parliamentary Socialists can only obtain great influence if they can
manage, by the use of a very confused language, to impose themselves on
very diverse groups; for example, they must have working-men constituents simple enough to allow themselves to be duped by high-sounding
phrases about future collectivism; they are compelled to represent themselves as profound philosophers to stupid middle-class people who wish
to appear to be well informed about social questions; it is very necessary
also for them to be able to exploit rich people who think that they are
earning the gratitude of humanity by taking shares in the enterprises of
Socialist politicians. This influence is founded on balderdash, and our
bigwigs endeavour — sometimes only too successfully — to spread confusion among the ideas of their readers; they detest the general strike because all propaganda carried on from that point of view is too socialistic
to please philanthropists.

In the mouths of these self-styled representatives of the proletariat all
socialistic formulas lose their real sense. The class war still remains the
great principle, but it must be subordinated to national solidarity. Inter-
nationalism is an article of faith about which the most moderate declare
themselves ready to take the most solemn oaths; but patriotism also imposes sacred duties. The emancipation of the workers must be the work

of the workers themselves — their newspapers repeat this every day — but real emancipation consists in voting for a professional politician, in securing for him the means of obtaining a comfortable situation in the world, in subjecting oneself to a leader. In the end the State must disappear — and they are very careful not to dispute what Engels has written on this subject — but this disappearance will take place only in a future so far distant that you must prepare yourself for it by using the State meanwhile as a means of providing the politicians with tidbits; and the best means of bringing about the disappearance of the State consists in strengthening meanwhile the Governmental machine. This method of reasoning resembles that of Gribouille, who threw himself into the water in order to escape getting wet in the rain.

Whole pages could be filled with the bare outlines of the contradictory, comical, and quack arguments which form the substance of the harangues of our great men; nothing embarrasses them, and they know how to combine, in pompous, impetuous, and nebulous speeches, the most absolute irreconcilability with the most supple opportunism. A learned exponent of Socialism has said that the art of reconciling opposites by means of nonsense is the most obvious result which he had got from the study of the works of Marx. I confess my extreme incompetence in these difficult matters; moreover, I make no claim whatever to be counted among the people upon whom politicians confer the title of learned; yet I cannot easily bring myself to admit that this is the sum and substance of the Marxian philosophy.

The controversy between Jaurès and Clemenceau demonstrated quite clearly that our Parliamentary Socialists can succeed in deceiving the public only by their equivocation; and that, as the result of continually deceiving their readers, they have finally lost all sense of honest discussion. In the *Aurore* of September 4, 1905, Clemenceau accuses Jaurès of muddling the minds of his partisans "with metaphysical subtleties into which they are incapable of following him"; there is nothing to object to in this accusation, save the use of the word *Metaphysical;* Jaurès is no more a metaphysician than he is a lawyer or an astronomer. In the number of October 26 Clemenceau proves that his opponent possesses "the art of falsifying his texts," and he ends by saying, "It seemed to me instructive to expose certain polemical practices which we wrongly supposed to be monopoly of the Jesuits."

Against this noisy, garrulous, and lying Socialism, which is exploited by ambitious people of every description, which amuses a few buffoons, and which is admired by decadents — revolutionary Syndicalism takes its stand, and endeavours, on the contrary, to leave nothing in a state of indecision; its ideas are honestly expressed, without trickery and without mental reservations; no attempt is made to dilute doctrines by a stream of confused commentaries. Syndicalism endeavours to employ methods of expression which throw a full light on things, which put them exactly in the place assigned to them by their nature, and which bring out the whole value of the forces in play. Oppositions, instead of being glozed over, must be thrown into sharp relief if we desire to obtain a clear idea of the Syndicalist movement; the groups which are struggling one against the other must be shown as separate and as compact as possible; in short, the movements of the revolted masses must be represented in such a way that the soul of the revolutionaries may receive a deep and lasting impression.

These results could not be produced in any very certain manner by the use of ordinary language; use must be made of a body of images which, *by intuition alone,* and before any considered analyses are made, is capable of evoking as an undivided whole the mass of sentiments which corresponds to the different manifestations of the war undertaken by Socialism against modern society. The Syndicalists solve this problem perfectly, by concentrating the whole of Socialism in the drama of the general strike; there is thus no longer any place for the reconciliation of contraries in the equivocations of the professors; everything is clearly mapped out, so that only one interpretation of Socialism is possible. This method has all the advantages which "integral" knowledge has over analysis, according to the doctrine of Bergson; and perhaps it would not be possible to cite another example which would so perfectly demonstrate the value of the famous professor's doctrines.

The possibility of the actual realisation of the general strike has been much discussed; it has been stated that the Socialist war could not be decided in one single battle. To the people who think themselves cautious, practical, and scientific the difficulty of setting great masses of the proletariat in motion at the same moment seems prodigious; they have analysed the difficulties of detail which such an enormous struggle would present. It is the opinion of the Socialist-sociologists, as also of the politicians, that the general strike is a popular dream, characteristic of the beginnings of a working-class movement; we have had quoted against us the authority of Sidney Webb, who has decreed that the general strike is an illusion of youth, of which the English workers — whom the monopolists of sociology have so often presented to us as the depositaries of the true conception of the working-class movement — soon rid themselves.

That the general strike is not popular in contemporary England, is a poor argument to bring against the historical significance of the idea, for the English are distinguished by an extraordinary lack of understanding of the class war; their ideas have remained very much dominated by medieval influences: the guild, privileged, or at least protected by laws, still seems to them the ideal of working-class organisation; it is for England that the term *working-class aristocracy,* as a name for the trades unionists, was invented, and, as a matter of fact, trades unionism does pursue the acquisition of legal privileges. We might therefore say that the aversion felt by England for the general strike should be looked upon as strong presumptive evidence in favour of the latter by all those who look upon class war as the essence of Socialism.

Moreover, Sidney Webb enjoys a reputation for competence which is very much exaggerated; all that can be put to his credit is that he has waded through uninteresting blue-books, and has had the patience to compose an extremely indigestible compilation on the history of trades unionism; he has a mind of the narrowest description, which could only impress people unaccustomed to reflection. Those who introduced his fame into France knew nothing at all about Socialism; and if he is really in the first rank of contemporary authors of economic history, as his translator affirms, it is because the intellectual level of these historians is rather low; moreover, many examples show us that it is possible to be a most illustrious professional historian and yet possess a mind something less than mediocre.

Neither do I attach any importance to the objections made to the general strike based on considerations of a practical order. The attempt to construct hypotheses about the nature of the struggles of the future and the means of suppressing capitalism, on the model furnished by history, is a return to the old methods of the Utopists. There is no process by which the future can be predicted scientifically, nor even one which enables us to discuss whether one hypothesis about it is better than another; it has been proved by too many memorable examples that the greatest men have committed prodigious errors in thus desiring to make predictions about even the least distant future.

And yet without leaving the present, without reasoning about this future, which seems for ever condemned to escape our reason, we should be unable to act at all. Experience shows that the *framing of a future, in some indeterminate time,* may, when it is done in a certain way, be very effective, and have very few inconveniences; this happens when the anticipations of the future take the form of those myths, which enclose with them, all the strongest inclinations of a people, of a party or of a class, inclinations which recur to the mind with the insistence of instincts in all the circumstances of life; and which give an aspect of complete reality to the hopes of immediate action by which, more easily than by any other method, men can reform their desires, passions, and mental activity. We know, moreover, that these social myths in no way prevent a man profiting by the observations which he makes in the course of his life, and form no obstacle to the pursuit of his normal occupations.

The truth of this may be shown by numerous examples.

The first Christians expected the return of Christ and the total ruin of the pagan world, with the inauguration of the kingdom of the saints, at the end of the first generation. The catastrophe did not come to pass, but

Christian thought profited so greatly from the apocalyptic myth that certain contemporary scholars maintain that the whole preaching of Christ referred solely to this one point. The hopes which Luther and Calvin had formed of the religious exaltation of Europe were by no means realised; these fathers of the Reformation very soon seemed men of a past era; for present-day Protestants they belong rather to the Middle Ages than to modern times, and the problems which troubled them most occupy very little place in contemporary Protestantism. Must we for that reason deny the immense result which came from their dreams of Christian renovation? It must be admitted that the real developments of the Revolution did not in any way resemble the enchanting pictures which created the enthusiasm at its first adepts; but without those pictures would the Revolution have been victorious? Many Utopias were mixed up with the Revolutionary myth, because it had been formed by a society passionately fond of imaginative literature, full of confidence in the "science," and very little acquainted with the economic history of the past. These Utopias came to nothing; but it may be asked whether the Revolution was not a much more profound transformation than those dreamed of by the people who in the eighteenth century had invented social Utopias. In our own times Mazzini pursued what the wiseacres of his time called a mad chimera; but it can no longer be denied that, without Mazzini, Italy would never have become a great power, and that he did more for Italian unity than Cavour and all the politicians of his school.

A knowledge of what the myths contain in the way of details which will actually form part of the history of the future is then of small importance; they are not astrological almanacs; it is even possible that nothing which they contain will ever come to pass — as was the case with the catastrophe expected by the first Christians. In our own daily life, are we not familiar with the fact that what actually happens is very different from our preconceived notion of it? And that does not prevent us from continuing to make resolutions. Psychologists say that there is heterogeneity between the ends in view and the ends actually realised: the slightest experience of life reveals this law to us, which Spencer transferred into nature, to extract therefrom his theory of the multiplication of effects.

The myth must be judged as a means of acting on the present; any attempt to discuss how far it can be taken literally as future history is devoid of sense. *It is the myth in its entirety which is alone important*: its parts are only of interest in so far as they bring out the main idea. No useful purpose is served, therefore, in arguing about the incidents which may occur in the course of a social war, and about the decisive conflicts which may give victory to the proletariat; even supposing the revolutionaries to have been wholly and entirely deluded in setting up this imaginary picture of the general strike, this picture may yet have been, in the course of the preparation for the Revolution, a great element of strength, if it has embraced all the aspirations of Socialism, and if it has given to the whole body of Revolutionary thought a precision and a rigidity which no other method of thought could have given.

To estimate, then, the significance of the idea of the general strike, all the methods of discussion which are current among politicians, sociologists, or people with pretensions to political science, must be abandoned. Everything which its opponents endeavour to establish may be conceded to them, without reducing in any way the value of the theory which they think they have refuted. The question whether the general strike is a partial reality, or only a product of popular imagination, is of little importance. All that it is necessary to know is, whether the general strike contains everything that the Socialist doctrine expects of the revolutionary proletariat.

To solve this question we are no longer compelled to argue learnedly about the future; we are not obliged to indulge in lofty reflections about philosophy, history, or economics; we are not on the plane of theories, and we can remain on the level of observable facts. We have to question men who take a very active part in the real revolutionary movement amidst the proletariat, men who do not aspire to climb into the middle class and whose mind is not dominated by corporative prejudices. These men may be deceived about an infinite number of political, economical, or moral questions; but their testimony is decisive, sovereign, and irrefutable when it is a question of knowing what are the ideas which most powerfully move them and their comrades, which most appeal to them as being identical with their socialistic conceptions, and thanks to which their reason, their hopes, and their way of looking at particular facts seem to make but one indivisible unity.

Thanks to these men, we know that the general strike is indeed what I have said: the *myth* in which Socialism is wholly comprised, *i.e.* a body of images capable of evoking instinctively all the sentiments which correspond to the different manifestations of the war undertaken by Socialism against modern society. Strikes have engendered in the proletariat the noblest, deepest, and most moving sentiments that they possess; the general strike groups them all in a co-ordinated picture, and, by bringing them together, gives to each one of them its maximum of intensity; appealing to their painful memories of particular conflicts, it colours with an intense life all the details of the composition presented to consciousness. We thus obtain that intuition of Socialism which language cannot give us with perfect clearness — and we obtain it as a whole, perceived instantaneously.

We may urge yet another piece of evidence to prove the power of the idea of the general strike. If that idea were a pure chimera, as is so frequently said, Parliamentary Socialists would not attack it with such heat; I do not remember that they ever attacked the senseless hopes which the Utopists have always held up before the dazzled eyes of the people. In the course of a polemic about realisable social reforms, Clemenceau brought out the Machiavelianism in the attitude of Jaurès, when he is confronted with popular illusions: he shelters his conscience beneath "some cleverly balanced sentence," but so cleverly balanced that it "will be received without thinking by those who have the greatest need to probe into its substance, while they will drink in with delight the delusive rhetoric of terrestrial joys to come" (*Aurore*, December 28, 1905). But when it is a question of the general strike, it is quite another thing; our politicians are no longer content with complicated reservations; they speak violently, and endeavour to induce their listeners to abandon this conception.

It is easy to understand the reason for this attitude: politicians have nothing to fear from the Utopias which present a deceptive mirage of the future to the people, and turn "men towards immediate realisations of terrestrial felicity, which any one who looks at these matters scientifically knows can only be very partially realised, and even then only after long efforts on the part of several generations." (That is what Socialist politicians do, according to Clemenceau.) The more readily the electors believe in the *magical forces of the State,* the more will they be disposed to vote for the candidate who promises marvels; in the electoral struggle each candidate tries to outbid the others: in order that the Socialist candidate may put the Radicals to rout, the electors must be credulous enough to believe every promise of future bliss; our Socialist politicians take very good care, therefore, not to combat these comfortable Utopias in any very effective way.

They struggle against the conception of the general strike, because they recognise, in the course of their propagandist rounds, that this conception is so admirably adapted to the working-class mind that there is a possibility of its dominating the latter in the most absolute manner, thus leaving no place for the desires which the Parliamentarians are able to satisfy. They perceive that this idea is so effective as a motive force that once it has entered the minds of the people they can no longer be controlled by leaders, and that thus the power of the deputies would be reduced to nothing. In short, they feel in a vague way that the whole Socialist movement might easily be absorbed by the general strike, which would render useless all those compromises between political groups in view of which the Parliamentary régime has been built up.

The opposition it meets with from official Socialists, therefore, furnishes a confirmation of our first inquiry into the scope of the general strike.

Sigmund Freud

In the decades since Sigmund Freud (1856–1939) gave his lectures "The Origin and Development of Psychoanalysis" at Clark University in Worcester, Massachusetts, in 1909, the United States has become the world center of psychoanalytic research and practice, and our age does not find anything particularly sensational in the notion of the unconscious or of infantile sexuality. Thus it is difficult to reconstruct how Freud's contemporaries reacted when he attacked the notion that they were autonomous in their behavior and destroyed the popular idea of the innocence of the child. Although Freud's emphasis upon the determined nature of human behavior and man's sexual drives was not entirely dissimilar to the Augustinian tradition in Christianity, his intentions were entirely secular and his goals were therapeutic. His views did not conform to those of the nineteenth-century optimists, who viewed man's potentialities as virtually limitless. Freud was slow to draw social and cultural implications from his work, but in his writings he emphasized the tensions produced by the requirements of civilization and raised questions about the extent to which man could accept the repression of his instincts that civilization requires.

The Unconscious, Infantile Sexuality, and Psychoanalysis

Ladies and Gentlemen: At this point you will be asking what the technique which I have described has taught us of the nature of the pathogenic complexes and repressed wishes of neurotics.

One thing in particular: psychoanalytic investigations trace back the symptoms of disease with really surprising regularity to impressions from the sexual life, show us that the pathogenic wishes are of the nature of erotic impulse-components (*Triebkomponente*), and necessitate the assumption that to disturbances of the erotic sphere must be ascribed the greatest significance among the etiological factors of the disease. This holds of both sexes.

I know that this assertion will not willingly be credited. Even those investigators who gladly follow my psychological labors, are inclined to think that I overestimate the etiological share of the sexual moments. They ask me why other mental excitations should not lead to the phenomena of repression and surrogate-creation which I have described. I can give them this answer; that I do not know why they should not do

From *American Journal of Psychology*, vol. 21 (April, 1919), pp. 206–13, 216–18. Reprinted by permission of University of Illinois Press.

this, I have no objection to their doing it, but experience shows that they do not possess such a significance, and that they merely support the effect of the sexual moments, without being able to supplant them. This conclusion was not a theoretical postulate; in the *Studien über Hysterie*, published in 1895 with Dr. Breuer, I did not stand on this ground. I was converted to it when my experience was richer and had led me deeper into the nature of the case. Gentlemen, there are among you some of my closest friends and adherents, who have traveled to Worcester with me. Ask them, and they will tell you that they all were at first completely skeptical of the assertion of the determinative significance of the sexual etiology, until they were compelled by their own analytic labors to come to the same conclusion.

The conduct of the patients does not make it any easier to convince one's self of the correctness of the view which I have expressed. Instead of willingly giving us information concerning their sexual life, they try to conceal it by every means in their power. Men generally are not candid in sexual matters. They do not show their sexuality freely, but they wear a thick overcoat — a fabric of lies — to conceal it, as though it were bad weather in the world of sex. And they are not wrong; sun and wind are not favorable in our civilized society to any demonstration of sex life. In truth no one can freely disclose his erotic life to his neighbor. But when your patients see that in your treatment they may disregard the conventional restraints, they lay aside this veil of lies, and then only are you in a position to formulate a judgment of the question in dispute. Unfortunately physicians are not favored above the rest of the children of men in their personal relationship to the questions of the sex life. Many of them are under the ban of that mixture of prudery and lasciviousness which determines the behavior of most *Kulturmenschen* in affairs of sex.

Now to proceed with the communication of our results. It is true that in another series of cases psychoanalysis at first traces the symptoms back not to the sexual, but to banal traumatic experiences. But the distinction loses its significance through other circumstances. The work of analysis which is necessary for the thorough explanation and complete cure of a case of sickness does not stop in any case with the experience of the time of onset of the disease but in every case it goes back to the adolescence and the early childhood of the patient. Here only do we hit upon the impressions and circumstances which determine the later sickness. Only the childhood experiences can give the explanation for the sensitivity to later traumata and only when these memory traces, which almost always are forgotten, are discovered and made conscious, is the power developed to banish the symptoms. We arrive here at the same conclusion as in the investigation of dreams — that it is the incompatible, repressed wishes of childhood which lend their power to the creation of symptoms. Without these the reactions upon later traumata discharge normally. But we must consider these mighty wishes of childhood very generally as sexual in nature.

Now I can at any rate be sure of your astonishment. Is there an infantile sexuality? you will ask. Is childhood not rather that period of life which is distinguished by the lack of the sexual impulse? No, gentlemen, it is not at all true that the sexual impulse enters into the child at puberty, as the devils in the gospel entered into the swine. The child has his sexual impulses and activities from the beginning, he brings them with him into the world, and from these the so-called normal sexuality of adults emerges by a significant development through manifold stages. It is not very difficult to observe the expressions of this childish sexual activity; it needs rather a certain art to overlook them or to fail to interpret them. . . .

Lay aside your doubts and let us evaluate the infantile sexuality of the earliest years. The sexual impulse of the child manifests itself as a very complex one, it permits of an analysis into many components, which spring from different sources. It is entirely disconnected from the function of reproduction which it is later to serve. It permits the child to gain different sorts of pleasure sensations, which we include, by the analogues and connections which they show, under the term sexual pleasures. The great source of infantile sexual pleasure is the auto excitation of certain particularly sensitive parts of the body; besides the genitals are included the rectum and the opening of the urinary canal, and also the skin and other sensory surfaces. Since in this first phase of child sexual life the satisfaction is found on the child's own body and has nothing to do with any other object, we call this phase after a word coined by Havelock Ellis, that of "auto-eroticism." The parts of the body significant in giving sexual pleasure we call "erogenous zones." The thumb-sucking (*Ludeln*) or passionate sucking (*Wonnesaugen*) of very young children is a good example of such an auto-erotic satisfaction of an erogenous zone. The first scientific observer of this phenomenon, a specialist in children's diseases in Budapest by the name of Lindner, interpreted these rightly as sexual satisfaction and described exhaustively their transformation into other and higher forms of sexual gratification. Another sexual satisfaction of this time of life is the excitation of the genitals by masturbation, which has such a great significance for later life and, in the case of many individuals, is never fully overcome. Besides this and other auto-erotic manifestations we see very early in the child the impulse-components of *sexual pleasure*, or, as we may say, of the *libido*, which presupposes a second person as its object. These impulses appear in opposed pairs, as active and passive. The most important representatives of this group are the pleasure in inflicting pain (sadism) with its passive exhibition-pleasure (*Schaulust*). From the first of these later pairs splits off the curiosity for knowledge, as from the latter impulse toward artistic and theatrical representation. Other sexual manifestations of the child can already be regarded from the viewpoint of object-choice, in which the second person plays the prominent part. The significance of this was primarily based upon motives of the impulse of self-preservation. The difference between the sexes plays, however, in the child no very great rôle. One may attribute to every child, without wronging him, a bit of the homosexual disposition.

The sexual life of the child, rich, but dissociated, in which each single impulse goes about the business of arousing pleasure independently of every other, is later correlated and organized in two general directions, so that by the close of puberty the definite sexual character of the individual is practically finally determined. The single impulses subordinate themselves to the overlordship of the genital zone, so that the whole sexual life is taken over into the service of procreation, and their gratification is now significant only so far as they help to prepare and promote the true sexual act. On the other hand, object-choice prevails over auto-eroticism, so that now in the sexual life all components of the sexual impulse are satisfied in the loved person. But not all the original impulse-components are given a share in the final shaping of the sexual life. Even before the advent of puberty certain impulses have undergone the most energetic repression under the impulse of education, and mental forces like shame, disgust and morality are developed, which, like sentinels, keep the repressed wishes in subjection. When there comes, in puberty, the high tide of sexual desire it finds dams in this creation of reactions and resistances. These guide the outflow into the so-called normal channels, and make it impossible to revivify the impulses which have undergone repression.

The most important of these repressed impulses are koprophilism, that is, the pleasure in children connected with the excrements; and, further, the tendencies attaching themselves to the persons of the primitive object-choice.

Gentlemen, a sentence of general pathology says that every process of development brings with it the germ of pathological dispositions in so far as it may be inhibited, delayed, or incompletely carried out. This holds for the development of the sexual function, with its many complications. It is not smoothly completed in all individuals, and may leave behind either abnormalities or disposition to later diseases by the way of later falling back or *regression*. It may happen that not all the partial impulses subordinate themselves to the rule of the genital zone. Such an impulse which has remained disconnected brings about what we call a perversion, which may replace the normal sexual goal by one of its own. It may happen, as has been said before, that the auto-eroticism is not fully overcome, as many sorts of disturbances testify. The originally equal value of both sexes as sexual objects may be maintained and an inclination to homosexual activities in adult life result from this, which, under suitable conditions, rises to the level of exclusive homosexuality. This series of disturbances corresponds to the direct inhibition of development of the sexual function, it includes the perversions and the general *infantilism* of the sex life that are not seldom met with.

The disposition to neuroses is to be derived in another way from an injury to the development of the sex life. The neuroses are related to the perversions as the negative to the positive; in them we find the same impulse-components as in perversions, as bearers of the complexes and as creators of the symptoms; but here they work from out the unconscious. They have undergone a repression, but in spite of this they maintain themselves in the unconscious. Psychoanalysis teaches us that overstrong expression of the impulse in very early life leads to a sort of fixation (*Fixirung*), which then offers a weak point in the articulation of the sexual function. If the exercise of the normal sexual function meets with hindrances in later life, this repression, dating from the time of development, is broken through at just that point at which the infantile fixation took place.

You will now perhaps make the objection: "But all that is not sexuality." I have used the word in a very much wider sense than you are accustomed to understand it. This I willingly concede. But it is a question whether you do not rather use the word in much too narrow a sense when you restrict it to the realm of procreation. You sacrifice by that the understanding of perversions; of the connection between perversion, neurosis, and normal sexual life; and have no means of recognizing, in its true significance, the easily observable beginning of the somatic and mental sexual life of the child. But however you decide about the use of the word, remember that the psychoanalyst understands sexuality in that full sense to which he is led by the evaluation of infantile sexuality.

Now we turn again to the sexual development of the child. We still have much to say here, since we have given more attention to the somatic than to the mental expressions of the sexual life. The primitive object-choice of the child, which is derived from his need of help, demands our further interest. It first attaches to all persons to whom he is accustomed, but soon these give way in favor of his parents. The relation of the child to his parents is, as both direct observation of the child and later analytic investigation of adults agree, not at all free from elements of sexual accessory-excitation (*Miterregung*). The child takes both parents, and especially one, as an object of his erotic wishes. Usually he follows in this the stimulus given by his parents, whose tenderness has very clearly the character of a sex manifestation, though inhibited so far as its goal is concerned. As a rule, the father prefers the daughter, the mother the son; the child reacts to this situation, since, as son, he wishes himself in the place of his father, as daughter, in the place of the mother. The feelings awakened in these relations between parents and children, and, as a resultant of them, those among the children in relation to each other, are not only positively of a tender, but negatively of an inimical sort. The complex built up in this way is destined to quick repression, but it still exerts a great and lasting effect from the unconscious. We must express the opinion that this with its ramifications presents the *nuclear complex* of every neurosis, and so we are prepared to meet with it in a not less effectual way in the other fields of mental life. The myth of King Oedipus, who kills his father and wins his mother as a wife, is only the slightly altered presentation of the infantile wish, rejected later by the opposing barriers of incest. Shakespeare's tale of Hamlet rests on the same basis of an incest complex, though better concealed. At the time when the child is still ruled by the still unrepressed nuclear complex, there begins a very significant part of his mental activity which serves sexual interest. He begins to investigate the question of where children come from and guesses more than adults imagine of the true relations by deduction from the signs which he sees. Usually his interest in this investigation is awakened by the threat to his welfare through the birth of another child in the family, in whom at first he sees only a rival. Under the influence of the partial impulses which are active in him he arrives at a number of "infantile sexual theories," as that the same male genitals belong to both sexes, that children are conceived by eating and born through the opening of the intestine, and that sexual intercourse is to be regarded as an inimical act, a sort of overpowering.

But just the unfinished nature of his sexual constitution and the gaps in his knowledge brought about by the hidden condition of the feminine sexual canal, cause the infant investigator to discontinue his work as a failure. The facts of this childish investigation itself as well as the infant sex theories created by it are of determinative significance in the building of the child's character, and in the content of his later neuroses.

It is unavoidable and quite normal that the child should make his parents the objects of his first object-choice. But his *libido* must not remain fixed on these first chosen objects, but must take them merely as a prototype and transfer from these to other persons in the time of definite object-choice. The breaking loose (*Ablösung*) of the child from his parents is thus a problem impossible to escape if the social virtue of the young individual is not to be impaired. During the time that the repressive activity is making its choice among the partial sexual impulses and later, when the influence of the parents, which in the most essential way has furnished the material for these repressions, is lessened, great problems fall to the work of education, which at present certainly does not always solve them in the most intelligent and economic way.

Gentlemen, do not think that with these explanations of the sexual life and the sexual development of the child we have too far departed from psychoanalysis and the cure of neurotic disturbances. If you like, you may regard the pyschoanalytic treatment only as a continued education for the overcoming of childhood-remnants (*Kindheitsresten*). . . .

Ladies and Gentlemen, I am of the opinion that there are, on the intellectual side, two hindrances to acknowledging the value of the psychoanalytic viewpoint: first, the fact that we are not accustomed to reckon with a strict determination of mental life, which holds without exception, and, second, the lack of knowledge of the peculiarities through which unconscious mental processes differ from these conscious ones with which we are familiar. One of the most widespread resistances against the work of psychoanalysis with patients as with persons in health reduces to the latter of the two moments. One is afraid of doing harm by psychoanalysis, one is anxious about calling up into consciousness the repressed sexual impulses of the patient, as though there were danger that they could overpower the higher ethical strivings and rob him of his cultural acquisitions. One can see that the patient has sore places in his soul life, but one is afraid to touch them, lest his suffering be increased. We may use this analogy. It is, of course, better not to touch diseased places when one can only cause pain. But we know that the surgeon does not refrain from the investigation and reinvestigation of the seat of illness, if his invasion has as its aim the restoration of lasting health. Nobody thinks of blaming him for the unavoidable difficulties of the investigation or the phenomena of reaction from the operation, if these only accomplish their purpose, and gain for the patient a final cure by temporarily making his condition worse. The case is similar in psychoanalysis; it can lay claim to the same things as surgery; the increase of pain which takes place in the patient during the treatment is very much less than that which the surgeon imposes upon him, and especially negligible in comparison with the pains of serious illness. But the consequence which is feared, that of a disturbance of the cultural character by the impulse which has been freed from repression, is wholly impossible. In relation to this anxiety we must consider what our experiences have taught us with certainty, that the somatic and mental power of a wish, if once its repression has not succeeded, is incomparably stronger when it is unconscious than when it is conscious, so that by being made conscious it can only be weakened. The unconscious wish cannot be influenced, is free from all strivings in the contrary direction, while the conscious is inhibited by those wishes which are also conscious and which strive against it. The work of psychoanalysis accordingly presents a better substitute, in the service of the highest and most valuable cultural strivings, for the repression which has failed.

Now what is the fate of the wishes which have become free by psychoanalysis, by what means shall they be made harmless for the life of the individual? There are several ways. The general consequence is, that the wish is consumed during the work by the correct mental activity of those better tendencies and which are opposed to it. The repression is supplanted by a condemnation carried through with the best means at one's disposal. This is possible, since for the most part we have to abolish only the effects of earlier developmental stages of the ego. The individual for his part only repressed the useless impulse, because at that time he was himself still incompletely organized and weak; in his present maturity and strength he can, perhaps, conquer without injury to himself that which is inimical to him. A second issue of the work of psychoanalysis may be that the revealed unconscious impulses can now arrive at those useful applications which, in the case of undisturbed development, they would have found earlier. The extirpation of the infantile wishes is not at all the ideal aim of development. The neurotic has lost, by his repressions, many sources of mental energy whose contingents would have been very valuable for his character building and his life activities. We know a far more purposive process of development, the so-called *sublimation (Sublimirung)*, by which the energy of infantile wish-excitations is not secluded, but remains capable of application, while for the particular excitations, instead of becoming useless, a higher, eventually no longer sexual, goal is set up. The components of the sexual instinct are especially distinguished by such a capacity for the sublimation and exchange of their sexual goal for one more remote and socially more valuable. To the contributions of the energy won in such a way for the functions of our mental life we probably owe the highest cultural consequences. A repression taking place at an early period excludes the sublimation of the repressed impulse; after the removal of the repression the way to sublimation is again free.

We must not neglect, also, to glance at the third of the possible issues. A certain part of the suppressed libidinous excitation has a right to direct satisfaction and ought to find it in life. The claims of our civilization make life too hard for the greater part of humanity, and so further the aversion to reality and the origin of neuroses, without producing an excess of cultural gain by this excess of sexual repression. We ought not to go so far as to fully neglect the original animal part of our nature, we ought not to forget that the happiness of individuals cannot be dispensed with as one of the aims of our culture. The plasticity of the sexual-components, manifest in their capacity for sublimation, may cause a great temptation to accomplish greater culture-effects by a more and more far reaching sublimation. But just as little as with our machines we expect to change more than a certain fraction of the applied heat into useful mechanical work, just as little ought we to strive to separate the sexual impulse in its whole extent of energy from its peculiar goal. This cannot succeed, and if the narrowing of sexuality is pushed too far it will have all the evil effects of a robbery.

I do not know whether you will regard the exhortation with which I close as a presumptuous one. I only venture the indirect presentation of my conviction, if I relate an old tale, whose application you may make yourselves. German literature knows a town called Schilda, to whose inhabitants were attributed all sorts of clever pranks. The wiseacres, so the story goes, had a horse, with whose powers of work they were well satisfied, and against whom they had only one grudge, that he consumed so much expensive oats. They concluded that by good management they would break him of this bad habit, by cutting down his rations by several stalks each day, until he had learned to do without them altogether. Things went finely for a while, the horse was weaned to one stalk a day, and on the next day he would at last work without fodder. On the morning of this day the malicious horse was found dead; the citizens of Schilda could not understand why he had died. We should be inclined to believe that the horse had starved, and that without a certain ration of oats no work could be expected from an animal.